Winslow Homer. *Upland Cotton*, 1879 (Weil Brothers Collection).

AN
AMERICAN
HARVEST

THE STORY OF
WEIL BROTHERS–COTTON

George S. Bush

PRENTICE-HALL, INC.
ENGLEWOOD CLIFFS, N.J.

Prentice-Hall International, Inc., *London*
Prentice-Hall of Australia, Pty. Ltd., *Sydney*
Prentice-Hall Canada Inc., *Toronto*
Prentice-Hall of India Private Ltd., *New Delhi*
Prentice-Hall of Japan, Inc., *Tokyo*
Prentice-Hall of Southeast Asia Pte., Ltd., *Singapore*
Whitehall Books, Ltd., Wellington, *New Zealand*
Editora Prentice-Hall do Brasil Ltda., *Rio de Janeiro*

Library of Congress Cataloging in Publication Data
Bush, George S.
An American harvest.

Bibliography: p.
Includes index.
1. Weil Brothers Cotton—History.
2. Cotton trade—United States—History. I. Title.
HD9079.W44B87   1982   380.1′41351′06073   82-9797
ISBN 0-13-027458-5   AACR2

Edited and designed by David Wright. Art director: Brianne
Carey. Production manager: Mary D. Morano. Picture layouts
by George S. Bush and Brianne Carey. Set in Electra by Elizabeth Typesetting Company, Kenilworth, New Jersey. Printed
and bound by Murray Printing Company, Westford, Massachusetts. Color plates by Phillips Offset, Mamaroneck, New
York.

To Margery,
who brought home the best little bales
ever from Trenton

Contents

Color plates

Preface

A KNOWLEDGEABLE READER is likely to find some errors in this book. If he is particularly keen, he may also discover contradictions, in implication if not in stated fact. Most are my fault—the results of the necessarily imperfect perception of the cotton world by an outsider. But some of the lapses must be blamed on Father Time and his sinister sport of distorting memories. Interviewing old-timers, I often heard the same stories over and over again, and they differed with each telling. I have tried to reconcile the discrepancies; however, such fudging can't help but end up as much fiction as fact.

I don't say this to impugn the veracity of any of the many who devoted countless hours to answering my questions, but merely to point out that history, perforce, is viewed through the eyes of its participants: subjective at best, prejudiced at worst, and in the end, alas, often veiled by cataracts. Certainly everyone I interviewed tried to do his best. Several interviewees even contacted me weeks later to fill me in on events they had originally forgotten.

Still, information on the earlier days—let alone the earliest—was hard to come by, and much detail was lacking. As a result, the past doesn't get as much coverage as it deserves, and today's protagonists, simply because more space is devoted to them, assume a somewhat disproportionate importance in the script: indeed, yesterday's prime movers were every bit, if not more, instrumental in shaping the course of the Weil companies. Partly to compensate for this short-coming, but largely because no human enterprise makes sense out of context, I have dwelled heavily on the historical and sociological aspects of cotton; understanding cotton's tempestuous environment may thus help the reader to a greater appreciation of the men who played their parts on that exciting stage.

Weil staffers who contributed to the book included, alphabetically, Tom Adams, Frank W. Bailey, Kay Ballard, Sue Bitterman, James D. "Pick" Butler, Wally Darneille, Julian Dewberry, Peter Frank, Stuart Frazer, David Hardoon, Manuel Held, Jim McGhee, Robert Mangum, Fred M. "Crackie" Parker, Mimi Randolph, George T. Wheeler, Jack Wilson, Marvin Woolen, and Lee Yarwood. Also in this category belongs Jack Rutkay, although he is not a Weil employee in the strict sense of the term: Jack does the floor trading for the firm on the New York Cotton Exchange.

Among the former Weil employees who gave generously of their time, A. M. Crawford, Sr., Alvin Weil, and Charles H. Greengrass have since died. It was touching how these men, and other old-timers as well, perked up as the interviews progressed and they had a chance to relive their most exciting years. Among them were Carl Baquie, Richard Block, A. M. Crawford, Jr., Fritz Ficke, George Hedick, Roland A. Hester, Arthur James, Joe D. McAteer, Thomas R. Moss, and Conril B. Smith.

I also want to express special thanks to Earle Billings, executive vice-president, American Cotton Shippers Association; Gaylon Booker, president, National Cotton Council; Patrick and Francis Devilder, Société Polycoton, of Lille, France; Robert du Pasquier, of Paris; Neal P. Gillen, vice-president and general counsel, American Cotton Shippers Association; Luis A. Gomez, retired vice-president, Chase Manhattan Bank; Roberto Herrera V., of Bogota, Colombia; the late Milo Howard, then director of the Alabama State Department of Archives and History; Joseph A. Moss, formerly with the U. S. Department of Agriculture, now consultant to the National Cotton Council; Mary Ann Neeley, research historian of the Landmark Foundation, the Montgomery (Alabama) preservation society; F. Marion "Dusty" Rhodes, president emeritus, New York Cotton Exchange; Marc Serck, cotton agent, of Ghent, Belgium; and Starke Taylor, retired Dallas cotton merchant and a former director of the New York Cotton Exchange.

Above all, my appreciation goes out to Adolph "Bucks" Weil, Jr., and Robert S. "Bobby" Weil, Sr., the sponsors of this book, who were incredibly patient when I went way beyond deadline. My gratitude, too, to other members of the family: Jean and Virginia Weil, the wives of Bucks and Bobby, who always made me feel welcome in their homes even at those times when my visits were importune, as some must have been; Leonel "Uncle Lee" Weil, the uncle of Bucks and Bobby, and Weil partner from 1919 to 1951; Carol (Mrs. Myron J.) Rothschild; Lucien Loeb, Leonel's brother-in-law, who also was an active Weil partner most of his life; R. Hugh "Pat" Uhlmann, brother-in-law of Bucks and Bobby; and his wife, Helen Jane, who hosted me in Kansas City where Pat is chairman of his own family firm, the Standard Milling Co.; and the young Weil generation: Bucks' children, Laurie (Mrs. Howard) Mandell, of Montgomery, and Adolph "Andy" Weil III, now a trainee in the company; and Bobby's children, Virginia "Vicki" (Mrs. Thomas) Langman, of Washington, D.C.; Rosalind (Mrs. Daniel H. III) Markstein of Birmingham, Alabama; and Robert S. "Bobby" Weil II, who graduated from squidgedom to Texas merchandising, and now functions as assistant to Bucks and Bobby.

Two old Weil friends also contributed valuable insights: Federal Judge Louis Oberdorfer, of Washington, D.C., who had gone to Dartmouth with Bobby; and Winton M. Blount, Montgomery entrepreneur (Blount Inc.), who had served as postmaster general in the first Nixon administration.

Some of the interviews turned out to be more than tape-recording sessions: with the Pat Uhlmanns; with Pick and Liesl Butler, who entertained me at their New York apartment; with Romain Van-driessche, Ghent cotton controller, who, after an afternoon of answering questions, in which his cousin, Leon, also participated, took me to one of the finest restaurants in Belgium; with Trudy (Mrs. Alvin) Weil, who received me in Memphis; with the Kronauers of Milan—Piera Kronauer, Mr. and Mrs. Federico Kronauer, and their daughter, Marzia—who devoted a whole day to me; with the Grayson family of Dallas, among them the children of legendary cotton man Al Grayson—Helen (Mrs. Tom) Rose and David M. Grayson; with Mrs. Nathan Rosenfield, of New Orleans; and finally, Peter and Liesl

Frank, who just naturally became good friends because we share so many interests; hopefully, now that this book is finished, we'll go skiing together.

Essential to the writing were the late Benjamin S. Barnes' typescript memoirs, "My 50 Years with Weil Bros."; the late Mildred Schwab's deathbed letter to Bucks Weil detailing her reminiscences about the early days of the Weils' New York office; a meticulously penned manuscript of more than one hundred pages by George H. Way, Weil's Liverpool agent from 1923 to 1961; a round-robin family letter about her youth by Hermione Weil Adler, of Birmingham, Alabama, daughter of Herman Weil, one of the firm's founders; Bobby Weil, Sr.'s, comprehensive memoranda on Weil court cases and his annotated collection of the Schoenhof family letters; plus a number of preliminary interviews conducted in 1977 by Sally Alcorn, a writer and researcher who later moved to Massachusetts.

Kay Ballard, already listed among Weil staffers, deserves a special mention. Throughout the process of research, writing, editing and production, she was my logistic alter ego in Montgomery, short-cutting delays and handling all manner of correspondence, shipping of materials, and filling in unanswered questions—not only labors of duty but also a self-imposed additional responsibility. As the long-time secretary of Bucks Weil, she had more than enough work to keep her busy without me.

Special thanks are also due for help in compiling the illustrations: to Memphis artist Georg Shook, who painted the rear view of the Weil building on Front Street; to Alabama artist Jack. C. DeLoney, for permission to include his painting *Riverbottom Cotton*; to the Musée de Beaux Arts de Pau, France, for the reproduction of Edgar Degas' *Le Bureau de Coton à la Nouvelle Orléans*; to John Hammett, of Weil Memphis, for supplying photos from his grandfather Wallace R. McKay's vast historical collection; to Jeanne Crawford, the widow of A. M. Crawford, Sr., and Trudy Weil, widow of Alvin Weil, for supplying family pictures from years past; and to the Defense Department, the National Archives, and the Alabama State Department of Archives and History for reproductions from their files.

I am equally indebted to Elizabeth Blair (Mrs. H. G.) Pannell, of Montgomery, for photographs from the Algernon Blair Collection; to

Tom Conner, national advertising manager (and in-house historian) of the *Montgomery Advertiser/Alabama Journal*, for providing reproductions from the newspapers' archives; to John Engelhardt Scott, Jr., of Scott Photographic Services, Montgomery, for rights to an old Montgomery street scene from his private collection; and to Walter A. Parrent, chief executive officer of the Bank of East Alabama; Mrs. Dee Dee Harper, the bank's marketing manager; Colonel R. Platt Boyd, U.S. Army Corps of Engineers, ret.; and Bill Sumners, assistant archivist at Auburn University, for historic illustrations of Opelika and Auburn, Alabama.

I can't pass up this opportunity also to acknowledge the indirect assistance of Carr Neel "Bud" Miller, of E. F. Hutton & Co., Universal City, California, an old family friend, who is not only the best, most conservative stockbroker I know but also extraordinarily considerate. The market was fairly interesting during the time this book was written and he'd often call me twice a day with his standard greeting: "Can you talk?" If, caught in the middle of a thought, I said no, he'd hang up without another word. Now, that's real help when you are concentrating on a script!

Last but not least, I want to express my gratitude to Martha Anne Freeman, of Santa Fe, New Mexico, a dear friend who had transcribed interviews for several of my previous books and on this project devoted much time to organizing the mountainous materials; to Nancy Lear of Doylestown, Pennsylvania, who took dictation and helped type and proof; to Joyce St. John, my secretary in Montgomery during the first-draft phase; as well as to Antoinette Roades, then also of Bucks County, who impinged on her own time as a successful magazine writer to help out when Ms. Lear was taken ill.

GSB

1

The Cotton Merchants

ONE BRIGHT, HOT DAY in the fall of 1972, Stuart Frazer, a young man only recently employed by Weil Brothers–Cotton Inc., of Montgomery, Alabama, drove up to a cotton gin near Roswell, New Mexico. He had barely slammed the car door shut when a big dog broke its chain and rushed him. Frazer scrambled onto the roof of his car and tossed his briefcase at the snarling beast. The ginner, awakened by the barking, eventually emerged in his sweaty undershirt. He grabbed the dog by its collar and tied it back up. Only then did he turn to Frazer. "Okay, boy," he said. "You can get off that damn car now. You're sure lucky. He's bitten four people this month."

Frazer climbed from his perch and handed the man his business card. The ginner peered at it, then shook his head in puzzlement. "What in hell is that?" he asked. Frazer explained that the name on the card, Algodonera Naçional, was Spanish for a cotton company. "Damn," the ginner said. "If I'da knowed you was a furner, I'da let mah dog eat 'cha."

Stuart Frazer is as American as they come. In the old days, before long hair on males once again came into fashion, he would have been called clean cut. A fifth-generation Alabaman, he had been born and raised in Montgomery, and was at the moment engaged in an occupation that's almost as old as the country itself, and originally and uniquely an American calling—the buying of cotton where it is grown (or, as they say in the trade, "made"), i.e. directly from farmers and ginners.

"No sir," Frazer replied with that deceptive mildness which properly reared Southerners are heir to. "I'm not a foreigner. I'm from here in the States. I work for a Latin American Company, but that company is associated with a U. S. cotton company."

The ginner still regarded him with a measure of mistrust, but relaxed enough to ask him in. "You look American, I guess," he conceded. "Well, c'mon and sit." He led the way to the porch, where Frazer promptly found himself crashing to the floor when the chair he chose collapsed under him. "Damn, boy," the ginner said. "First you make me beat mah old dog half to death, and now you tear up mah favorite chair. You're some character."

They sat in silence for awhile, and then the ginner asked Frazer how much he'd be willing to pay for cottonseed. "We don't buy seed here," Frazer said. "In the States we only buy raw cotton. We buy our seed in Nicaragua."

"Niggeraga?" the ginner chuckled. "I thought you said you weren't no furner. Goddam, boy. First you tell one story, and then you tell another."

Needless to report, the two men didn't come to terms. When Frazer refused to buy seed at $100 a ton, the ginner informed him that if he ever showed up again, he'd let the dog have at him. "Damn furner," he muttered as the young man climbed back in his dusty car.

Pretty good story, and probably mostly true, although Stuart Frazer is acclaimed far and wide for his embellishments—and that's quite an honor in the cotton business, where overgrown tales come by the bale and are as much a stock in trade as Strict Low Middling. But think about this story for a minute, and you begin to see that, underneath it all, it's sad, not funny.

Here is Stuart, a 100-percent American, if you will, working for a firm founded in the Deep South a century ago, dealing in the raw material that triggered the first major expansions of the United States and that has greatly influenced, directly and indirectly, the nation's course ever since. But he is buying cotton for a foreign company (albeit owned by an American company), and by virtue of that fact is suspect as an alien. Well, you might ask, what do you expect from a ginner in the boonies?

But this is not the point. What's so serious about Stuart's tale is that the ginner was, instinctively, absolutely right. He rebelled against a world in which cotton was no longer truly an American business. For the past twenty-five years, big merchants like the Weils have bought much of their cotton in other countries, and almost half the cotton they sell goes to foreign mills.

To be sure, export always has been a vital factor in the cotton business. The dollars thus earned bought the country's first luxuries and provided the funds needed to launch its earliest industries: cotton was the economic base of the Industrial Revolution. When Isidor and Herman Weil, immigrants from Germany, founded Weil Brothers in Opelika, Alabama, in 1878, the United States not only grew more cotton than any other nation but spun most of it. Nearly the whole crop came from the Southeast and went to mill towns in New England. But today, the United States is no longer the largest producer of cotton, and only a small handful of textile mills still exist in New England.

The cotton industry, by its nature, flourishes in societies where cheap labor is abundant and technical skills are scarce. This holds true even with mechanization. As first the United States and later Western Europe grew affluent, the cotton market's center of gravity shifted initially across the Atlantic and then ever farther east until, today, cotton has come full circle to where it was presumably first used—the Chinese mainland. Weil survived, when most American cotton houses didn't, because it adjusted to these changes. That Weil remains headquartered in Montgomery is an anachronism rooted in sentimentality and force of habit, and made possible by the invention of telephone and teletype. The firm could function as easily, and more logically, out of Memphis, Lubbock, or Fresno. Even Hong Kong would be quite appropriate, if it weren't for its awkward time difference from Europe and America.

In one of the Weils' biggest weeks ever, the company in late November 1979 sold more than 21,000 metric tons of cotton. Although this five-day tour de force was by no means typical, its very distortions illustrate what's been happening in the cotton business. Of that week's 95,000 bales, 71,500 were destined for the Far East— China, Taiwan, Hong Kong, and Korea. The People's Republic alone accounted for 52,800 bales. By contrast, only some 1,500 bales dribbled to the United Kingdom, Belgium, the Netherlands, and France, the countries that had been among America's (and Weil's) biggest export customers until only a few years ago. What's more, nearly all of the 71,500 bales sent to the Orient came from Texas, the balance from the mid-South and California. Not a single bale originated in Alabama, Georgia, or the Carolinas, King Cotton's one-time stronghold. Nor did domestic mills, now largely concentrated in the Southeast, buy any "Eastern" cotton. The 20,000 bales Weil sold to American spinners that week came out of the Memphis territory and from California.

That same week, the Weils' Central American operation shipped 1,500 bales of Guatemalan cotton to Italy, and their Mexican company 600 bales of Mexican cotton to Mexican mills. Meanwhile, Unicosa, Weil's affiliate in Switzerland, sold 1,000 bales of Israeli cotton to Italy, and was engaged in trading for substantial quantities of cotton with Turkey and Bangladesh, and buying yet more from Israel.

Weil ranks among the seven giants of international cotton merchandising. Since the First World War, it has almost always been among our country's top three. Handling at times more than one million bales in a single season, the firm could make the *Fortune* 500 almost every year were it a public company. Because most other cotton houses also are closely held, and because their volumes and profits vary from year to year (not necessarily in direct relation to each other), it is impossible to define precisely the relative positions of the merchants.

Four of the largest are foreign: Ralli Brothers–Coney, of Britain; Bunge & Born, originally a Belgian firm now headquartered in Argentina; Volkart, of Switzerland; and Esteve, which operates out of headquarters in Mexico City, Dallas, and Geneva. Among U. S. firms, Anderson Clayton, out of Houston, was the undisputed General Motors of the cotton business until the early 1970s, but has since dropped out of the picture, concentrating instead on other enterprises. George H. McFadden, of Memphis, the nation's oldest existing cotton house, which for many decades occupied the undisputed number-two spot, is now more involved with poultry and operates under a new name, Valmac. Another big Memphis merchant, Cook & Co., has withdrawn entirely from cotton, along with all other commodities. Cook had to retrench a few years ago after suffering substantial losses in soybeans when a group of investors that included Bunker Hunt (more recently of silver fame) took an opposite position and came out the winner. Cook has since devoted its efforts to less volatile markets: insecticides and insurance.

For the past ten years, a brilliant newcomer to the cotton scene, W. B. "Billy" Dunavant, also of Memphis, has been the most successful U. S. merchant in terms of volume, and possibly also dollars. He achieved sudden prominence by taking neck-out positions that older, more conservative firms like Weil Brothers–Cotton, Inc., are unwilling to risk. Thus, Weil and Hohenberg Brothers Co., a centenarian Memphis family firm which was acquired by Cargill in 1976, are trailing Dunavant, if not by much, and are now perennial contenders for the second spot.

Also important in the field are Allenberg Cotton Co. of Memphis (acquired in 1981 by the Louis Dreyfus Group but still operating under its own name); and the Dallas firms of Volkart Taylor Cooper Inc. (until recently Starke Taylor & Co.), H. Molsen & Co., and Cotton Import Export Co. In addition, there are the cooperatives: Calcot (California Cotton), of Bakersfield; Swig (Southwestern Irrigated Growers), of El Paso; the Plains Cotton Cooperative Association, of Lubbock, Texas; and Staplcotton, of Greenwood, Mississippi. All these cooperatives do their own marketing. But since they sell cotton to merchants as well as directly to mills, it is impossible to come up with reliable comparative statistics. Suffice it to say that where there were once scores of American cotton merchants, only a few names ever crop up these days in shop talk.

That it's an exclusive fraternity goes without saying—exclusive not because it's a closed shop, but because of the substantial credit lines needed to engage in this business on more than a minimal scale. For the past decade, the world's annual cotton production has ranged between about 55 and 65 million bales. Almost half of this is grown in Russia and China. But at a market price of, say, seventy cents a pound, that still leaves more than 10 billion dollars worth of cotton in the Free World's commercial channels.

When but a handful of merchants broker the flow of this "free" cotton, it only stands to reason that everybody in the business knows each other—and that they watch one another like hawks. Not long ago, for instance, Adolph "Bucks" Weil, Jr., threw the futures market into a thirty-minute uproar when he paid a visit to the New York Cotton Exchange, then still at 37 Wall Street (but since moved into the World Trade Center). As is his habit when he is preoccupied, Bucks strolled restlessly back and forth, in this instance near the pit where cotton futures are traded. Nervously gnawing at his lower lip, chin on chest, his gaze inward and withdrawn, his jacket flung open and his hands tucked into the rear pockets of his pants, he was the picture of a man wrestling with momentous decisions. Was Weil about to buy? to sell? No doubt a fortune was at stake. Why else would the big man be here in the flesh, in his button-down 100-percent cotton shirt, rather than leave matters in the hands of James D. "Pick" Butler, the Weils' big wheel in New York for more than twenty-five years? For a tense half hour, cotton quotations roller-coastered as the traders around the pit yelled their bids and asks, trying to anticipate the Weils' intentions. Suddenly, Bucks' frown metamorphosed into the very special million-dollar smile that had earned him his nickname when still a boy. He extricated his right hand, raised it in joyous greeting, and rushed out the door. The market had convulsed over Bucks waiting for his lunch date.

Bucks, born February 8, 1915, and his brother, Robert S. "Bobby" Weil, born November 29, 1919, are the third generation to run the Weil family partnership and its spinoff corporations and subsidiaries. Were you to walk into their office on Montgomery Street, you would be taken aback, at first glance, by its deceptive dinginess. Not only is Weil quartered at the wrong end of downtown, in the opposite direction from the State Capitol, but it occupies the upper floor of a blandly ugly, superannuated two-story structure, whose street level is rented to a bank complete with drive-in window. A staircase, barren but for an antique nameplate of polished brass, brings you to a narrow, windowless corridor whose most distinctive features are a venerable plug-in switchboard, a Hammond wall map of the world, a stuttering Dow Jones commodities teletype, and a tape ticker of the type popularized in tycoon cartoons of the Depression era. Beyond the map, and out of sight until you reach that end of the hall, hangs a spinach-green blackboard, where whoever happens to be looking at the ticker at the moment chalks up the latest cotton-future quotations. A roofed wing chair, resembling the fin-de-siècle strand chairs still fashionable on continental Europe's Channel beaches—except that this specimen is of Winesap-red leather—enhances the sense of genteel but valiant poverty, or conversely, suppressed wealth. Certainly, no prospective IBM or Xerox employee would be caught dead applying for a job in such archaic surroundings.

Nor are the rooms whose doors open off this hall steeped in modern-office plush. Even the organization's key staffers work in space that most businesses would regard askance today: desks often older than the men who use them, creaky chairs, whitewashed walls, everywhere a clutter of papers, dusty sills that would brighten a white-gloved shavetail's day. The Weil brothers' inner sanctum appears hardly more imposing, although its long-frayed Chippendale-period chairs finally have been reupholstered. The two-sided partners desk, where the Weils sit facing each other day after day, is so heaped with memos, newspapers, teletype takes, carbons of contracts, letters to be signed, letters to be read, discarded envelopes, shoved-aside file folders, and piles of snipped-out postage stamps, that only an acute antiquarian would recognize the desk for the valuable antique it is. Take a second look around, and other splendors are revealed: originals by Renoir, Degas, Monet, Pissarro, and Gilbert Stuart. Winslow Homer's classic "Upland Cotton," however, is the only relatively permanent piece. Only rarely does any one of the paintings occupy its space for long, since the works are often touring museums, while other canvases, pulled from stacks along the walls of the next-door conference room, replace them.

This extraordinary chamber is equipped with an antique dining table too large for the space, plus a matching sideboard, bearing an aging bottle of Harvey's Bristol Cream and a few goblets. The sideboard is crowded so tightly against the table that anyone sitting at that end endangers the gleaming finish of both the sideboard and his chair with the slightest twitch. The most precious of the paintings usually hang on these walls, albeit cheated of adequate lighting, for the Venetian blinds are drawn against the sun that once made Southern cotton grow, and the chandelier above the table sprouts but dim candle-shaped bulbs. The room's most unexpected feature, as office fixtures go, is an original casting, on a pedestal, of a naked young man by Rodin.

One of the intriguing aspects of the conference room is that it's hardly ever used for conferences. It serves mostly as a luxurious booth

During a rare moment of tranquility, Bobby Weil, Sr. (right), for once uninterrupted, dictates letters while Bucks, on the other side of their venerable partners desk, plows through piles of paper awaiting his attention.—*Author's photograph*

for confidential phone calls, since privacy is hard to come by anywhere else.

No one ever knocks before entering Bucks' and Bobby's domain, where often three conversations take place all at once: Bucks on the phone with New York, Bobby talking to Memphis, plus a couple of staffers discussing whatever problem they came to obtain guidance on, while waiting for one of the partners, or preferably both, finally to hang up. Several times a day, the room reverberates with amplified voices from the squawker phone that's switched on when both Weils want to listen: the Mississippi Delta drawl of Tom Adams, the Weil boss in Memphis, whose every phrase carries the insistent cadence of a country preacher's invocation; the Hong Kong–British accent, since Midwesternized on the campus of the University of Wisconsin and further modified at Berkeley, of David Hardoon, the Weil man in the Orient; the didactic drone, exaggerated by the squawker, of Peter Frank, a one-time Nazi refugee and later a field-commissioned U. S. paratrooper, now head of Unicosa in Zug, Switzerland; Gordon Redmond, Weil's Texas-lanky manager in Lubbock, reporting on an overnight freeze; the gutsy laugh and tumbling English of Roberto Herrera V., cotton agent and entrepreneur for all seasons in Bogota, Colombia; the tender Tennessee twang of Jack Wilson, head of Weil Hermanos (formerly Algodonera Weil), phoning in from a trip to Central America; the silky staccato of Federico "Chicco" Kronauer, who represents Weil in Milan, Italy, as his father and grandfather had before him.

Within the same hour, Bucks will put in a straddle order, bemoan the imminent collapse of Western Civilization, give a buy order to his stockbroker in New York, dawdle over a Parke-Bernet catalog, solicit donations to the United Way, make arrangements to testify in Bangkok on a claim against Thai mills, and deliver himself of a brief lecture on Albrecht Dürer's engravings. In that same hour, Bobby might approve a major purchase of Iron Curtain cotton for resale to Swiss and Italian spinners, work on obtaining his entry permit for a trip to Red China, trade with a London art dealer for an Andrew Wyeth, and consult with a Bremen lawyer on a German litigation.

For refreshments, there's coffee in paper cups from a brewing apparatus tucked into a recess of the hall, and Cokes from a dilapidated refrigerator that stands with a drunken tilt in the most important room in any cotton house—the sample room, where cotton samples, cut from bales in warehouses, are examined for color, trash content, staple (length), and character of fiber, the criteria that determine its eventual use and relative worth. The sample room's walls are lined with tiers of racks, like bunks on a troopship, and in past days often used for the same purpose, for they are cushioned with bundles of cotton, a most inviting berth for snoozing between chores. Cotton that's already been examined piles up ankle-deep on the floor until it's swept away at the end of the day for resale as cotton waste. In the peak season, from September to March, you almost feel like you're walking on clouds. The samples are "classed" on long tables, an art that every cotton man must make his second nature, and whose findings are expressed in a terminology as standard in Osaka and Liverpool as it is in Dallas and Memphis. Not surprisingly, since cotton, as an international commodity, originated in the young United States, the traditional British measurement rather than the metric is used: staple is defined in fractions of an inch wherever cotton is produced or sold.

A special school in Memphis teaches classing, and its eight-week to twelve-week sessions are populated nowadays by as many foreign students as Americans. Rare is the cotton man who did not attend this institution, long famous as Murdoch's and succeeded since early 1980 by the Memphis Cotton Exchange School. But the incipient cotton man doesn't only attend classes. Regardless of his prior education, even if he comes equipped with a doctorate in economics from some European university or an MBA from Harvard, he must serve for a couple of years as an apprentice—a "squidge" in the jargon of the trade. Much of a squidge's time is spent in the sample room, for that's one of the hardest parts of the business to master, involving, as it does, the skills of hand and eye, the senses of touch and sight, and, above all, experience and more experience. Incredible as it may seem, chief classers at Weil must be able to gauge staple to $\frac{1}{64}$ of an inch.

Among the firm's half-dozen samplers and sample-room porters, there's nearly always one foreign squidge; this is a time-honored practice in all cotton houses and has made the cotton world a club. Family connection often plays a part. The aforementioned David Hardoon, for instance, came aboard as a trainee (after a brief career as a television reporter in Vietnam and Japan) under the auspices of his father, David George Hardoon, Weil's long-time agent in Hong Kong. The fact that young David is part Chinese—indeed a descendant of a godchild of the last Dowager Empress Tzushih—and speaks perfect Mandarin as well as Shanghainese and Cantonese helped considerably of course. Recently also Chicco Kronauer's nephew, Carlo Mor, now working with his uncle in Milan, squidged with Weil in Montgomery and Memphis after earning his doctorate in law at the University of Genoa and apprenticing in Liverpool, England's cotton port.

We'll meet all these people again later, as they figure in the continuum of the Weil enterprise. Suffice it to say here that such cross-fertilization is integral to cotton merchandising and endows its orbit with a special glow. With the exception of the oil business, no other arena is quite so peripatetic, bringing together grassroots America with the rural and commercial cultures of other civilizations. Even the least sophisticated of Weil employees, straight out of country schools, soon find nothing particularly strange about dealing with faraway places and far-out personalities that, for the average American, are vaguely familiar only from movies and television.

Not so, however, the town of Montgomery itself. When the Weils pulled out all stops for their firm's centennial celebration in November 1978, the Montgomery *Advertiser* shivered with excitement that such an exotic enclave existed almost unnoticed in the community's midst.

Among the more than one thousand guests at this two-day fête were visitors and Weil staffers from fourteen foreign countries, as well as twenty-three of the fifty states, plus Washington, D.C., and the Virgin Islands. The guest list gives a clue to the geography of cotton: the Carolinas, where it all began; Georgia, Alabama, Mississippi, Arkansas, and Tennessee, where the fiber later ruled or greatly influenced the area's economy; Texas, Arizona, and California, where most of the U. S. cotton is grown today; the District of Columbia, where cotton production and manufacturing is legislated and administrated; New York, where it is hedged; Italy, France, and Britain, which used to process most of it; Spain and the Low Countries, which still manage to sustain some of their textile mills; Hong Kong, Japan, and Taiwan, among today's biggest importers of raw cotton and biggest exporters of cotton materials; Nicaragua, Colombia, Guatemala, and Mexico, whose agricultures still encompass the fiber; Switzerland, whose import and export expertise (and tax structure) make it as important in cotton merchandising as it is in nearly all international endeavors.

What pleased the Weils perhaps more than anything else was that not only their customers, suppliers, bankers, brokers, agents, and old associates showed up, many paying air fares for themselves and their families that ranged into the thousands of dollars, but that traditional competitors also responded to the invitation: Hohenberg, Starke Taylor, Allenberg, and Ralli Brothers–Coney, whose A. K. J. McBride flew in from Liverpool for the occasion.

At Montgomery's Civic Center, rented for the gala reception and ball, guests gorged themselves on goodies that covered three lavishly decorated, seemingly endless tables: caviar mousse, oysters, clams, and shrimps ladled from huge buckets, liver pâté on immense platters, canapés, antipasto, country ham and biscuits, tenderloin cubes, chicken breast au vin, mushrooms stroganoff, fresh fruit and enough cheeses to make even a Frenchman feel at home. As the *Advertiser* breathlessly reported, "From the buffet room, guests were ushered into the grand ballroom where 135 individual tables, seating 8 each, were covered alternately with gold, green, and flamestitched cloths, each table with a center piece of small daisy mums, pittosporum, and cotton bolls . . . [a New Orleans orchestra] played from a bandstand flanked with [potted] magnolia trees and fronted with antique cotton baskets filled with flowers . . . ." Earlier, Colonel Bob Barmettler, in periwig and eighteenth-century red coat with gold epaulettes, had boomed out introductions as the guests wound their way past bales of cotton to the reception line and bar tables beyond. The newspaper concluded that "Possibly one of the most elaborate social events of its kind, this Centennial Ball will long be remembered for its international flair"—and, the reporter might have added—for its confusion and inevitable gaffes. As the guests mingled, a veteran Southern belle, adrip with mink, approached a handsome black gentleman, aglow in white dinner jacket, and with the social acquisitiveness of a professional hostess announced, "You must be the ambassador from Chad." Nonplussed, her prey responded, "No, ma'am, I works in the sample room at Weil."

As if one shindig weren't enough, there was yet another the next evening, cocktails and a buffet dinner at the Standard Club, following a three-hour cruise on the Alabama River aboard a sidewheeler. The city's two leading motels had been preempted by the Weils; a fleet of cars stood ready to ferry visitors wherever they wanted to go. Hospitality suites stayed open around the clock, a great comfort to guests suffering from jet lag. As Bobby's wife, Virginia, wryly remarked after it was all over, "For one hundred years the Weils have worked at keeping a low profile, and here we blew it all in one weekend."

Not quite. The customary anonymity of the cotton business soon returned to enfold Weil once again. Who, indeed, gives cotton much thought these days except growers and spinners? But it wasn't always so.

At Weil's gala centennial in Montgomery's Civic Center, Colonel Robert S. Barmettler (right), attired in traditional British footman's garb, called out the names of more than 1,000 guests as they approached the receiving line to be greeted by Bucks and Jean Weil (bottom left), Bobby, Sr., and Virginia Weil (bottom center), and Leonel and Cecile Weil (bottom right); the latter here welcoming Alabama Governor and Mrs. Fob James. Meanwhile, the four Weil vice-presidents posed with the firm's 100th-birthday cake, appropriately baked in the shape of a cotton bale (above, left to right) Jack Wilson, Jim McGhee, Marvin Woolen and Tom Adams.—*Photos by The Robertsons*

2

Reprise: Gossypium Rex (1793–1864)

MOST OF HISTORY derives from man's quest for raw materials; it would be frivolous to claim more significance in that regard for one commodity than for another. Tobacco prompted the colonization of Virginia, but surely America would not have remained a blank on the map even if Indians hadn't cultivated the weed. Gold opened California, but probably there'd be surfers off Santa Monica today even if Sutter hadn't struck it rich in the foothills of the Sierra. The possibilities of extrapolation are infinite. Would there be automobiles if oil hadn't been found in Pennsylvania? How much lower would the dollar have dropped if, God forbid, the prairies hadn't lent themselves to the growing of wheat?

But if you really want to engage in some fancy second-guessing, take cotton. Without it, there would have been no Dixie, no booming slave trade, no Civil War, no carpetbaggers, no Martin Luther King, no George Wallace, no Andy Young. There'd be no racial strife in the big cities, and the Third World would have little motivation to back the Arab cause. Cotton brought great wealth, and, along with it, equally great misery. Its fiber clothed the world in jeans and left the United States wearing a hair shirt.

India and Egypt grew and spun cotton long before Christ. Marco Polo found it in China. Columbus encountered it in Cuba and on Hispaniola (Haiti) but not surprisingly was far more intrigued by the cigars the Cubans puffed and the gold the Haitians panned from their rivers. In fact, cotton was something of a footnote in his report to

Ferdinand and Isabella. Still dependent on homemade spinning wheels and looms, people clothed themselves in whatever fibers were nearest at hand, and in Europe these were wool and flax. Thus while cotton did bring some profits to early English planters on Barbados and St. Kitts in the 1600s, it did not catch on as a major import from the New World until the spinning mule and the power loom were developed in Britain a century and a half later. At about the same time (1793), Eli Whitney invented the gin for the efficient extraction of the fiber from the boll. With this constellation of technology, cotton came into its own.

Cotton is lighter than wool, softer than flax. It is durable, amenable to dyes, and easily washed. Its structure is not readily impaired by moisture or heat. Its natural twist gives it great strength. It can be cool or warm, coarse or gossamer-delicate, depending on the weave. Although flax is more forgiving of soil and climate, it is harder to process. Sheep, while they can graze almost anywhere, do not yield much wool per acre, and shearing them calls for more labor per pound of wool than picking does per pound of cotton. Besides, sheep kick and cotton doesn't. Cotton's economic advantages over other fibers were overwhelming even with the early machinery, and this

Eli Whitney, pictured in his workshop at right, patented his cotton gin in 1793. At about the same time, the spinning mule was developed in Britain. Within a generation, cotton mills such as the one shown in the 1835 engraving (opposite) prospered all over New England.—*The Bettmann Archive, Inc.*

applied particularly to American cotton because the "peculiar domestic institution" of the Southern states (as John C. Calhoun put it) permitted the harvesting of their rich crops with the cheapest labor of all.

Slavery was not an American invention. Contrary to recent legend, its roots and greatest miseries were far from Tara—in Africa, among the Negroes themselves. On the Dark Continent, children were routinely wrenched from their mothers; to be sold into bondage was a common fate. Indeed, the practice of slavery continued in Africa well into this century. In his *Wind, Sand and Stars* (1939), the French author Saint-Exupéry tells how he saw an old and useless black slave being turned out into the desert by his Moslem master to die of starvation. Nor was slavery on this and other continents restricted to blacks. This is not cited as an apologia for the South's "peculiar institution" but merely to put it into context. Slavery was practiced in the outposts of all colonial empires, and in North America it was by no means peculiar to the South. Newport in Rhode Island, not Charleston of the Carolinas, was the hub of the slave trade. Every New England colony had its share of black serfs; in New York, African slaves accounted for almost 10 percent of the population.

Enlightenment is a slow process, and never slower than when it hurts. As the tenet of free and equal creation inflamed the imagination of American colonists, it inevitably engendered a revulsion against the ownership of one human by another. It only stands to reason that this repugnance was more pronounced in the North, where slaves were not so much an economic asset as a status symbol. Even before the Revolution, the North was being urbanized. Shipping was its biggest industry, manufacture was increasing, and most farms were small enough so that the farmer's family could do all the work. Not so in the South. Virginia and North Carolina lived off tobacco, and South Carolina reaped rice, both crops that demanded large acreages. Here, for the moment, the Negro's labor was essential: there were not enough whites. Even so, abolitionist societies sprang up throughout the early South, and many Southern leaders, including Thomas Jefferson and George Mason, spoke freely for that cause. The slave trade was banned by Delaware, Maryland, and Virginia, along with all the Northern states, by 1783, and South Carolina barred it from 1787 to 1803. At that time, there were still fewer than 70,000 slaves, and Oliver Ellsworth, of Connecticut, predicted at the Federal Convention of 1793 that rising immigration soon would cause such a labor glut as to make slaves redundant. What Ellsworth did not know was that at this very moment Whitney was putting the finishing touches to his cotton gin, and that the Napoleonic Wars would disrupt emigration to the New World.

Had sense prevailed rather than greed, slavery might still have withered, but King Cotton exploited not only labor but the land. In every region fit for the crop, the richest acreages were absorbed by plantations within the first generation of settlement. As unremitting one-crop cultivation depleted these lands, the wealthy planters and their entourages of slaves moved on to greener pastures, ever pushing west. Small farmers then appropriated the eroded hillsides and raped the fields.

Now arithmetic came into play. On generous soil, and provided the labor force was properly organized, a field hand could cultivate ten acres and make five or more bales of cotton. On second-generation land, the yield was less than half that and demanded far more sweat. Two or even three hands now kept busy on a dozen acres. Hence, the labor requirement of the Cotton Kingdom no longer followed a linear progression as new acreage was opened; it jumped geometrically. Moreover, the small farmers, each with six to a dozen slaves, owned more slaves in the aggregate than did the gentry, whose glamorized *Gone With the Wind* image has become our culture's conceptualization of the antebellum South. And that's a crucial point.

The gentry were but a small minority: a handful of descendants of the colonial aristocracy, the Washington pattern perpetuated in his Lee kinsmen. Then there were South Carolina's proud yet humble Huguenots; tidewater Virginians like the Lees; and a smattering of wealthy Louisiana-French Creoles; plus a backbone of self-made men like Jefferson Davis, whose parents lived in a log cabin, and John Hampden Randolph who turned a $27,000 debt into the biggest plantation in Louisiana's Iberville Parish and presaged Kaiser-Permanente by employing a resident physician to care for his 195 slaves. The gentry, on its own, just might have seen reason and freed their slaves, but a small, scared farmer wasn't about to do that, and ever less likely to do it as the slave population burgeoned and he felt immersed in a hostile black sea—hostile, for while the small farmer was not as ruthless toward his Negro serfs as Saint-Exupéry's Moslem, neither was he a generous and forgiving master. He couldn't afford to be.

There was yet a third stratum, way at the bottom of the social scale, an ominous presence, like teenagers lurking in alleys. Those were the "po-whites," the white trash, who lived in hovels, owned no slaves, and, if they worked at all, worked the poorest lands nobody else wanted. Possessed of nothing but their Caucasian skin, it was their only pride, and they exuded hatred of the Negro. Political control resided with the gentry (except in Alabama, Missouri, and Arkansas) only at the sufferance of this rural proletariat. When the time came, Southern gentlemen would lead the small farmers and po-whites in battle, but each would fight for a subtly different cause: the gentry to defend the principle of Southern sovereignty; the small farmer, to defend his land and livelihood; the po-white, to slay the abolitionist dragon.

Indeed, slavery as such was by no means the core issue in the conflict between North and South, any more than the fate of Europe's Jewry under Hitler occasioned World War II. The first shot of the Civil War was fired at Fort Sumter on April 12, 1861. But as late as August 22, 1862, Lincoln wrote to Horace Greeley, "My paramount objective in this struggle is to save the Union, and it is not either to save or to destroy slavery." Not until the week after the Battle of Antietam, which began on September 17, 1862, did Lincoln issue the Emancipation Proclamation, and this mainly as a foreign policy maneuver. The Union victory at Antietam (Sharpsburg) narrowly averted Britain's entry into the war on the side of the Confederacy; in the delicate balance of international relations, this was the time to rally Europe's liberals to the Union's cause. No, slavery was not the fulcrum. The issue was, as always, economic, and the power that economic strength entails.

As the century progressed, King Cotton's canter had turned into a gallop. Cotton sped from South Carolina into Georgia, and across the new Indian cessions in Alabama, Mississippi, and Louisiana on into the Mississippi Valley. Its advance then forked. One spearhead raced up the Mississippi to Memphis. The other pushed up the Red River of Louisiana into Indian territory, then past the boundaries of Mexico into the plains of Texas. The year after Washington first became president, the South had raised about 3,000 bales of cotton. In 1820, the cotton crop topped 32,000 bales, some 16 million pounds (at roughly 500 pounds per bale). By 1850, the output exceeded 2 million bales, more than 1 billion pounds, and by 1860, it had more than doubled again to 4.6 million bales or 2.3 billion pounds. *

Over those years, the Liverpool price of upland cotton fluctuated between eleven and nineteen cents a pound, and averaged about twelve cents. By conservative estimate (1.5 billion pounds @ twelve cents), the cotton business put $180 million into U. S. coffers in any

---

*Alston Hill Garside and Samuel Eliot Morison differ on the exact figures. The approximations cited above constitute a compromise. See Garside, *Cotton Goes to Market* (New York: Frederick A. Stokes, 1935), p. 6; and Morison, *The Oxford History of the American People* (New York: Oxford University Press, 1965), p. 500.

given year of the 1850s. In 1860, that income rose to $250 million. In our day of cheap dollars and billion-dollar companies, this may not sound like much. But then it was a veritable fortune, and constituted fully three quarters of the nation's export income. It was cotton that bought all of America's luxuries, from silks to furnishings, and much of the machinery that formed the basis for the country's industrialization. The cotton income profited the North no less than the South. It sustained the border slave states—Delaware, Maryland, Kentucky, and West Virginia—which supplied labor, food, and mules. It propped the wobbly economy of Virginia, which had found itself with a surplus of slaves when its tobacco business flagged and the indigo gave out, and which could survive only by the selling or hiring out of slaves to the lower South. But the real benefits fell to New England and New York. A planter was lucky to receive half the Liverpool price. The rest went for transportation, brokerage, and the interest on monies advanced on future crops, and almost all of this ended up in Yankee pockets. That's where the ships were and the banks, for although the Southern gentry kept talking about establishing shipping lines and banks of their own, they plowed all their profits back into the soil; into land and the slaves needed to work it.

In the meanwhile, however, New England, New York, and Pennsylvania had increasingly put their surplus into manufacturing enterprises of various kinds, including cotton mills. To protect these infant industries, Northern congressmen pushed through ever-higher tariffs on imported goods. The idea of a tariff had been Alexander Hamilton's. Back in 1791, he had proposed it, ironically, as a bid for Southern support over the heads of Jefferson and Madison. He envisioned an industrially developed South to countervail the power of the Northern merchants and bankers. Neither the South nor the North supported Hamilton's plan. The South saw it as a plum for Northern interests, and the Northern ship owners had a stake in free trade. The next time the idea came up, in 1816, it was promulgated by, of all people, John C. Calhoun. He wanted cotton mills for his native South Carolina, and sold the bill to Congress on the basis that a tariff would bind the Republic together by keeping out foreign goods, thus creating a home market for both the country's agricultural and manufactured products. Calhoun's tariff passed, proving that lawmakers then were no wiser than they are now: among the bill's supporters were representatives from states that would eventually secede to escape the tariff, and among its most vociferous opponents were congressmen from states that would benefit hugely from it.

Northern interests did not make that mistake again. The South, however, did. To begin with, the tariff was strengthened in 1824. Four years later, as Andrew Jackson readied himself to wrest the presidency from John Quincy Adams, Jackson's cohorts in Congress introduced a bill that put higher duties on raw materials than on manufactured goods, although tariffs on the latter, too, were raised. This was of course patent nonsense—the United States had no reason to protect itself against imported cotton. But the South swallowed the bait. Actually, the bill's sponsors didn't want it to pass. It was their hope that this two-sided measure would endear Jackson to the South (which it did), and that the North would defeat the legislation because it seemed to favor agriculture, and that this defeat would then be blamed on Adams. Those two-bit Machiavellis couldn't have been more mistaken. Not that they cared. Jackson beat Adams anyway. The North supported the bill, and the tariff, soon to be denounced as the "tariff of abominations," became law. With it, the die was cast.

Two weeks after the tariff's passage, Britain's William Huskisson issued a barely veiled warning in the House of Commons: in the face of this tariff, the island would have to turn to other sources for its imports. Not that the English mills had any intention to quit buying Southern cotton—there was no other source. What Huskisson intended by his own admission was to prod the South to make an all-out effort to repeal the tariff, and, if that didn't work, to separate from the North. South Carolina's McDuffy was quick to pick up Huskisson's message. He aroused his constituents with his "forty-bale theory" that had the North, in effect, stealing forty out of every hundred bales of cotton; this, he insisted, was the penalty exacted by the tariff, which decreased British cotton purchases while raising the price the South had to pay for imported consumer goods. Fellow South Carolinian John Randolph went even further. All the North's wealth, he screamed, had been plundered from the South. Academe, too, soon spouted the party line. At an antitariff meeting in Columbia, the president of South Carolina College, Thomas Cooper, asked "Is it worth our while to continue this union of states where the North demands to be our masters and we are required to be their tributaries?"

However, only South Carolina quivered in this first spasm of revolt. Impoverished by the westward march of cotton, its fields spent and its mills aborted, it had the least to lose and the most to gain. Calhoun (anonymously, for he was Jackson's vice-president) proposed nullification, the already discredited device by which a state could challenge the constitutionality of a federal law and make it inapplicable within its borders. The move was squelched by compromise. Jackson arranged for a nominal lowering of the tariff (20 percent over ten years) after Georgia had made the incipiently dangerous proposal to call a Southern Convention. South Carolina, thus able to claim victory, gladly retreated from the firing line. It was just as happy not to have to secede on its own, for it had no ally other than Georgia. For the moment, the Union was strengthened. But Jackson, who was a lot smarter than he is given credit for, knew that the struggle between North and South had only just begun. "The next pretext," he predicted, "will be the Negro."

Jackson had the situation pegged but didn't use the correct word. The issue of slavery was not a pretext. It was real. True, as yet there was no viable movement to force the South to abandon slavery, but for the South this was no consolation. Slavery was the base of its agricultural economies—not only cotton, but sugar, tobacco, and rice as well. Once a state had enjoyed the fruits of bonded labor, it perforce allied itself with others of like interest. So, if the South ever hoped to defeat the protective tariff, a preponderance of the territories applying for admission to the Union had to be accepted as slave states; or, if not most, then at least half of them, lest sooner or later the South be overpowered. Thus, as the curtain rose on the next act, the scene was the West, which both North and South now strove to create in their own image.

The political pattern for westward expansion had been set by the Missouri Compromise of 1820, which held the Union together at a time when both sides threatened secession. Planters from Louisiana, where slavery existed under French law and which had been admitted in 1812 as a slave state, migrated to the Territory of Upper Louisiana. They came with their chattels in tow and established themselves on the fertile bottom lands of the lower Missouri and on the western bank of the Mississippi near the old fur-trade outpost of St. Louis. It was only logical that when these people applied for admission to the Union as the State of Missouri, they would incorporate slavery into their state constitution. As Congress was about to vote on Missouri's admission, James Tallmadge of New York offered an amendment that would have effectively ended slavery in the new state within a generation.* The amended bill passed in the House and lost in the Senate. At this point, Congress luckily adjourned, and the hotheads on both sides had the better part of a year to cool off. Eventually a compromise was reached that allowed Missouri's admission as a slave state, but prohibited slavery in any territory of the United States north of 36° 30', Missouri's southern boundary. To keep the balance in the Senate, the state of Maine, which had detached itself from Massachusetts, was accepted into the Union at the same time. The South was content with the arrangement. It had achieved its purpose. Arkansas was about to come its way, and there still was Florida.

But as North and South came to blows over the protective tariff, the slave states suddenly realized with the clarity of hindsight that the Missouri Compromise had been a terrible mistake. Arkansas, offset by Michigan, came into the fold in 1837. Now the only slave territory left was Florida, while the free territories of Michigan, Wisconsin, and Iowa were knocking at the door. Once the Indians' hold on the Great Plains was broken, who knew what might happen?

For the moment, fate sided with the South. The accidental explosion of a cannon aboard the U.S.S. *Princeton* wiped out all Northerners in John Tyler's cabinet while the presidential party was aboard the frigate.

"Tyler Too" had two great ambitions. One was to be elected president in his own right, the other to become a country builder. He wanted to annex the Republic of Texas, which had recently secured its independence from Mexico. What better way to accomplish both than to appoint Calhoun as his new secretary of state? Calhoun, the eminent Democratic stalwart, could deliver him the Democratic nomination, of which he was by no means certain. Moreover,

---

*The amendment barred further import of slaves into Missouri, and required that all Negroes subsequently born in that state would be freed at age twenty-five.

Calhoun, unlike the former secretary, was all in favor of a cotton-growing, slave-owning Lone Star State.

Calhoun couldn't make Texas palatable to the Northerners but he figured out a way to ram it down their throats. After concluding a treaty acceptable to Sam Houston, he had President Tyler acclaim it by joint resolution of Congress, which didn't require a two-thirds majority. As for the nomination, Calhoun came through on that, too, but while he could deliver the politicians, he was unable to swing the popular vote. Tyler surrendered the White House to Polk on March 1, 1845, the day after he had signed the annexation treaty with Texas.

This was to be King Cotton's last real triumph. Iowa joined the Union in 1846, Wisconsin two years later. The admission of California in 1850 as a free state that extended far below 36° 30′ was a stunning blow. To prevent secession right then and there, Henry Clay devised a brilliantly tinkered compromise (made palatable by Daniel Webster's oratory), whose peace offerings turned out to be largely spurious, if not originally so intended. The compromise held the door ajar to slavery in New Mexico, if and when it was admitted to statehood (which didn't happen until fifty-two years later). The

The "Approach to Montgomery," drawn by A.R. Ward, date unrecorded.—*Alabama Archives*

compromise also gave the South a long-desired federal fugitive slave law to be enforced in the free states—but enforceable to any significant extent only with local cooperation. It provided for Congress to assume the horrendous national debt Texas had inherited from its days as a republic—except that this settlement mostly benefited Northern banks that held the bulk of Texas paper.

In effect, the Compromise of 1850 gave the South nothing but another ten years of tenuous peace and deceptive prosperity, ten years during which hatreds grew and positions hardened on both sides. Ironically, for eight of those ten years, the South all but controlled the White House, and through it found sympathy in the Supreme Court; the Whigs' collapse and the Republicans' as yet adolescent flailing had put the Democrats firmly in the saddle. Thus, the South won the Dred Scott Decision, which held that a Negro did not become free, and did not have the rights of a citizen, simply by virtue of being taken into a free state. Even the restrictions of the Missouri Compromise were found unconstitutional, albeit a little late in the game. But such nominal victories only served to increase the tensions. Radicals flourished on both sides as reason gave way to stubborn pride. The

Montgomery in the early 1850s, looking toward the State Capitol.—*Alabama Archives*

North developed a frightening righteousness, a missionary dedication of Puritan-liberal mix that has been entrenched ever since in U.S. policy. John Brown, a murderous messiah who had distinguished himself earlier in a Kansas massacre of Pottawatomi Indians, was acclaimed a martyr when he was hanged for his terrorist attack on Harpers Ferry. The South, in turn, fell prey to a siege mentality, a paranoia remarkably akin to that of Germany between the two World Wars. Slavery had been an economic tool; now it became a faith. Mails were censored for abolitionist propaganda. Criticism of slavery was suppressed. Prominent abolitionists were tried in absentia and bounties placed on their heads.

The Civil War's first fusillades were fired as early as 1855 in Kansas, as a consequence of the Supreme Court decision that had declared the Missouri Compromise unconstitutional, and had opened the territories of Kansas, Nebraska, and Oregon to slavery. The South had no interest in Kansas as such; it was not cotton country. But slave owners came anyway, along with their human property, and the Freestaters gave them battle. It was an unofficial overture but, for all that, no less evocative of the slaughter to come than the Japanese bombing of the U.S. gunship *Panay* on the Yangtze in 1937 would be of Pearl Harbor.

After federal troops had moved in to quell the fighting, the Kansas skirmish and the Dred Scott issue gave rise to the Lincoln-Douglas debates, and thus catapulted Honest Abe from relative obscurity as a Midwestern lawyer-politician to Republican prominence. Although Lincoln's new testament of antislavery was delivered "with malice toward none," he was anathema to Dixie. "A house divided against itself cannot stand," he said, predicting that the nation must "become all one thing, or all the other." The implication was clear. Lincoln, both morally and politically, sided with all free. His election would be unacceptable to the South.

After his victory over Douglas, South Carolina was first to repeal its ratification of the U.S. Constitution. Six other states seceded before Lincoln assumed office: Mississippi, Florida, Alabama, Georgia, Louisiana, and Texas. In the two months after the Sumter attack, Virginia, Arkansas, North Carolina, and Tennessee followed suit. Five slave states did not: Delaware, Maryland, Kentucky, Western (now West) Virginia, and Missouri. A perusal of the lineup shows that

CHARLESTON

MERCURY

EXTRA:

Passed unanimously at 1.15 o'clock, P. M., December 20th, 1860.

AN ORDINANCE

To dissolve the Union between the State of South Carolina and other States united with her under the compact entitled " The Constitution of the United States of America."

We, the People of the State of South Carolina, in Convention assembled, do declare and ordain, and it is hereby declared and ordained,

That the Ordinance adopted by us in Convention, on the twenty-third day of May, in the year of our Lord one thousand seven hundred and eighty-eight, whereby the Constitution of the United States of America was ratified, and also, all Acts and parts of Acts of the General Assembly of this State, ratifying amendments of the said Constitution, are hereby repealed; and that the union now subsisting between South Carolina and other States, under the name of " The United States of America," is hereby dissolved.

THE

UNION

IS

DISSOLVED!

The Civil War's first broadside was fired by the *Charleston Mercury*. At right, scene in front of the Alabama Capitol the day the Ordinance of Secession was passed.—*Montgomery Advertiser/ Alabama Journal*

this was indeed to be a cotton war. Of the eleven Confederate states, only four were grounded in other economies.

And cotton was to be Dixie's blockbuster weapon. The graycoats who streamed from their plantations and farms, leaving hog and hominy behind, were, to begin with, strictly on tactical deployment. The South's intended strategic strike force reposed in the bulging warehouses and on the great wharves of Charleston, New Orleans, Mobile, and Memphis—millions of bales of upland cotton. Complacent in this richness, the South failed to follow up its stunning victory at Bull Run. General Joe Johnston called for an immediate invasion of Pennsylvania before the Union had time to organize its forces, but Jefferson Davis disagreed. All the South had to do, he fervently

believed, was to hold its position. Hunger for cotton would soon bring Britain in on Dixie's side.

Jefferson Davis would have made a lousy futures trader. He didn't recognize that the bumper crop of 1860 still glutted the market. His Jefferson-style embargo gave him no leverage at all. Had he rushed his cotton to Europe and sold it, if need be, at cut-rate prices, the conflict might have taken a different course. With the proceeds he could have bought the arms and ammunition his troops needed, and brought the materiel home before the Northern blockade was effectively in place. But Davis was so smug that he didn't even impose a war tax in 1861. By the time he realized what was happening, the blockade had made it nearly impossible for the Confederacy to sustain commerce across the sea. As for Davis' expectation that the British Empire wouldn't condone the blockade, this also was in vain. Britain, as a maritime power, respected naval conventions: This was not a paper blockade, which she might have violated since her sympathies were on the Confederacy's side, but a real one, which brooked no neutral interference.

For a whole year, until it was too late, Davis stuck to his fatal "hold back cotton" policy. Only then did he decide to dump it, and by that time this was easier said than done. True, no blockade has ever been complete, and this one wasn't either. Blockade runners, low of freeboard, were built in Nova Scotia and on the British Isles to steal in and out of Southern ports in the darkness of the moon. But because of their low construction, these vessels could carry only limited cargo. Cotton dribbled out and war materiel in (along with an astounding quantity of luxury goods), but the traffic gained less for the Confederacy than for the blockade runners and their intermediate ports in the Bahamas and on Bermuda, which enjoyed a prosperity they had not known since the days of buccaneers and would not know again until the age of condominiums. Blockade runners were paid as much as $5,000 in gold for a round trip. To skipper such a vessel was a short and glamorous existence; on the average a runner lasted four journeys before being captured or losing his ship on shoals. For a time, Dixie's one secure gateway was the mouth of the Rio Grande. There, Richard King, who had established the giant King Ranch in 1853, owned a fleet of river steamers, which he put under the Mexican flag. Immune under these colors, he ferried thousands of cotton bales to Tampico and Vera Cruz, but an amphibious attack in 1863 all but plugged that leak. By 1864, only 24 of the 1,395 vessels that had attempted to run the blockade were still in action. It was all over but for the final shots.

Intervention by European powers could have turned the tide. Napoleon III flirted with that idea when he'd sent Maximilian to Mexico. Spain's sympathies also lay with the Confederacy, but rather than become involved, Spain took advantage of the Union's inability to enforce the Monroe Doctrine: for four of the Civil War years, Dominica was once again a Spanish colony. Britain came close to mediating the conflict, but mediation would have implied recognition of the Confederacy, and Britain shied away from this decisive step. As the end drew near, the weather also conspired against Dixie. Britain, along with the continent of Europe, suffered three seasons of poor harvest, and food for empty bellies took precedence over cotton for stilled mills.

This food came from the American Midwest, where McCormick's mechanical reaper had meanwhile come into general use. Bumper crops of wheat and corn, tens of millions of bushels, were loaded aboard ships at Northern ports to fight the famine across the Atlantic. Even before Lee surrendered at Appomattox, Britain's music halls echoed with a new popular song: "Old King Cotton's dead and buried. Brave young corn is king."

3

Of Patriarchs and Peddlers

IN THE 1860s, as Dixie rushed toward its doom, the hamlet of Otterstadt, in the Rhenish Palatinate of the Kingdom of Bavaria, had just recovered from its most recent disaster, an epidemic of bubonic plague. While King Cotton, astride that most treacherous of all steeds, that of prosperity, could envision no end to his reign, even Otterstadt's most simpleminded burghers knew that permanence is an illusion. The tiny town's past, like that of all habitations along the world's trade routes, was one of war and pillage. Situated on the middle Rhine, where the great river flows in a wide, flat valley toward its confluence with the Main, the settlement stood in the natural gateway between the Vosges and the Black Forest. The Roman legions had marched through here, scattering bits of armor on fields whose rich soil hid the relics of yet earlier, more primitive battles and pursuits: stone axes, bronze and iron picks. The Franks came along about 500 to 800 A.D., and one of them, Authari, gave the village his name, since transmogrified to Otter, like the small furry beast that, in those days, still hunted pink-meated salmon in Lorelei's river. The Palatine Counts, electors in the Holy Roman Empire, ruled the region in the Middle Ages. Then the Palatinate was appropriated by Bavaria. In the Thirty Years' War (1618–1648), Otterstadt was sacked and burned by the Count of Mansfeld. It was incinerated once again in the War of the Spanish Succession (1701–1714) and later Napoleon, en route to Moscow, grabbed it for France in passing. After his defeat, the Bavarians took it back.

You'd think that all this brutal coming and going would have discouraged settlement of the Rhenish Palatinate, the Rheinpfalz. But the land was generous, and the climate, tempered by the Rhine, benign. Mists wrapped the country in a gentle veil that shimmered as the morning sun broke through to heat the moistened fields. Potatoes, wheat, rye, flax, and sugar beets flourished without undue prompting. Grapes, brought by the Romans, provided sweet solace. Even tobacco managed to take root. Besides, the river was full of fish, and Otterstadt had been something of a fishing village until the Rhine's course was altered in the 1840s to make it more amenable to traffic. There is no record of how many people lived in Otterstadt before the plague, but after it had passed, a clerk in 1787 counted forty-one survivors and inscribed their names in the books of the medieval cathedral at Speyer, the nearby bishopric and capital of the duchy. By 1860, despite the ravages of the Napoleonic Wars, the population had grown to about eleven hundred, and you might say that Otterstadt was almost cosmopolitan by the standards of that time, for its citizenry included nine Protestants and sixty-five Jews.

Among the latter were four Weil families that may well have been related. How closely is a moot question. Weil is one of the more common German-Jewish names, and an impressive number of Weils today can trace their ancestry to the Palatinate. The one thing that the Otterstadt Weils definitely shared, in addition to their faith, was their means of livelihood. Several of the paterfamilias were butchers, which is not as surprising as it may seem since Jews, because of their dietary laws, had always slaughtered their own meat and thus tended naturally toward that trade, just as matzoh got them into baking. There was Benjamin Weil, born in 1792, who was not a native but came from the village of Landsheim, also in the Palatinate. Then there were two brothers, Leon, born in 1823, and Aron, born in 1814, the sons of Solomon (spelled Salimon on his gravestone), who lived from 1780 to 1856. Finally, there was Abraham Weil, born in 1832 to Wolfgang Weil and Gertrude Gutherz, and in all probability the descendant of one Isaac Weil, who lived in Otterstadt in the early 1700s, before the pestilence. It was this Abraham who was destined to be the progenitor of the Weils of Weil Brothers.

Like a kaleidoscope, fate creates its permutations from past pat-

The white house with the big courtyard doors above was the Otterstadt home of
Abraham Weil. Its current owners, Karl and Anna Katz, posed for the author next
to their modest grocery, which now occupies the building's storefront.

terns. Each vision alone may appear capricious, but viewed as a continuum the changing imagery makes perfect sense. That's what makes history so fascinating—its ineluctable chain of cause and effect. But we can look back only so far, and beyond that lies speculation. Abraham's two eldest sons had barely reached their teens when he sent them to Huntsville, Alabama, an obscure outpost in a distant, mysterious land only recently ravaged in a *Bürgerkrieg* so bloody that even war-inured Europe watched with awe. Isidor Weil, born April 24, 1856, was but thirteen when he journeyed across the Atlantic; his brother Herman, born September 14, 1857, just twelve. True, children matured earlier then. It was expected of them. But still they were children. What could make a provincial German Jew, in an era of tolerance in Germany, tear these boys away from their mother and bid them farewell, perhaps never to see them again?

It wasn't that the family went hungry, that there were too many mouths to feed. The same year Isidor and Herman embarked for America, Abraham built a new house, a drab one to be sure, on Otterstadt's somnolent main street, and moved his wife and their other children, six by then and one more on the way, into the living quarters behind the store. Evidently the Weils were reasonably comfortable—as comfortable as a village shopkeeper's family could be. But they were no by no means well-to-do. Was it then a dream of milk and honey that prompted Abraham? Or was it less a dream than the realization that life in Otterstadt was hopelessly stultifying, a dead-end street? If so, why not simply send the boys to nearby Mannheim, to Frankfurt, or to Mainz? Did Abraham mistrust the Germans? Was he plagued by anti-Semitism? Or did he feel the German states were moribund? And even if he did ship his sons off to America, why to Alabama?

Intriguing speculations—but only the last question is answered: Abraham's two younger brothers, Isaiah (known as Isha) and Hermann (after whom the younger Herman was named) had emigrated to America, probably in 1866 or 1867, and owned a general store in Huntsville, in northern Alabama. Abraham's brother-in-law, Moses Lemle (originally Lemmle), was also in the States. He had come to Cincinnati before the Civil War, and eventually settled in Opelika, a tiny town in eastern Alabama, where he also opened a country store. Abraham entrusted his young sons to their American uncles' care.

But again this only begs the question: Why Alabama? From the Palatinate's perspective, it hardly could have seemed the most propitious place to seek one's fortune. European Jews, with their group ethic, were generally not inclined to frontier adventurism. Although the ghetto, as an enforced institution, had been abolished in Germany for more than a century, they still tended to cling to each other in tight insular communities. Of course, there were Jews in America, notably in Boston, Cincinnati, Baltimore, and New Orleans; less so, however, in the Deep South. True, the Confederacy's attorney general and secretary of war, Judah P. Benjamin, had been a Jew, and supposedly the first settler in what is now Montgomery County was one, too. The latter, Abraham Mordecai, a native of Pennsylvania, is said to have arrived in 1785. According to some accounts, Indian braves cut off one of his ears for consorting with a squaw; another story has it that he married her. In any event, Mordecai was an anomaly, and if the Weils had heard about him, which is highly improbable, they would have been properly discouraged. On their faded photographs, they don't look much like sabras.

Not that Alabama was frontier, but it wasn't far from it. Statehood had come only about fifty years earlier, in 1819, five years after Andrew Jackson defeated the Indians in the Battle of Horseshoe Bend of the Tallapoosa River. As late as 1832, the Creeks in eastern Alabama were still fighting settlers. The final Indian treaty wasn't concluded until that year. Mobile flourished as a seaport before the Civil War, but the state's interior was something else again. The westward march of cotton along Alabama's "Black Belt"—a broad band of fertile, dusky soil that slants across the crumbly red clay of the region—had brought with it a modicum of civilization, even a railroad, the Western Railway of Alabama, which connected West Point, Georgia, with Montgomery. But the state was only sparsely settled, and even its biggest towns were far smaller than those of provincial Germany. In early 1861, when Montgomery enjoyed its brief glory as the Confederacy's first capital, the city only had about 10,000 inhabitants, most of them po-whites: although Alabama had its share of prosperous planters, it was not a gentry state. What wealth there had been, the Civil War wiped out. Montgomery had burned its own cotton warehouses before surrendering to Wilson's Raiders.

Union troops laid waste to plantations. Slaves in overrun territories fled the fields. Carpetbaggers and military occupation finished the job. No—in the late 1860s, Alabama surely was no Shangri-la.

To be sure, Montgomery was mildly cosmopolitan. It had harbored a small Jewish community prior to the Civil War. Their congregation, Kahl Montgomery, was founded in 1852 and their temple built in 1860. Lehman Bros., the investment bankers, had their beginnings in Montgomery among the first cotton factors, whose function it was to finance the crops of growers. Jacob Greil, founder of the wholesale house of Greil Bros. (dry goods, then groceries, then liquor, and ultimately pharmaceuticals) had served as a captain in the Confederate Army. Sarah Guggenheim Roman, whose daughter, Esther, was to marry into Uncle Isha's branch of the Weil family, was born in Montgomery in 1853. David Weil, who helped organize Goetter, Weil & Co., another old Montgomery wholesale firm, arrived in 1850; he could well be distantly related to the Weils of this story, for he also had his origins in the Palatinate. Indeed, Albert Strassburger, a great-grandfather of Virginia Loeb Weil, the wife of Bobby Weil, Sr., was acting mayor of Montgomery at one time during the War Between the States.

Montgomery was a true inland port, joined to Mobile Bay by the eminently navigable Alabama River, even if such a journey by steamboat took ten days. But not so Huntsville, whose only link to the outside world was the temperamental Tennessee: it flows tortuously toward the Ohio, and its waters thence arc over to the Mississippi. This town was way out in the boondocks, and far less likely to attract immigrant Jews. Indeed, as we shall see, Isha and Hermann came to settle there by chance.

No matter what Abraham's reservations about Otterstadt and Germany might have been, and no matter how brightly Isha and Hermann may have pictured Huntsville in their correspondence, he must have been an extraordinarily courageous man to gamble his sons' futures on such a mysterious locale, so far beyond the sea and deep within the distant continent. Not only must he have been courageous, but strong-willed and single-minded, too. A few years after Isidor and the younger, one-*n* Herman had joined their uncles, he also sent his third-born son, Adolf, to Huntsville. That parting

Four Weil generations gathered in Otterstadt shortly after the First World War: great-grandfather Abraham, grandfather Isidor, father Adolph, and Adolph's elder son, Bucks.

must have been particularly painful. Adolf, a bookish, sickly child, was the apple of his eye, the "Flower of the Flock," as family reminiscences have it.

Since Otterstadt only had a common lower school, Adolf trudged to Speyer every day, nearly five miles each way, so he could attend classes at the *Gymnasium*. The boy was always racked by coughs, but no one suspected that he suffered from tuberculosis. So, he too was shipped to America, where the disease soon overpowered him. When Uncle Hermann brought him back to Otterstadt to die at home, Adolf's mother fell to her knees before the frail young man and clutched him. She looked up at her brother and sobbed, "What have you done to my son?"

But even after Adolf's death a few months later, America remained Abraham's vicarious mecca. Yet another son, Emil, born to Abraham in 1864 in his first marriage to Magdalena Lemmle, was sent to Alabama when he reached his teens. Of Abraham's and Magdalena's nine children, only three remained in Germany. Widowed in 1882, Abraham remarried three years later, and all of the children of this union with Johanette (Helene) Freundlich, eventually emigrated to the United States.

So, amazingly, did most of the other Otterstadt Jews, and we may safely presume that their exodus took place largely at Abraham's instigation. He was the most respected member of their community. Had they been sufficiently organized to have a formal *Kultusgemeinde*, he would surely have been its president. Even the synagogue was in his house (the new one), a chamber on the second floor that looked out over the small inner courtyard. Although this temple seems to have been consecrated, there was no rabbi. Abraham led the men in reading the Torah and the Sabbath Prayer Book. The women sat behind a partition, a slight that was to anger Herman's daugher, Hermione (Mrs. Julian Adler, of Birmingham, Alabama), when her father took the nine-year-old girl to visit *Grosspapa* Abraham in Otterstadt. Hermione marvels to this day that the devout ladies did not seem humiliated in the least.* But then, of course, Gloria Steinem was not yet even a twinkle in her father's male-chauvinist eye.

As the years passed, emigration shrunk Abraham's flock. The tiny temple finally accommodated everyone in comfort. Abraham died in 1926, so he never knew what a great service he had done with his mania for America. Almost as if he had been clairvoyant, he had helped save the Jews of Otterstadt from the Holocaust. Only three Jewish families still lived there when Hitler came to power in 1933, and only one Otterstadt Jew, a Moritz Weil of unknown lineage, died in a concentration camp.

That's what the records say, which to this day are kept on large pink index cards in Otterstadt's former city hall. The cards show birthdays, death dates, occupations, marriages, children. There's also a space for religion, but apparently that wasn't prominent enough. Sometime in the 1930s, the cards of all Jews, even those long dead, were pulled from the files, and crossed out with corner-to-corner x's, drawn meticulously with the aid of a ruler. The clerk then carefully wrote *Jude*! in the center of each card before putting it back in the file.

---

*From "The Weil-Simon Saga," a short informal typescript, written for her family by Hermione Weil Adler.

Abraham's house at 43 Mannheimerstrasse still stands, one of a bleak row of almost identical two-story houses. Its owner is Karl Katz, a grocer, whose father had bought it from Abraham's widow shortly after his death. Abraham's temple is now a store room. There isn't much in it. The grocery doesn't appear very prosperous. In one of the two show windows that flank the door, Katz keeps a big Marlboro display box. In another, there's a Martini cardboard sign. That's about all.

The Count of Mansfeld wouldn't bother with Otterstadt anymore. It's now off the beaten track. In fact, it no longer exists as an independent municipality. In 1972, it was absorbed by the more

Hidden in the municipal files of Otterstadt, there rests an astounding document. It is the civic record of Abraham Weil's life: the dates of his birth, death, and marriages; the vital statistics of his first wife, including the names of her parents; and, on its obverse (not shown), a listing of his children. Nothing special about that. What makes that pink 5-by-7 index card so remarkable is that when Hitler came to power eight years after Abraham's death (and all of forty-nine years after his first wife's decease), a Nazi bureaucrat carefully ruled an X over the card, and in its center scribbled *Juden!*—Jews! Perhaps even more surprising is that the author was easily granted permission to photograph this embarrassing relic.

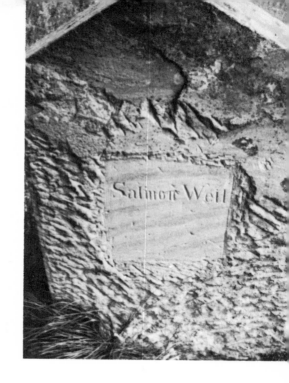

Otterstadt's Jewish cemetery, surprisingly left intact during the Hitler years, is tended by August Flory, keeper of a Catholic cemetery across the road. The gravestone that marks the burial site of Abraham Weil and his second wife was the last to be erected, in the spring of 1931 (bottom left). The oldest recognizable headstone (right) is that of Salimon Weil, not a direct ancestor but probably a relative, who died in 1856.—*Author's photographs*

prosperous neighboring village of Waldsee, a bedroom community for workers at BASF, I.G. Farben's offspring, ten miles to the north in Ludwigshafen.

At the edge of what once was Otterstadt, the Jewish cemetery stands unkempt. Wildflowers grow on the graves. The cemetery is bordered by a ancient wall and protected by an iron gate. Some tombstones have crumbled, but all are in place. A visitor can't help but be surprised that the graveyard wasn't vandalized, let alone plowed up, in Hitler's time.

August Flory has the answer. Caretaker of the Catholic cemetery on the other side of the pleasant country lane, he also guards the key to the Jewish burial grounds. "In Germany," Flory says proudly, "cemeteries have always been protected by law."

Like most Jewish immigrants of the 1800s, the three uncles, Isha and Hermann Weil and Moses Lemle, started life in the New World as peddlers. This term evokes an image from fuzzy photographs: scrawny, bearded men pushing carts through the sepia-tinted turmoil of New York City's Lower East Side. But Isha, Hermann, and Moses didn't look at all like that. The Jews in those pictures, ageless in their long coats and dark hats, their pale foreheads framed by earlocks, were refugees from the pogrom-punished ghettos of Poland and Russia, and they did not come to this country in appreciable numbers until nearly the turn of the century. The earlier Jewish immigrants, like the three Weil uncles, were largely of southern German origin, natives of the Bavarian Palatinate and neighboring Elsass-Lothringen before it became Alsace-Lorraine. They spoke neither Hebrew nor Yiddish, and they had long discarded the traditional costume of the devout. In America, as in Germany, they endeavored to blend with the local population, even as they maintained their religious integrity.

The uncles did not linger at the port where they debarked, presumably New York or Boston. All three proceeded almost immediately to Cincinnati, with its established community of German Jews. If, as must be presumed, Isha and Hermann came shortly after the Civil War, Isha, born in 1835, was in his early thirties, and Hermann, born in 1845 or 1847, in his early twenties. Uncle Moses, the first to set foot on these shores, had also emigrated as a young man. The Archives and History Department of the State of Alabama lists a Moses Lemle, who was born in Bavaria in 1840 and died in Opelika in 1884. This Lemle, whose grave is in Montgomery's Oakwood Cemetery, is almost certainly the uncle who figures briefly but prominently in our story a few pages hence.

Isha and Hermann did not peddle their merchandise from push-carts. It appears that they traveled in bourgeois respectability by railroad train and river boat, transporting their merchandise in trunks and satchels—cloth for pretty dresses, yarn, silken thread, thimbles, needles, tatting, all manner of dry goods. Thus they drummed their way up the Ohio to the confluence with the Tennessee River and then up the Tennessee. How long the voyage took them and how often they made it is anyone's guess. Cincinnati was their base, and that's where they stocked up on supplies. It's more than 1,000 river miles from Cincinnati to Huntsville, and when Isha and Hermann had saved enough money, it was there that they decided to open a general store, perhaps because there wasn't too much competition, or maybe they just liked the place. They kept on going back to Cincinnati, however, to replenish their merchandise and to court the Wertheimer sisters, Emma and Belle, who had been born in Ohio but were also of Palatinate descent.

Isha and Hermann were always very close. They lived out of a common purse, and continued to do so even after they married the Cincinnati girls and brought them to Huntsville. Eventually, as children came along, they decided to move out of their communal house, and built two identical houses across a yard from each other. Then they flipped a coin to see which of them would move into what house.

The two brothers were still bachelors when Abraham's sons, Isidor and the younger Herman, showed up in their Sabbath best, albeit no doubt soiled and rumpled from their long voyage. Whether the boys crossed the ocean on their own or one of the uncles fetched them is not certain. In any case, their arrival was well timed. In 1869, the South was over the worst of its postwar agonies and beginning to recover. On the social and political level, the problems of emancipation were by no means solved, but the economy was picking up again;

there was food on the table, and maybe a little extra to spend. What the South had feared most had not come to pass. Unlike in the West Indies, the freed slaves, who outnumbered whites almost everywhere, did not revolt, and in many areas not overrun by Union troops they continued to work for their former owners. Elsewhere, Negroes, if anything, were worse off as a whole under the carpetbagger regimes imposed under Congressional Reconstruction than they had been before the war, and when the freedmen discovered that their votes did not gain them the "forty acres and a mule" they had been promised by their liberators, they soon abandoned the Republicans who backed radical measures to enforce equality. Increasingly, they drifted back into the fold of the "Conservatives," who represented the old regime. After all, whether chattel or free, they had to eat. Often, in fact, they worked harder than before: now they could be fired. And so the South stabilized—despite inequality, despite the emergence of the Ku Klux Klan, and despite periodic outbursts of brutality such as Negroes had never known when they were still slaves. Not until after the Second World War did the blacks call in the debt owed them by King Cotton. By then, of course, the interest far outweighed the principal.

Isha's and Hermann's Huntsville store prospered with the economy's resurgence. This was not plantation country, so there were many more potential customers. Eventually, the store specialized in clothing—men's and women's suits and dresses, shoes and boots, coveralls, ginghams, and finery. The fact that the local economy depended on small and medium farms had yet another advantage. Rural northern Alabama, separated by some two hundred miles of densely forested mountains from the Black Belt of southern Alabama, had escaped the ravages of incontinent cultivation: it wasn't on the main route of King Cotton's westward march. But the fields of northern Alabama were highly productive and small acreages provided excellent yields. Indeed, most of today's Alabama cotton crop comes from that section of the state.

But in the 1870s, the Black Belt's decline was not yet a concern. Its cotton harvests increased with each passing season. By 1875, they nearly reached the presecession level. Meanwhile, Isidor and Herman learned English and helped out in their uncles' store. Very likely they had no idea that they would soon be in the cotton business.

About the only explanation of how this came about is that the two Huntsville uncles didn't need help as much as the Opelika uncle, Moses Lemle, who so far had to manage all by himself. Moses also had started a dry goods store, and this one was in the center of the cotton country. Presumably he wrote to Huntsville, requesting assistance. There was yet another uncle, Issac (Isaac), Abraham's youngest brother, who had also joined the Otterstadt exodus and somehow wound up in Columbus, Mississippi. It's possible that Isidor and Herman went there first from Huntsville. In any event, they didn't stay. Sometime in 1875 they arrived in Opelika, and that's where they would found the cotton firm.

On the face of it, this wasn't exactly the best time to go into business in Opelika. Unlike Huntsville and Montgomery, this rural hamlet of less than 2,500 souls was still embroiled in the politics of Reconstruction. But venturing into an enterprise is like any other investment: you hope to buy cheap and sell dear. Chances are that neither Moses, nor Isidor and Herman, quite thought of it that way, except in terms of their merchandise, but that is in effect how it all turned out.

The first settlers had come to Opelika about 1837, when there were still plenty of Indians around who had either not heard of the peace treaty or couldn't care less. When they asked for handouts and the pioneers didn't comply, the rejected supplicants got even by burning homesteads and often killing their occupants. Such risks, however, did not deter immigration, and by 1840 there were enough people in the general area to warrant the establishment of a post office. The settlement was then called "Opellikan," a name derived from the Creek phrase for "large swamp," although the bog referred to wasn't anywhere near town. Eight years later, the West Point and Montgomery Railroad Company (eventually known as the Western of Alabama), extended its single track from Franklin to Opelika, but the link to West Point, Georgia, was not completed until 1861. Meanwhile, a line had also been constructed between Columbus, Georgia, and Opelika, but even so the aborning community could only muster fifty votes in the election of 1860. Early city ordinances testify to futile attempts at respectability. Fines were decreed for the firing of pistols, guns, blunderbusses, and bows and arrows on the streets, and it was illegal to sell liquor in quantities smaller than a quart without a license; the law said nothing about gallons, which then retailed for about $1.50. That no one took the firearms ordinance too seriously was made evident by subsequent events. Even after Isidor became a cotton merchant, Opelikans still toted six-shooters and some of them proudly notched their guns for kills.

But let it not be said that Opelika lacked civic pride. In 1861, it proposed its selection as the capital of the Confederacy, a noble gesture that wasn't taken too seriously beyond the city limits. Even so, their patriotic fervor undiminished, the Opelika Volunteers marched off to join the Sixth Alabama Regiment and were thus stationed in Virginia, far from home, when General Rousseau's Union Cavalry swooped on southeastern Alabama to cut the West Point and Montgomery Railroad. Rousseau's troops, encountering little opposition, not only wrecked the trackage but Opelika's depot and the warehouses as well. The town had barely pulled itself back together again when seven months later, on May 1, 1865, the Second Indiana Cavalry arrived on yet another foray. This time, a handful of Confederate pickets tried to defend the town, only to be driven back and soundly thrashed, with much attendant damage.

Now, we all know how much rebuilding can be accomplished in ten years. Look at Germany and Japan after World War II. But Opelika's rulers were not nearly so benevolent. The carpetbag-scallawag regime remained entrenched here until the election of 1874, by which time Moses Lemle certainly was in Opelika, and Isidor and Herman probably were too. For young immigrants, that election must have been quite an experience. The radical Republicans threatened to cut off the ears of every black who voted the Democratic ticket, and Negroes by the dozen were locked up the night before election and kept drunk until marched to the polls by hit men of the carpetbagger mafia.

The Democrats won, but this didn't solve Opelika's problems. The city was deeply in debt and the newly elected office holders had no idea what to do about it. By 1882, there was so much bad feeling that both slates of candidates in the election of that year claimed victory, and the town found itself not only with two sets of officials but two police forces as well, whose main duty was to fight each other. At this point, Opelika no longer was even a respectable hole in the road. Traveling salesmen, leery of becoming involved in brawls, avoided the place, and railroad passengers were officially advised to duck while their trains passed through town. In January 1883, the sheriff of Lee County telegraphed the governor that "it is impossible to keep peace. . . [that there was] shooting in the streets in every direction." Alabama's governor, who previously had apparently paid no attention to widely published newspaper reports that Opelika was run by "knights of the bar room," now called out the Montgomery Grays and dispatched them to the unruly little town. The Grays arrested the troublemakers, and peace finally came to Opelika eight years after Appomattox.

Yet, during all this turbulence, the Weil business grew and prospered in the midst of Opelika's embattled "downtown." The establishment occupied the two floors of a modest building at the southeast corner of Railroad Avenue and North Eighth Street, overlooking the tracks and warehouses, where the Opelika Hardware Co. now makes its home. Since 1878, and perhaps even before then, Isidor had been in charge. All we know for sure is that at some point Moses Lemle turned over his store to Isidor and Herman, and moved to Cincinnati for some years. Very likely this happened in 1877, shortly after the death of his twenty-two-year-old wife, Helen.* In any event, it was the following year, 1878, that marked the birth of the original Weil Bros. as a partnership of Isidor and Herman. The company was to be engaged in two distinct, but, as we shall see, closely related businesses: a general mercantile store and a cotton

---

*In Cincinnati, Moses remarried. His second wife, Carrie Oppenheimer, was Helen's sister. Later, Moses must have returned with Carrie and a daughter of his first marriage, Minnie, to Opelika, for he died there in 1884. Minnie is still remembered in Montgomery for having driven that city's first electric automobile.

Insufficient and often contradictory records make it impossible to trace the Lemle line. The Alabama Department of Archives and History notes a Samuel Lemle, born in "Rulzhan" (probably Rülzheim), Bavaria, in 1849, who died in Opelika in 1876. Also named in the archives are Judah Leon Lemle (no vital statistics); Isaac Lemle (1844–1909), who may well have been Moses' brother Issac; and one Babette Lemle, who is recorded as the wife of Moses, but if indeed she was, then there must have been a second Moses Lemle. Babette is shown as having a daughter, born in 1871, who died in Opelika in 1901. That's the biggest puzzler of all, for our Moses Lemle is supposed to have had a sister by the name of Babette.

brokerage, with the store located downstairs and the brokerage upstairs, both on Moses Lemle's former premises.

One may safely assume that neither Isidor nor Herman knew anything about cotton when they moved from Huntsville to Opelika. Nor, since arriving there, could they have availed themselves of tutelage; there was no mentor in the house. Whatever knowledge Isidor acquired—for it was he who took on the cotton end of the business—he garnered on his own. Alabama grew only one kind in those days, a fairly uniform crop known the world over as "Alabama cotton"; no other specifications were required. There was no need yet for the skill of "stapling," the deft, repeated pulling apart of a small cotton sample cut out of a bale until only a few strands, now straight, are left in the classer's hand. From these strands, he can (or thinks he can) tell at a glance the length, i.e. the "staple," of the fiber to $\frac{1}{32}$ of an inch. Alabama cotton was presumed to be $\frac{7}{8}$ of an inch and usually was. The yet more sophisticated measurement of "micronaire," which quantifies the wall thickness of the hollow fiber and thereby its capacity for absorbing dyes, was a concept not yet even dreamed of, and which technology wouldn't make possible until two generations later. In the earliest days, Isidor didn't even have to be too concerned about the "grade," the inherent quality of the cotton as manifest by the cotton's color, its texture (smooth for easy spinning), and the foreign matter, such as leaf fragments and soil particles, it contained. As for the financial aspects of the brokerage operation, these too were not yet terribly complex. To begin with, there wasn't all that much money involved.

It's interesting to speculate that Isidor might not have gone into the cotton business had the South not been poverty-striken after the war. Who knows, he might have ended up owning a department store. What made him a cotton man was that the farmers around Opelika had no money. Growers, whether of cotton or any other agricultural commodity, have always required financing of their crops, and in the Cotton South this was one of the functions of the factors, like the Lehmans in Montgomery. But during Reconstruction most factors were as broke as everybody else, and the South's banking system lay in shambles. To keep food on the table, clothe his kids, and to buy seed and such, the farmer had to get help somewhere. At the same time, the need for credit was more pressing than ever, since many of the larger plantations were now rented in parcels to tenant farmers. Without slaves, and without the wherewithal to pay wages, this was often the only way to cope with extensive acreages. Meanwhile, the tenants had to start from scratch, making it through the year before they could collect on their shares of the crop.

Not that Isidor went into the money-lending business, advancing cash against the coming harvest, as he did later. Rather, at the beginning, he advanced merchandise from the Weil store, and when the crop came in he collected cotton in payment for the debts. He then sold this cotton to nearby mills in Columbus, West Point, and Tallahassee, and to factors at Savannah and Charleston. That's how it all started.

But before long, the synergy between brokerage and store also began working in reverse. Isidor not only accepted cotton in settlement but bought crops from the farmers and always paid them in cash at the back of the store. On the way out, they had to run a gauntlet of sales clerks, and some of the money went right back into the Weils' cash drawer. Later, as the cotton volume increased, the brokerage moved into offices above the mercantile store. But by then the farmers were more prosperous. While they traded upstairs with Isidor, their wives, along for the festive and profitable trip to town, did their shopping down below. After the farmer had clomped back down the metal steps that were affixed to the outside of the building on its alley side, he joined his lady and paid her bill. This give-and-take didn't make Isidor a "sharp" operator by any means. The transaction, although it involved cash, was akin to barter. Even today, country stores are often the small farmer's banker, and astute country elevator operators, particularly in the Midwest, have long stocked fertilizer and salt blocks, feed for livestock and chickens, and lumber for fencing and construction. Weil Bros. never expanded its mercantile activities to that degree. Indeed, as time passed, the cotton business so outgrew the dry goods end of the Weil operation that the store became a mere sideline and finally was sold.

In 1887, after Opelika had calmed down and looked like it would stay that way, Isidor decided it was high time to start a family. He was then in his thirty-first year. His bride, Eda Oppenheimer, was twenty-six. Like his Huntsville uncles' brides, Eda hailed from Cincinnati.

The Weils were, and to a remarkable degree still are, the kind of

Brother Emil stayed with the firm.

close-knit family you don't find much anymore. Isha and Hermann had carried that closeness to the extreme, not only marrying sisters, but then living out of a common purse in almost identical neighboring ménages. Isidor and Herman were a mite more modern. Herman went his own way when it came to courting and found his bride in New Orleans, not in Cincinnati. The two young brothers were then married within a week of each other, gave their brides identical wedding rings, and shared alike in the proceeds of the business; when Isidor took a dollar, so did Herman. Still, they lived separate lives. Isidor's house was on the southeast corner of Second Avenue and Sixth Street, now a parking lot for a beauty salon, a health spa, and a hearing aid company. But, even today, the breastworks once thrown up for the futile defense of Opelika still bulge in the shrubs at the end of Sixth Street. Herman and his wife, nee Bertha Simon, made their home near Fourth Street and Avenue A. The decayed, deserted cottage that stands there now may well be where his first son, Louis, was born in 1888. But not long thereafter Bertha's mother died. She was only forty-five and left five young children and a husband many years older than she. Someone had to take care of the family, and there was no one but Bertha to do it. And so, early in the 1890s, Herman bade farewell to Weil Bros. with a heavy heart and moved to New Orleans, where he joined a general merchandise business that had been founded by his wife's grandfather.

By then, reinforcements had arrived from Otterstadt. Isidor's youngest brother, Emil, was Abraham's latest contribution to the Weil

Herman Weil moved to New Orleans.

effort.* It wasn't his last. Siegfried Weil, born circa 1889, the male offspring of Abraham's second marriage, also was shipped off eventually to join the Alabama contingent. Siegfried, however, was less than fascinated by the cotton business and soon drifted off to parts unknown.

Emil stuck, thereby completing the second set of Weil brothers. He served his apprenticeship under Herman in the dry goods business, proved himself extraordinarily adept at bookkeeping, and, when Herman moved to New Orleans, became Isidor's partner, taking over the operation of the store. By all accounts, no two brothers could have been less alike—except perhaps the two generations of Weil brothers, Isidor's sons and grandsons, that were to follow Isidor and Emil. The only point of resemblance was that both of them wore spectacles.

Isidor, although not athletic, was of sturdy build, and by virtue of his forceful personality appeared much stronger than he really was. Of medium height, he always stood erect, making the most of every inch and letting it be known that he would not shrink from any man. He had inherited Abraham's single-mindedness: once set on a course of action, he only rarely could be swayed. "Be sure you're right," his motto was, "then go ahead." In today's lingo, he'd be pigeonholed as a workaholic; except for his family and friends, nothing mattered to him

---

*The Weils have always thought of Emil as the youngest son of Abraham's union with Magdalena Lemmle, but Otterstadt's municipal files reveal that there was yet another boy, Ludwig, born in 1867, who died in infancy.

but making the business grow. His sole avocations were the study of history and the reading of classics. All else struck him as a nuisance. He even forgot to apply for his naturalization papers, and his two Opelika-born sons were in school before he got around to swearing the Oath of Allegiance in 1896, some twenty-five years after his arrival in the United States.

Emil was softer, more lenient, conciliatory, a perfect foil in the bad-guy, good-guy game that must have been played even then. Always frail, he seemed to shrivel in middle age. His appearance in later years reminded some of his friends of Mahatma Gandhi. His was a difficult lot, for, next to Isidor, almost anyone would seem diminished. As Isidor's Eda, arrogant and waspish, once said of her brother-in-law, "Only Isidor could have made a millionaire of Emil." Still, there was more to Emil than met the superficial glance. Once when a Montgomery wag met Emil coming out of the showers at the Standard Club, he looked him up and down, shook his head in wonderment, and remarked wistfully, "Some men have everything."

Be that as it may, the division of responsibilities between the two brothers was well advised. Since Emil tended to hesitancy in a business that doesn't tolerate vacillation, he was better off in the backroom with the ledgers. Besides, a cotton trader won't stay healthy long if he frets too much. Day in, day out, unpredictable factors come into play, from fickle weather to the whims of speculators. Growers may "lay down" on their commitments, refusing to deliver to the merchant at the contracted price. Mills may reject shipments for marginal and sometimes trumped-up reasons. It always has been, and always will be, a rough business, and in the early days, when Isidor started from scratch on Opelika's Railroad Avenue, it wasn't only rough but tumble.

4

Railroad Avenue

EVEN IF ISIDOR had not been a Jew, he could not have attained success as a cotton merchant in the Reconstruction South without making his share of enemies. In this beaten land, any degree of prosperity was suspect, and if the envied man appeared to thrive on the product of the sweat of others then he was presumed to be villainous indeed. Ordered out of northern Alabama by a hothead, Mr. I. (as Isidor was later often called) bought himself a pistol. When negotiating for cotton in the forbidden territory, he placed the weapon on a bale so everyone knew where he stood. Even in Opelika, his life was threatened more than once. Yet he refused to carry his gun except when he went alone to the office late at night or traveled cross-country with a satchel full of cash to pay for cotton.

Once when a farmer, who had strutted around Opelika announcing to one and all that he would kill Isidor, showed up at the office, Isidor had him sent in, ordered everyone else out of the room, and coolly remained seated behind his desk, with his right hand fanned over an open drawer. The intruder, convinced that Isidor wouldn't hesitate to shoot him, was persuaded easily enough to leave. What really amazed Isidor's helpers was that their boss escorted the would-be assassin out into the alley and then even shook hands with him in parting. Isidor later explained that he had noticed that the man was right-handed, and that he had accompanied him only to make sure that the farmer wouldn't draw his gun: he'd stayed behind him all the

Contract of Copartnership
of Isidor & Emil Weil —
Making the firming Of Weil Bros —
of Opelika Ala —

1st Term of Copartnership to expire four
years from date. this copartnership
however can be terminated any fiscal
year by either of the partners giving
the other partner notice that ~~that~~ a
desolution of the said copartnership is
desired. at the end of the fiscal year.
such notification however must be given
on or before the first day of October
preceeding the desired dissolution — such
dissolution then to take place on the
first day of February following the
notification. Should no ~~such~~ notice be
given. this copartnership shall remain
in force until the first day of Feby 1898.

2d The Capital of the ~~firm~~ shall be furnished
jointly. three fourth by J. Weil one fourth
by ~~E. Weil~~ E. Weil. no interest for defic-
iency in capital to be charged to either partner
and neither of the partners is allowed
to withdraw any capitol from the business
except for ~~current~~ expenses of his family
unless he may have an amount above
the required capitol as stated above — that is
J Weil three fourth & E Weil one fourth

3d the Stocks, Bonds, and real Estate owned and aquired by the firm up to date (Feb 1st 1894) the proceeds and interest and dividents of same Shall be devided as follows — Isidor Weil is to receive four fifth and Emil Weil one fifth ——

4th The Profits of the firm, with the exeption of the Bonds, Stocks, & real Estate now owned by said firm — is to be devided, after deducting expenses — bad outstanding debts, and allowing for Shrinkage in value of stock of Merchandise on hand into four parts. Isidor Weil to receive three fourth and Emil Weil one fourth as their respective shares —

5th It is further agreed. Should unfortunately death take either partner away. the business may be carried on by the surviving partner in all its branches. as during the lifetime of both partners for three years longer from the time of death of either partner. with like conditions, this however only with the full consent of the wife of the deceased partner Agreed to this First day of February 1894

Witness
N. Weil.

Isidor Weil
Emil Weil

Isidor and Emil periodically made new partnership agreements. This is their contract of 1894.

way, ready to stop him from reaching, and that's also why he shook the man's hand. Nonplussed, the fellow wouldn't have had time to tug the revolver from his belt before Isidor ducked back into the building.

Such calculation was characteristic of Isidor's approach to life. His mind worked every minute, and all the more efficiently under stress. On another occasion, in Columbus, Georgia, where he had gone to collect on an overdue ninety-day draft from a mill, he was refused payment and told to get out. When Isidor stood his ground, the spinner drew his pistol, pointed it at Isidor and grunted, "Go on, git!" Isidor shook his head. "I'm going to stay right here until I have the money," he said. "Now that you've threatened me, you know you have to pay me." The spinner was smart enough to get the message: his credit would be ruined if he turned away the merchant at gunpoint rather than pay him what was due. A few minutes later, Isidor climbed back on his buggy, cash in hand.

His companion on these journeys was a freedman, John Tarver, who had been born on a plantation in Macon County near Tuskegee in about 1860, left there when he was seventeen, and found his way to Opelika where Isidor hired him as a porter—the company's first employee. So far as Southern mores permitted, the two young men soon were almost inseparable, like Robinson Crusoe and his man Friday; in a sense, both were still learning to live in alien worlds, the nearsighted Jewish boy from Otterstadt in rural Alabama, the black boy in his new-found freedom.

Although in the society then prevailing it was impossible to promote John Tarver into a "white man's job," he enjoyed special status as the Weil organization grew and had become a legend by the time old age forced him to retire. Thus, while Tarver never officially was named head classer, the man responsible for the quality of cotton shipments, he was de facto head of the sample room, where cotton is classed for grade and staple and cleared for shipment on the basis of the samples. He was one of the few employees who could talk back to Isidor and get away with it. One day, after they had been together for many years, Tarver committed the truly unforgivable sin of letting one of his men smoke in the lint-laden atmosphere of the sample room, where piles of cotton are ever ready to flash. In an understandable rage, Isidor called Tarver to his office and told him that they could no longer work together. Tarver pushed back the painter's cap he was fond of wearing, thoughtfully scratched his head, and said, "Mr. Isidor, I's sorry to hear you're leaving. But I's a fixture around here."

Tarver was so possessive of Isidor that he would not permit anyone else to clean the boss' office. He insisted on doing it himself in a nightly ritual with a worn-out, totally useless duster that only had a few feathers left on it. "Colonel" Tarver, as he came to be called, took his position very seriously, and would not allow newly hired Negroes, like Hillary Craig and Will Hawkins, later faithfuls, to talk to him until they had passed a lengthy period of probation. Noblesse oblige. Tarver was well into his sixties when a sample room fire did erupt at Weil Bros., by then in Montgomery. One man leaped from the second-story window, breaking his leg. Another, too scared to jump, could be seen against the flames. Old Tarver brushed the firemen aside and rushed into the building, slung the panicked young man over his shoulder, and carried him through the blaze to safety. Tarver's clothes were half burned off by the time he reached the street, but, miraculously, he was not hurt. "Are you crazy?" screamed a frantic Isidor. "I am old," John Tarver explained. "My children are grown. But he has a young wife and three kids."

On their horse-and-buggy expeditions, Tarver would take the money and Isidor the reins. If they were held up, Isidor reasoned, no one would think that a white man would trust a black man with cash. The trips were long, the buggy slow. Often they slept in the woods. Sometimes Isidor would even send Tarver out by himself, carrying thousands of dollars to the growing string of Weil outposts. On a trip in about 1902, Isidor put every penny the Weils had in Tarver's lap. Isidor had drawn out all the money from the bank in Opelika and decided to look for new quarters in Montgomery. One can't help but wonder if this old family story is apocryphal: Isidor sleeping under the stars with his black sidekick, a small fortune between them. Why didn't he simply ask for a draft? But Tarver's daughter, Johnailene Wilson, tells it, too. So perhaps it's true after all.

Isidor had made that money—which was probably less than we would assume today—not because he was an expert judge of cotton, nor because he was adept at figures; many other men were thus qualified, yet did not prosper. Rather, Isidor was successful because, with his entrepreneurial talent, he perceived the pattern of the cotton

To

STATE OF ALABAMA,
Lee County.

By the _1st_ day of _October_ 188_8_. _I_ promise to pay to _Weil Bros_ or bearer, the sum of _One hundred and five_ _00/100_ DOLLARS.

And as to the collection of this note _I_ hereby waive all homestead and exemption allowed _me_ under the constitution and laws of the State of Alabama.

Witness _my_ hand and seal this _13th_ day of _April_ 188_8_

Thos. C. Brown
J B Butler

Jeff + Morgan 𝐋.𝐒.
his mark 𝐋.𝐒.
𝐋.𝐒.

NOW, to secure the prompt payment of the above note when the same becomes due _I_ hereby bargain, sell and convey to the said _Weil Bros_ the entire crop grown and raised by _me_ and all _my_ right, title and interest in crops grown by tenants under _me_ or co-tenants with _me_ in Lee County, Alabama, and also the following property situated in Lee County, to wit:—

one Black mare mule 6 years old name Dot
one Mare " Mule 12 years old Kit Buck
one Bay " mule 12 " "
one two Horse Wagon and Harness.
one Red Cow (and Calf) Gusto
one " Cow " name Fannie
one sow and five Pigs
all Crops of every Kind

The above is free from incumbrance except—
as to 8 Bales Cotton rent due R F Smith

To have and to hold to the said _Weil Bros_ heirs and assigns, forever: Upon condition, however, that if _I_ pay the amount due upon the above note on or before the said _1st_ day of _October_ 188_8_ when the same falls due, then this conveyance is to be void; BUT, if _I_ fail to pay said note in full, then the said _Weil Bros_ is hereby authorized to take possession of said _Property_ above described, and after giving _5_ days' notice of the time and place of sale by _Three written notice_ to sell the same to the highest bidder for cash at the Court House door of said County, and to execute titles to the purchaser, and devote the proceeds of said sale to the payment, 1st, of the expenses of recording, advertising, selling and conveying, and all other costs that has or may accrue; 2nd, of the amount, with interest, that may be due on said note; and, lastly, if there be any surplus of said proceeds, the same is to be returned to the undersigned. It is further agreed that if the said _Weil Bros_ shall advance to _me_ anything over and above the amount named in said note, this conveyance shall stand as security for the same as fully as if included in said amount.

IT IS FURTHER AGREED, that when the said crops herein conveyed are planted _will convey to the said_ the legal title to the same for the purposes herein named. We hereby waive all right of homestead and exemption under the constitution and laws of the State of Alabama, as to the collection of this claim.

WITNESS _my_ hand and seal this _15th_ day of _April_ 188_8_

Witness

Thos. C. Brown }
J B Butler }

Jeff + Morgan 𝐋.𝐒.
his mark 𝐋.𝐒.
𝐋.𝐒.

STATE OF ALABAMA, } ss. I. _for said county hereby_
LEE COUNTY, certify that
whose name signed to the foregoing conveyance, and who known to me, acknowledged before me on this day, that being informed of the contents of the conveyance executed the same voluntarily, on the day the same bears date. And the said known or made known to me as the wife of the within who being by me examined, separate and apart from her husband, touching her signature to the within mortgage, acknowledged that she signed the same of her own free will and accord, and without fear, constraint or threats on the part of her husband.
Given under my hand, this day of 188

When Isidor advanced money on crops, the loan was secured by mortgage. Most farmers were unable to write in those days, and, as in this document of 1888, signed with "his mark," attested by witnesses.

business as it had developed under the impact of the Civil War. Had he been in the business all along, with his attitudes thus burdened by precepts rooted in the past, it is possible that he might not have grasped the new demands so quickly. But he was a newcomer and saw the business for what it was, not what it had been.

Before the Civil War, when factors advanced on crops, growers owned the cotton until it reached a buyer. The factor attended to the selling and the shipping, and collected his percentage. This system was entirely appropriate to the slave economy when a spinner could obtain all the fiber he needed from the crops of a few large plantations. Now, with the splitting up of most big acreages, this was no longer possible. Someone had to combine the output of a multitude of small farms to make up mill orders, and that's where the new breed of cotton merchants like Weil came in: they owned the cotton between its piecemeal purchase and bulk resale and, unlike the factors who lent money, they borrowed money against the cotton for the brief period they held it.

With cotton at about five cents a pound, or twenty-five dollars a bale, Isidor considered himself fortunate when he grossed more than fifty cents a bale. The answer, then as now, was volume, and to move the cotton promptly after its purchase, within a day or two if possible, for otherwise warehousing and financing charges would eat up the small profit within this modest gross. To keep the cotton coming, Isidor soon opened a buying office in Columbus, the first of a network that, before long, would cover Eufaula, Dothan, Selma, Mobile, Decatur, and Montgomery (the primary function of the city office being to buy supplies from other merchants when additional cotton was needed to supplement stock on hand).

Isidor also understood that the decline of the cotton factor left a hole in export trade as much as in domestic trade, and he was quick to jump into the breach. Astoundingly, within just two years of the founding of his company, he began selling cotton abroad. There is no record of how he established contact with his first customer, Cotonificio Cantoni, a Swiss-owned mill in northern Italy. We do know that this spinnery's buyer, a Swiss by the name of Friedrich "Fritz" Kronauer, had only recently gone into business on his own, opening a cotton firm in Milan in 1878, the same year the Weils launched their company. Fritz Kronauer became the Weils' first foreign agent; his sons Rodolfo and Carlo eventually served their apprenticeships at Weil; and his grandson, Federico "Chicco" Kronauer, represents the firm to this day.

Yet even as Isidor first began shipping cotton to Italy, Weil Bros. did not yet have a sample room. Such classing as was done took place on an open platform between the train tracks that run along Opelika's Railroad Avenue and the warehouses that faced them from opposite the business district. John Tarver then marked the bales for shipment in the warehouse, directing a small crew of porters and scale hands. As classing came into its own, Walter Cullars was hired for this essential function; subsequently he ran the Weil office in Montgomery when the company was still headquartered in Opelika, and later the Opelika office after Weil had moved to Montgomery. Other early staffers included Bob Lindsay as weigher and Cliff Edwards as checker.

At the junction of two rail lines, Opelika rapidly developed into a major cotton distribution center. The narrow gauge of the Western of Alabama had been widened to conform to that of the Atlanta and West Point, making through-traffic possible. Essentially, the railroad network of today was in place by 1890, although ownerships since have changed: the Central of Georgia is now part of the Southern Railways System between Birmingham and Columbus; and the Western of Alabama joined with the Atlanta and West Point to feed into the Georgia Railroad from Atlanta to Augusta, all three now part of Family Lines. Five warehouses lined the tracks at Opelika, and the largest interior cotton press in the South was about to go into operation.

The existence of such a facility was essential not only to Weil Bros. but to the growers of the area, since all cotton destined for shipment to other than nearby mills had to be compressed into smaller bales than came out of the gins. Heretofore the compressing had been done in Columbus, which necessitated transportation of the voluminous bulk cotton and added to transportation costs. Moreover, the railroads discriminated against Opelika in favor of Columbus and Montgomery. The latter cities, being classified as seaports thanks to their connecting waterways, could ship at marine tariffs that were consider-

Buying cotton from farmers in the 1870s or 1880s, this
unidentified merchant did his own weighing. The picture, a
remarkable example of early documentary style, was made by a
Memphis photographer by the name of Coovert who apparently
took hundreds of pictures dealing with the cotton trade.—
National Archives

ably lower than inland rates. To overcome these handicaps, the
Opelika Compress Company was incorporated in 1890 with Isidor
Weil as president. Its major stockholders, in addition to Weil Bros.,
were K.C. Hitt, of Augusta; and Hudmon Bros. & Co. and H. J.
Brady, both of Opelika. The compress became a political football
even before it disgorged its first bale, but, as it turned out, the
railroads lost the scrimmage and Opelika scored the touchdown.

While the compress was under construction, the Central of
Georgia warned the company that it would not stop cotton in Opelika
for processing but continue its shipments to Columbus. In the

A cotton plantation on the Mississippi, painted by an artist named Walker in 1883.—*The Bettmann Archive, Inc.*

meanwhile, Reid Barnes, an Opelika lawyer in the Alabama Legislature, had introduced a bill giving the state's Public Service Commission regulatory powers over the railroads. When the Central of Georgia learned that such action was pending, the railroad proposed a deal. It promised to stop cotton in Opelika if Barnes would withdraw the bill. Barnes was an honest fellow, however, and deeply concerned about the whole issue of discriminatory freight rates. He refused, and the commission's powers were enacted. Before long, not only were the freight rates equalized but the Central of Georgia was enjoined from bypassing Opelika. Indeed, the compress turned out to be so profitable, processing 50,000 to 70,000 bales a year, that the railroad eventually bought it.

In those days, the cotton business began in early August and was pretty well over by early March. Growers sold all of their crop at harvest. If they held back any cotton in anticipation of higher prices later, it wasn't much. The mills, too, purchased their year's needs during this season, so there was no point in keeping Weil Bros. staffed the year round. No cotton merchant did. With the exception of John Tarver, all hands worked on contracts that ran no longer than eight months. At the end of every season, each employee individually negotiated in the privacy of Isidor's office how much the firm ought to pay him in the coming fall. This annual wage and commission "trading"—as any give-and-take is called in cottonese—remained a tradition at Weil until the late 1960s, although by then, of course, the business was no longer seasonal. Trading was a sport almost as much as a necessity, akin to bargaining in a bazaar. But more than that: it was a duel of firmness and wit, an interlude of heightened awareness, an adrenalin charge. Cotton men earned reputations as "hard traders" and "poor traders," and Isidor, as did his successors, laid great store by this distinction. It was only reasonable to assume that a man who traded hard on his own behalf would be equally adept at trading on behalf of the company.

Country buyers—the men who went out into the boondocks to round up crops—traded for a guarantee plus commission on a specified number of bales. The heads of branch offices, like Charles E. Porter, the first manager in Columbus, George Cobb in Macon, Elbert Driver in Selma, H. P. Blue in Union Springs, and Walter Cullars in Montgomery, traded for salaries plus percentage of profits. Inside employees—clerks, weighers, checkers, stenographers—traded

One single bale of cotton, which probably fetched thirty-five dollars at most, was worth a wagon trip to market for these sharecroppers in 1910.—*The Bettmann Archive, Inc.*

for their wages. Even the hardest traders had to be content with but a few dollars. No one, as yet, was getting rich. But the dollar still was worth a dollar; except for periodic panics (one about every fifteen years), the country was still fat and sassy, nobody had yet invented payroll deductions, and any serious proposal of federal income taxation would have kicked off an epidemic of secessions. When Benjamin S. Barnes, the son of a Suggsville physician who had served as a surgeon in the Confederate Army, joined Weil as a secretary in 1898, the young man, then seventeen and the graduate of a three-month course at an Atlanta business college, earned thirty dollars a month for eight months—but he only paid ten dollars a month for room and board. "A careful person," Barnes recalled in his un-published memoirs after his retirement in 1954 as manager of the Atlanta office, "could save a little...and supplement these savings with summer work" in businesses whose cycle peaked at that time of

year: ice plants, fruit packers, summer hotels. Barnes himself was lucky. Isidor kept him on as part-time secretary for twenty dollars a month and obtained for him odd secretarial jobs at the Court House. When fall came, Barnes was able to buy himself an overcoat. Not everyone was that ambitious. One Weil employee, who preferred to take it easy during the summer lull, told Isidor when the time came for trading, "I am not so much concerned about what you are going to pay me next year; what I want to know is how much you're going to loan me right now."

As summers were sleepy, so were the other seasons hectic, the pace mounting as the year's end approached. The work day started at eight in the morning and never stopped before eleven at night. Sundays were not sancrosanct; nor was Saturday, the Jewish Sabbath. Christmas was about the only time when no one showed up except Isidor. Even today, there is nothing about Weil Bros. that suggests a modern

Reconstruction Era woodcuts illustrate plantation life of the 1870s. Above, Negroes pick cotton as a white overseer watches. At left, a plantation superintendent hires transient sharecroppers.—*The Bettmann Archive, Inc.*

corporation. Organization men don't cotton to this business and never have. Save for routine jobs, work is done in spurts, with lots of sociable chit-chat between, but hardly anyone quits regularly at 5:30, and key employees frequently still come in on Saturdays for a few hours. Bucks and Bobby Weil still work in the same room, as Isidor and Emil did after the store closed for the night and the latter came upstairs to put the company's books in order. No task that takes longer than a few minutes has ever been finished without interruption: telephone calls, teletypes, cables, urgent confabs. Of this array of routine intrusions, only phone calls were missing in the Opelika days. At the turn of the century, the telephone was just beginning to be used commercially, and was as yet useless for long distance. With luck, it was possible to ring through to Columbus, but then neither party understood the other. Telegraph, conducted by Morse code, was the basic means of communication. Opelika's Western Union man tapped his key in an office on South Eighth Street, in the building where Ward Moore Real Estate and Insurance now is ensconced. A succession of messenger boys with telegrams and cables clattered up and down the metal steps to Isidor's office; the staircase soon loosened and clanged, making the premises reverberate like a busy boiler shop.

During the active movement of cotton, farmers with samples clamped under their arms vied with the messengers for space on the rickety steps. The farmers were especially numerous on rainy days when they couldn't work in the fields, and on Saturdays when their wives wanted an outing. Isidor did practically all the buying of this "street" cotton, a term that originated in Memphis on whose Front Street farmers used to display their cotton on carts and sidewalk tables or make the rounds of the factors and cotton merchants, who jammed this street wall to wall. Between trading with his visiting farmers, Isidor, gauging the market, set the limits within which his country buyers could strike their deals. He also did the selling to the mills, writing the telegrams himself, and, if all that weren't enough, composed cables to Kronauer in Milan and later other agents as well, and watched over Otto Loosen, the firm's first staffer charged with handling the details of the export trade. Out at the warehouses, meanwhile, thousands of bales of "wagon" cotton, brought in from nearby farms, were sold to buyers on samples. At the compress, where the country buyers' purchases were unloaded, thousands of bales more were concentrated for reshipment after being weighed, classed,

In the course of the past hundred years, the Weil firm's first
abode, at the corner of Opelika's Railroad Avenue and
Eighth Street, has been modernized. Only the upper story,
where Isidor made his cotton deals, is still reminiscent of
the era.—*Jernigan Photography*

and put in even-running grades of fifty- and one-hundred-bale lots.
"At the end of the day," according to the late Ben Barnes' nostalgic
manuscript, "he [Isidor] could tell you to the bale how much cotton
he had bought and sold without referring to any record of the day's
business. At first I thought he was guessing, but not so. He didn't do
much guessing, and was nearly always correct."

Competition was keen, not so much in Opelika itself, but from
every cotton center in the South, along the Mississippi, and over in
Texas. With profit margins small, every penny counted, and Isidor
kept as careful track of office overhead as he did of bales. When
Barnes first came aboard as secretary, he found to his astonishment
that the single typewriter in the office, even then an ancient model
(the first machines had been tinkered together in 1868), apparently
had never been cleaned, let alone oiled, and was so rusty that all the
keys stuck. Barnes, who would have quit right there if he'd had
enough money to go home to Suggsville, fixed the machine
temporarily, then spent the next four months lobbying Isidor to trade
it in on a new model before the Old Man finally gave in. Evidently
the latter was as impressed with Barnes as the young man was with
him, and Ben Barnes did not remain a secretary for long. One year
after his arrival, Harry Herzfeld, the firm's first invoice clerk, left to
help out his aging father who ran the bank in Alexander City, and

Opelika's Railroad Avenue in 1900 (above) and during a parade that year (top left), shortly before the Weils removed their headquarters to Montgomery. Below is a view from Railroad Avenue, looking up Ninth Street, photographed at about the same time. Center left is a picture of the interior of the Shapard Banking Company. There is no record of which of the gentlemen might be W. B. Shapard, nor of the date this photograph was made, but by 1886 it was the Bank of Opelika, as the Report of Condition at bottom left indicates. Now the Bank of East Alabama, it was the Weils' first bank.—*Top left, courtesy Colonel R. Platt Boyd, whose mother was the queen on the parade float; center and bottom left, Bank of East Alabama; above and below, Auburn University Archives*

South Ninth Street, Opelika, Ala.

Isidor picked Barnes to replace Harry and gave him an impressive raise, ten dollars a month, soon followed by another in the same amount. This did not mean, however, that Ben was relieved of his secretarial duties. The difference was that he now held two jobs.

Although the firm made enough money to enable Isidor and Emil to take their families to Europe in alternate summers, visiting Otterstadt and calling on agents and mills, Weil Bros. was not yet sufficiently strong to withstand so much as one truly adverse season. A malfeasance on the part of a warehouse employee almost wrecked the firm in the lage 1890s. Isidor had delivered cotton to a Georgia mill, which had no use for it immediately but wanted the bales put in its warehouse. When Isidor chanced to drop in some weeks later, the cotton was gone. The mill's owner insisted that he knew nothing about it and refused to honor Isidor's receipt. Once again, a gun came into play, but John Tarver rushed to the Old Man's aid and broke up the confrontation. A few days later, the warehouseman threw himself into the Chattahoochee; this solved the crime but didn't alleviate the financial problem. However, W. B. Shapard, founder of the Shapard Banking Co. (later the Bank of Opelika, and now the Bank of East Alabama), who had been the first banker to give Weil Bros. a credit line, backed the firm also on this occasion. Years later, Isidor was happy to have the chance to repay this favor in kind. When the Bank of Opelika, by then in the hands of J.B. Greene, its erstwhile cashier, buckled in the face of a run, Isidor prevailed on his New York bank, the Importers and Traders National, to dispatch funds by overnight train from Atlanta, thus saving the Opelika institution from almost inevitable collapse.

So far as anyone can tell, Weil Bros. was the only cotton merchant headquartered in Opelika. Of course, other merchant firms maintained branches in the town and had buyers scouring the surrounding countryside, just as Weil sent representatives into their respective bailiwicks. It's interesting to note that the only published history of nineteenth-century Opelika mentions the compress as one of its leading industries but not the cotton firm.* Opelika also had its own

---

*This "History of Opelika from 1836 to 1900" was written by Florence Weldon as a thesis for an M.S. degree at Auburn University (then College) in 1939, and was published in installments on two occasions in the Opelika *Daily News* (now the *Opelika-Auburn News*) in November/December 1940 and in October/November 1953.

mill, built in 1900 and equipped with 6,500 spindles, but Weil had no interest in this enterprise except as one of its suppliers. The brothers were busy enough as it was. In the spring of 1901, the mercantile store was sold to Barney Rothschild, of Columbus, so that Emil could devote his full time to working with Isidor. Export volume was growing by leaps and bounds, as was Weil's business with cotton mills in New England. At its beginnings, this business had been handled through J.C. Graham & Company, of New York, whose founder, Colonel Graham, had been a cotton man in Selma and Montgomery in the 1850s and who had moved north shortly after the Civil War. When the colonel's firm was liquidated after his death in 1901, Isidor decided to open Weil's own office in New York to handle sales to northern mills as well as futures transactions on the New York Cotton Exchange—an increasingly important aspect of the business as Weil's potential exposure to losses grew with the firm's ever-mounting volume.

For this purpose, Isidor and Emil chartered a separate corporation, the first of many such spinoffs from the parent company. Weil Bros. itself had been a partnership since its inception.* Periodically the two brothers worked out new agreements between them, usually for twelve-month periods. In their fiscal year ending September 1, 1901, the firm's capitalization stood at $100,000, with Isidor's interest recorded as 75 percent. Of that sum, Weil Bros. invested $25,000 in Weil Brothers & Co., later known as Weil Brothers Cotton Co., to finance the New York operations, while limiting the partners' losses should anything go awry. This was of particular concern since the new corporation's business would be conducted by a newcomer to the organization. He was Edwin Shields, formerly of J.C. Graham, who, although he was given shares in the corporation, did not invest any money of his own. Not that Isidor mistrusted Shields. What worried him was that Shields, however "honorable, honest and straight-forward," could succumb to the commodity trade's most rampant disease: the urge to gamble. As Isidor wrote to Charles Storrow & Co., when he informed this superb Boston cotton agent of Weil's new relationship with Shields, " . . . we must not forget that a man, at all times, or most of the time, at the exchange is more or less tempted,

---

*Weil Bros. still exists as a partnership. However, the operating company was incorporated in 1950 as Weil Brothers–Cotton, Inc.

even against inclination, to speculate, and though it may be only in a small way or start in a small way, it may eventually grow."

Isidor hadn't gotten where he was by risking hard-won capital, and he wasn't about to start now. As it turned out, he needn't have been concerned on Shields' account. Shields apparently was never even tempted to gamble. He was that rare breed—a truly cautious cotton man. But he surely knew his business. Working through Storrow, he nearly doubled Weil's New England sales within a year to more than 50,000 bales.

Clearly, Opelika no longer sufficed as a base. But this was not the only reason why Weil Bros. removed its headquarters to Montgomery in September 1903. As Jews, the Weils had felt isolated in Opelika all along. Only four other Jewish families lived in the little town, not enough to support a temple or form the base for a congregation. Isidor and Emil read the Sabbath Prayer Book with their families on Friday nights, and, to give their children religious training, sent them to the local Methodist Sunday School. Isidor even went so far as to drill his two sons in the catechism. Only on the High Holy Days did the Weils travel to Montgomery to attend services at that city's oldest temple, Beth Or. While the demands of the spirit thus may have been appeased, it was no way for the flesh to go. To Jews of that generation, it was still important that their young find Jewish mates. This particularly loomed as a problem after Isidor's third and last child, a

Isidor Weil sold his early cottons to be processed as shown here. It was almost exclusively woman's work. In the 1882 woodcut at left, a young lady tends a New England spinning frame. The 1881 woodcut at right by H. Bradley pictures an exhibit from the Atlanta National Cotton Exposition of that year, which compared the old and the then-new technologies of spinning.—*The Bettmann Archive, Inc.*

daughter, was born in 1894. While his boys, Adolph, born in 1888, and Leonel, younger by two years, might eventually go courting in Cincinnati or New Orleans as their elders had done, such would not be seemly for Helen; nor was it likely that enough eligible young men of the Jewish faith would ever show up in Opelika to present her with much of a choice. Emil had less reason to be concerned on that score. He only had one son, Alvin, then eight years old; his daughter, Mathile, would not be born until 1906. In any case, Isidor was the unquestioned leader of the tribe. And so he and faithful John Tarver set out on their apocryphal horse-and-buggy journey to Montgomery, toting the firm's fortune in a "handbag," while Emil and the other Weils, less burdened by legends, presumably boarded one of the several daily trains that stopped in Opelika en route from Atlanta to Montgomery.

That the story of Isidor's move to the capital should be embellished is not really surprising. A new century had just dawned, and in this instance not only on the calendar. The gasoline automobile, already invented and soon to be in mass production, spelled the end of the American frontier. Isidor was the family's last pioneer. His horse and buggy symbolized the passing of an era.

5

Bibb Street

Isidor's younger son, Leonel Weil, now in his nineties, is the family's last link to its Opelika days. He can still remember Buffalo Bill and Annie Oakley performing at the Lee County Fairgrounds, and earning his first wages, ten cents a week, by coming down to the office on Saturday mornings to index the telegrams which, in those days, were written in longhand with copying ink and pressed onto tissue paper with a wet rag so that copies could be kept. Even then Leonel was the calmer, more deliberate of the two brothers, given to analysis, distrustful of hunches and quick decisions. Adolph, the first born, was more of an adventurer; he lived not only by the dictates of brain and heart but those of temperament. Once, as a boy, he and some friends found a handcar sitting unattended on a siding of the Atlanta and West Point. For a lark, he pumped the little car back and forth across a trestle, causing a passenger train to screech to a halt. Having tasted this triumph, for which he was nearly arrested, he figured out a yet more effective way to stop traffic: he laid himself across the tracks, then let his young legs carry him out of range of the engineer's wrath. It was a boyhood in the Tom Sawyer–Huck Finn tradition, for even by the standards of a rural society, Opelika was hardly more than a hole in the road. It only had about 2,500 inhabitants, a far cry from the 15,000 of today. There was as yet no Uniroyal plant, no Orr Radio, and no Opelika Manufacturing Co.

Not that Montgomery was all that much of a metropolis either, but after their move to the capital, the Weils' life inevitably become more formal. Adolph had attended the Alabama Polytechnic Institute (now Auburn University). Leonel, who had taken his lessons in Opelika from a Mr. Smallwood who used his own little house as a school, now attended Starke School, a prestigious private institution one block from the State Capitol (and across the street from the church in which Martin Luther King was to preach years later). Already in Opelika, the Weils had come up in the world. They had moved from the one-story frame cottage in which the boys were born to a much larger two-story house with a large yard. Now, in Montgomery, they occupied a mansion at 902 South Perry Street, in those days the city's poshest residential neighborhood. Isidor had bought the big home almost immediately upon his arrival from a former mayor, John Clisby.

In the days of sternwheeler steamboats, the Alabama River was Montgomery's highway to the outside world. Much of the state's cotton was shipped on its deep, broad channel 410 miles to Mobile on the Gulf of Mexico. The photographs above were taken about 1898. Yet older sketches (right) were published in the *Illustrated London News* in May 1861.—*Montgomery Advertiser/Alabama Journal*

LOADING COTTON ON THE ALABAMA RIVER.

COTTON-SHOOT ON THE ALABAMA.

FOOT OF THE SHOOT: RECEIVING THE COTTON-BALES ON BOARD THE STEAMER.—SEE NEXT PAGE.

There was even a fountain in the garden. That token of genteel success must have meant a great deal to Isidor. When he sold the house seventeen years later and retired to the apartment life at the Exchange Hotel, he had the fountain pulled up and installed on the no-less-gracious property of his son-in-law, Lucien Loeb, a wholesale grocer's son, the man Helen was to choose among her many swains.

Not all the Weils lived quite that elegantly. Isidor's sister Rosa, born in Otterstadt in 1862, was married to a Montgomery man by the name of Henry Simon. They had a small plot of land on which they raised their own vegetables and kept some livestock and poultry. In later years, as the city expanded, Rosa made a deal with the municipal government: in return for giving up part of her property for a street, she was permitted to keep her animals. When she died in 1956, she still had a cow and some chickens on this mini-farm in the middle of town.

Mule-drawn cotton wagons vied with electric trolleys for
room on Montgomery's downtown streets in the early
1900s. The above photograph, circa 1903, looks north on
Court Street, with the steeple of the First Baptist Church
in background, and northwest on Commerce, where the
Moses, Vandiver and Temple (Le Grand) Buildings are
recognizable. At left is Court Square, circa 1912, looking
up Montgomery Street. It shows the Exchange Hotel, the
First National Bank (now the First Alabama) and the
Capitol Clothing Store (now Capitol City Club).—*Photograph above from the private files of John Engelhardt Scott,
Jr.; left, Weil Collection.*

Isidor moved the firm's headquarters into a building on the south side
of Bibb Street, on a site now occupied by the Union Bank's parking
garage. Western Union had the lower floor, a most practical arrangement since telegraphic communication was still of prime importance,
although long-distance telephone service was at last coming into its
own.

The Weils' arrival in Montgomery was timed to coincide with the start of the new cotton season. Bibb Street and the other thoroughfares near Court Square bustled with mule-drawn wagons. Warehouse buyers and small speculators hopped on and off even as the wagons moved, cutting into the bales, drawing samples, making their bids. No sooner was a load bought than the vehicle rattled off to the warehouses along the Alabama River and the railroad tracks, where the farmers dumped their bales and received their money. Thus not only had the Weils' venue changed, but their style of doing business as well. Almost overnight, the company had joined the big league of cotton merchandising. In Opelika, Isidor had accumulated his mill orders largely by picking up a few bales at a time; now he purchased only big quantities, mostly from warehouses. Meanwhile, the firm's network of buying outposts was expanding, too: to Dothan, Demopolis, Greenville, Uniontown, and Union Springs, Alabama; to Tupelo, Holly Springs, and West Point, Mississippi; and to Columbus, Georgia.

Walter Markstein, a great uncle of the Daniel Markstein who would marry one of Isidor's great-granddaughters three generations later, came aboard to manage Dothan. Bob Driver sat in Greenville, Bob Dunlop in Uniontown, J. P. Woodall in Eufaula, John Motlow in Tupelo, H. P. Blue in Union Springs, C. E. Porter in Columbus, Albert B. Frenkel in West Point, W. S. R. "Will" Beane in Holly Springs, and a fellow by the name of Coleman in Demopolis. Elbert Driver continued buying out of Selma, but at Macon, George Cobb replaced Myron D. Kahn, and the composition of the main office changed as well. Thomas Vickers, a brother-in-law of Isidor's wife, kept the long-and-short account, an increasingly important function as hedging became ever more necessary with mounting volume. Ben Stoll succeeded Ben Barnes as stenographer when the latter was promoted to chief clerk.

Lawrence W. Weil, Uncle Hermann's firstborn, had come from Huntsville to work for Isidor and Emil as bookkeeper in 1901: Isidor now was the mentor to his mentor's son. Lawrence took naturally to the cotton business, and, in the intervening two years, learned so much about street buying that Isidor left him in charge of Opelika. This arrangement, however, did not last for long. Only a few seasons later, Lawrence and his brother Harry, who also worked briefly for the

Isidor Weil's first home in Montgomery, at 902 South Perry Street, was the former residence of Mayor John Clisby. Not long after moving in, he posed for the family portrait above with his wife Eda and daughter Helen, later the wife of Lucien Loeb and mother of Jimmy Loeb. Isidor's sons were included in a photograph taken earlier, while the Weils still lived in Opelika: Adolph stands behind Helen, and Leonel sits next to his father.

THE STANDARD CLUB.

Weil's first Montgomery quarters were on Bibb Street, in a building that previously housed the Standard Club (above). Weil took the upper floors while Western Union occupied street-level premises, a most convenient arrangement since telegraphic communications were vital to the firm. The building was later decapitated (below) and eventually razed. As it happens, Weil's current main office at 311 Montgomery Street occupies the site on which the ever more opulent Standard Club had its building for many years (right) after it moved from the Bibb Street location in 1902.—*Counterclockwise: Montgomery Advertiser/Alabama Journal; Scott Photographic Services; Algernon Blair Collection, courtesy Elizabeth Blair Pannell*

Weils, joined up with Adolph Lehman of the aforementioned Montgomery investment baking clan to form their own cotton merchant firm, Lehman, Weil & Co., which was eventually re-organized as L. W. Weil & Co., and is no longer in existence. This was but the first of three occasions when Weil Bros. spawned rival companies from its own ranks that involved members of the family— some defections must be expected in any organization of bright, ambitious men. When Lawrence left, Walter Cullars, the chief buyer in Montgomery, took over Opelika, and under his auspices it remained the concern's most productive agency until Weil Bros. expanded to Memphis, Dallas, and Houston. Before long, Weil's annual volume ranged from 250,000 to 500,000 bales, with Opelika alone handling 50,000 bales or more.

Like any other sphere of activity that involves relatively few key positions, the cotton business has been a continuous round of musical chairs in which outsiders rarely get the chance to grab a seat for long. Pursuing this narrative, we'll encounter the same names again and again in different positions and locations, and frequently with different companies. As we already know, cotton factoring gave rise to Lehman Bros. Such ties, not only to stocks and bonds but

inevitably to other commodities, were and are by no means uncommon in the business. For instance, Opelika's chief classer, John Roberts, who had replaced Walter Cullars when the latter went to Montgomery as buyer, was the uncle of the Beane brothers, Will, Frank, and Alpheus. Will Beane first worked in Opelika as a clerk, and later did the buying in Holly Springs and New Albany, Mississippi, where he remained until World War I broke out in Europe. He then had a splendid idea. He quit Weil Bros., and joined with his brothers to buy a cotton gin and oil mill whose byproduct, cotton linters, Beane Brothers promptly sold to Canada for gun cotton. Beane Brothers eventually evolved into Fenner & Beane, and later still into Merrill, Lynch, Fenner & Beane, now simply known as Merrill, Lynch. By the same token, Harry Weil eventually quit Lehman, Weil & Co. to become a prominent commodity futures broker in New York. Cyrus A. "Cy" Case, another Opelika clerk, threw in with Eli Bashinsky of the Bashinsky Cotton Co. to form Bashinsky, Case & Co., for years one of Weil's strongest competitors.

For the most part, however, rivalries were friendly, and often resolved themselves with self-deprecating humor. One such story concerns Bashinsky and Weil. Bashinsky, unlike Weil, was involved almost exclusively in export. One summer, when the European market had temporarily dried up, Eli Bashinsky received an urgent call from one of his perennial suppliers, Fox Henderson, of Troy, Alabama, informing him that the grower wanted to sell 3,000 bales immediately. Bashinsky could see no way of handling that consignment, but bluffed for time by telling Henderson that he'd contact a number of domestic mill friends (of which he had none) to see what he could do. After going into a huddle with his associate, Charles Golson, Case's predecessor, Bashinsky decided that his only hope was to get Weil to buy the lot. For three hot nights, Bashinsky haggled over the phone with Isidor, trying to squeeze as many points as possible out of the deal. Isidor, no less of a staunch trader, stuck resolutely by his figures. When Bashinsky finally gave in, he leaned back, sweat streaming from his unquestionably Semitic nose, and proudly smiled at Golson. "You know, Charlie," he said, "that Weil is a regular damn Jew."

Emil, who had taken on the financial and administrative functions of the firm after the divestment of the Opelika store, was as tight-fisted as Isidor was tough. The office on Bibb Street occupied the former quarters of the Standard Club, the city's first and only Jewish club. From this organization, the Weil offices has inherited four impressive chandeliers, all of which were kept burning routinely in the evenings until the last stalwart finally called it quits. One night when Ben Barnes stayed late with Marshall Stiles, another addition to the growing firm, Emil happened to walk in, and he promptly turned off all the lights but one. Stiles, somewhat chagrined, informed Emil that the electricity was charged at a flat rate and that it didn't cost anything to keep the lights burning. Emil fixed his eyes solemnly on Stiles and said, "We may be on a flat rate, but I've still got an interest in it." Somewhat puzzled, Stiles asked, "What interest?" Whereupon Emil shook his head in wonderment at such ignorance, and said, "We buy the globes."

Not that pennies didn't count in the cotton business. The whole profit structure was, and is, based on points. By the time the Weils had established themselves in Montgomery, Isidor's aim was to gross (before overhead but after shipping and other transactional expenses) 12.5 points, or about 63 cents a bale, more than had been the rule in his early Opelika days, and considerably less than today's goal of at least 100 points, i.e. $5 per bale. But the dollar was still as hard then as any currency could possibly be, and a year's revenues of, say, $185,000 on a volume of 300,000 bales was a substantial sum. Just how much Weil actually made was a secret outside Isidor's immediate circle and, as was the custom in closely held firms of this type, he would inform his associates of the profits they'd made by code. Any cryptanalyst worth his ciphers could have broken these codes in no time flat, since they were based on letters substituted for numbers, with the values of the letters determined by their position in a nine-letter word. Isidor's code was marginally more sophisticated than other business ciphers: his key was a short German phrase.

To domestic mills, Weil sold lots in the thousands of bales, with single transactions grossing in the six figures. Isidor tried his best to maintain volume even when the crop wasn't up to par, and usually he succeeded. Not taking open positions, and relying on a small margin rather than potential speculative gain, he had to keep as much cotton on the move as possible. One year, for instance, an early frost overwhelmed much of Alabama's growth before the bolls were fully open, with the result that there was an abundance of light tinges to deep stains. The tinged cotton presented no particular problem, since there was always a market for that quality. But cotton with blue splotches in it also was abundant and had to be sold, although most mills at home and abroad shied away from such strong coloration on the assumption that it would make uniform dying difficult. Isidor finally persuaded the Amoskeag Manufacturing Company, of Manchester, New Hampshire, to take 25,000 bales of the blue at a good price. This broke the deadlock. Henceforth, other mills also bought the spotted cotton, and Weil had a good season after all.

As a result of such coups, the Weil name soon spread throughout the cotton world. Japanese firms had begun establishing buying offices in Dallas and other Texas locations, hiring Americans to do their buying and classing. The representatives of these companies, like Southern Cotton Co. (a Japanese concern despite its name), Japan Trading Co., Mitsui & Co., the Gosho Co., and Suzuki Co., would come to Montgomery to purchase Eastern Belt cotton, and with increasing frequency they called on Weil Bros., as did the buyers from England, Germany, France, Spain, and Italy.

Little attention was paid in those days to the staple of Eastern Belt cotton. Sales were made under the broad stipulation of ⅞″ to 1″ to domestic mills, and the metric equivalents (28 mm to 28-30 mm) to European markets. Thus, with but few exceptions, orders could be filled from general stock without staple selection. The exceptions were cottons merchandised by Weil under local growth designations, such as "Coosa Rivers" and "Tallapoosa Rivers" (from the Childerburg and Alexander City areas) and "Canebreaks" (from around Uniontown and Demopolis). These were of tougher and slightly longer staple, around 1¹⁄₃₂ inches, and because the longer staple produced a better cloth, called for a quality premium. Today, all Alabama cotton runs from about 1¹⁄₃₂ to 1³⁄₃₂ inches, but this was the beginning. With Weil's introduction of special Eastern Belt cottons, and the fact that the firm now also handled the longer-fibered cottons from the Mississippi Valley, classing for staple length became a necessity for the firm, and has been ever since.

Woodbury Ga. May 7th. 1906.

Contract entered into between Weil brothers of Montgomery Ala, as party of the first part: and J.A.Gill of Woodbury Ga, as party of the second part.

Party of the second part agrees to sell Twenty Five (25) bales of cotton, basis fours, Ten Cents per lb, F.O.B Woodbury Ga. Nothing below 3s, with the following differences,--5s 1/8 off basis: 6s 1/4 off basis. Sale of said 25 bales, based on N.Y October 10.56.

Should the market decline 1/8 ¢, then the party of the first part agrees to put margin with Woodbury Banking Company, for deposit against such difference in price.

Should the market advance 1/8 ¢, then the party of the second part is to put margin with the Woodbury Banking Company equivalent to the advance.

Party of the second part agrees to deliver the above mentioned 25 bales by the 15th day of October 1906 as stipulated above.

For the faithfull fulfillment of this agreement both parties hereby affix their signatures

Signed in duplicate, this 9 day of May. 1906.

Weil Bros

J. A. Gill

This highly unusual contract dates back to 1906, when Weil Brothers still bought crops before they were harvested, a practice the firm has long since ceased. What made this particular crop purchase agreement so extraordinary is that it required the seller to put up margin in case the market advanced, and the buyer in the event the market declined. Moreover, the contract varies from most modern crop purchases in that it calls for a specific number of bales and an extremely narrow range in quality.

Indeed, it's the distinctions of staple and grade that form the basis of modern cotton merchandising and are essentially the reason for a cotton merchant firm's existence. If all cotton were alike, a mill could buy indiscriminately from any and all growers. It is the merchant's function in the scheme of things to form the conduit from the growers of various types of cotton to the mills that want those types. In short, it's the merchant's job to cull the world's collective crop for desired qualities. Since much that happens henceforth in this account hinges on how Weil Bros. pursues this purpose, this is a good time to take a brief look at the mechanics of the business.

6

Basics

Rare is the skill whose practitioner doesn't claim it as an art rather than a science. In most cases, of course, that isn't so except in the loosest sense. For instance, a toolmaker's fractional measurement either is precise or it isn't; the component he machines either fits or it doesn't, and there is no room for personal interpretation. Not so, however, when it comes to classing cotton.

The classer stands at a big table in the sample room, pulls a wad of cotton down to a few fibers, lines them up in a thin sheaf between thumb and index finger, and almost without looking judges the staple to be 1$\frac{1}{32}$ inches long. Amazingly, he usually is right. But sometimes he isn't. In fact, he might pull the very same sample again the next day and class it 1$\frac{1}{16}$ inches. Again, he is right—or is he? Classers of equal expertise have been known to argue about a difference as infinitesimal as $\frac{1}{64}$ of an inch. When one insists that the cotton is a "full" 1$\frac{1}{32}$ inches, and the other that it's a "shy" 1$\frac{1}{16}$ inches, that's what their squabble amounts to.*

You'd think that by now an instrument could have been devised to give the exact measurement. Indeed, such a machine exists. It's called a digital fibrograph. But the trouble is that the sample must be prepared (i.e., combed out) for the machine, and even greater

---

*To be licensed, a classer (in the opinion of his examiner) must be able to class to $\frac{1}{32}$, but he won't last long in the business if he can't call cotton to $\frac{1}{64}$ of an inch.

deviations can occur during this preparation. Another cotton man once bet Marvin Woolen, one of Weil Brothers' four vice-presidents, that he could tell by the way a fibrograph girl combed cotton whether she was in a sexy mood that day. Marvin took him up on the bet and lost. Stapling by hand remains the more reliable method.

Length, moreover, is not the only consideration. Cotton comes in many variations of color, brightness, purity, resilience, tensile strength—qualities that depend on the seed, the vagaries of weather, the type of soil, and how the cotton is cultivated, harvested, and ginned. If, as happened the year Isidor sold Amoskeag the blue cotton, there's frost before most of the bolls have opened, much of the crop comes with "spot" in it, i.e, with areas of distinct coloration. If there has been too much rain, the cotton isn't as bright. If the cotton is picked by hand, as it used to be the world over and still is in developing countries, and provided the picker has been careful, there are few impurities. But if the pickers have been sloppy, or if the plant has been stripped by a machine, the cotton is permeated with bits of leaf, grass, bark, and other extraneous substances, and the gin saws have to work extra hard to clean it. This, in turn, causes tiny knots and curlicues in the fiber, known in the trade as "neps and nips," which make it more difficult to spin.

On the basis of these characteristics, the classer grades the cotton according to a scale of designations that ranges from "Below Grade" at the low end to "Good Middling" at the top. Between these extremes, there's Good Ordinary, Strict Good Ordinary (strict meaning "better than"), Low Middling, Strict Low Middling, Middling, and Strict Middling. In addition, there are split grades like "Low Middling Bright" that fall between the basic designations. "Low Middling Bright," for instance, would indicate that the cotton is low middling but brighter than you'd ordinarily expect from that grade.

In addition to staple and basic grade, a sophisticated measurement called micronaire ("mike" in the trade) has been applied in the past twenty-five years to define the thickness of the fiber.* With about 400 possible combination of grades and staples, plus seven different micro-

---

*Thickness here does not mean diameter. Drastically enlarged, cotton fiber has a configuration something like a soda straw. Micronaire measures the walls, not the hollow middle.

naires, this means—in theory—that there are something like 2,800 variations of cotton. It stands to reason that classing isn't all that precise.

But within limits of practicality, subtle distinctions are important, since a textile mill can't just spin any quality but must work with a specific type of cotton to produce its goods. Below-grade cotton of short staple is fine for mops, rag material, and sandbags (such as were made for the outposts in Vietnam). Lower grades may be used in industrial goods, like tires in the old days and fanbelts today. Mills also will buy lower grades for heavy constructions, like denims. Strict low middling, the predominant grade, goes into mass-produced cotton goods and cotton-synthetic mixes. Finer constructions, such as quality shirtings and sheets, call for better grades and longer staple.

The economics of the cotton business are firmly based on supply and demand. The way a conservative merchant like Weil makes money is by estimating the demand for the various grades of cotton in relation to their probable availability—an exercise of educated guesswork that helps him decide what price to pay for his cotton and what he can expect to get for it. But because he can very easily be wrong, and the price of cotton often varies greatly from day to day, he reduces the risks he incurs in buying, and conversely in forward selling (what he has not yet bought), by hedging his transactions on the futures exchange. This is essentially an auction market whose price fluctuations reflect the collective opinion of all who trade there: farmers, merchants, mills, and speculators.

Over the years there have been a number of exchanges, including the New York Cotton Exchange and New Orleans Cotton Exchange in the United States, the Liverpool Cotton Exchange in England, the Le Havre Cotton Exchange in France, and the Bombay Cotton Exchange in India. Today, the sole active market is that of the New York Cotton Exchange, whose futures prices are focused on Strict Low Middling, 1⅟₁₆. In relation to this "base" quality, higher grades and/or longer staples are worth more; lower grades and/or shorter staples less. But the prices of the various cottons never remain completely parallel, since their individual demand-and-supply patterns can vary sharply.

That's where a merchant's expertise comes into play: in recognizing

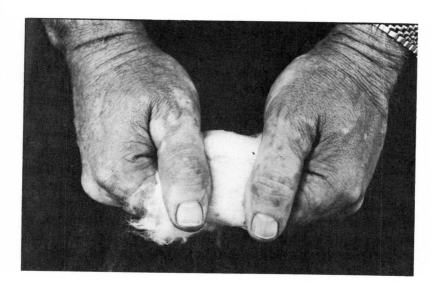

Memphis Territory cotton, 1¹⁄₁₆ inches in length, is stapled by the experienced hands of George Wheeler, second in command of Weil's Memphis office. Top picture shows the cotton wad before being pulled. Below, the fibers are being separated. At left, with the fibers thinned down and smoothed out and the impurities removed, is the end result of this skillful process.—*Author's photographs*

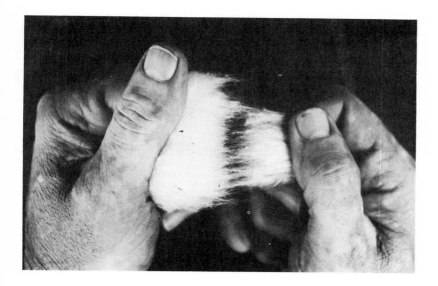

and forecasting price relationships between various qualities and growths of cotton. He must make his living—take his profit and pay his expenses—out of the price difference between his actual purchases and actual sales and those of the futures he hedged them with.

This difference is called the "basis" and is expressed in points (one-hundredths of one cent) per pound of cotton "on the month" or "off the month" (i.e., above or below) the price of the futures contract. For example, it only stands to reason that Strict Low Middling 1$\frac{1}{16}$ is worth less at the gin at origin than delivered on contract. To complete delivery, the cotton has to be warehoused, insured, financed, and then freighted to one of four designated delivery points in the United States (where it is reclassed). Hence, it would usually sell "off the month." On the other hand, that same bale of Strict Low Middling 1$\frac{1}{16}$ landed at a textile mill in Hong Kong or Genoa, or even in North Carolina, would be worth more than the price of a New York contract. With all the additional charges built into its price, it would sell "on the month." Covering with futures thus enables a shipper to secure a basis for transactions as well as to hedge them.

Moreover, the ability to hedge makes the cotton merchant a vital link in the marketplace. Without incurring undue risk, he can make a firm price to the mill as much as eighteen months in advance. Far from being a superfluous middleman, he helps to keep the cotton commerce stable.

The house rule at Weil to hedge each bale was laid down by Isidor, and has been followed whenever possible since. But it isn't always. In recent years, as Weil increasingly has dealt in foreign growths, many of the transactions could not be matched against New York futures since their respective price fluctuations sometimes bear no relation to each other. The same applies to certain domestic specialty cottons that often do not follow the market. By the same token, short-staple below-grade cotton is also seldom hedged. But otherwise, the rule still holds. Weil will buy, say, 10,000 bales of spot cotton only if it can sell 100 contracts (100 bales each) on the futures market the same day at a price that provides a sound basis. In selling forward to a mill at a certain fixed price, the firm will buy enough futures contracts to cover the sale.

For example, Weil might buy cotton from a grower at "200 off the market" (200 points below the futures price) and sell to a spinner at "200 on the market" (200 points above the futures price). If the cotton is bought at a fixed price and sold at a fixed price, futures should be sold when the cotton is bought, and bought when the cotton is sold. The spread of 400 points has to cover the cost of distribution; otherwise, there would be a loss. Over the years, the cost of distribution has increased very considerably as a result of much higher warehouse and compress charges and interest rates. The profit per bale remains minimal and varies from transaction to transaction. At times of higher prices, for instance, very wide spreads are often possible, leaving more room for gain. But such extras aside, the basis operator depends, like any low-margin enterprise, on volume: the more cotton he moves, the more money he stands to make.

Can he lose? Certainly, but the worst that can happen is that the spread between the price at which he can buy or has bought cotton and the landed mill price is insufficient to cover the cost of distribution. That is why there is an old saying in the business that a basis operator may be bent a little but he will not break. He will never get as rich as a position taker might—the speculator who buys and sells without hedging—but, more important, he will not be bankrupt.

In cotton, as in everything else, beauty is in the eyes of the beholder. One classer's Strict Low Middling may be another's Low Middling Bright. To be sure, there are now international standards, and every sample room has its collection of boxes in which "biscuits" of cotton from different regions are displayed for each grade, so that if the classer isn't sure of his judgment he can compare his sample to the standard biscuit.* Hardly anyone but a "squidge," as apprentices are called in the cotton business, ever looks at these boxes. An experi-

---

*The standards, defined by the U.S. Department of Agriculture under the U.S. Cotton Standard Act, have been subscribed to by the East India Cotton Association Ltd. (India), Gdynia Cotton Association (Poland), Bremer Baumwollbörse (Germany), Associaton Cotonnière De Belgique (Belgium), the Liverpool Cotton Association Ltd. (U.K.), Japan Cotton Spinners Association (Japan), Association Française Cotonnière (France), Associazione Cotoniera Italiana (Italy), Centro Algodonero Naçional (Spain), Osaka Sampin Exchange (Japan), the Japanese Cotton Traders Association (Japan), the British Textile Employers Association (U.K.), and De Vereeniging voor den Katoenhandel (Netherlands). China, although not an official subscriber, also operates under the definition of the U.S. act.

enced classer sticks by his own judgment, even if the classer at the other end of the table disagrees.

If two classers working for the same outfit can have their differences of opinion on length and grade, the likelihood of controversy is yet greater when the classers represent divergent interests—those of the merchant and the spinner. Ordinarily, neither is out to cheat the other, if for no better reason than that merchants need mills as steady customers, and the mills soon would find themselves hard up for suppliers if they consistently turned back shipments. But it's in the nature of their respective pursuits that the merchant tries to obtain the highest prices for his cotton, and the spinner tries to buy the best cotton he can for the least money.

Now, only the spinner knows for sure what he really needs, or more precisely, what minimum quality he can get away with for his purposes. And that's where the art of cotton merchandising comes in, for the merchant must match his classer's judgment of the cotton to the spinner's presumed need, regardless of how the latter labels his order. Thus, a merchant may offer lower than his competitors and win the order if he is convinced that the mill will accept cotton of marginally lesser quality than specified. Of course, if the merchant is wrong and the shipment is rejected, the mistake can cost him plenty. By the same token, the merchant may ship to the mill's precise specifications and still get in trouble simply because two classers saw the same cotton differently. Since the shipper guarantees specified quality and weight to the buyer at destination, the rejected cotton, in the event of dispute, is submitted to arbitration. Despite the headaches that arise in such a case, one thing is sure. As Isidor liked to say, "If you never get rejections, you know you are giving cotton away."

7

Mr. I. & Co.

ISIDOR WASN'T LIKELY to "give cotton away." Even so, rejections of his merchandise, especially by those mills that dealt with him regularly, were quite uncommon. That's because he soon devised a system of classifying cotton to conform to his customer's requirements, which enabled him to deliver consistently the same cotton they had been happy with previously. In later years, of course, as the mills' demands grew more exacting, classification became ever more precise. The Weil house mark "Sox," for instance, would designate a shy 1¹⁄₁₆, or a government-standard 1¹⁄₁₆, while "Kite" identified a true 1¹⁄₁₆. "Nancy" was a "bank walking" (i.e. high-quality) Middling. The mark "Ella," on the other hand, meant that the cotton was equivalent to the slightly less demanding government-standard Middling. Although not quite that sophisticated, the Weil system in Isidor's time had already gone far beyond the requirements of government class. While the Agriculture Department established one all-inclusive "light spot" grade, Weil early on distinguished between "faint spot," "very light spot," and "light spot." Needless to say, Weil shippers and classers had to be very special experts, not only to distinguish the nuances but to know exactly which customer wanted what.

But Isidor's strength went far beyond his appreciation of the various mills' requirements. He had an uncanny perception of the marketplace, a subtle hunching he had developed in Opelika when his buying hinged on the question of whether he could make fifty cents a bale. He'd look at a farmer's cotton and quickly calculate what portion

of it he could sell to whom and for how much. If the figures came out right, he bought; when they didn't he turned his back on the deal.

In those times, the cotton was sold within a day or two of its purchase, keeping insurance and warehousing costs at a minimum. As the mills grew more discerning and classing for grade and staple became necessary, such rapid movement was no longer possible. This not only added to the cost of doing business but made it advisable to hedge all purchases, since the firm might be in possession of large quantities of cotton for several months, during which prices could fluctuate enough to wipe out a merchant's slim margin. True, some successful firms of that time, such as Lesser, Goldman & Co., of St. Louis, bought cotton, albeit in smaller amounts than was Isidor's practice, like grocers purchase their shelf stock—they'd be long whatever they bought until they managed to sell it. Not so Isidor, one of whose favorite saws was "If it isn't worth hedging, it isn't worth buying." The Old Man, as everyone started calling him when he was barely in his forties, instantly covered almost every bale he bought with a corresponding short sale on the futures market; conversely, when he sold a mill order before he had the cotton to fill it, he bought futures that very same day to even his position, thus guarding against the eventuality of a price rise.

Years later, by then truly an old man, Isidor coined a phrase that has remained the firm's unofficial motto to this day. His nephew Alvin, Emil's son, a superb and flamboyant salesman, had sold 10,000 bales to a Georgia mill for a good price—a significant quantity for a single transaction. Alvin happily went to bed that night without hedging the sale, confident that this could be accomplished the next morning. What Alvin did not contemplate was that the futures market could turn so thin that not enough cotton would be offered to cover his sale at a price that would make it a winner rather than a loser. Only the cunning of Shap Dowdell, the firm's New York manager at

Isidor Weil at his rolltop desk (left), circa 1920. By then, his sons Adolph and Leonel were in effect running the company from the partners desks previously occupied by Isidor and his brother Emil.

that time, saved Weil Bros. from taking a bath on Alvin's deal. Dowdell, instead of stepping up to the pit and bidding heavily into the market, which would have pushed prices sky-high, remained on the sidelines and waited for offers, quietly taking up those that were within reason, and keeping his fingers crossed that the market wouldn't run away from him. His strategy worked. Prices remained fairly stable. When the gong rang at the end of the trading day, Dowdell at last had 10,000 bales together. At the Montgomery office, Isidor shook his trembling finger in young Alvin's face. "Lookahere," the Old Man said (he always said "lookahere" when he wanted prompt attention): "Lookahere, you never play craps with bales of cotton." The fact that Isidor pronounced craps "crabs" didn't detract from his message.

Isidor's gambling, if you care to call it such, was to trust his judgment of how much cotton the mills would eventually take up. Although he proclaimed repeatedly that "there's nothing more uncertain than a sure thing," he never doubted his acumen in this regard. When the textile economy looked promising, and futures prices no more than covered carrying charges, he went aggressively into the spot market, accumulating bales by the tens of thousands. *

Not that Isidor always got what he wanted. One time, at the height of a seller's market, he found a large quantity of high-grade cotton in the stocks of a warehouseman by the name of Hardaway. It was precisely the kind of cotton one of Weil's mill customers was after; all Isidor had to do to work the transaction was to pin down the prices at both ends. Thus, in order to have time to negotiate with the mill, he asked Hardaway to make his offer firm until the next day. "I'll tell you what, Mr. Weil," the warehouseman drawled. "I'll keep that offer open just as long as you can hold your stiff —— over a candle." Since then, any impossible term has been known in the trade as a "Hardaway option."

Isidor's perspicacity did not only manifest itself in cotton merchandising. He possessed a keen sense of all markets, not least the stock

---

*In recent times, with their high interest rates, heavy buying would be indicated, for instance, if cotton could be bought for 66 cents a pound while three-month futures were quoted at 69 cents and six-month futures at 70.8 cents. Why would a grower sell under these conditions? Because he needs cash flow like the rest of us.

Lucien Loeb, brother-in-law of Adolph and Leonel, was a partner in the firm for many years. His forte lay in the important function of dealing with the banks.

market, and gained widespread respect for his acumen in finding undervalued issues. One famous Montgomery story had him walking into Fenner & Beane one day, telling the manager that he wanted to buy 500 shares of a stock that he identified by its symbol—let's call it UP. Mr. Shinbaum, a very recent émigré who used to sit around Fenner & Beane a lot, overheard the order. When Isidor had left, he rushed to the manager and asked him, "Was that Mr. Weil?" The manager said it had been. "Mr. I. Weil?" Mr. Shinbaum asked. "Yes," said the manager. "Did I hear him place an order to buy five hundred shares of UP?" Again the manager agreed. Mr. Shinbaum, who had no idea what UP was, said, "Buy me one hundred shares."

In the next few days, the market fell out of bed and UP with it. After Mr. Shinbaum saw his investment eroding point by point, he decided to get out. As he placed his sell order, he said to the manager, "You know, that Mr. I. Weil—he ain't so shmart." Blissfully unaware of Shinbaum's assessment of his wisdom, Isidor held on to the stock a while longer and, as usual, made a profit.

He was no less astute in spotting talent. Over the years, as we shall see, he built the cadre that would propel Weil to the forefront of cotton merchants—men whose names have become legends in the business, like Shap Dowdell, Al Grayson, and A. M. Crawford, Sr. To be sure, like many family-firm entrepreneurs of his era, especially those of European antecedents, he was a practicing, if not necessarily confirmed, nepotist. That his and Emil's sons would come into the business was taken for granted. So was the advent of Isidor's son-in-law, Lucien Loeb. But Isidor's family loyalty went far beyond the boundaries of immediate blood lines and his daughter's mate. Weil Bros. became a veritable haven for any relative who wanted a job. We have already encountered his cousins, Harry and Lawrence Weil, Uncle Hermann's sons, who later started a cotton brokerage of their own. Then there were Herman Simon, the son of Isidor's sister, Rosa, and the aforementioned Thomas Vickers, the British brother-in-law of Isidor's wife, who kept track of the firm's hedging. Two cousins, who also happened to be nephews of Emil's wife, came aboard too: Richard and Herman Block, both in the Memphis office. Moreover, if Emil's Stella could run a placement service for her folks, so of course could Isidor's Eda. She contributed a brother-in-law, Aron Metzger, who became the buyer in Huntsville, as well as a nephew, Joe Oppenheimer. Nor was the younger generation excluded. Isidor's daughter-in-law, Rossie Shoenhof, Adolph's wife, brought in her cousin, Julian Schwabacher, a chicken farmer from Massachusetts who tried life in Memphis for a while before retreating to New England. In turn, Lucien Loeb, Isidor's son-in-law and later a partner in the firm, had no difficulty in obtaining a niche for his brother Raphael.*

If some of the family members showed a true aptitude for the business, so much the better, but of course it was nothing Isidor could count on. Twice, in fact, he made pretty bad mistakes. His half-

---

*An extended family tree of the Weil clan presents a tangle of relationships that would startle even the most phlegmatic geneologist. That Uncles Isha and Hermann married sisters, Emma and Bella Wertheimer, presented no special complications. But intertwining branches started sprouting in the next generation like lianas in the jungle. The above-mentioned Aron Metzger was not only Eda Weil's brother-in-law (being married to her sister, Minnie Oppenheimer), but also Isidor's first cousin (being Aunt Babette's son).

Moreover, there are five nuptial connections between the Weils and the Loebs. To

brother, Siegfried, perhaps in revolt against his Wagnerian name, deserted first the Imperial German Army, then the U.S. Army, and eventually his wife. As if that weren't enough, he tried to kidnap Walter (Bunks) Weil, Jr., a fourth cousin in New Orleans, for $10,000 ransom before he was persuaded to drift off to parts unknown. Isidor also must have regretted hiring yet another young man in deference to relatives' wishes. That fellow stole Eda's pearls and was banished to Panama. Years later, R. Hugh (Pat) Uhlmann, who married one of Isidor's granddaughters, reinforced his reputation as the clan's quipster when (from his home in Kansas City) he mailed a Panamanian picture postcard to the Weils, reporting that he had chanced to meet the pearl thief and now understood at last why they put locks on the Canal.

But such black sheep were exceptions. In Isidor's glory years, those between his move to Montgomery and the outbreak of World War I, he not only made Weil Bros. one of the country's most respected cotton firms but recruited and trained the cadre that soon would build the business far beyond anything that he might have envisioned. One of these men was William Shapard (Shap) Dowdell, the New York manager who saved the day when nephew Alvin didn't hedge his 10,000 bales. As it happened, Shap Dowdell was the grandson of W. P. Shapard, the Opelika banker who had granted Weil Bros. its first loan. But that's not why young Shap went on the payroll. For several weeks, in fact, the Old Man wasn't even aware that Shap was around, for the latter had unofficially taken the place of his older brother, W. C. Dowdell, who for compelling personal reasons had to leave his job as assistant bookkeeper from one day to the next. Once Isidor discovered Shap's talents, promotions were fast in coming. By the time of World War I, while Isidor's sons, Adolph and Leonel, were in the service, Shap virtually managed the Montgomery office.

---

begin with, Isidor's sister, Lena, married Michel Loeb, a Montgomery wholesaler of hardware who had immigrated from Reichshofen, Alsace. Next, Lucien Loeb, Michel's nephew, married Isidor's daughter, Helen. Then Herman's son, Louis, married Lucien Loeb's sister, Blanche. In the current generation, Robert S. (Bobby) Weil, Isidor's grandson, is married to Virginia Loeb, and Herman Block (see above text) to Virginia's sister, Frances. Virginia and Frances are the daughters of Lucien Loeb's first cousin, Victor, also a native of Reichshofen. More about the Loebs in later text.

Weil's license to do business in New York dates back to October 1901 when the company sought registration in the Empire State in order to join the New York Cotton Exchange.

After Germany's capitulation, Weil Bros. sent Shap to Liverpool, England's cotton port, to establish the firm's first foreign branch. In 1923, Shap took over the New York office and soon became a leader of the big city's commodity community. Serving as vice-president of the New York Cotton Exchange when the federal government engaged in one of its periodic investigations, hoping to uncover villainy on the exchanges, Shap came off so well in his verbal duels with Senator Hugo Black, the later Supreme Court justice, that he was elected president of the New York Cotton Exchange, the first Southerner so honored. His election was celebrated at a Montgomery barbeque to which much of the Alabama cotton fraternity was invited. As usual on such occasions, a high-stakes crap game was part of the fun. Between rolls, Shap peeled off a ten-dollar bill and handed it to John Tarver. Another black asked Tarver how come a white man would give him so much money. "That's the president of the New York Cotton Exchange!" Isidor's old sidekick answered, "and I learned him all he knows." Shap died of a heart attack on New Year's Eve of 1937 at the age of fifty-three, thirty-two years after he had rushed from Opelika to Montgomery to cover for his brother.

Allen M. Grayson, long famed in the cotton business as the "Sage of St. Paul" (the street on which the Dallas Cotton Exchange was located), was another of Isidor's stalwarts. He was long and gawky, had a stutter, and could be brutally frank. When the emaciated sixteen-year-old came to work in Weil's Selma office in 1901, his first job was to clean spitoons, then still standard fixtures. From the very beginning, Al Grayson was intent on becoming a millionaire. He probably succeeded, for, like all managers, he shared in the profits from his transactions. Being one of the best buyers around, they came to a bundle. A Hoagy Carmichael–type, with long, nicotine-stained fingers, he was in frail health most of his life, suffering from asthma so bad that for a time it was mistaken for tuberculosis. But this did not stop him any more than his pronounced stammer, which he turned to his advantage. It became his trademark—a singularly effective vehicle for delivering wry one-liners that soon found currency wherever cotton men gathered.

Once, lined up against the wall of a men's room at a cotton convention, he groped in his fly without much success. Transmogrifying embarrassment into humor, he turned to Adolph, who was standing next to him. "There's times," Al Grayson stuttered, "when I don't know if I am Al or Al... Alice." He called New Orleans the "city of imps, pimps and shrimps," and when Frank Davis, a Carolina mill man, long since dead, repeatedly rejected consignments of Weil cotton, Al Grayson destroyed that poor fellow's reputation once and for all by remarking, "If I ordered a shipment of sons of bitches and Frank Davis wasn't the first to fall out of the car, I'd reject the whole lot."

Some of his one-liners were deadly serious. Phoning in from Dallas, where Adolph had assigned him because of its beneficial climate (or so it was then believed) when Weil expanded westward, Grayson would report that "it's raining in Dallas." He managed to get that much out without stumbling over his tongue, and it was really all he needed to say: rain in Dallas was the harbinger of a good Texas crop.

Like so many cotton men, Al Grayson was an iconoclastic cuss. On one occasion, when Al phoned Isidor from New York and couldn't seem to get out what he had to say, the Old Man lost his patience. "If it's going to take you that long to say something on the telephone," he remarked rather unkindly, "it would be cheaper if you'd come to Montgomery." Al grabbed the next train, shaming Isidor when he suddenly showed up at the head office. Grayson's wit could cut deeply. Once again in a men's room, this time at a private club in Dallas, a Ku Kluxer invited him to join the Klan. "Hell, no," Al sputtered. "First of all, I am married to a Catholic. Second, I'm working for a Jewish firm. Three, I've got Negroes working for me. And fourth, I wouldn't come with any outfit that has to do its recruiting in a crapper." As Shap in New York, the font of futures, so Al Grayson became president of the Dallas Cotton Exchange, the seat of Texas-cotton spot transactions. And, like Shap, he died on the job, in 1951 when he was 65.

The third of Mr. I.'s old crew was A. M. Crawford, Sr., who was born in Marion, Alabama, in the 1880s and joined Weil in his late teens as Isidor's stenographer. Crawford was to end his career as head of the Memphis office, which, with Alvin Weil, he built into the firm's largest and most profitable branch. There was little humor about this tall, angular cotton man, who had been raised a Baptist and hated Demon Rum. This alone made him something of an anomaly in the business, whose ship of state fairly floated on corn likker in those days, its sails tumescent with the hot breath of lust. In Memphis, the opulent Peabody Hotel on Front Street's cotton row was the trade's favorite watering hole and primrose palace, the place to entertain mill buyers with the paid favors of complaisant ladies, of which there was no shortage. Crawford, whose steely gaze could make men quake in their boots, had no use for such shenanigans.

Almost from the beginning, he had been Isidor's troubleshooter, being advanced from stenographer to auditor when he discovered that the firm was being taken by one of its branch managers. After a stint as assistant manager in Dallas under Grayson, he was sent to

Memphis to put that house in order. No sooner had he arrived and looked out the window onto Front Street, than he noticed what appeared to be a bundle of rags lying on the sidewalk. "What's that down there?" he asked. "That's so-and-so," one of the sample room men answered with great mirth. "He's a staple chaser." Crawford had the drunk taken home in a taxi, and then all hell broke loose. He stormed into the sample room only to find most of the men out cold in the racks, sleeping it off on soft cushions of cotton—long a favorite retreat in staple houses. It didn't take long for Crawford to shake up the office. Almost overnight, it was full of new faces.

By the time he retired, he was close to ninety and burdened by his age. He took one last trip to Montgomery to attend the firm's 100th anniversary celebration. At that time he was asked what he remembered about Isidor. He pondered the question for several minutes. "The Old Man," he said, "was very acute, very smart." Then, after a long silence, he added, "And I never smelled whiskey on him."

On the formal photograph that hangs in the Weil Bros. office, Isidor looks like an elderly German schoolmaster. A bushy white mustache adorns his lip, and his eyes are magnified behind thick glasses. It is difficult to imagine that he wasn't always this age, that there was a day when he refused to leave Dadeville when a farmer, furious at how low the firm had classed his cotton, vowed to kill him if he stayed the night. That same farmer, years later, went bankrupt with a mill venture in Roanoke. Defeated, he turned to Isidor, of all people, for help, and was not refused.

Evidently, like most men, Isidor mellowed with age. As a young father, he didn't spare the rod. When his sons got a beating in school, he administered another at home. But his grandsons remember him as sweet and mild. "To me," says Bobby Weil, "he was like a teddy bear." On those Friday evenings when Isidor and Eda didn't go to temple, they'd come to their son Adolph's house for dinner. At Chanukah, Isidor would light the candles and sing "Rock of Ages." Often he sang to his grandchildren; it was always a march, and he beat the tempo with the pendant of his watch, a throwback to the Palatinate. When Bobby, a second lieutenant in the Army Reserve, went on active duty in World War II, Isidor, who was then still in the business, called the young man into his office. "He'd always welcome me in the same way," Bobby says. "It was a little formality he had. He'd say, 'Bobby, come here. Sit down,' and I'd sit down, and then he started asking questions. He'd go into everything with me, very thoroughly, and then he would kiss me goodbye." That time, after the young man had told him he was going into the service, and after he'd hugged "Pa," as his grandchildren called the Old Man, Isidor looked at Bobby through watery eyes that were worse than ever, now that he suffered from a detached retina. "Lookahere," he said. "Don't take any foolish chances."

8

Cavalcade I

THE FIRST WORLD WAR proved as much a watershed in the microcosm of Weil Bros. as it did in the fate of nations. Philosophies changed and rulers fell, and so they did here as well. Adolph, Isidor's eldest, had first squidged for the firm in the summer of 1905 when he was seventeen, after attending Auburn and then Columbia. Similarly, his younger brother, Leonel, affectionately called "Lee," came aboard in 1911, at age twenty-one, with a business degree from Harvard, along with a slightly battered nose from playing football.

In those years, the cotton business was still seasonal. With the low interest rates then prevailing, carrying cotton was cheap, and the mills bought their supplies as the cotton was produced. Nor did most growers care to hold their crop in the expectation of higher prices later. Thus, along with everybody else in the shop, Adolph and Leonel worked long and hard for eight months, spending practically every evening at the office (or one of the branch offices) except Christmas. They learned the business from the ground up, and couldn't have had a more knowledgeable teacher than Isidor. But while Isidor was wonderfully astute and informed about cotton merchandising, he was, at least by modern precepts, not a good manager, whose prime responsibility, after making a profit, must be to insure continuity by grooming a successor. That Isidor refused to delegate authority and ran the outfit essentially as a one-man show had been entirely appropriate so long as only his brother Emil was involved, for while the latter was good at figures, and ever meticulous about details, he was not an instinctive cotton merchant: Emil hadn't been infected by the adventure of the business as had Isidor.

But even as Adolph, and later Leonel, matured, Isidor still clung firmly to the reins. To be sure, his confidence in himself was well founded. Apart from the time he'd been defrauded in Columbus, the only major losses he ever suffered had been due to natural disasters. Salt water ruined a large quantity of cotton about to be shipped from Galveston when the great flood of 1900 devastated that port city. Another time, army worms destroyed 5,000 bales at a cost to Weil of $50,000, a considerable sum at that time. But those Isidor considered acts of God, beyond any man's control, even his own. Thus, totally relying on his own judgment, Isidor never gave his sons the chance to prove their competence where it ultimately counted—in the perception of the market's movements as translated into the setting of limits, i.e. at what prices cotton could be purchased and sold.

In the summer of 1914, it was Isidor's and Eda's turn to vacation abroad and to renew friendships with the firm's overseas agents.

Auburn University campus (then Alabama Polytechnic) circa 1905, shortly after Adolph attended the school as a sophomore.—*Auburn University Archives*

Leonel spent the first weeks with them, but as the summer wore on and the new crop approached harvest, he bade his parents farewell in Switzerland and left for home to help get the office ready for the season. Isidor and Eda, and their twenty-year-old daughter Helen, were scheduled to follow a couple of weeks later. Leonel boarded his train from St. Moritz on August 1. Four days later, as the German army invaded Belgium, he was on the high seas aboard the Cunarder *Lusitania*, whose sinking, nine months later, was to precipitate that war's first major diplomatic confrontation between the United States and Germany. Not until the *Lusitania*, blacked-out and zigzagging, arrived in Halifax instead of New York did Leonel and the other passengers have their suspicion confirmed that war indeed had broken out.

For Isidor, meanwhile, Switzerland became a luxurious prison, walled in by warring countries. For all practical purposes, passenger traffic across the Atlantic from continental ports had ceased. Only the neutral nations, the Netherlands, Sweden, and Norway, still operated civilian ships, and it was impossible to reach their ports except by way of Germany, which had closed its borders to such transit. To escape the isolation of St. Moritz, Isidor, Eda, and Helen moved to Lausanne. Meanwhile, the cotton season was in full swing, and Isidor was chafing at the bit. Frantic that the business would falter if he were not there to lead it, he fired off telegram after telegram to Montgomery, but this mode of communication was hardly instantaneous. For the first time, the day-to-day decisions so crucial to effective trading were completely out of his hands.

Not until the season was nearly over did Germany at last allow trains to pass through to Holland. There, the stranded Weils finally managed to obtain bunk space in the hold of a Dutch freighter, and so Isidor travelled to America yet a second time in steerage. On his return to Montgomery, he found to his surprise that the firm not only was surviving but doing very well—far better than competing houses.

What had happened was that the outbreak of hostilities had stampeded the cotton market into one of its periodic panics. Just as Isidor and Eda had been unable to find space on a ship to America, so cotton found no room on ships to Europe; in any event, foreign mills weren't buying. Export trade was paralyzed, and domestic business faltered with it. Cotton prices went into such a precipitous decline that the exchanges in New York, New Orleans, and Liverpool suspended trading for an indefinite period. With the exchanges closed, there was no way to hedge purchases from growers. Under such conditions, almost no one wanted to buy. This, in turn, sent cotton prices lower still.

Adolph and Leonel had sensed what was coming even before the markets closed. As prices started their plunge from that year's high of about fourteen cents a pound, Isidor's sons kept going short into the ever-declining market. Uncle Emil was desperate. With every successive bottom, he was convinced it was the last. But here, despite his orders to the contrary, Adolph was still selling. By the time futures trading was halted, the young man had committed Weil to the delivery of 18,000 bales, and, in addition, had 2,500 bales of hard-won mill orders on its books. With all the force Emil could muster, he forbade any further selling. The market then stood at about eight cents. As Shap Dowdell later told it, Adolph was "walking up and down the office like a caged lion, tearing his hair" and insisting that cotton was going to five cents. For once, Emil prevailed—if not for long. No sooner had he rushed off to New York, presumably to find some way to cover his nephew's shorts, than Adolph managed to secure another order of 5,000 bales from Pacific Mills. Emil's telegrams to Adolph were to no avail; the latter simply disregarded them. Discouraged, Emil repaired to Atlantic City, his favorite retreat, leaving the arena to his nephews.

As they had predicted, cotton hit five cents, but they also knew that once the hysteria subsided, prices inevitably would rise again: with vast armies to be clothed, there'd soon be great demand for cotton. At that point, when everyone else thought prices would go lower still, Adolph ordered all Weil offices to buy every bale they could find. And just as he had been alone in selling on the way down, he was now practically alone in buying at the bottom; more often than not, Weil's branch managers, like Ben Barnes in Dothan, were the only buyers willing to take up farmers' crops. When the exchanges reopened in November, Adolph not only had all his shorts covered, but fairly bulged with cotton. Sure enough, prices rebounded with a rush. By the end of the season, they were back to eleven cents a pound. Adolph and Leonel had whipsawed the market. Weil's profits for 1914/15, high in the six figures, were the firm's heftiest to date.

Nor was this the end of Adolph's and Leonel's tour de force, proving that they could run the company as well, if not better, than the older generation. In the three years from that fateful August of 1914 to the autumn of 1917, the firm's capital more than doubled—a gain that was nearly all the young men's doing. For, with Isidor's return from Switzerland, the Old Man's stance had suddenly and unexpectedly changed. It's no exaggeration to say that he all but abdicated. True, he would spend every day at the office and continue to set Weil's overall policy for many more years, but he would fill the role of consultant rather than chief executive. The operating officers, in charge of the crucial buy-and-sell decisions, were to be his sons.

Isidor's letting go couldn't have been a matter of old age. After all, he was not yet quite sixty, and he enjoyed robust health but for his eyes. The likeliest explanation is also the simplest: he was immensely relieved that, however inadvertently, he had found out at last that the business he had worked so hard to build would be in safe hands.

The Old Man's benign leadership combined with his sons' acumen to make 1916/17 yet another banner season. Here's Ben Barnes' account of the first part of this success story:

> During November and December 1916 I had bought several lots of cotton "on call" from a good many of my customers (in the Dothan area), as the cotton market continued to advance and they were riding with the advance, expecting to fix prices of this cotton later and take their profits. As soon as I got back to the office I checked these "call" purchases with my bookkeeper and found they were all well margined and in good shape. The next morning, February 1st, 1917, the Germans declared unrestricted submarine warfare, breaking the cotton market from around 17¢ to 12¢ per pound, and in a matter of minutes had wiped out all margins on the "call" purchases and thrown them into a considerable loss. I immediately called the Boss [Isidor] to get my bearings and know how to proceed, and in this crisis he measured up to his full stature. He told me not to close out a single customer, not to call for any additional margin, to tell them to take it easy until this period of hysteria had passed and then we would talk about a remedy.
>
> The news of the big break...soon reached all over the territory and the telephone began to ring. One customer, a banker of Dothan, ran all the way to my office and when he got there was so

exhausted he couldn't talk. The news I gave him revived him completely. Then I proceeded to tell all my "call" customers what my instructions were, and while all of them felt greatly relieved, their individual reactions took different forms. Some shouted for joy, some darn near passed out and one emotional individual cried like a child, but they were all unanimous in praising Weil Brothers for their broadminded attitude.

It took the country much less time than at first anticipated to become adjusted after this crisis. In very short order the New York and New Orleans Cotton Exchanges passed a rule limiting to 2¢ per pound any one day's advance or decline, and gradually the market recovered all it had lost, eventually going much higher. *

In the few days cotton hovered around twelve cents, Adolph's and Leonel's decisiveness once more came into play, resulting in an even greater coup than they had carried off in their debut season. With minimal hedging, they added thousands of bales to the firm's long position, and as the market recovered, they cashed in. When the United States declared war on Germany in April, a pound of cotton fetched more than twenty cents. By summer, it hit thirty cents. Weil still had some cheaply bought cotton on hand in late fall, when the price went to thirty-four cents.

As if to underline the perspicacity of the new protagonists, Weil's profit, despite the carried-over stock and a rising market, declined dramatically after they were called by Uncle Sam—Leonel as a sergeant at a cavalry remount depot near Montgomery, and Adolph as a lieutenant stationed at camps near Atlanta and Jacksonville. During their absence from the office, the firm did the smallest volume of business it had in many years. What caused this setback is impossible to tell in retrospect. One reason may well have been that Isidor, once he had relinquished day-to-day management, did not return to it, even while his sons were away. Rather, he left the affairs of the company largely in the hands of Shap Dowdell. Not that this serves to explain the temporary decline: Shap was a cotton man par excellence. In any event, things did not begin to pick up again for Weil until after

---

*From "My Fifty-Six Years With Weil Brothers," the unpublished memoirs of Benjamin S. Barnes.

Adolph and Leonel were discharged from the army in early 1919, the year that was to mark the official ascendancy of the next generation.

Since 1911 (until which time Adolph had been paid like any other employee, if perhaps a little more: $1,800 a year), his remuneration had been 7½ percent of net, with an annual $2,500 guarantee. Leonel, shortly afterward, had "traded" for and won a similar salary. Now, with their accomplishments of 1914 to 1917 behind them, this clearly was not enough. Adolph, acting on his own behalf and that of his brother, argued that they were entitled to a far larger share of the business. The resulting contretemps caused a family rift that never fully healed.

As is customary in family firms where siblings are involved both horizontally and vertically, Isidor, as Adolph's and Leonel's father, stayed out of the negotiations, and Adolph had to do his trading with his uncle—a most delicate situation, since the only reason the two young men actually deserved a bigger interest was that they, not Uncle Emil, were doing most of the work. In an affectionate letter that typified Adolph's lifelong dependency on both the heart and mind of his younger brother, he wrote to vacationing Leonel on July 15, 1919, "I'm tired, Lee, very tired of you and I shouldering the burden of this business and Papa still working hard and Uncle Emil sitting complacently by, reaping the benefits, and doing what he pleases . . . I am trying and I shall try to avoid even the slightest breach no matter what comes—for Papa's sake. I want you to figure out both mine, Papa's and Uncle Emil's plans from every angle. Then write me fully your advice. Do this at once, hear?"

To avoid a breach was easier said than done, particularly since most of the negotiations took place by mail (Emil was once again in Atlantic City), and the written word is far more unyielding than the spoken. It wasn't long before the correspondence turned acrimonious, fired by the younger man's brashness and the older man's anxiety. Adolph employed every bit of leverage to gain his ends, from the recitation of his and Leonel's feats (customary in trading) to the finally inevitable accusations that Emil wasn't earning his keep. "If you'd let me alone," he wrote, referring to the short sales of 1914, "I'd have made you a millionaire then. . . ." Adolph topped his arguments with the threat that, if their demands weren't met, he and Leonel

Alvin Weil was acclaimed far and wide as the best cotton salesman of his day.—*Photo by Gittings*

would leave the firm the following season and start a cotton brokerage of their own: "Lee and I can certainly do two fifths as much business as Weil Bros. are doing and make just as much and, the chances are, more with less risk and less work and worry...."

Emil, in turn, resorted to deprecations of Adolph's and Leonel's contribution, a common strategem in trading ("You state you are working hard, the work nowadays is nothing compared to when the biz was started...you seem to forget that the firm...was built up by Isidor and Emil Weil, it's quite easy to keep the ball rolling after a firm is favorably introduced and organized...."). Emil then gave vent to his hurt feelings, indignation and avuncular censoriousness. "Your rather insulting letter," he wrote to Adolph, "hardly deserves a reply and was least expected from you, whose part I have always taken and whose interest I have always had at heart...."

But Emil's real interest did not lie with Adolph and Leonel, or even with himself, for he was well fixed and not particularly eager to have much to do with the business anyway. Rather, his big fear was that if so much of the enterprise went to his nephews, then his own son, Alvin, just twenty-four and fresh out of the navy, was sure to end up the third wheel on an apparatus designed as a bike.

Not without cause did Adolph earn the nickname "Iron Man" in the coming years. As his correspondence with Emil continued into August, he softened his phrases but stood pat on all basic demands. Emil could not help but yield, for Adolph meant it when he said he was ready to quit. Not that, if he and Leonel established their own business, they would steal Weil accounts. Such was not their nature. Very likely, had they set out on their own, they wouldn't even have opened a competing office in Montgomery but moved to another city.

In September 1919, Emil finally gave up the fight. Adolph and Leonel were allotted 20 percent participations with $10,000 annual guarantees. Isidor retained 30 percent. Emil saw his share cut back to 20 percent, but of course continued to draw interest on the money he had invested in the company, and that interest came off the top before the net was figured. As for Alvin, he received 10 percent and was out of the running for top management.

But Alvin's great talents were not wasted. Although of unprepossessing appearance—he was far from handsome and quite small—he was blessed with such an infectious smile and was so bubbly with good humor that everyone he met was instantly his friend, or girlfriend, as the case may be. Among his most tongue-wagged adventures as a young man was the time when he roared down Montgomery's main drag, Commerce Street, in his Stutz Bearcat, with Zelda Sayre, the later Mrs. F. Scott Fitzgerald, on his lap; to add spice to the gossip, she wore a flesh-colored bathing suit.

No one was immune to Alvin's charms. His favorite gambit with anti-Semites was a disarming one-liner. "You know," he'd say with a puzzled grin, "Jews are always accused of robbing gentiles. What I want to know is where you guys got all the money we take away from you." Besides, Alvin was enthusiastic about sport and the club life that went with it. What better use for an ebullient, gregarious youngster than to put him into marketing? Indeed, this is what was done. Not resentful in the least that he would never be a senior partner (perhaps even secretly relieved), he took charge of the Weil selling organization. Wherever personality counted for more than product or price, he was on the scene himself: with Goodyear and Firestone when cotton was still used to make tires; as goodwill ambassador to mills whose buyers always looked forward to Alvin's jolly visits. His tire company accounts alone—a quarter of all industry sales—ran as high as 200,000 bales a season. He was, by consensus, the best cotton salesman of his time.

As fate would have it, Alvin's son, Kenneth, who eventually joined the family firm to follow in his father's footsteps, turned out to be allergic to cotton. He'd gone to Yale and then served as an ensign in the navy in World War II before being assigned to the Houston office to learn the business under William J. Reckling, by then one of the big stars on the cotton firmament. But within a year asthma got the better of Kenneth, and he is now a New York City stockbroker with the house of Drexel Burnham Lambert.* Meanwhile, Alvin's other son, John, had no interest in cotton. Thus, Alvin's retirement in 1954 marked the end of Emil's line in the firm.†

---

*For the next decade, Alvin operated under his own name in an advisory capacity to numerous mills. He died in 1980 after a long illness.

†More *Our Crowd*: I. W. "Tubby" Burnham, of Drexel Burnham Lambert, is married to cousin Dick Weil's sister, Lawribel.

It's a Wall Street truism that almost anyone can make money in a bull market; the test comes when the bears take over. The years when Alvin cultivated customers out of the Memphis office, whose executive suite he shared with A. M. Crawford, and when Adolph and Leonel directed the company from their partners' desks in Montgomery: these nearly four decades ushered in the end of American cotton business as Isidor had known it. In those years, the Deep South's soil would be depleted, labor strife would rout New England's mills, cheaper synthetics would encroach on cotton, there would be weevils and dustbowls, depression and war—and, in the midst of all this, government controls and price supports would make futures trading redundant, close the exchanges, and thus once again keep cotton merchants from hedging their transactions. That Weil, unlike many other firms, survived this trying period is remarkable enough in itself. That it prospered verges on the astounding.

In any business, success accrues to the credit of its leadership. What made Weil so fortunate in that regard was the meshing of Adolph's and Leonel's peculiar talents, two men congruent only in their acuity, but wholly unlike each other in personality and temperament: Adolph, headstrong and impulsive, easily angered, unable to brook opposition and loath to compromise; Leonel, gentle and deliberate, always soft-spoken, patient with his lessers, the kind of man who could infuriate with his long silences because, unlike most people, he wouldn't speak until he had a problem all thought out. Their physical appearances, expressive of the men within, were equally at odds: Adolph, tall, trim and darkly handsome, elegant in his suits of continental tailoring, a commanding presence. When he was young, women often compared him to Rudolph Valentino. Older, his proud bearing resembled General MacArthur's: head high, ramrod straight, feet apart, his hands resting on his hips, lord of all he surveyed. Leonel, in contrast, was of less than medium height, broad shouldered, slow in movement as in speech, modest of demeanor, satisfied to watch from the sidelines. Leonel would fish the moody Southern ponds for bream and crappie, happy in the uncomplicated company of Alabama sharecroppers; indeed he himself had wanted to become a farmer upon leaving Harvard, but Isidor had pushed him into the cotton business. Adolph also loved fishing and the great outdoors, but there was no mistaking when he strode across furrowed

Rarely do photographs capture personality as effectively as these. Adolph, brash in his matinee-idol youth (left), was no less imperial at the height of his career (right). But advancing years and grandfatherhood made even Weil's "Iron Man" shed his armor. In the party snapshot below he is in his seventies, posing with his ever kindly brother, Leonel (left).

fields that he was landed gentry. Surprisingly, these two very different brothers could work as one. When a decision was to be made, Adolph functioned with computer speed. His analysis of any given situation seemed to be spontaneous. Leonel, meanwhile, took his time, asking innumerable pertinent questions, leaving Adolph chomping at the bit. In the end, Leonel usually agreed with his brother. When he didn't, chances were that Leonel was right. But no one ever heard them argue in anger. At worst, when they disagreed on a purchase or sale and Leonel wouldn't budge from his position, Adolph might say, "Okay, Lee, if you don't want it, I'll take it on my own account." This was empty oratory: he never did. He respected their relationship too much for that, and his brother's judgment.

When the two brothers took control, the future looked auspicious—if that may ever be said about the cotton business where, as in any enterprise based on commodities, each season, and indeed each day, is its own finite universe. In the autumn of 1919, Europe was beginning to recover from the war. Foreign mill business was picking up, and it was not unusual for a branch office like the one in Savannah to handle as much as 10,000 export bales at one time. As soon as the sale was arranged, orders went out to the country buyers, who then sent in samples of the cotton received each day. By the time the shipments arrived at the ports, the lots had been reclassed from the samples and made ready for delivery to shipside. This streamlined method was ideal for merchants, since it helped them to avoid the cost involved in warehousing. Orders in hand, they bought only what was wanted in even-running grades, which permitted a quick turnover at little cost. The demand continued into 1921, but by that time the boll weevil, having already made himself at home in Alabama, jumped across the Chattahoochee River and invaded Georgia and the coastal cotton-growing regions. In Georgia alone, production dropped from about one million bales to less than 50,000. This crop failure, coupled with a minor recession that hit the country at about

Leonel always enjoyed a good laugh. Now in his nineties, he continues to chuckle at human foibles. At right he is shown in his middle years at the fullness of his powers.

that time, was a real setback, and, while only temporary, it had far-reaching consequences. To combat the weevil, the farmers not only used an insecticide, calcium arsenate, but they also tried to deprive the insect of the diet on which it depended: they replaced cotton with other cash crops on much of their land. Rotation, of course, had been long overdue. A century of cotton culture had impoverished the soil. Now the one-crop system was dead, and cotton would never again be the mainstay of the Deep South.

This didn't mean that the region's fiber business would collapse instantly, but it was the beginning of the end. Ben Barnes, whom the weevils had chased from Dothan to Savannah, removed his headquarters to Fayetteville, North Carolina, to remain close to still productive areas. But both export and domestic business continued to stagnate well into the fall of 1924, and buying was necessarily limited to cotton that could be purchased on a sufficiently cheap basis to deliver on contract in New York at a profit. It was then, and not for the last time, that the Russians, who were still largely dependent on Southeastern cotton, came to the rescue of a moribund season. As Barnes tells it,

Ben Barnes, Weil's in-house chronicler, whose career spanned more than fifty years.

Almost immediately cotton began to pour... from Columbia, S.C., and from that time until July 4th, 1925, my office was a beehive of activity. The initial sale to the Russians was the beginning of many more sales. . . . The receiving of this cotton was done by H.W. "Shike" Wells. . . . From our standpoint it was a pretty piece of business and there were never any differences of opinion that couldn't be adjusted with a few drinks and a good dinner. . . . On July 1 we completed our delivery to the Russians, and as everything had been paid for we thought the end had come. However, on the morning of July 2nd, Shike Wells came into our office all excited saying they had miscalculated the capacity of the boat and one thousand more bales had to be bought and put aboard the steamer that day. Wells thought that was an impossibility and for a few minutes I did also, as our stock (in that area) was almost nil. My mind clicked for once, though, and I recalled seeing 1000 bales of high grade compressed cotton stored at the East Side Compress (in Savannah) bearing South Carolina Co-op tags. . . . I had no authority to pull the samples, but took the chance anyhow. In the meantime, I would call Arthur Mazyck, Sales Manager for the Co-ops at Columbia and see if they wanted to sell. . . . We talked about five minutes, discussing business in general, when I casually asked him if he had finished for the season. He said, "All but a thousand bales of Middling Inch staple..." and he would like to sell. I asked him to give it to me under good offer, good for the day, and I would see what could be done. . . . Mazyck named a fair price and pretty soon [Barnes was informed that he] could deliver 400 Strict Middling and 600 Middling Inch staple without any trouble. . . . I tacked on 2¢ per pound to Mazyck's price and told Wells to contact... New York. He did, and in less than three hours I had bought and sold the 1000 bales at almost $10 per bale profit... and at five o'clock that afternoon the cotton was loaded aboard ship and the money in the bank. . . .

The export business revived with a vengeance in 1926, when demand was so insistent that the crop was nearly all picked, ginned, and marketed by the end of December. When the season was over, the United States had exported more than eleven million bales, an unprecedented, and since unequalled, record. It's almost unheard of to go through a whole season without some poor sales, but that year

Weil Brothers

Weil Brothers Cotton Co.

42 Cotton Exchange, New York

Montgomery, Ala.

CROP LETTER

Montgomery, Ala., March 16, 1918.

Gentlemen:

The weather during the last month has been more favorable for preparation of the land and considerable plowing has been done. Our reports indicate that a great many mules and horses have been bought by farmers all over the country, and also to the effect that a great deal more fertilizer will be used than last season. This is not only locally the fact, but it seems to be universal in the entire belt. Delivery of fertilizer is slow; it is said that the quality is far superior to that of the previous two years.

There has been quite a change in sentiment as regards the area to be planted in cotton. It looks to us that there will be a substantial increase over last season. This is especially the case in the boll weevil districts, for the reason that the boll weevil last year was not very active, and it is furthermore claimed that the severe winter has destroyed the pest to a considerable extent. This, however, remains to be be seen.

Spot cotton seems to be in good demand, especially for the higher grades of white and tinges. Of course there is a great deal of difficulty experienced in the exportation of cotton, the matter of getting licenses and then ship room is hampering cotton buyers from making engagements unless they can get both simultaneously.

Eastern and Southern mills have been free buyers and are heavy consumers.

Yours truly,   WEIL BROTHERS.

For many years before the Department of Agriculture began to issue crop letters in the 1930s, Weil Brothers sent semimonthly reports, like this 1918 example, which had a wide distribution and were eagerly followed. Isidor Weil authored the earliest of these. Later, Lucien Loeb took on the responsibility, and after his retirement various members of the Weil family continued the practice. The crop letter still remains a Weil Brothers institution.

Weil didn't have a single unprofitable transaction on its books. However, 1926 was a last glorious spasm. Beginning with 1927, the export business in the Eastern Belt began a steady, gradual decline, which lasted until October 1929, when the stock market crash and the ensuing Depression knocked the last stilts out from under the wobbly world economy. As buying power dried up both at home and abroad, America's innate capacity to produce more agricultural goods than could be consumed resulted in unprecedented misery for the country's farmers.

Casting about for some means to ease the plight of agriculture, the Hoover Administration (not Roosevelt's, as many people have since come to believe) established the Federal Farm Board and gave it $500 million to spend as it saw fit, thereby inaugurating the era of government regulation of agriculture, the first industry to fall prey to Uncle Sam's avuncular ministrations. In itself, the Farm Board was by no means harmful. Several fine minds had contributed to its creation, including John D. Black, then a Harvard professor; Arthur M. Hyde, Hoover's secretary of agriculture; E.E. Kennedy, of the Farmers Union; O.F. Bledsoe, of the Staple Cotton Cooperative Association; and C.O. Moser, of the American Cotton Growers Exchange. On the Senate side, the bill had heavy backing from the cotton states: Thomas Heflin of Alabama and Walter F. George of Georgia. As they saw it, the $500 million would be lent to farmers to compensate them for the crops they couldn't sell. Since there was no way for the farmers to repay the loans, the crops, which constituted the security, were taken over by the government. Even so, the Farm Bureau's kitty soon was exhausted. But temporarily Uncle Sam's infusion did alleviate rural misery to a degree, and, in so doing, contributed to the belief, prevalent since then, that the country could not function without government intervention—a logic akin to gulping antibiotics so you won't get sick. Moreover, no one gave much thought to the possibility that the economy might be allergic to such medicine, as indeed it turned out to be.

Meanwhile, as the Farm Bureau's funds were depleted, cotton glutted the market. In the case of cotton, as of all other commodities, supply and demand are the fundamentals of trade. With an imbalance of supply overhanging the market, the basis price can do nothing but drop to a point where merchants can buy sufficiently under the price of futures to permit delivery at no loss to them. As demand continued to flag, cotton thus piled up in huge quantities at contract delivery points. Until the Farm Board had been organized, the only such points were New York and New Orleans, the seats of the futures exchanges. Now the Board also authorized delivery on contract at Norfolk, Charleston, Savannah, Mobile, and Houston—ports where, it was hoped, foreign buyers would show up sooner or later.

Cotton came pouring in so fast that there were not enough warehouses to store it—a profusion that benefited no one as buyers stayed away in droves even as prices sank to one of the lowest levels in history: five cents a pound or twenty-five dollars a bale. Prowling through these Himalayas of unwanted bales, some twenty classers of the Department of Agriculture were at work just in Savannah, certifying cotton for contract delivery. It was of course far more than they could handle. And this is where ingenuity helped Weil Bros. to sail through the doldrums.

Adolph and Leonel—we must speak of them jointly for they were as one in all major decisions—came up with the idea of offering assistance to the government classers on a commission basis. Having little or no cotton of their own to keep them busy, Weil staffers at the ports were thus contracted out to the Department of Agriculture to process bales at fifty cents each. If nothing else, this kept the men off the unemployment rolls, bought their groceries, and maintained them in the organization. Then, in Savannah, Ben Barnes discovered an even better opportunity to make a few dollars, and Montgomery was quick to seize on his suggestion. We'd best let Barnes tell this story.

> A group of cotton merchants and factors, headed by . . . Anderson, Clayton had, either by outright purchase or lease, gotten control of all the compresses and warehouses in Savannah. It was a move to throttle competition in . . . compressing and storing cotton by channeling practically all business to the large Savannah Warehouse & Compress Co. To make a show of living up to the lease terms requiring operation of the smaller plants, a truck would be loaded once each month to make the rounds of these plants, get up steam, press a few bales at each place and then take the compressed bales back to the main plant. A small quantity of linters or waste was stored to carry out the storage requirements. . . . Our firm, as well as several of the smaller firms, were not stockholders but forced to concentrate our cotton at the big plant, and we didn't like it. These people had such a monopoly they became careless about lease renewals. Robert Perrin, a close friend of mine, was Secretary & Treasurer of the Corporation, owning the East Side Compress. Bob told me that the lease on the East Side plant would soon expire, and they were very much dissatisfied with the operation by the other people. I jumped at the opportunity to tie up this plant with an option good for sixty days. The plant was ideal for us—directly on the river where boats could dock for loading, high roofed warehouses and plenty of humidity not only to maintain the weight of the bales, but would show fair weight gains when held a few weeks. I rounded up my friends Charlie Golson of Bashinsky, Case & Co., and Malcolm Logan of M. J. Logan and Co., to go in with me and hied myself to Montgomery to lay the plan before the firm.

Every member of the firm from the Old Man down to young Alvin sat in on the conference. Weil Brothers had had some disturbing experiences with compresses in the past and were a little dubious about taking on something that might give them trouble. They looked at that proposition from every angle, mulled over the matter until nearly time for my train to leave for Savannah, finally giving me the green light to go ahead and close the lease. In no time at all the firms interested had signed a lease for one year, with the privilege of renewing for as long as we wanted it. Not a word was said to anyone about our having leased the East Side plant. On March 15th when Col. Arthur Gordon (of Anderson, Clayton) nonchalantly told Bob Perrin to draw up a renewal lease, and he was informed that our group had already signed up, panic broke out in the enemy camp.... Before we could make tentative plans to operate the plant we were approached by Mr. W. H. Glenn, President of the Savannah Warehouse & Compress Co., and Mr. T. E. Fugate, General Manager, to sublease to them.... We all met at the Atlantic Cotton Association convention in Augusta for a discussion of terms. Leonel came from Montgomery to be with me.... After the usual preliminary discussion lasting for a couple of hours, punctuated with many highballs, those representing the Big Plant made us a proposition to assume our lease and allow us 10% of the profits emanating from the operation of all plants in Savannah. With this before us the meeting adjourned in order to give our crowd time to discuss and consider their offer. In private conference we thought their proposition was good, but decided to make a counterproposal that we share in 10% of all profits, but would not be called on to share *any losses*, they to assume the monthly rent as also all other conditions of our lease. They agreed to our terms and later developments showed that we had made a trade that turned out to be quite beneficial to our group for the twelve years that this business lasted. We had already organized the East Side Comp. Co., with C. O. Golson as President, Malcolm J. Logan, Vice President, and myself Sec'y-Treas., with a paid-in capital of $100.00, or $33.33 each, with the privilege of increasing the capital to $50,000.00. Based on the paid-in capitalization, the percentage of profits accruing to the stockholders was so fantastic as to defy the imagination.*

*Barnes, *ibid.*

American production of cotton goods boomed in 1941 as uniforms were needed to clothe millions of servicemen for World War II at the same time that civilian demand burgeoned with the end of the Depression. At left is a magazine creel of a warper at Callaway Mills in La Grange, Georgia, and below the creel of a spinning frame at the same plant, also of that vintage. At right, a workman dollies rolls of carded cotton to the production line of the Pepperell Manufacturing Co. plant in Lee County, Alabama.—*National Archives*

These measures alone couldn't have kept Weil afloat without at least a minimum of regular buying and selling. Every transaction had to be figured to the point; on small volume, .01 cents per pound is all that more important. On July 1, 1931, the Savannah office still had several thousand bales of certificated cotton on hand, all hedged with July futures in New York. These could have been tendered on contract, and the profits included in the fiscal year ending that month. However, the distant future months were selling at prices well above the current contract month. May 1932 looked best to Leonel. At 144 points under July, it would be worthwhile to keep the stock and transfer the hedges; even with carrying and warehousing charges there would be more left over. That kind of thinking is done routinely in a cotton house, but the need for it now was greater than ever.

Yet, no matter how earnings were maximized, they could not compensate for the drastic shrinking of the export trade from Atlantic ports. As the Depression abated somewhat in the mid-1930s, it became evident that it would be wiser to concentrate on supplying domestic mills. By then, many of New England's mills, squeezed by union troubles and labor costs, had moved to the Southeast, where wages were lower, and, moreover, the sources of supply close at hand, thereby reducing shipping costs. The mill migration which had started in the late 1920s, would continue until after World War II; today only a small handful of textile manufacturers remain in the Northeast, most notably among them Bates Manufacturing and Edwards Manufacturing (both Maine), and Kendall (Massachusetts)—but even Kendall had opened a branch in North Carolina. Just about everybody was trooping south: Pacific Mills, Hanes, and Pepperell, which was merged with West Point Manufacturing Co., of West Point, Georgia.

Weil, as other merchants, benefited from this change to a degree: their offices in the Southeast could buy and sell from under the same roof. For a time, this advantage held, but as local crops grew ever smaller and harder to obtain, and as the mills eventually began to replace cotton with synthetics, the merchant offices in the original cotton states declined in importance, and the center of gravity shifted westward—to A. M. Crawford's Memphis, to Al Grayson's Dallas, and later to Houston and Fresno. Within the Eastern Belt, too, there was a constant redeployment of Weil's forces. Dothan, Alabama, deprived of its reason for existence by the weevils, had been the first to go. Savannah, in the face of faltering exports, was next. Macon, the subsequent pivot of Southeastern operations, fell by the wayside in 1942, when Atlanta took its place. This outpost lasted as a full-fledged branch office only for three years, and, ironically, it was a surge of unprecedented prosperity that occasioned its demise.

With World War II in high gear, Uncle Sam had all but preempted civilian production; meanwhile, the demand for consumer goods piled up, and textile mills profited hugely in the process. The manufacturers were permitted to reinvest a goodly portion of their earnings. Even so, they had enough left over for handsome dividends, and Atlanta fairly swam in money. With ten million men in the armed services, and a minimum of two GI outfits for each, this came close to the Nirvana of the cotton business—to sell just one shirt to every Chinese.

The dilemma lay in the fact that, as mentioned before, the Southeast no longer produced all that much fiber. Its crops then averaged about three million bales in a season, while the mills easily used three times that and kept hollering for more. Anyone who has passed Economics 101 will tell you that under such circumstances the mills would have to pay premium prices for their cotton. But not so. Real life isn't always that simple. What happened was that a new kind of carpetbagger suddenly showed up. Gaggles of small dealers, with no overhead but the roofs of their trucks, inundated the Eastern Belt. They bought all the freshly produced cotton their little vehicles could hold, and then raced to the nearest mill to sell the cotton the same day. Often with several such trucks vying for position at a mill's dock, the law of supply and demand on the scene superseded its bigger brother in the general marketplace. The cotton wildcatters, able to survive on minimal margins, undercut each other mercilessly, and the mills weren't about to pay more than they had to. On this basis, the merchant houses couldn't possibly compete. The only business left to them was selling for forward delivery, from two months ahead to contracts maturing twelve months later, known in cotton parlance as "round-the-clock" sales: the little dealers had neither capital nor credit for such transactions, and weren't interested in them anyway.

What's more, the large mill groups, such as Bibb of Macon, Callaway of LaGrange, and West Point, engaged increasingly in direct buying, especially spot—again a matter of less overhead.

This isn't to say that forward contracts were Weil's only source of revenue in those exciting times. The firm's offices in Alabama, Tennessee, and Texas, being out of range of the fast-buck operators, could and did pick up spot cotton for prompt delivery at prices that allowed enough profit for survival. But there was no way for Weil to keep Atlanta open as a profit-sharing merchandising office whose managers participated in the turnover of the cotton they bought and sold. By fluke—as we shall shortly see—it lasted out another season, but since World War II, it has been strictly a sales agency, whose sole purpose is to sell the cotton purchased elsewhere by the Weil organization. There are three other such Weil selling agencies in the Eastern Belt. One operates out of the firm's Montgomery headquarters; the other two are in Gastonia, North Carolina, and in Greenville, South Carolina—all vitally important territories to Weil, although the company today does only about 50 to 60 percent of its business with U.S. mills, a considerable shrinkage from the largely domestic marketing that prevailed from mid-Depression until the Marshall Plan revitalized Western Europe in the late 1940s. The steady drop of Weil's domestic percentage has been symptomatic of the American cotton mills' decline in the textile markets.

No single broker handles all of one mill's cotton. Some years it's more, some years it's less, and some years he sells the mill nothing at all. These fluctuations depend less on personal relationships (although of course they are a factor, too, as in any business) than on whether the mill is able to meet the broker's price and still show a margin of profit. Trust also has something to do with it: both sides have to be fairly sure that the other will meet its obligations. Indeed, there are a number of mills (mostly foreign) that Weil will not do business with because of prior experiences. But, all this aside, the overriding fact is that the cotton consumption of domestic mills today is only a little more than half of what it used to be. This decline came about as the result of several events in Adolph's and Leonel's time that conspired to make synthetics cheaper than natural fiber. Some of these events were technological developments. Others were government actions which, in seeking to protect the American cotton farmer, accomplished precisely the opposite.

Which brings us to the circumstance that kept the Atlanta merchandising office open one year longer than would have been possible in a free-market economy. Late in the 1943–44 season, the government found the price of cotton favorable for unloading a large quantity of the "loan cotton" it had accumulated over several years. To move those thousands upon thousands of bales stashed in warehouses from North Carolina to Texas, the Commodities Credit Corporation (CCC), a government-chartered entity, was authorized to issue catalogs citing grade and staple of the various lots so as to sell them in the open market. Weil's purchases out of this stock were considerable: there was obviously no problem reselling the cotton to all the mills that were starving for fiber. And that's how Atlanta turned in its last profitable year, doing both buying and selling—buying cotton from the government, and placing it with manufacturers who had government contracts on their books but lacked the raw material to fill them.

If you are not in the commodities business, chances are that what you have just read makes no sense to you. Not that it ever made sense to cotton people either—that during all these war years, when cotton was so desperately hard to get even for combat fatigues, several million bales were stagnating in government storage, courtesy of the New Deal.

More than anything else, it was the legislation promulgated under Franklin Delano Roosevelt that would dominate Weil's affairs for almost four decades, and whose effects—although most of the programs have now been discontinued for some years—still determine the course of the cotton business and will forevermore.

9

CCC (Catch as Catch Can)

KILL THE BABY PIGS, poison the potatoes, plow under the crops—such was the government's policy that came in with FDR in 1932. The rationale was that farmers were suffering, not getting enough money for what they had to sell because they had too much to sell. All of which was true enough. So the answer was again straight out of Economics 101: create a scarcity, and prices will rise. What Henry Wallace, then Roosevelt's secretary of agriculture, forgot to take into consideration was that, thanks to the Depression, nobody had the money to pay the higher prices.

But no matter. The scorched-earth approach died soon enough. For one thing, the public, sentimental as always, didn't like the idea of piglets being slaughtered while they were still pink and cute. But more important, the Supreme Court, despite FDR's efforts to recreate it in his own image, struck down the most blatantly odious features of the New Deal's Agricultural Adjustment Act of 1933.

The basic law, pushed through in the first famous "One Hundred Days" of the new administration, provided for payments to farmers who volunteered to withhold acreage they would otherwise harvest. If a crop was already planted (or a sow already enceinte), they were rewarded for making sure the product never reached the market. In the case of cotton, the money to be paid to farmers came from a tax imposed on cotton mills and their cotton consumption. It soon became apparent, however, that many farmers still clung to an antediluvian faith in the free market and would have none of the Agricultural Adjustment Administration's silver. As FDR put it, they were "standing on the same old pot." It must be presumed that the press doctored up this statement just a little: Roosevelt had an excellent vocabulary and knew very well what people did on pots. In any event, the law had to have teeth in it to make the farmers budge. Those teeth were put in place by, among other similar laws, the Bankhead Cotton Control Act of 1934, which penalized farmers who grew more cotton than the quota allocated to them. The quota, a poundage allotment, was a percentage of how much cotton the farmer

The first government check to a cotton farmer for witholding acreage went in July 1933 to William E. Morris of Nueces County, Texas, with FDR doing the honors. Marvin Jones (far left), chairman of the House Agricultural Committee, and Henry A. Wallace (far right), secretary of agriculture, got in on this historic picture too. The check, as others that followed it, was financed, ironically, by a tax imposed on cotton mills and their cotton consumption.—*National Archives*

Adolph in the 1930s, when mere mention of That Man in the White House was enough to send him through the ceiling.

had made in the past. Within the quota, he could produce and market free of penalty. But say he had an unusually good crop, he then either had to pay a fine to the ginner, who in turn passed it on to the government, or he could buy poundage from a neighbor with a short crop and add that poundage to his own, thus achieving a higher limit before he was penalized.

This intricate system was the idea (or at least they took most of the credit for it) of three cottonbelt senators, the likes of which you see nowadays only in the movies: John H. Bankhead II of Alabama, incongruously the uncle of emancipated Tallulah Bankhead;* Ellison D. "Cotton Ed" Smith of South Carolina, then chairman of the Senate's powerful Agriculture Committee; and Elmer Thomas of Oklahoma, who succeeded Smith as that committee's chairman. Also

---

*Actress Tallulah Bankhead was the daughter of Congressman William B. Bankhead, who also got in on the act and later served as Speaker of the House (1936–1940).

heavily involved were Senators Huey Long (Louisiana) and Kenneth McKellar (Tennessee), along with Congressmen Wall Doxey (Mississippi) and Marvin Jones (Texas). Senator John Bankhead, a farmer-populist like most of his cohorts, had been trying, and quite probably sincerely, to improve the cotton farmer's lot ever since he had entered public life as an Alabama legislator in 1904. A modicum of self-promotion did enter into his efforts along the way: farmers were given Bankhead Certificates, redeemable in cash, for acreages they didn't plant, a sure way to make them remember his name when they cast their ballots.

The Agricultural Adjustment Act, and the Cotton Control Act with it, expired in 1936. The Supreme Court ruled that it was unconstitutional to tax mills and then hand the proceeds to farmers. Taxes, the Court found, had to go into the General Fund; if then someone felt like giving farmers money, they had to make a separate law. On similarly legalistic grounds—this was in the days before social considerations began to color some of the Court's decisions—the Justices ruled that the federal government was usurping states' rights in making a contract with farmers to take acreage out of use. As usual in such a case, FDR had a snit, said a few more unkind things about "Old Tories," and sent his crew back to the drawing board. The resultant new Bankhead Act of 1938 vaulted the Supreme Court's hurdle by penalizing the farmers not for what they grew, but only for what they actually put on the market; at the same time, the successor of the Agricultural Adjustment Act halted the tax on mills and provided precisely what the Supreme Court had found lacking: legislation to give farmers money out of the General Fund, but this time not to bribe them to keep acreage out of production; rather, the money went to the farmers as "loans" when the free market price of cotton (and other commodities) dropped below a certain point, a system much like the one promulgated by Hoover's Farm Bureau.

The prices the farmers were supposed to get were based on a complex "parity" formula, the kind which takes platoons of Ps with PhDs to dream up, that related the farmer's resultant net income to a theoretical average net income he would have earned on a similar crop in the years 1909–1914. That this base period was a generation past didn't seem to faze anyone in the slightest. Needless to say, market prices in the 1930s refused to climb anywhere near the 52 percent of parity that applied to cotton. That allows you one guess as to what happened, but we'll tell you anyway. Between the Bankhead Act, which penalized marketing, and the price-support legislation, which rewarded production, the 1937–38 country-wide cotton crop was the heftiest in history—between seventeen and eighteeen million bales—much of which went into government warehouses as "loan cotton" (if you speak cottonese) or "surplus" (if you are of bureaucratic bent). Equally predictable, as commodity prices rose with the end of the Depression and the onset of World War II, the parity percentage farmers were deemed entitled to was upped accordingly: a no-win situation for the taxpayer who thus not only paid for the shirts and socks he wore but also for those he couldn't afford. In 1941, parity was pegged at 85 percent, and in 1948 at 90 percent—but that's getting ahead of our story, in which Weil's Atlanta office, ironically, made money for another year by buying and selling "loan cotton" when the government felt that, if it dumped some of its cotton on the market, the price would not be affected sufficiently to hurt the farmers.

You could say that was fair enough: the farmer got paid more than he would have otherwise, the government got some of its money back, Weil (and other merchants) made a profit, and everybody lived happily ever after. But they didn't. That's the trouble with intellectual fairy tales: their endings aren't what their authors expect.

As befits our protagonists, however, Adolph and Leonel saw what was coming—in essence, if not in detail. Adolph in particular, with his quick temper, exploded into anti-Roosevelt diatribes, convinced that the New Deal legislation would lay the American cotton business low, and indeed the whole country with it. He was so worried about Weil Brothers' future that he insisted on sending Bucks, his older son, to law school. Not that legal training isn't helpful to a cotton merchant, but Adolph wanted Bucks to be able to make a living, no matter what happened, when he graduated from Harvard.

As it luckily turned out, Adolph was overly pessimistic—a trait he passed on to Bucks. But essentially he was right: the American cotton business, and the textile industry as well, have been in a steady decline since the 1930s.

Yet, even with all their acuity, Adolph and Leonel couldn't have foretold all the direct and indirect consequences of the New Deal legislation. Their reaction must have been founded on instinct rather than reasoning. In those days, for instance, rayon was still in its infancy and nylon embryonic. Nobody could have predicted with certainty that the artificially high cotton prices would stimulate the chemical industry to develop cheaper substitutes that eventually would all but replace cotton in mass merchandise, or , for that matter, that such materials were technologically possible. A more reasonable assumption would have been that the propped-up prices would prompt other, less developed countries blessed with warm climates to emphasize cotton culture. But even so, Adolph and Leonel couldn't possibly have foreseen the scope of this displacement—or, for that matter, that exotic countries like Korea and Taiwan, then not even on the map, would someday develop textile industries whose cheap products would replace domestic goods even in old Opelika. Even less could the two brothers have predicted that the outflow of dollars for foreign textiles would contribute to a dangerous foreign-trade imbalance in our time.

The immediate consequences of the New Deal's agricultural experiments were not on that grand scale, of course. The dollar was then still the world's hardest currency. But the new laws did make it increasingly difficult for cotton merchants to stay in business. To be sure, as pointed out earlier, Weil did all right. In all the years of Adolph's and Leonel's leadership, there was only one season when the firm didn't show a profit, and some years it showed a substantial profit indeed. But this was possible only because as soon as World War II ended Weil made a determined effort to find cheaper cotton abroad than could be obtained at home. Cia. Algodones Extranjeros in Central America was the first such venture. But more about that later.

What, meanwhile, made the domestic business increasingly difficult was that the artificially pegged high price of government cotton eventually caused the futures market to dry up. Not that a cotton merchant—as opposed to a speculator—tries to get rich by playing futures. But to survive, he is dependent on the conditions that make a futures market essential: the vagaries of an ever-changing spot market. When prices are determined by decree, and the mills know almost exactly how much cotton will cost when they need it, the merchant has little room for his basis operation. No longer can he find bargains to resell to spinners on more favorable terms than his competitor; nor can he work the widely divergent prices of the grades for which he tries to find buyers against the known price of the standard-grade futures contracts.

Moreover, the government's marketing of loan cotton by catalog made the merchant's life more difficult in yet another respect, in that it encouraged direct purchases by textile mills of stocks from the CCC. Many spinners, especially since moving to the South, already had their own "mill buyers." This practice now burgeoned. An outsider may well ask, why not cut out the middleman and get the cotton cheaper? The answer is that it's cheaper only if the mill can obtain *precisely* the cotton it wants and in *precisely* the quantities it needs. Catalog buying sometimes made this possible, at least to a degree. But under ordinary circumstances, direct buying costs a mill as much as going through a merchant. Here's why. The merchant accumulates his cotton by buying from farmers who may produce anywhere from fewer than a dozen to many thousands of bales. There may be as many as fifty type variations in this stock, which the merchant then sorts out and resells to mills and other customers (pharmaceutical cotton houses, for instance) according to their needs. All these intermediate functions from buying to storing, from reclassing to shipping, have to be undertaken also by mills that purchase directly; and, as has often happened, if the mills inadvertently end up with cotton they don't want, they then have to play merchant and try to resell it. Consequently, mill buying declined again when cotton eventually returned to the free market, although some of the largest mills, such as Cannon and J. P. Stevens, continued this practice until the early 1980s.

In 1944, at the height of the World War II, the restrictions on raising cotton were suspended, and only the loan and the price support system remained in effect. There was no need then to force farmers into other commodities. Higher prices for food crops took care of that. It was because of the resultant cotton scarcity that the Commodity Credit Corporation, the legal entity that the government had chartered to make nonrecourse loans to farmers, felt free to release so much of its cotton in that final glory year of the Atlanta office. But the scarcity soon turned into superabundance as the parity price moved up in 1948, and again in 1949, while, at the same time, vast new acreages were brought into production in Arizona, California, and the Texas Panhandle. Needless to say, marketing quotas were put back into effect again to halt the flood.

But as so often happens when man tries to tame the sea of history in which we're all aswim, this action was taken at exactly the wrong time. For one thing, Western Europe's resurgent spinning industry was coming back into the market and export demand was strong. For another, that most fickle of all factors, weather, turned sour simultaneously. Last and most serious, North Korea attacked South Korea in June 1950, and the United States found itself at war again, even if no one called it by that name, just as this miserably lame crop was maturing. No constellation of circumstances could have been less fortuitous. The squeeze was so severe that, for the first time (and only time so far), the government felt compelled to slap an embargo on cotton exports. If, by then, Weil hadn't begun to ship considerable quantities of Central American growths, Adolph and Leonel hardly would have been able to do any exporting at all.

Not surprisingly, acreage allotments and marketing limitations were once again suspended in the face of this shortage, and all sorts of incentives devised to prompt farmers to plant more cotton. Among these carrots was a section of the Defense Production Act of 1950 that allowed new gins to be amortized almost as they were built. As may be expected, this fast write-off spurred heavy development in the new cotton areas of the West. The weather also cooperated: bumper crop followed bumper crop. Naturally, most of this cotton went under the loan program and ended up in government hands. By 1956, the warehouses were plugged to the rafters with nearly 10 million bales of government cotton. With another 4.6 million bales in privately held stocks, this added up to the greatest cotton carryover to date—14.5 million bales—a record that has since been exceeded only once.* At

---

*The all-time carryover record of 16.8 million bales was set in 1966 when the CCC held 12.3 million. This was the climax of yet another period of government hoarding that had started in 1964. In the 1967 season, the CCC's stocks were halved, and by 1968 the government only held 205,000 bales. Loan cotton hasn't been a problem since (see later text). United States Department of Agriculture Economics Research Service. *Statistics on Cotton and Related Data 1920–73*. Washington, D.C.: Government Printing Office, 1974. P. 43.

the same time, the total world supply of U.S. cotton also set a record with 28.3 million bales.* The consequences of this overhang were predictable: prices plummeted on the foreign markets, and export of U.S. cotton slumped as the gap between foreign and domestic prices widened.

But rather than collapse the umbrella that parity pricing held over foreign cotton, Congress passed an export subsidy program introduced by Senator James Eastland and Congressman Jamie Whitten, both of Mississippi. As if that weren't enough, the lawmakers also presented Secretary of Agriculture Ezra Taft Benson with a new Soil Bank program that rewarded farmers for taking land out of production. Apparently no one considered the possibility that a farmer might not be interested in relegating cotton acreage to the Soil Bank if he could make more money by selling a crop at a subsidized price. It certainly never occurred to Eisenhower to veto the legislation.

In any event, farmers didn't suffer. Farm bills aren't designed that way. But it didn't take long before the ill effects of the new medicine on the domestic textile industry became apparent. As the subsidized cotton reached foreign markets, foreign mills happily spun U.S. cotton, and soon that very same cotton, by then fashioned into garments, came back across the oceans once again to our shores. The foreign-made cotton goods were, of course, much lower priced than equivalent items of U.S. manufacture. Not only had they been made from fiber that cost considerably less than what American mills had to pay, but they were manufactured with cheaper labor, and in brand-new mills equipped with the latest machinery—also largely paid for, via foreign aid, by U.S. taxpayers. In 1961, the subsidy alone cost about $225 million. With the loan at thirty-three cents while export cotton went for around twenty-four cents, the difference was about forty-five dollars a bale for the approximately five million bales shipped abroad that season. †

No doubt, there are any number of ivory tower pundits who'd like nothing better than to make a case against Weil and other cotton merchants for contributing to this sad state of affairs. True enough,

---

*Again this record was broken in the mid-1960s, with the world supply of U.S. cotton at 29.5 million bales in 1964, and 30.2 million bales in 1965. *Ibid.*

†*Ibid.* and Joe Moss, until his retirement in 1972 director of the Cotton Division, Agricultural Stabilization and Conservation Service, U.S. Department of Agriculture.

Weil sold subsidized cotton to mill customers in foreign countries. But firms that would survive must function within the framework of the marketplace, and if that framework be ill designed, the blame must rest with its designers.

In any event, selling CCC cotton was hardly ever very profitable. With the price standardized, there was no need for a futures market, and, without the futures market, there was no basis to work with. The spinners bid according to the government pricing, and the merchant could take it or leave it. He had to make it on the fundamental bid, or not at all. The key lay in the competence of the merchant's classers: in reclassing the already government-classed cotton, they might, and frequently did, discover lots of superior grade that would fetch premiums when channeled to the proper customers.

In particular, Weil managed to take advantage of cotton's inherent proclivity to change color from bright white to a homogenous creamy hue when it has been stored for some time. This "light spot," as it's called, is deemed not to be quite as valuable. That's not necessarily so, however. Dyed, it's as good as bright cotton of the same quality and staple. Still, since it's not appropriate for some uses, the government, upon reclassing it for sale, released it for about 100 points less. The trick was to find that potentially valuable cotton in the millions of bales warehoused all over the countryside. If Weil managed to buy such discounted cotton, the firm could turn right around and sell it for 50 points more to any number of mills and everybody'd be happy, with the mill receiving perfectly fine cotton at a discount while Weil made 50 points on the transaction.

How Weil went about this was simple enough in retrospect—so simple that it bordered on the ingenious. Since it takes cotton many months to discolor, it stood to reason that it could be found only in warehouses where cotton had been stored for a long time. So Weil checked through stacks of periodically issued government catalogs that listed the various offerings. By comparing the stored quantities over a period of time, it was possible to deduce which warehouses were likely to hold the oldest cotton. Weil then bought a few bales to sample the stock. If it was creamy as expected, they went in heavy—customers for it were easy to find.

Credit for this highly successful strategy accrued to Jimmy Loeb, Lucien Loeb's son and Adolph and Leonel Weil's nephew, who was always alert to competitors' activities and an expert at drawing them out. On this occasion, Charles "Chuck" Hohenberg inadvertently let it slip to Jimmy that Hohenberg was engaged in such selective buying. Similarly, Jimmy Loeb picked up from Eddie Shipper, of Florence, Alabama, that 1958 Texas equities had big gains built into them. Jimmy, who then handled some of the catalog buying of Texas cotton, made three seasons out of this profitable bit of intelligence.

It was the capability of locating special cottons, along with Weils' astuteness in analyzing bids, which saw the company through those difficult years. The rule, as always at the firm, was to buy all the cotton it could. Thus, although profits per bale weren't big, the firm by no means walked the tightrope.

Weil's repeated success in buying and moving government cotton was to have some uncomfortable consequences. On the six o'clock news on March 28, 1956, it was announced that Weil Brothers–Cotton Inc., along with seven other corporations and four individuals, had been indicted by a federal grand jury for alleged violations of the Clayton Anti-Trust Act. The indictment contended that the accused had engaged in an unlawful conspiracy to restrain competition in the merchandising of government cotton valued at twenty million dollars. As usual on Wednesdays, Bucks and Bobby Weil went to play poker at the Standard Club that night. "It was very hard," says Bobby, "to keep a poker face."

Besides Weil, the indictment named E. F. Creekmore & Co., a New Orleans firm; A. Campdera and Co., Sternberg-Martin and Co., R. L. Dixon and Brothers Inc., and Crespi & Co., all of Dallas; J. A. Baker & Co. and Pell Cotton Co., of Charlotte, North Carolina; Robert D. McCallum, the Memphis partner of McFadden, and R. O. Beach, Sr., that firm's Houston partner; and at the fulcrum of the alleged price-fixing conspiracy, Morris Wolf, the owner of Wolf and Co., a New Orleans spot cotton broker, and his assistant, John P. Godchaux. Named as coconspirators, but not indicted, were about twenty other cotton merchant houses, including Hohenberg Bros. and Cook & Co.

Shocking as it was, the news did not come as a complete surprise. The grand jury had been convened on the case some months before, and Bobby as well as Weil's Nathan Rosenfield had appeared before it in New Orleans to testify. Bobby was astounded to find Julian Hohenberg calmly reading *Huckleberry Finn* in the anteroom while waiting for his turn with the jurors. The story behind the indictment was this:

The CCC issued its bulky catalog listing government cottons for sale about every other week. In between, the CCC mailed voluminous lists of deletions to the catalog subscribers. To figure out what stocks were available, the prospective buyers then had to go back into the catalog and strike out the deletions. It was a complex, time-consuming job that left much room for error. Morris "Pete" Wolf, the indicted New Orleans spot broker, had devised a system that, by means of an IBM computer, quickly reconciled the deletions with the catalog listings, and the resulting compilation was mailed free of charge to anyone who used his services as a broker to take up the cotton from the CCC. Wolf's commission was fifty cents a bale— which amounted to, say, $25,000 for 50,000 bales at one clip. With close to one hundred clients, Pete was pulling in a fortune with every government sale. It was no secret in the trade that Frank Biggs, then the director of the CCC's cotton sales, was more than a little upset that Wolf made so much money. Biggs suggested to the Justice Department that Wolf was not merely distributing revised catalogs and funneling the resulting bids to the CCC, but that he was specifically advising his clients on what lots to bid on and how much to bid. If true, this indeed would have been a restraint of trade. It was a plausible enough charge: such collusion could have taken place. Except that Bobby knew that this was not how the business had been done.

When it was decided that Bobby would answer the subpoena on behalf of the firm, he consulted T. B. Hill, a leading Montgomery attorney. Hill, after being told that Bobby felt Weil had nothing to hide, advised him to give the Justice Department a waiver of immunity if he was asked for it. He also told Bobby to go back to his hotel room immediately after the hearing to write detailed notes on his testimony. The government transcript of the hearings, Hill said, would not be made available to the witnesses in the event that an indictment was returned.

Although the Justice Department investigator, Charles Beckler, put Bobby on the defensive with a number of ambiguous questions that required evasive responses because they couldn't be answered precisely, Bobby felt that he had acquitted himself quite well. He went to the Roosevelt Hotel to write his notes as instructed, and returned to Montgomery without worrying too much about any further consequences to Weil. "When they didn't ask me for a waiver of immunity," he says, "I figured that we were not their target. I found out later that they couldn't indict me personally anyway, but could indict my firm. I didn't know the distinction. The second thing, the line of questioning, even though it was hostile, never seemed directed against us. It was more toward Wolf. And of course we didn't know anything that we had done wrong."

The morning after the newscast, Bobby had a call from Louis Oberdorfer, a Dartmouth buddy who had married Leonel's daughter Elizabeth. Oberdorfer, now on the federal bench, was then associated with the Washington law firm of Cox, Langford, Stoddard and Cutler. He said he'd heard the family firm had been indicted; that he wasn't soliciting the case but wanted to warn the Weils not to say anything about the case to anybody since a careless statement now could make things very difficult later. Louis also wanted to talk to Adolph. Bobby told him that he couldn't: Adolph, with a brand-new indictment hanging over the firm, had calmly gone off fishing with Leonel. Louis laughed when he heard this, and said, "They really made them in those days."

Oberdorfer's firm did get the case. Lloyd Cutler, of later prominence as Jimmy Carter's White House legal counsel, was famous for his work in antitrust cases, and Louis Oberdorfer was no legal slouch himself: six years after the Wolf fracas, he was about to be proposed for nomination to the Supreme Court by his friend and close associate, Robert Kennedy, then attorney general, when the latter's brother, John F. Kennedy, was assassinated and the function of Supreme Court appointments fell to Lyndon B. Johnson, who had no love for Bobby.

As soon as Louis Oberdorfer took on Weil as a client, he immediately spotted a serious legal flaw in the government's handling of the case. We shall let him tell it:

"I asked Bobby at our first meeting what he was asked and what he answered to the grand jury. He says, 'I can't tell you.' Why couldn't he tell me? 'I swore on an oath that I would keep the proceedings secret.' I asked him, did he tell his father or his brother? His answer was no. I told him, 'I don't see how we can represent you if you can't tell us the facts.' At that, he got indignant. There was no subterfuge about it. He had no sense—and certainly I didn't at that moment—of the legal issue. Here was a man who had taken an oath and he was going to stick by it.

"What had happened was, there had been a rule that authorized the administering of an oath of secrecy to the witnesses. But a few months before this proceeding the rule had been changed. Witnesses could no longer be sworn to secrecy in federal cases, and the dumb cluck who was running the case for the Anti-Trust Division didn't know that, and he swore Bobby to secrecy.

"We broke the case on that. It wasn't much of a case for the government on the merit side anyway, but you don't know that about an antitrust case when you start. You can be reasonably innocent and still be swept right into it, never knowing you had a little piece of the action or part in some crucial conversation. The oath wasn't the only ground for the dismissal of the case, but that's what did it. It was like a tough football game, and we sacked their quarterback on the first play. They had some more plays left, but they never got momentum, and they never got into the twenty-yard line. Finally they gave up."

What defeated the government's other plays was in the Adolph-Leonel tradition. Bobby reasoned that by detailed analysis of trading patterns, he could refute the government's contention that the bids were rigged. Bobby knew that Weil used a pyramid system of bidding—so much at one price, so much more at a different price, and so on depending on which way the market was heading. This in itself contradicted the possibility that Wolf could have directed how much Weil would pay for what. On examining the bids of the other merchants, Bobby found that each had his own equally independent approach to buying government cotton. Cook, for instance, would bid across the board at minimum prices, figuring whatever cotton they got was going to be the cheapest. Hohenberg, and also McFadden, went high on particular kinds of cotton and wouldn't bid on others at all. Once Bobby had thus established the premise of his argument, the accounting firm of Haskins & Sells was hired by the defendants to analyze the records of all the bids from 1948 to 1956 that were covered by the indictment. This study bore out Bobby's thesis of individual patterns.

As a final blow to the government, it came to light that the Department of Agriculture had in fact approved Wolf's operations, knowing that the computerized system would expedite the CCC's sales. F. Marion "Dusty" Rhodes, later president of the New York Cotton Exchange, was then head of the Agriculture Department's cotton section. To clarify the point, the defendants' lawyers and the government's lawyer went to Dusty's office. But when one of the defense attorneys asked him about the department's involvement, the government lawyer jumped up and said, "I forbid you to answer that question." Here's Bucks' account of what happened next:

"So this sort of knocked the stew out of our boys, and we all went back to the Mayflower and had a drink and said this was a government railroading. About that time, the phone rang and they asked to speak to old man Creekmore. It was Dusty Rhodes, and Dusty says, 'Jerry, I shouldn't be calling you, and I'm not drunk, but I'm just as mad as I can be. So if I sound a little excited, this is why. I can tell you what the answer was to the question they didn't let me answer today. We did give Pete Wolf license for his procedure. We put our blessings on it, and if you go to court you just call me as a witness, because I'm going to tell the truth, and they're not going to hush me up."

Throughout all this back-and-forth, which went on for twenty months, the government went through all the customary routines. The first was intimidation, the threat of adding a civil suit to the criminal charge, and the last, the time-honored dodge of saving face.

Early on, the Justice Department had offered to let the defendants off with $5,000 fines if they pleaded guilty, and indeed there had been several of them almost ready to go along with this ploy. They reasoned that if the government said they had been doing something wrong, it must be so; the fine was insignificant compared to what it would cost not to knuckle under, and in any event there was an element of glamour in confessing guilt of antitrust. But Adolph had not been satisfied with this easy out, although he could have saved legal fees that eventually totaled $75,000. He went to Washington to see the chief of the antitrust division to find out precisely what Weil was supposed to be guilty of. No answer was forthcoming, and the two men did little but growl at one another. Later, the government suggested that the defendants plead *nolo contendere*, throwing themselves on the mercy of the court. Again there were a number of potential takers, and again they were persuaded to hold out. As Jerry Creekmore said, "I'll see those bastards in hell first." Finally, the Justice Department lawyers agreed to withdraw the case if the defendants would sign a consent decree, i.e., promise never to do again what they hadn't done in the first place. And that was the end of this expensive hassle.

Here's a neat touch to cap the tale: Pete Wolf didn't even have to sign the consent decree. How indeed could one arm of government demand of him to refrain from doing what another arm of government had asked him to do?

The gigantic sales of government cotton were to continue for some years after this contretemps, reaching their peak in 1967 with 12.3 million bales. By then the government, staggering under the load of the surplus, had begun to see the error of its approach. Under legislation promulgated by Senator Allen Ellender, chairman of the Agricultural Committee, the subsidies were abandoned and cotton allowed to reach its own price; direct payments were to be made to recompense farmers if that level dropped below parity. *

As it turned out, there was no need for such payments then, and there hasn't been since. The 1967 crop came a cropper, and even as

---

*A system of direct payments to farmers so as to liberate the market had been proposed, unsuccessfully, already in the 1950s by F. Marion Rhodes when he served as director of the Cotton Branch of the Agricultural Adjustment Administration under Benson. Rhodes left government in 1960 to preside over the New York Cotton Exchange, and he held that office until 1975. Retired, he now lives near San Diego but continues as president emeritus of the Exchange in numerous advisory functions.

the CCC's overhang was being sold, a mad scramble for cotton began. As prices jumped from one day to the next, and without a futures floor decreed by parity, growers had to hedge. The New Orleans Cotton Exchange no longer existed, having given up its ghost in the late 1950s, but the New York Cotton Exchange had weathered the crisis, thanks largely to the sale of the building it owned and occupied at 60 Beaver Street. With the renewed trading of futures, Weil was back in business as a basis operator, as it had been meant to be.

Leonel had retired in 1951, but came to the office every day, except on Thursdays, when he devoted himself to the farm he and Adolph had bought near Montgomery. Adolph was still active, although his sons by then had taken over the company's day-to-day affairs. With the return to normal—if such a term may be used in connection with something as erratic as the cotton business—the firm's continuity was assured for the foreseeable future, an assurance made possible by Adolph's and Leonel's early perception of the path where history must carry them.

Cotton merchants have to follow cotton as unerringly as camp followers follow camps. In Adolph's and Leonel's era, this meant away from the Eastern Belt, whose vestigial production was kept alive only by price supports, and to the West, whose vast acreages lent themselves to modern techniques of mechanized agriculture, and on to Latin America, whose populace was still too hungry to be displaced by machines.

10

Born to the Boll

But for the thirteen years of the loan cotton doldrums, from 1954 to 1967, when it was often very difficult for one office or another to show profits, Weil managers have participated in the earnings of their individual operations, and by more than a few nominal percentage points at that. * They had the chance to become rich men, even millionaires, in their own right. This potential of direct reward made them entrepreneurs rather than employees, almost as if they were in business on their own—a marvelous incentive for anyone endowed with initiative and brains. The firm has insisted only that a few basic policies be followed; the house rule on hedging is a case in point, and even that one is flexible to a degree. Other than honesty and fidelity to this Weil doctrine, the managers have been saddled with one obligation: to stay in constant touch with the head office, so that there would be a perpetual give and take of business intelligence and advice.

Given such freedom, it is only to be expected that each manager had his own mode of operation. Al Grayson, the Sage of St. Paul, was

---

*In 1954, Weil's top managers, rather than sharing in the profits of their own operations, were issued stock in Weil Brothers–Cotton, Inc., which had been chartered as a corporation in 1950. They were A. M. Crawford, Sr., Nathan Rosenfield, Carl Baquie, Vasser Gunter, and A. M. Crawford, Jr. No further stockholders were admitted, and in 1967 the firm returned to its original mode of executive compensation.

Unlike proverbial organization men, cotton merchants are an individualistic bunch, each with his own personal and operational style. Weil's managers were no exception. Despite their different predilections and strategies, A. M. Crawford, Sr. (left), Bill Reckling (top center), Nathan Rosenfield (bottom center), and Al Grayson (right) were all hugely successful.

a high-profit, high-quality, low-volume operator. Although big volume has been a Weil tenet since Isidor's time, the firm did not mind Al's selective approach for he had such an ingrained sense of cotton that he never took a sale unless he was pretty sure he'd make good money on it. Al was so shrewd about price trends that even the heads of almighty Anderson Clayton used to call him regularly to get his point of view on the market.

In contrast, A. M. Crawford, Sr., went for high volume, regardless of low margins. Extraordinarily aggressive, he did not shy from iffy sales. Also unlike Grayson, who ran a tight ship, Crawford was not a penny pincher. His one big hangup, besides temperance, was to keep his staff busy. In the summers, when there was often little to do, he used to be driven to distraction when he found his squidges, classers

and office people playing checkers. Occasionally he sent his buyers on wild goose chases just to keep them occupied. His extensive Memphis organization had no resemblance to a pyramid. Everyone, including the newest squidge, knew fully well that in the end he was responsible to Crawford, not to the interposed supervisor.

What made Crawford's success all the more amazing is that he never learned to class cotton. He'd come up as an auditor, and didn't even try. When he took over Memphis in 1928, that office was still known as Weil Brothers & West. Weil had provided the capital and collected two thirds of the profits; the local partner, B. B. West, was entitled to one third. In this instance, however, this seemed not to have been enough, and B. B. had been juggling the books for some time. The complexities of cotton merchandising have always lent

themselves to devious maneuvering, what with purchases coming in from all over the countryside, shipments always on the move, and forward sales for delivery on a multitude of dates—although such shenanigans are less likely with today's more sophisticated controls. Indeed, West's malfeasances may well have remained undiscovered had he been more cautious, and if A. M. Crawford hadn't been so good with figures. It turned out that B. B. West had taken a heavy position in low grades, but had kept them off the books; he was trying to make a killing on his own account while pretending that he was acting for Weil. Had the weather lived up to his wet and miserable expectations that 1927 season, he would have made a bundle, with probably no one the wiser. But then skies brightened, and low grades got so scarce that there was no way for him to deliver the cotton he had contracted for. The matter came to Adolph's and Leonel's attention when mills started calling Montgomery wanting to know where the Memphis cotton was that had been promised them. Concerned, Adolph and Leonel dispatched A. M. Crawford from Texas to take a close look at the Memphis books—and that was the end of B. B. West. Even before all the evidence was in, he tried to kill himself and bungled once again. The case never came to trial. The bonding company compensated Weil for its losses on transactions, and B. B. West's brother, S. Y. West, a cotton merchant himself, made restitution for the Weil funds B. B. West had employed.

The Weil Brothers sample room in Memphis, shown here in a photograph taken probably in the late 1940s, was reputedly the country's longest. The discerning eye, aided perhaps by a magnifier, may spot A.M. Crawford standing to the right of the second table, looking across to Alvin Weil, who is pulling at a sample.

Keeping one's hat on was apparently good form in those days. The classic example was John Wagner, shown at right in front of the sample racks in a 1940 snapshot, who was self-conscious about being bald and never bared his pate.

But more important than the reparations was the fact that this incident catapulted A. M. Crawford into the forefront of the firm's managers. In the interregnum between West and Crawford, John Wagner, the Memphis head classer, ran the show. Wagner, who hailed from Chesterville, Mississippi, was compact of figure and tough of demeanor and was feared but loved. Although outwardly an unpredictable and often erratic disciplinarian, he was a born mentor who always tried to help the young men coming into the business get squared away. Among his charges was to be a host of cotton prominences, including Tom Adams, his nephew-in-law and now head of the Memphis office; Julian Dewberry, now in Fresno; Adolph Weil's son Bucks, as well as many men who have since left the firm to seek and sometimes make their fortunes elsewhere. Sensitive to his bald pate, Wagner never took off his hat—a subject of much merriment around the shop, and not conducive to the respect a boss must instill in his staff. Nor was Wagner a merchandiser and marketer; these were not his ambitions. The sample room was his kingdom, and he didn't mind at all that his elevation to head of the office was only temporary.

A. M. Crawford, while short on sampling expertise, fulfilled all the other qualifications, including that of being an unquestioned leader. From the time he went to Memphis, everything came up greenbacks. Before long, A. M. garnered a reputation in the business comparable to Grayson's, and although the two men were good friends, there was considerable rivalry betwen them. Crawford used to complain that Grayson always took the good orders and left the bad ones to him. What actually happened was that Adolph and Leonel, upon receiving an order, would consult with both men and give it to the one they thought could profit most on it. Grayson and Crawford understood these mechanics, of course, and played their respective games accordingly.

As Weil's activity expanded after World War I, the organization naturally grew with it. Isidor's two old stalwarts were joined in the managerial ranks by members of a new generation. Among these was Charles Greengrass, who worked as Grayson's assistant until the latter's death, and then succeeded him in Dallas. Greengrass adopted Grayson's style and leavened it with a certain measure of license. A native of Liverpool, Britain's cotton port, he'd been in America only a short while when, in the 1920s, the Soviet textile syndicate sent one of its purchasing missions to Texas. Greengrass, accompanied by Leonel, went to Houston to meet the Russians. Apparently they were ill received. Neither can remember the details at this late stage except that the Russians seemed to have made insulting remarks about Weil Brothers. Greengrass, then in his early thirties and inclined to be rash, was of a mind to suspend further talks. Leonel, more placid, disagreed. He suggested taking a long walk to cool down their tempers before meeting the Russians again in the afternoon. Sure enough, by that time the visitors were over their snit. Suddenly all smiles, they bought several thousand bales at very favorable prices. But Greengrass wasn't done with them yet and wanted to get even.

The Russians had insisted that they didn't want cotton from the Aransas Compress; they'd heard somewhere that it wasn't suitable for what they wanted, which wasn't true. So that night, Greengrass craftily trucked 7,000 bales from the Aransas Compress to Taft, had them retagged there with the name of the local compress, and delivered them to the Russians, who didn't know the difference anyway (there wasn't any) and accepted the order without a single rejection. Greengrass admits that if he had been unable to deliver the cotton he would have been fired—and rightly so.

Greengrass, a resourceful man to say the least, also claimed to have invented the somewhat dubious practice of blending cotton by reginning it. Amoskeag, then a major New England mill, had contracted to buy a respectable quantity of "Rose Ruby," the Weil designation for a certain type of Strict Middling light-spotted cotton. When the time came to ship it, Dallas didn't have it, and there was none to be found. But, in Greengrass' words, "We had a bunch of Strict Middling fifteen sixteenths and some red cotton on hand, and I don't remember how this came about, but I went down to Galveston, and inasmuch as I had done a bit of reginning at times, I thought we could make the Rose Ruby. Well, it took several white bales and a tingy bale, and after getting the formula correct, I went ahead and had the shipment reginned. It was several thousand bales—enough to fill a whole Moore-McCormack steamer to New Bedford, Massachusetts. Every single bale passed. Amoskeag could use it very well, and they were certainly better off to have this cocktail than nothing at all."

As a native Englishman, Greengrass was by no means an oddity in Texas, whose cotton culture attracted numerous Western Europeans, among them, incidentally, Otto Goedecke, a German to whom the idea of reginning has been commonly attributed. Goedecke wasn't with Weil; he worked for cooperatives and later went into business for himself in Hallettsville. It might be pointed out in this connection that reginning was not a Weil practice, although there were no rules against it in the Greengrass days. Today, reginned cotton must be so identified.

Another Weil recruit after World War I was Nathan "Boy" Rosenfield, who soon became one of the firm's prime movers. A native of Lafayette, Louisiana, he had begun his cotton career with Sylvan Newberger and Son in New Orleans, where he soon was made a partner. But the Newberger firm fell on hard times, wiping out Nathan's holdings, and in 1935 he applied for a job in Memphis, where A. M. Crawford hired him. Two years later, Rosenfield was called to Montgomery to take charge of the Eastern merchandising when the manager at the head office, Mose Blumenfeld, went into business for himself.

Of all Weil managers, Rosenfield was perhaps the best cotton technician—and no one was left in doubt that he knew it. Stocky in stature and Napoleonesque in bearing, he was not a man to argue with. If somebody asked his opinion of some other recognized cotton expert, he would reply, "He's the second-best judge of cotton I know." If the questioner then wanted to know whom Rosenfield considered the best cotton judge of all, he would regard his interrogator with disdain and say, "Modesty forbids." Bobby Weil, who trained under Rosenfield, once showed him a sample and asked, "What do you think this cotton is?" Nathan Rosenfield replied, "You don't mean 'what do I *think* it is.' You meant to say 'what *is* this cotton?'"

Needless to say, people who worked for Rosenfield didn't always like him, but they soon learned to respect him as much as he respected himself. Interestingly enough, despite his phenomenal knowledge of cotton and an equal talent for hair-splitting deals, he was constantly worried about his decisions and therefore terribly conservative. This may well have been because of his sad experience with Newberger's, which went broke because it had sold forward large quantities of bright long-staple cotton that didn't materialize when the crop matured.

In a move that astounded many people in the business, Nathan Rosenfield was appointed manager of the Houston office in 1952. What made this transfer so remarkable was that for all his professional life he had been a staple expert and was so recognized by the mill people who held him in great esteem. In New Orleans and Memphis, he had dealt with $\frac{1}{16}$ cotton or longer, and in Montgomery with staple of at least $\frac{1}{32}$, but in Texas he had to handle $\frac{7}{8}$ to $\frac{15}{16}$—an altogether different ball game. Yet more astounding was that he caught on instantly, and soon was as firmly established in the new arena as he had been in the old. Later his office was the first Weil branch to buy CCC cotton on government class. He had discovered what some men in other cotton houses already knew, namely that the government sometimes classed its loan cotton much "harder" (i.e. lower) than was customary in the real world. As a result, there were gains built into much of the warehoused cotton, which could be turned to profit once the cotton was reclassed.

Nathan had taken over the Houston office from another brilliant comer in the cotton field, William J. Reckling, a native of Savannah, Georgia, who had trained in Liverpool and later Le Havre, where he had been sent by Weil to work with the firm's French partners, Maison Du Pasquier. But more of that aspect of Reckling's career later. In the late 1930s, Bill Reckling was recalled from Europe to put his knowledge of foreign markets to use as Al Grayson's assistant in Dallas. When, after World War II, Reckling desired an office of his own to concentrate on the booming export business, the firm established him in Houston as W. J. Reckling & Co. This pseudonymous operation was actually wholly owned by Weil and managed like any of its other branches, with Reckling working on a minimal guarantee and participating in the profits. In this case, however, since it was assumed that Al Grayson had a franchise with respect to Texas cotton, Dallas also shared in the earnings of the Houston office, if to a lesser extent.

As Al Grayson was famous for his wit, so Reckling was recognized in the trade for his unflappable, gentlemanly manner. This may well have been his nature, but chances are that he had absorbed some of it during his years in Europe, whose cotton fraternity tends to cloak itself in the *mondain* rather than mundane. Deep down he was probably as tense as most people in the business, but one never would have known it. Unlike everybody else, he refused to be involved from early morning until late at night, and stuck to regular office hours.

Bill Reckling was what might be most aptly termed an opportunist in his transactions. While it was Grayson's style to obtain the best-priced order and find the most favorably priced purchase to fill it—a policy that called for great patience and a steady participation in the market—Reckling would sit on the sidelines for weeks, not doing much business at all. But then, when he saw his chance, he'd leap in for all he was worth, and nearly always came out a big winner.

On one occasion, for example, a local Houston broker, Campbell Riddick, offered him a large quantity of Arizona cotton at a bargain price. Reckling's classers, among them Tom Adams who would later head the Memphis office, agreed with him that the bulk of this cotton

Tom Moss was the first of several Dyersburgers—all imported by Moss—to make their careers with Weil. At right is how Dyersburg, Tennessee, looked early in the century when cotton farmers rolled their wagons up Court Street.

could be certificated and tendered on futures contract. With the backing of Adolph and Leonel, Bill Reckling bought the whole lot and hauled in a big profit. He even made money on the split qualities that he could not put on contract but for which he soon found other export markets. It was altogether a remarkable performance. As it turned out, A. M. Crawford was less than pleased with Reckling's coup. Crawford considered Arizona part of his territory and he felt that Reckling was horning in. But Reckling quite properly pointed out that, although the cotton had been grown in Arizona, he had bought it in the Houston market. Crawford acquiesced. Not being the type to allow any opportunity to pass him by unchallenged, he soon delivered Arizona cotton on contract himself.

Reckling's resignation from the firm in 1952 was a blow to Weil, albeit understandable. Reckling left for a position few men could have resisted: that of Anderson Clayton's top man in Europe. But his departure came at a most unfortunate time. Al Grayson had only recently died, and Leonel, as well as Lucien Loeb, Adolph's and Leonel's brother-in-law, retired. It was the first of two management crises in the company, more of which in detail later. Suffice it to say here, in this account of cotton men and their accomplishments, that this first time around, unlike the second, plenty of executive backup was available. Greengrass temporarily succeeded Grayson in Dallas until all the Texas functions were consolidated in Houston under Rosenfield the following year. Adolph's sons, Bucks and Bobby, in

their thirties, by then had gained enough experience to begin filling Leonel's shoes and to absorb Lucien Loeb's responsibilities between them. At the same time, Jimmy Loeb, Lucien's son, was called back from Houston, where he had assisted Reckling, to run the Eastern operation under Bucks' and Bobby's supervision. With A. M. Crawford firmly in the Memphis saddle, this lineup would direct Weil's domestic merchandising during most of the remaining years of Adolph's career.

Just as the nation's oldest cotton lands had spawned the Weil organization's cadre in Isidor's time, so the Memphis territory would be the future generation's fount in Adolph's. Ben Barnes, we recall, was born in Suggsville, Alabama. Shap Dowdell came from Opelika. Al Grayson started out in Selma. A. M. Crawford was a native of Marion, Alabama. Nathan Rosenfield had learned the trade in New Orleans. But as cotton's venue shifted ever westward, their successors from Ray G. White, who took over from Barnes in Atlanta, to James D. "Pick" Butler in New York, to Julian Dewberry in Fresno were born and/or trained in A. M. Crawford's domain.

Nearly everybody started out as a country buyer, or as a street buyer if the job called for shopping Front Street rather than scouting the countryside for cotton. Many of the men who came to Crawford were sharecroppers' sons who wanted to make a better living than two acres and a mule provided. But they came from all walks of country life. What they had in common was that they were born go-getters in the tradition popularized by Horatio Alger. The story of Thomas R. Moss is typical of that entrepreneurial but ever down-to-earth breed.

Tom Moss was born in 1899 in Dyersburg, Tennessee, where his father and two uncles owned the local general store, the largest between Memphis and Paducah, Kentucky. His feet rattling around in oversized brogans, "plow shoes" as the farmers called them, he started running errands for that emporium when he was eight years old. He grew up in the tangy scent of salted-down hog, slabs of bacon big enough to last a season, which he lugged out to the farmers' wagons. His first experience with cotton was hefting bolts of "brown domestic," an unfinished cloth from which country people sewed their own sheets and pillowcases. Summers, Tom and his brother would raise a garden—corn, asparagus, Irish potatoes, sweet potatoes—and they'd sell their produce to the grocery department. With the proceeds, they bought their winter clothes.

Tom went to Milligan College, a church school out from Johnson City where Bob and Alf Taylor came from, the brothers who ran against each other for governor of Tennessee at the time of World War I. Tom fell in love with Alf's daughter, Mary, and when Alf won he went courting her at the governor's mansion, a special thrill if short-lived: he was only eighteen and got turned down. He did the next-best thing to joining the army: he went far away, to Philadelphia, where somebody had just started up a factory to build planes with pontoons so they could land on water. Eventually, toward the end of World War I, Uncle Sam wanted Tom anyway, too late for fighting, and soon he was back home again, this time working at his Uncle Dave's oil mill, where cottonseed was processed into vegetable shortening. Three years later he was hired as a squidge by Andrews & Gabbert Cotton Co., which has since disappeared from the scene.

Unlike many other cotton companies, however, Andrews & Gabbert didn't go broke. They got out in 1925 after making a pile of money, which was no consolation to Tom Moss, by then an experienced street buyer. He went over to Weil Brothers & West in the Falls Building, and John Wagner hired him to set up a buying agency on his old turf, in West Tennessee. It was a smart move. With Uncle Dave's oil mill, the Moss family had lots of connections with farmers and ginners in the area, and if anyone would be welcomed as a buyer from the big city, it was Tom Moss.

On an average day, he bought about 500 bales, and on a really good day as many as 2,000. This was only during part of the year, of course, so you can't multiply by 365 to arrive at his total volume. But Moss' annual production of around 30,000 bales was way above what would be normally expected, for he was an exceptionally astute buyer. The season after B. B. West's departure, for instance, too much rain fell in Moss' territory and spoiled much of the cotton. Inexorably, the resultant shortage drove up the price and made every lot a merchant could handle all that more valuable. Moss knew well that discoloration of cotton caused by rain is rarely uniform. So he made an interesting arrangement with his country cronies. He optioned to buy their crops under the provision that he would pay only for those bales the mills did not reject.

When Adolph saw the samples Moss had brought in from about two dozen gins, he thought the cotton looked too cloudy to be taken up. Moss' explanation that the farmers were willing to take a chance on its sale didn't strike him as too likely. "I wouldn't give a man that kind of leeway on my time," he said, picking up on the local lingo. But then he shrugged and let Moss and Crawford go ahead, and much of the cotton was taken up by mills without causing any problem. Henceforth buying with a "weather clause," as it is called, was widely practiced. But Memphis never took advantage of the trading leverage that such purchasing evidently gave the merchant: a farmer watching his crop go to hell is willing to take almost anything for it. Sure, Moss traded. If a farmer wanted fifty points above the market, Moss would do his utmost to trade him down to twenty-five. But cotton changes; given a dry spell, the cloudy cotton will turn white so long as it's still in the boll. When that happened, Moss would call Crawford from West Tennessee and tell him that he intended to pay twenty-five points more than the original option provided, and Crawford always gave his okay.

The Moss generation was a hardy bunch. Incredibly, four of his Weil contemporaries are still active. Joe D. McAteer, now in his middle eighties, knew Isidor long before he ever came to work for Weil. McAteer, a native of Lewisburg, Tennessee, grew up in Fort Smith, Arkansas, and as a young man after World War I bought cotton for Lehman-Stern, of New Orleans. This eminent firm was connected with the New York investment house of Lehman Bros., whose local New Orleans partner, Edgar Stern, was married to one of the daughters of Julius Rosenwald, of Sears Roebuck.* When Lehman-Stern, for unknown reasons, decided to get out of the cotton business, Edgar Stern sent McAteer to Leonel, with whom he'd gone to school, and McAteer was hired as head classer for Dallas. Then, in 1935, the head classer in Memphis fell ill, and Wagner asked McAteer to come up for a week to fill in.

McAteer never went back to Texas. He became a specialist in buying and selling low grades, and in this function gave Adolph quite a few headaches. Once he accumulated 4,000 bales of GUSes and HUSes, the old Weil code words for Low Middling Spotted and Strict Good Ordinary Spotted, which, with the market headed down, he decided to get rid of quickly and ship to China as Low Middling. The lot was aboard ship by the time Adolph happened to call, wanting to know what McAteer had done with that cheap cotton, which wasn't considered good for much of anything, except maybe curtains and sacking. When McAteer told Adolph about the China deal, Adolph all but gave him his walking papers, expecting a "terrible claim" from the furious Chinese any day. But the cotton arrived, the Chinese spinners duly paid for it, and, if they objected, Memphis never heard: any claim, if there was one, disappeared in the confusion of the Communist takeover. On another occasion, McAteer made everyone doubt his sanity when, sent to the Carolinas to sell cotton, he suddenly phoned in to report that he'd just bought some instead— and not from farmers, but from a mill that despaired of using it. But McAteer had remembered seeing demand for similar low-grade fiber recently at the brokers' tables in Memphis; he brought samples back with him from Greenville, and shortly afterward sold the lot at a net

---

*The Sterns of New Orleans were cousins of M. and B. Stern, of Liverpool, whose progeny, David and Phillip Stern, are principals of Eccles & Stern, Weil's correspondents in the United Kingdom.

profit of five dollars a bale. McAteer left Weil in 1965. Then sixty-six, he decided to start his own cotton company, concentrating largely on low grades, and is still at it.

Richard Block, another of the Memphis old-timers and a Weil relative, had made himself independent earlier, back in 1944. He teamed up with Bert Unobsky, whom Bucks Weil had met at Dartmouth and squidged with under Wagner, to found Block & Unobsky, which still exists. Dick Block, born in 1908, had started as a squidge, then became a country buyer out of Brownsville, Tennessee, handling parts of Tennessee, Mississippi, and Arkansas. Later, when exports picked up just before World War II, he moved back to his native Memphis to supervise all country buying for that branch. His younger brother, Herman Block, had also worked for the Memphis branch as a young man: at Weil Brothers, nepotism didn't die with Isidor.

Still representing Weil in a telephone-equipped cubbyhole office at Newport, Arkansas, is seventy-eight-year-old Fred M. "Crackie" Parker, who has covered that territory as a country buyer since 1933— the counties of Lawrence, Jackson, Woodruff, and White, which are among the best cotton lands in Arkansas. Crackie canvasses about thirty-six gins (it used to be close to eighty when the volume was greater), and comes to Memphis once or twice a month in the fall, at the climax of the growing season, to bring in some types and show how the cotton is coming. He always returns home the same afternoon, as he did even when he was young. The city never held any charm for him. Born on a farm in appropriately named Cotton Plant, Arkansas, he has remained a country boy at heart.

Also still working is Robert Mangum, the dignified head porter at the Memphis office. Always polite but never subservient, Mangum at eighty is one of that eclipsed class of Southern blacks nowadays glibly dismissed as Uncle Toms. There's no denying that Mr. Mangum (as everyone calls him) could have done much better for himself had he been born white. With his keen mind, imposing figure, and resonant voice, few careers would have been closed to him. But he was born the grandson of a slave on a sharecropper patch near Portland, Arkansas, hard by the Louisiana state line. He was one of six children; that much he knows. But four must have died early, for he only remembers his older sister. Nor can he remember his mother and only barely his father; after the latter's death, he was raised along with several other children by his maternal grandparents in Memphis.

This must have been at about the same time young Tom Moss started to make himself useful amidst the bolts of brown domestic at the store in Dyersburg, when Al Grayson graduated from cleaning spittoons at the Weils' Selma office, and when Isidor and Emil, nearly forty years out of Otterstadt but still thick-tongued with Teutonic accents, moved from Opelika to Montgomery. That these diverse cultures merged is one of the fascinations of the cotton business. If Mangum never rose far above the nominally lowest rungs of the trade's ladder, it was not by design but circumstance. Call it economic determinism if you will: sharecroppers kept sharecropping long after machinery could have replaced them simply because there were so many of them and they had to eat and thus were ready to deliver cheap labor. The blacks, more tied to tradition and habitude than the whites, and saddled by an even greater lack of education, share-cropped longer than most. But the removal of the orphaned Mangum children to Memphis at least liberated them from the shanty. In the fall, grandmother and all the children still crossed the Mississippi to make extra money picking cotton, but within a few years adolescent Robert Mangum would find work finishing fancy tables at a veneering factory for two dollars a day, then quite a respectable wage. By 1919, he was learning to class cotton in the Memphis branch of a Liverpool firm. Then he worked some years for C. S. Blount, a prominent Front Street merchant. When the latter died, John Wagner sent for Mangum, who had already established a reputation for reliability. Since then, he's done a little of everything, from wrapping samples to classing to cleaning.

Now he no longer has the strength to work as hard as he once did, and a few years ago, being a prideful man, he wanted to quit because

Robert Mangum (right), dean of Memphis cotton-firm porters, has been with Weil for forty-nine years, during which time he put three children through college. Now in his eighties, he is still on the job.—*Author's photograph*

he felt he wasn't doing his job. But Bucks told him that at home he'd only get bored, and that he should stick around and take time off whenever he got tired. This was no paternalistic gesture, proffered out of guilt for being white. It's a tradition in the cotton business that men may work as long as they care to, and if they can only manage a couple of hours a day, then so be it. There's a good reason for this custom: a young man may be brilliant but an old cotton man is experienced, and in a business so full of nuances there's no substitute for that.

The Memphis office of Weil Brothers remained in the Falls Building until 1935, occupying three floors on the north side. The sample room was on the seventh floor, above the roof of the building that faced it across the street; this was before the introduction of artificial lights that simulate the northern exposure required for classing. Weil then moved its quarters to a Front Street building all its own, cattyways across from the Memphis Cotton Exchange (which trades in spots, not in futures). Weil didn't acquire the building until fairly recently; for many years, the Episcopal diocese was the firm's landlord. The quarters here are no more grandiose than those in Montgomery. Tom Adams, A. M. Crawford's successor, makes his million-dollar deals from a windowless office so small that it barely seats two visitors. Crawford, after retirement, had to be content with a cubbyhole jam-packed with telex equipment and dusty cartons.

It was at first intended that A. M.'s son, Allius M. "Allie" Crawford, Jr., would eventually take over the Memphis office—and not for nepotistic reasons either. Exposed to cotton merchandising since earliest childhood, he was one of the Weil organization's brightest young men. Allie had started squidging for his father immediately after graduating from the University of Tennessee, with a bachelor's in commerce and science. In 1940, he was sent out into the country for the first time, demonstrating entrepreneurial initiative that even rocked his crusty father.

The market then was about ten cents a pound, or fifty dollars a bale, nearly as low as it had been at the depth of the Depression. But it was headed up and gathering momentum. Allie happily headed for

Portersville, Missouri, with his father's explicit instructions: "Don't you buy a damn thing. Look around and give me a ring." As it happened, A. M. Crawford was in rather desperate need of 1⅛ staple. He had hedged a fair volume of forward sales in that type on too narrow a basis, and now was trying to buy in the cotton as best as he could. Allie recalls:

"So I got there and this ginner has about one thousand bales. I got a pull of it, and God, it was long! The market was nine-point-seven-five cents. The ginner said, 'I've got ten cents in it and I'd like to get that out.' I said, 'Well, I can't pay you that.' Remember, I had been instructed not to buy anything, but I knew this was a helluva bargain so we finally settled for nine-point-seven-five cents for the thousand bales and he gave me an option on another thousand.

"In this particular area there were five gins within half a mile of each other. I knew if this ginner had that cotton, the others would have it too. I raced over to the railroad station, an old Frisco station, to use the telephone. It was an old crank job, but it was the only place where I could talk in private. The phone kept ringing and ringing and I couldn't get Memphis.

"Nothing else to do except get over to the next gin fast. Hell, that cotton was just as long as the other. They had fifteen hundred bales, and I bought that. Back to the phone I went, and still no Memphis. To make a long story short, by the time I finally got through to the office, I'd spent two hundred and fifty thousand dollars and had five thousand bales. I told my father. He said, 'You've done what?' I had to repeat it. He just wouldn't believe that anyone would go counter to his instructions. 'Oh my God,' he kept saying, 'did you really do that?' and I kept saying yes. In the end, he calmed down a little and said, 'Well, I tell you what you do. If you're right, keep on buying, and if you're wrong, don't come back here,' and he hung up.

"I was sure I was right, or anyway I thought I was right, and by the end of the afternoon I had seven thousand bales. I stuffed some samples in the back of the car and drove back. When I got back to Memphis, it was dark by then, they were all waiting for me. We never even took the samples out of the trunk. My father pulled about three or four. Somebody held a flashlight. 'Oh my God,' he said—that's as far as he ever went with cussing—'are you lucky! Go back quick and don't miss nothing.' I turned right around, drove back the same night, and in three days I had about twenty-five thousand bales, every bit of that beautiful long cotton before anybody else caught on."

Allie's next stop was Fresno, California's cotton capital. The Weil branch here was opened in 1948, as the San Joaquin Valley came into its own after World War II. At first, with Kite Morton in charge, Fresno was merely a buying suboffice, like the one Moss had in Dyersburg, where a fellow could sit behind a desk and work the telephone. But as volume burgeoned, Adolph and Leonel decided to expand the operation to incorporate shipping and sent Allie out from Memphis in 1952 to take charge. Here he was soon to get a demonstration of hard trading, Adolph-style.

Visiting Fresno that fall, Adolph accompanied Allie to a local club where they encountered Dinny Dinsmore, who years earlier had worked under Al Grayson in Weil's Dallas office. Dinny was now manager of the Producers Cotton Oil Company, a giant handler, ginner, and cottonseed processor—and an immensely efficient operation. After extracting the oil from the seed obtained from their gins and preparing the cottonseed meal, they were left with cottonseed husks. Not even these were wasted. Producers used them to fatten cattle that neighboring farmers entrusted them to feed, paying an agreed price per pound of gain in weight. Moreover, the manure from the cattle pens was the right of Producers to keep, and the annual sale of that natural fertilizer alone netted five figures.

Dinny and Adolph talked about old times, and then Dinny asked Adolph what he thought of the cotton market. Every few sentences Dinny would come back to the same subject, and Adolph detected an increasing note of worry in his voice. In Adolph's inimitable way of drawing people out, he learned from Dinsmore that the directors of Producers had limited his futures market position to a certain number of bales, but Dinny, feeling more bullish than his restricted position would allow, had bought some 8,000 bales of Memphis-territory cotton unhedged. This had been strictly speculation, for Producers didn't merchandise Memphis. And now the market had gone against Dinsmore, and he was not only stuck on the price he had paid for his purchase, but was not experienced in merchandising Memphis cotton. It so happened that Weil's Memphis office was currently stuck on the basis, and Adolph recognized that here was a chance to make a pickup. They arranged to meet at Dinny's office the next morning.

In those days, not much of the cotton was government-classed, and Dinny offered the cotton to Adolph on his own class. Adolph didn't accept that. Knowing full well that they easily could get into protracted haggling on that point, Adolph discounted Dinsmore's description by half a grade, and bid him one price for the first 2,000 bales of Weil's selection, a lower price on the next 3,000, and a much lower price for the last 3,000. The more Dinsmore resisted Adolph's low offers, the more Adolph feigned disinterest, looking impatiently at his watch and making ready to go. Beads of sweat were popping out on Dinsmore's brow, for he knew he couldn't let this trade get away. But Adolph knew it, too. Allie said afterwards that the scene was so pitiful he had to leave the room.

Dinsmore finally gave in on Adolph's price, but there was more to come. Adolph knew that there was a good gain in weight on Memphis cotton that year and insisted that the lot be invoiced at the weights shown on the original warehouse receipts. Dinny struggled vainly for reweights, but eventually had to give in, of course. Putting the frosting on the cake. Adolph then said, "Now Dinny, you understand I'm buying this FOB terms," which in those days was worth fifteen points over warehouse terms to the buyer. After Dinsmore, completely defeated, had agreed to all of Adolph's demands, he walked out of the office and bumped into Allie. "For gosh sakes," he said, "deliver me from that man!"

There is an interesting footnote to this story. After Adolph's departure from Fresno, Bobby arrived there the following week and paid a courtesy call on Dinsmore to advise him that two classers would soon arrive from Memphis to take up the cotton. Before the subject was even broached, Dinsmore told Bobby, "Your Dad and I nearly came to a trade last week, but he was too tough, and I have decided not to sell the cotton." Bobby said, "According to Dad, he bought that cotton from you, and a trade is a trade." When Dinny still held out, Bobby insisted that they telephone Adolph immediately. But to face Adolph again, even on the phone, proved too much for Dinny, and the takeup was completed that week.

In 1962, Allie Crawford, by then a vice-president of Weil Broth-

Thomas C. Adams, Weil's senior vice-president and manager of the Memphis operation, is probably the only man who ever bested Adolph in a trade. As it later turned out, Tom would have been better off accepting Adolph's proposition.

ers—Cotton, Inc., was reassigned to Memphis to take over slowly from his father. But logical as such a move appeared to be, the Crawfords weren't the Weils. Where family succession is taken for granted when it comes to owners, it doesn't go down so easily when employees are involved. As resentments and jealousies smoldered in the Memphis organization, Allie eventually decided to resign his position and return to California where he liked it better anyway. Soon he was back in Fresno, running his own cotton-buying business.

His move was accepted without rancor but created the pressing problem of finding a new manager to run Weil's linchpin office, whose responsibilities included not only the Central Belt—Louisiana, Mississippi, Arkansas, Tennessee, and Missouri—but also the irrigated crops from California and Arizona.

Adolph's first choice for the post was Tom Adams, then Nathan Rosenfield's assistant in Houston. That Tom was a go-getter had been evident since he'd started squidging in the firm's Memphis office shortly before World War II. Most recently, his energy and business acumen had been attested to by the fact that his regular job in Houston wasn't enough for him. He'd gone into real estate and construction in that booming Texas city as a sideline, and was by now fixed well enough to retire in utmost comfort had he wanted to.

Adams was then forty-seven, a stocky, comfortable-looking man whose trip hammer brain was belied by the country drawl of his Tupelo inheritance. Having been around long enough to remember the old days of basis operations, he was a rarity among cotton men even of his own generation, let alone those who had followed him into the business. Most youngsters, who had squidged after World War II and then graduated into buying, lumped futures with other relics of the past. But Tom, by birth and circumstance, had bridged whole eras in the cavalcade of cotton. While still in grade school, he would make his own cotton on his father's farm. Whatever the boy raised was his, provided he did all the work. When he plowed, it wasn't with a tractor but a mule. To feed the mule, he planted corn along with the cotton. In 1933, at age thirteen, he had four bales he could call his own and he sold them for ninety dollars—altogether,

Waiting for the *Robert E. Lee*, cotton bales repose on the Memphis levee. In the heydays of river traffic, the Mississippi was crowded with steamers (top right), which often carried record loads. The sternwheeler *T.P. Leathers*, burdened with 4,000 bales, once sat so deep in the water that it was immersed to its gunwales (center left), and, in what was a record to that date, the steamer *Chickasaw* carried 1,613 bales on November 4, 1885 (bottom left). Cotton was also shipped out of Memphis by rail, having been delivered to the sidings on wagons.—*Photos courtesy of John W. Hammett, of the Weil Memphis Office, from the collection of his maternal grandfather Wallace R. McKay*

3943

Front Street in Memphis, the trading hub of Delta cotton, as it looked at the turn of the century when bales were cut and sampled on its sidewalks by street buyers. Today, bales are shipped directly from growers to customers, and only samples reach the diminished number of merchants that still operate on the street. The volume of Memphis transactions however, has not appreciably declined.

not apiece. He took the money to Sunday School to show the teacher, and the next morning he deposited his four twenties and a ten in the bank. From that moment on he paid all his own expenses and never again took a dime he hadn't earned from anyone.

Sharecropping his father's land during summer vacations, along with some twenty tenants scrabbling for a living, he never went much beyond four bales in a season. A sharecropper family with three children old enough to work, say, ten and up, could tend maybe twelve acres at best, including the land put into feedcorn for the mules, and they only ended up with a dozen bales in a good year. Doing all the work by himself (although he gained efficiency by swapping chores), Tom was limited to about three acres. Eventually he went off to the University of Mississippi, but by then cotton was in his blood. He quit in his junior year and hitched a ride to Memphis, ninety miles away, to call on his maternal uncle, John Wagner, who supervised the buying and classing for Crawford.

This was about as good an entree as a country boy could have had but his uncle wouldn't give him a job without prior experience. Wagner was an excellent cotton man, but he was scared of the Weils, and if there was one thing he dreaded it was to have another green squidge around for whose mistakes he might be blamed, particularly if that squidge was a relation. Every time Adolph came to town, you could almost see Wagner quaking, and as it was Adolph's way to talk directly to the men in the sample room, there was often hell to pay after the Iron Man left. Inspecting tagged samples, Adolph would sometimes ask the nearest classer how he judged that cotton, without letting on what he, Adolph, thought of it himself or revealing what was on the tag. It happened more than once that the classer would call it differently from what Wagner had and that Adolph sided with the classer. After such contretemps, life in the sample room wasn't too pleasant.

In those days Memphis was still a cotton market town, the biggest one around. The barges and steamboats were gone by then, and the cobblestone levee between Front Street and the river was no longer covered with bales destined for New Orleans. Cotton was now being moved by rail on the Illinois Central and the L&N in cars that carried 50,000 pounds of compressed fiber. By then, too, farmers were beginning to bring their cotton to town on trucks, although there were still occasional wagon caravans from the nearby countryside, sometimes as many as fifteen wagons to a string, each pulled by two mules and creaking under six bales. Street buyers ambled along Front Street's "Cotton Row," carving samples and concluding bargains on the spot. More and more, though, that business was moving indoors into sample rooms on the street floor. Everybody had offices here in the four blocks north of the Falls Building, names still remembered and names since forgotten but sometimes still inscribed on weathered doors: McFadden & Oates, Bashinsky & Case, Clayton, S.Y. West. And there were hundreds of small brokers and FOB agents who bought from farmers and gins and resold to the merchants. Mill buyers would be wined and dined at the Peabody Hotel and frequently fixed up with girls. For some cotton men, it was cussing and fighting, for others women, for others drinking, for some all three, and men were still sleeping it off in the sample rooms. Even Crawford hadn't been able to stamp that out completely.

Young Tom Adams, turned away by his uncle but now at least armed with a reference, went to work for another merchant down the street, A. C. T. "Tread" Beasley, who himself had once worked for Weil. About a year later, Wagner finally considered it safe to hire Tom and put him on the payroll. Tom had been working for Weil less than a week when Al Grayson called from Texas and asked Wagner if he had someone to go down to Opelousas, Louisiana, where a good deal of cotton was for sale. Grayson needed a few thousand bales of Middling 1¹⁄₁₆ for shipment to France; if Memphis didn't want it, would they kindly buy the cotton for the Dallas office. Wagner, precipitously, volunteered to send Tom.

The trouble was that, at this juncture, Tom Adams had no idea what Grayson was talking about: cotton was cotton, and it either looked good or it didn't. But off he went to Louisiana, bravely bought 1,500 bales for starters, and shipped samples off to Dallas by Railway Express. He so informed Grayson by telephone and told him that he had better look at those samples very carefully since he, Adams, had never bought cotton before. On hearing this news, Grayson suffered such a fit of stuttering he had to hand the receiver to his assistant, Charles Greengrass, who in turn was so upset he hung up altogether. Luckily, after all this excitement, the cotton turned out to be okay, and Adams was instructed to pick up all he could he get his hands on. Still, it was Tom's last country-buying trip for some years. From now on he was a prisoner in the sample room until, as a first step, Wagner saw fit to send him on the street to look over the offering of the FOB houses and the farmers and ginners who marketed their crops on Cotton Row.

When Tom still worked for Beasley, Adolph sent his older son, Bucks, fresh out of law school, to squidge under Crawford's steely-eyed gaze: it was the one office where Adolph could be sure that Bucks would never be treated as the boss' son. Bucks found a room in the same boarding house where Tom lived; they each earned sixty-five dollars a month, the standard squidge wage at that time, and they each paid four dollars a week for room and board to two fussy ladies on Peabody Street, who specialized in mothering squidges and Sears Roebuck apprentices. Lunches at the sandwich shop across the street cut heavily into the young men's remaining budgets, and there was rarely enough money left even to go to the movies on. Bucks was the only one who had a car and he chauffeured everybody else around. In return, Tom and Bucks were sometimes able to get in free at the Peabody's Skyway rooftop nightclub, where some of the other squidges were moonlighting as bouncers. But most evenings they spent in their room, where Bucks used to make Tom study the bible of the business, Alston Hill Garside's *Cotton Goes to Market*, and then quiz him for lack of something better to do. And that's how Tom Adams came to learn about the futures market and basis operations, knowledge that later stood him in good stead.

The tutelage came to an end when Bucks was drafted into the army in July 1941. Tom, two months later, enlisted in the Army Air Corps, just a few weeks before Pearl Harbor. He returned to Weil Brothers in 1945 after serving as a Flying Fortress bombardier in North Africa, Sicily, and Italy. Tom had long looked forward to his discharge, but it was something of a comedown just the same: from bemedaled captain once again to lowly squidge. Soon, however, he was promoted to street buyer, and after six years on that job was transferred to Houston as an assistant manager.

When Adolph offered him the Memphis post in 1967, neither man knew that within a few weeks the cotton market would break away from the fetters of parity pricing. Thus, in their ignorance, both men traded from the wrong position. Adolph, not expecting immense profits, offered Tom an arrangement heavy on profit-sharing and light

Historian David Cohn, in 1935, called the Peabody in Memphis "the Paris Ritz" of the Mississippi Delta. First opened in 1869, rebuilt in 1925, it was the South's grandest, most cosmopolitan hotel, and as such the meeting place, licit and illicit, of the cotton fraternity. Representatives of mills, merchant houses, and compress companies frequently gathered in its private dining rooms; they danced to big bands in the rooftop Skyway nightclub; and business visitors from out of town who were so inclined were often provided by their hosts with private female entertainment. With the stagnation of the domestic cotton business during the Commodity Credit Corporation era of the 1950s, the Peabody lost its Front Street clientele and soon its splendors faded.

Recently refurbished, it is once again the showplace of the Delta—albeit now wholly respectable and no longer the semiexclusive bailiwick of cotton men whose numbers are greatly diminished. The hotel's traditional ducks again bathe in the

elaborate fountain of its lobby, and its restaurants cater to international taste; you can even order bagels, lox, and cream cheese for breakfast.

Not that cotton men were ever given to fancy dining, to wit the ketchup and steak-sauce bottles in the picture below. That particular high-powered assemblage, presumably photographed in the late 1940s or early 1950s, was attended by (from left) Howard Willey, president of Union Service Industries (Union Compress); Russell Gregg, president of Anderson Clayton; George Thatcher, chief buyer for the spinning mills of Bates Manufacturing Co.; Alvin Weil, Weil's top sales executive and partner in residence in Memphis; unidentified; Buckner Potts, of Anderson Clayton; unidentified; W.C. Graves, of A.C.T Beasley; A.M. Crawford, Sr., Weil vice-president; and Memphis merchant A.C.T. "Tread" Beasley—*Hotel photos courtesy of the Memphis Room, Memphis/Shelby County Public Library and Information Center.*

on salary. Tom, equally mistaken, held out for a high salary and a small percentage. So far as he was concerned, there wasn't enough money in the proffered contract to make his move to Tennessee worthwhile. As it turned out, Tom had learned trading only too well. He beat Adolph at his own game—an unsual accomplishment indeed. And yet, ironically, Tom lost by winning.

At their final negotiation, Adolph played his hole card. "So far, we've talked to nobody else," he said. "But I want to tell you that now we've got another person we want to talk to. If we don't get together with him then we'll check with you again." To this date, no one knows if this was a bluff. Tom certainly didn't. Apprehensive though he was of the possible consequences, he replied, "Mr. Adolph, if we can't get together right now, I'm not talking any more. I'm quitting." Nothing more was said and Tom got what he wanted—a large salary and a small percentage. In the ten years that followed, his fortitude in trading would cost him close to one million dollars.

Remember, this was 1967, and Tom walked smack into the season that saw the Commodity Credit Corporation sell its twelve-million-bale horde into a liberated, spurting market. He had hardly settled down at his new desk when he brought in $640,000 from the sale of 25,000 bales, practically all of it sheer profit, and with another 75,000 similar bales to go. It was success on a scale that Weil had never experienced before. Tom had performed an unprecedented coup—and here he was largely on salary.

As Tom tells it (and to him it's still the most exciting moment of his long career, even more thrilling than when he was named senior vice-president four years later), "We had about a hundred thousand bales of Low Middling one-and-one-thirty-second and one-and-one-sixteenth Eastern growth. We'd bought it from Commodity Credit. I don't know why. It was not the most desirable type of cotton, and a very hard article to move. I kept puzzling, how can we move that cotton? Understand, we had been selling some cotton out and were making two and three dollars [a bale]. And then it dawned on me: if we were big enough fools to buy it, in a manner of speaking, then there's got to be another fool big enough to buy it the same way from us, straight off the tag list [the catalog, issued by the CCC, listing cotton for sale]. I said to George Wheeler [Tom's second in command], 'Let's offer it to

our salesmen in the Carolinas on the same basis. We'll offer it exactly
as it is and we will turn the whole invoice over to the mills.'

"So we got on the phones, and we explained to the salesmen what a
tag list was and how we could sell it and gave them a price. We said
we'd put it in the warehouse or even in the mill at whatever date it was
wanted, and we'd put the carrying charges in the bank. Two days later
Bill Wyatt called in from the Greenville office and said he had some
interest from Arkwright Mills. We sold that twenty-five thousand bales
at one clip just the way we'd bought it, never touching it, billing it
right onto the mills. Then we went to work on the rest, and started
buying more at the same time. We sold it with the carrying charges to
start. They [the mills] started paying interest on the storage the day we
sold it. In some cases, we hadn't yet even paid for it. It was the first
time that a tag list had been peddled and sold as you bought. There
couldn't be a cheaper way to operate.

"Mr. Adolph called up every couple of hours and kept saying,
'Tom, be careful. Don't trade too hard. If one of our competitors
hears about this and undercuts you, what would you do?' I said, 'I'll
tell you what I'd do. I'd go down to Goldsmith's and buy me some
black crepe paper and hang it on the front door and run like hell.'

"He just laughed. This was September 1967. He died just a few
months later. It's nice to know that he had this last thrill. Anyway, we
kept selling and he was so excited because it was a new way of doing
business and just a hell of a slug of money, at that time something
gigantic.

"Our competitors knew about it less than an hour after we started. I
heard rumors in the street. They were pretty close on the bales and
also the money. They could figure it out because they knew the price
we paid—it was a published record. We never let much go at the same
time. We threw that bait out in tens and twenties and thirties
[thousands of bales] and every time we could sell it for more. Our
competitors started doing it the following week, buying from the CCC
and immediately turning it around, but we had the jump on them,
and we made more money than anybody else."

As others caught on to the selling-on-government-class routine and
also started bidding, the scarce Strict Low Middling 1$\frac{1}{16}$ eventually
petered out. Weil, buying about 50,000 bales every two weeks, had to

go into shorter staples and lower grades. But since that's all there was, this cotton also kept turning over promptly and at ever higher prices. On one transaction alone, which involved 50,000 bales of Low Middling 1¹⁄₃₂ shipped to a mill in the Carolinas, Weil was reputed to have cleared one million dollars. "As a matter of fact," says Bucks, "we didn't do quite that well. We'd already sold some of that 50,000 bales to another customer and had to buy it in on the market to fill the order. But it was still a good deal."

Weil could have done better yet had caution not prevailed. In December, Spray Mills, of Spray, North Carolina, one of Weil's best and most exacting clients, came into the market for their April, May, June, and July requirements, offering a premium price for Strict Low Middling Bright 1¹⁄₁₆, which was particularly scarce. Tom Adams opposed making this forward sale. He was afraid he'd be unable to obtain the cotton to fill it. Bucks agreed. Not so Adolph, although he had no intention either of disappointing Spray. "Go ahead and sell it," he told Bucks. "You don't have that cotton now, but don't worry about it. By the time you'll need it, you'll find it."

As fate turned out, it was the last time Adolph had the chance to advise his sons. Only a few weeks later he died of a heart attack. "Dad was absolutely right," Bucks says. "We should have sold that cotton. We could have made a fortune out of it. Dad knew that the scarce grade would become available late in the season. This sort of thing happens all the time. As certain qualities turn scarce, shippers try to put aside those qualities in the hopes of selling them at an advanced price later. All that hoarded cotton then shows up toward the end of the season, and the situation sometimes turns around completely."

Of course, nothing humans undertake ever works out without the cooperation of circumstance. It could have been one of those rare instances when no one had stashed away enough cotton to cause a dip in price. Nor, for that matter, could Tom have pulled off his tour de force in the first place if market panic hadn't set in and resulted in a price explosion. Why, indeed, had there been such a stampede for the loan cotton? One likely answer is that the shortage came as a real shock after years of glut. But once aboard the gravy train, Tom had the sense not to get off. He kept on buying as much as he could and only drew away from the risk of selling something he did not have.

In the Weil tradition, Tom Adams' two assistants, George Wheeler (right) and Ken Weatherford, work across from each other at partners desks in the Memphis office.—*Author's photographs*

But exactly ten years later, much to his regret, he did exactly that. In the 1977/78 season he became so convinced that the market was about to break that he took a substantial short position. Before he knew it, speculators had gotten hold of the market and were bidding it up, and Tom had to jump in to cut his mounting losses. It was the one year Memphis wound up in the red. Tom still shakes his head about it. "It happened," he says sadly, "because I messed up every cardinal rule I had. If I am recognized as any sort of cotton man, it's as a basis operator. At Weil we have a rare situation. We have three things of which most others only have one or two. We have a buying force as good as anybody's, a sales force second to none, and the third thing is ample finances, where the bank is not calling up and saying 'That's enough, you're up to your line.' When you have all that going for you, you can afford to play it safe. So you work a little harder, and buy more and sell more, and you make it anyway."

Tom's second-in-command is George T. Wheeler, a towering loose-limbed fellow who, like most of his cotton contemporaries, had spent much of his youth on a cotton farm. Wheeler was born in 1929 at Paragould, Arkansas, but his family soon moved to Finley, Tennessee, a tranquil corner straight out of Mark Twain between Dyersburg and the Mississippi River. At Dyersburg, where he went to high school, George Wheeler met Tom Moss' daughter, Carroll, and they married. Almost predictably, this being the cotton business, Tom sponsored his son-in-law at Weil's, and after one year at the Memphis State, the young man started his apprenticeship in John Wagner's sample room. A stint in country buying followed. Then George worked as a classer and shipper. When A. M. Crawford semiretired in 1962 and Allie Crawford ran the office, George Wheeler was named his assistant manager and placed in charge of all country buying and domestic sales. These mainstays of the Memphis operation are still his responsibilities today.

Since the country-buying days of Moss and McAteer, soybeans have displaced cotton in much of the old Memphis territory. Of the nation's total crop of about twelve million bales in a normal season, this region typically produces three to three and a half million, only

about half of what it used to. In contrast, California's San Joaquin
Valley grew from next to nothing just sixty years ago to almost three
million, and Arizona (including California's Imperial Valley) to more
than one million. This feat, moreover, was accomplished on less
acreage than would be required elsewhere: irrigated soil produces
about two bales per acre, as against the one bale that's considered
standard for the Eastern and Central Belts, and even less for Texas.

The crop of King Cotton's one-time kingdom, the Eastern Belt, is
indeed puny by comparison—about 500,000 bales in an average year.
To balance Montgomery's shrunken volume with that of Memphis,
the Houston office was closed a year after Nathan Rosenfield's death,
and the Eastern office took on all of Texas, along with the cotton that's
grown in the adjoining Oklahoma Panhandle, a total of about six
million bales. Of the Texas cotton, more than half is the short-staple
type raised in the Lubbock region. The rest, improved by seed
culture, is longer—something like the Memphis cotton—and comes
from the Rio Grande Valley and the Coastal Bend.* Thus, the bulk of
both Montgomery's and Memphis' business originates far from their
doorsteps these days, with Lubbock, under Gordon Redmond, and
Fresno, under Julian Dewberry, the firm's key buying centers.

Like most cotton men, Julian Dewberry, Allie's successor, hails
from cotton country: Searcy, Arkansas. His cousin was a commission
buyer; his bride, the daughter of a cotton farmer and ginner. The
cousin, who occasionally bought for Weil, introduced him to A. M.
Crawford, and Dewberry went to work for Weil in 1949 when he was
twenty-two. After squidging, he worked Front Street and the Mississippi Delta as a buyer until his transfer to the West Coast.

Julian Dewberry shares offices with Allie Crawford, although Allie
does most of his purchasing for McFadden. Their somewhat thread-
bare headquarters are on a desolate street of dilapidated warehouses.
Here, as elsewhere in the Weil domain, visitors need not be
impressed with decor. Out front, presiding behind a worn but sturdy

---

*The 1978/79 crop, for instance, came in as follows: California, 2.7 million bales;
Arizona, 1.07 million; Texas, 6 million; Mississippi, 1 million; Arkansas, 650,000;
Tennessee, 150,000; Alabama, 285,000; Georgia, 115,000; North Carolina, 40,000;
and only nominal quantities from elsewhere.

Julian R. Dewberry, headquartered in Fresno, handles Weil's buying of California cotton.

Allie Crawford, A.M. Crawford's son, worked for Weil for many years and now has his own cotton company which shares quarters with Weil's Fresno office.

metal desk, sits Barbara Dilldine, the joint secretary and all-around factotum. There is no other staff and not even a sample room. In recent years, most cotton has been purchased on "government class," a free service originally provided to farmers under the Smith-Doxey Act, sponsored by Senator Cotton Ed Smith and Congressman Wall Doxey (D-Miss.). Classers of the U.S. Department of Agriculture prepare a green card for the bales, specifying grade, staple, and micronaire, and that's how the cotton goes to the merchants. If the cotton is of lower quality than the government classer decides, the merchant has to take his licks; if it's better, he's that much ahead. Reclassing isn't done until the lot is culled for resale—unless, like Tom Adams did in his spectacular Memphis debut, the merchant finds it advantageous to market the cotton as he bought it, "on the green card."

Thus, as a buyer, Dewberry receipts and pays for the cotton, and then the receipts and class cards go through the bank to Memphis. The samples, meanwhile, are shipped directly from the compress via truck, or, if there's a hurry, by air freight. In turn, when it comes to delivering the cotton, Memphis makes up the order from Dewberry's receipts, which then go to whichever press is holding the lot. And the copies of all that are mailed to Fresno, where Barbara arranges the movement. For export, everything is trucked to the port, where it's usually containerized for overseas shipment. Domestic orders still go mainly by rail, but also sometimes by truck when it's worthwhile, as when truckers moving textiles to the West Coast are looking for back hauls.

The bulk of Dewberry's volume is San Joaquin Valley cotton, known in the trade as SJV. Under normal conditions—and it is California's peculiar grace that conditions are monotonously normal—cotton varies no more from crop to crop than California wines do in their vintages. SJV Acala is Acala no matter how and when you pull it: $1\frac{1}{8}$ to $\frac{3}{32}$ in staple, and uniformly premium grade—the top of the line for shirtings and sheetings. That it is of consistent desirability is not only the result of weather and soil, which are the same that originally made Egyptian cotton so famous, but that SJV seed descends from the premium cottons in the Middle East. Acala, which is the only cotton that, under California law, may be planted in the San Joaquin Valley, resulted from genetic tricks played on the Oriental chromosomes at a planting and breeding station at Shafter, outside Bakersfield. Acala generally brings a hefty premium, sometimes as much as eight cents, over Memphis territory cotton, and is the favorite of mills in Japan and Korea, which alone buy more than two million bales a year between them.

Arizona's cotton, for the most part, comes from seed developed by the Delta Pine and Land Company (DP&L) of Greenville, Mississippi, as is the cotton grown by Calcot, the huge California cooperative in the Forty-Niner State's Imperial Valley. Hence, the Imperial Valley cotton, although Californian, is lumped with Arizona's. In total these crops comprise only about 1.4 million bales, just a little more than ten percent of U. S. production, and it was even less than that in the years immediately after World War II, when the new seed had just begun to sprout.

There has never been any need to maintain an Arizona office, but in the early 1950s Weil did have its own branch in Phoenix—a beau geste on Adolph's part, hard-headed businessman though he was. Shortly after World War I, Weil had hired a young German, Helmut Kruse, a protege of Weil's agent in Bremen, George Hartmann. Many youngsters from the German cotton port emigrated to the United States at that time, including also Fritz Ficke, who later worked for Weil. Helmut, frail from wartime starvation, suffered from tuberculosis, and Montgomery's hot-moist climate depleted his strength to fight the disease. On several occasions, Adolph sent him to the Denver Jewish Hospital at Weil's expense; each time he recovered only to relapse. In the end, he could carry on no longer, and in order to keep him employed, Adolph opened a one-man office in Phoenix in 1949, where Helmut worked as buyer until his retirement, when the office was abandoned. It never had really been needed. The Arizona business could be handled as easily and more cheaply through a commission buyer—and was before and after Helmut.

As intermediary between producer and processor, a cotton merchant bridges two vastly different worlds—one shrewd and simple, the other shrewd and complex. For the grower, cotton is the end-all of his labor.

In his callused hands, the fibrous fluff is no abstraction: it is totally concrete. But for the mill man, the commodity is but one factor, albeit basic, in the mass marketing of manufactured goods. He is no less concerned with pricing, the efficacy and availability of raw materials, the vagaries of fashion, the demands of labor, the cost of money, and the existence or lack of tariffs. Moreover, while he may be no richer than a big farmer, he generally has more cash flow and lives a more opulent life. He is either the owner, a descendant of the founder, or (especially since World War II) a well-paid professional executive. He has studied liberal arts in college, often transacts business on the golf course, and is more likely to be a Mason than an Elk.

To function in this sphere calls for a different kind of man from the one who could trade successfully with growers. To be sure, some cotton men have been capable of both—Grayson and Reckling, for instance, or Isidor, Adolph and Leonel, for that matter. In most cases, however, cotton men of urbane background have been unable to breach the rural barricades while bright and ambitious country boys, who were originally trained as buyers, have had success in adapting to mill circles.

Before the consolidation of textile mills into public companies, the owners of the mills bought the cotton themselves, or delegated this responsibility to their treasurers, and even when a professional mill buyer was involved, one of the two top men usually took a direct hand in the transaction. During that era, Weil was represented largely by independent sales agents who were as entrenched in their communities as the mill people themselves. The first of these agents in New England was Charles Storrow and Company, of Boston, one of whose principals, an ardent Yalie, was F. J. O. Alsop, the uncle of writers Stewart and Joseph Alsop. Already in the Storrow days Weil had begun to send its own men to work with the agents and become accustomed to their sophisticated arena. Among these staffers thus dispatched was Clarence Grayson, a half-brother of Al. True to form, Al could not resist exercising his sense of humor also on the sell side of the fence. When Storrow sent him a telegram saying that on this, Clarence' first trip to New England, they would like to make a good showing, but that Al's prices were 100 points too high, would he please cut them to help out his brother, Al whipped back a telegram: "Clarence only half brother. I'll give you 50 points."

Under Storrow's auspices, Pepperell Manufacturing Co. and Pacific Mills were among Weil's most valued customers, and Weil in turn among their most valued suppliers. The relationships were so close that when Bobby was still in Harvard Business School and contributing to a study on Pepperell as part of his industrial management curriculum, he was made a welcome guest by Amory Coolidge, the company's president. Moreover, Lindsay Dexter, who bought for Pepperell well into the 1960s, although of a fine old New England family, had close connections to Montgomery, being related to Andrew Dexter, one of that city's two founders. And at Pacific

F.J.O. Alsop, managing partner of Charles Storrow, once called Adolph the "Iron Man," and that nickname stuck.

Mills, which for years made the famous Pacific cloth used for wrapping silver cutlery, Ben Whitney was a particularly close friend of Adolph's—close enough to tell him off, something that few men dared. One day when Adolph went into a long discourse on the errors that Pacific made in the selection of various cottons for their constructions, Whitney listened patiently until Adolph was finished. Then he told him that he didn't know what he was talking about. Adolph always remembered this encounter and used it as an object lesson to teach his sons never to pretend to authority they didn't have.

Regardless of how little use Whitney seemed to have for Adolph's self-proclaimed milling expertise, he had nothing but respect for his knowledge of cottons. The consistent quality of Weil shipments had been a byword in the industry since Isidor's day; to keep that reputation required not only exquisite discernment but honesty, and these were the prime tools Weil's salesmen worked with. Nothing so much illustrated the standing of the firm as did a highly unorthodox clause a Georgia mill once insisted on putting into a contract with a new merchant firm. When Weil cousin Richard Block and Bucks' fellow squidge Bert Unobsky quit the Memphis operation to go into business on their own, one of their salesmen, Jack Scheuer, also a Weil graduate, was trying to sell Middling $^{15}/_{16}$ to Jordan Mills, of Columbus. The buying for Jordan was handled by N. C. Coffin, a merchant retained for that purpose, who in turn had hired Bob Collins, a former Weil classer, to work with him on the assignment. Collins, after conferring with the mill executives, demanded that Block & Unobsky, who at this point were untried, guarantee that the cotton they delivered would be equal to Weil's famed "Nancy Dan" style. Only after they had committed themselves on that point was the deal concluded.

As in New England, the spinning mills around Gastonia, North Carolina, were in the hands of individual families and clans, such as the highly respected Lineberger group. Here Weil was represented for many years by Andrew "Dutch" Gullick, of Gullick & Torrence, who was related to and/or a close personal friend of all the mill owners. Dutch Gullick also ran a small warehouse owned by Weil, where cotton was stored for the mills to draw on, and occasionally to house lots they had rejected. Charlotte, although not far from Gastonia, was a territory unto itself, with the firm of Labouisse & Couch acting as Weil agents. John Labouisse and Charlie Couch not only had entree into every mill and mill owner's home, but Charlie, when he wore his other hat, was the buyer for the Corriher and Lynn Mills. Charlie, an avid bird hunter, spent much time on a direct private telephone line with Adolph, Leonel and Alvin, who also loved the sport; then, more than today, business was social, and while on mill trips the Weils spent as much time, if not more, hunting with their agents and customers as in trading cotton.

Spartanburg, South Carolina, had its own circle of cotton mills, too, all of them on the friendliest terms with E. P. "Fleece" Murray, a very kindly man who spoke in a hoarse voice and was probably the most tenacious salesman ever to represent Weil. There, as in Gastonia, the mill owners constituted a social set, and it often followed that when Walter Montgomery of Spartan Mills decided to buy, other mills in the community would follow his example. Bobby Chapman, whose family owned the Inman and Riverdale Mills, worked with Fleece Murray for a time and sold cotton for Weil Brothers. After Fleece died, Bobby went back to the mill as cotton buyer; in his spare time, he's one of South Carolina's top amateur golfers.

In the other parts of South Carolina, the mills were covered by the Greenville firm of Donkle & McCabe. Gordon McCabe, named after his grandfather, a famous Confederate poet, was one of the most prominent cotton men of his time. He not only understood cotton and was extremely energetic—often driving 600 miles of country roads in a day, with as many as four selling stops en route—but he knew how to persuade mill owners to buy as well as his principals to sell when he thought the time was right. Adolph and McCabe were particularly close, and when the latter received an offer in the late 1950s to go with J. P. Stevens, he traveled to Montgomery to ask Adolph for advice. Adolph encouraged him to accept the job, and McCabe soon rose to the vice-presidency of J. P. Stevens, buying wool and synthetics as well as cotton, and continued as a spokesman for the textile industry in Washington until his death in 1979. McCabe's partner, Ike Donkle, also was highly competent and well connected; he had played football at Georgia Tech. His son, Rusty Donkle, now a commission agent in Greenville, is one of the few people still in that line of business.

For, as the textiles industry became increasingly concentrated after World War II, commission agents disappeared from the scene along with the old-time mill magnates, with whom they had been socially linked. The estate tax structure, as well as a host of other factors, such as efficiency of scale, resulted in the mergers of family-owned mills into bigger companies, and the purchasing function, which today encompasses synthetics as well as cotton, was relegated more and more to professional buyers on the mills' staffs. This reshuffling completely changed the business. How different it became is illustrated by the fact that many of the new buyers, who entered the field after 1954 while the futures market was dormant, had no idea of how to buy "on call." By the time the market revived in the late 1960s there were few old-timers left—men like Charles Thompson of Goodrich, Ben Kyser of Graniteville, and Bob Smith of M. Lowenstein—who could train the new generation of mill executives in this vital area of operations.

Montgomery and Memphis had always done their own direct selling. Montgomery dealt primarily with the Alabama mills and with Thomaston in Georgia. Memphis, where Alvin Weil was in charge of the merchandising, shipped to high-volume customers like Goodyear, Goodrich, and General Tire, as well as some smaller organizations like Standard Knitting and Roxboro Mills. Other than in Montgomery and Memphis, Weil had operated only two selling offices of its own before World War II. The Georgia mills, with the exception of Thomaston, had been handled out of Atlanta ever since Ben Barnes' time. For a brief period, Weil also maintained a selling office in Greensboro, North Carolina, but this branch was discontinued when its manager, Bert Unobsky, resigned to go in business for himself to buy for Cone Mills, the major account he had serviced.

In the late 1940s, Ray G. White was brought from Memphis to Atlanta as Barnes' assistant. To this day Weil's sales manager in Georgia, Ray had been thoroughly imbued with Adolph's approach to bringing cotton to market. Adolph was always convinced, and rightly so, that the best way to find out a mill's requirements was to go into a mill's opening room and see the cotton it bought, and he never tired of emphasizing the importance of this tactic to his salesmen. In Ray's case, it so happened that one of his accounts was the Federal Penitentiary in Atlanta, which usually bought on sealed bid. After Weil missed that business by large margins several times, Adolph called on Ray to rectify the situation forthwith. "Mr. Adolph," Ray interrupted him, "I know exactly what you're going to say, but there's only one way to getting into that opening room and I won't do it."

Don Klyce, Greenville   Tom Pitts, Greenville

Weil's domestic sales team:
the legendary Ray G. White (right)
and today's boll carriers (below)

Left to right, John D. Holt, Atlanta; O.L. Jackson, Atlanta;
and Carroll C. Hudson, Jr., Gastonia

Not that opportunities to become eligible for such entry didn't abound in the cotton business as in any other where individuals have the nod and nix on large transactions. For instance, there was a cotton buyer for a Georgia mill who had dreams of buying into the mill and one day taking it over. He approached Ray to see if Weil would "lend" him $25,000 for the purchase of stock. Of course, Ray understood immediately what that buyer had in mind—a kickback strategy. This became even more apparent when the buyer, in the presence of Nathan Rosenfield and Bobby Weil, agreed to pay a very fancy price for a large quantity of low-grade cotton he didn't even bother to class. At that opportunity, he again broached the idea of the loan, whereupon Bobby and Nathan sent him to Leonel in Montgomery. Leonel heard the man out and waved him off, saying that he would not dream of making the money available without first obtaining agreement from the buyer's boss. That was enough to scare the fellow away from Weil, but apparently did not still his ambition. The following year he gave every single ounce of the mill's business to another cotton merchant house, making it apparent that this was where he had finally obtained the "loan."

Like George Wheeler, Adams' right-hand man in Memphis, Ray White hailed from Dyersburg, Tennessee, and he too was brought into the Weil organization by Tom Moss. In fact, Ray was the first of a long line of Dyersburgers, all introduced by Moss, who were to be especially instrumental in the firm's push for direct sales. After Ray White, Moss next brought in William W. Wyatt, who became Ray's assistant after training in Memphis, Dallas, and Houston.

From the very beginning, Bill Wyatt's jovial manner and natural trading ability singled him out as a comer. Thus, after Gordon McCabe joined Stevens and Fleece Murray had passed away, he was picked to head the new selling office Weil then opened in Greenville, South Carolina. As his assistant, Bill enlisted Don Klyce, yet another young man from Dyersburg. In just a few years, the sales of the Greenville branch, which also covered the mills in the Spartanburg area, exceeded those in White's territory. Billy Wyatt was more than a salesman. He wasn't out merely to make a sale, but wanted the sale to be profitable for the firm, and on many occasions told Memphis, Montgomery and Houston that he would not take a sale because he

Georg Shook. *The Great Escape*, 1974 (Weil Brothers Collection).

felt it was too cheap or sensed that there might be hitches in delivery. Moreover, he was equally honest and outspoken with the mills, and as a result became probably the most respected salesman in the state. Now the buyer for M. Lowenstein, the big mill group, he will be long remembered for being the marketer of the CCC cotton in Tom Adams' 1967 tag-list triumph. Tom Pitts, also of Dyersburg, has since succeeded Wyatt as Weil's Greenville ambassador par excellence.

More recently, Weil opened its own office in Gastonia, first under Tim Gilmore and then under Carroll Hudson, to cover the entire state of North Carolina. Acting as assistant under Ray White in Atlanta today is John Holt, who is not a Dyersburg native himself but married one.

Internal affairs were no less well tended. Here again Adolph and Leonel had excelled in their choices of Harris Washburn as head bookkeeper and Vasser Gunter as auditor and comptroller. Washburn had gone to Alabama Polytechnic Institute (now Auburn University) with Adolph and remained a lifelong friend. On the job, Washburn occasionally seemed cantankerous and gruff, but those who knew him well recognized this as a front. Certainly he was about the most popular member of the Montgomery Lions Club, where he came out of his shell and roared along with the best of them. As has often been the case in the organization, Washburn's connection with Weil was passed down in the family. His granddaughter-in-law, Mrs. Eugenia Rittenour, is now on the Montgomery bookkeeping staff.

Like Washburn, Vasser Gunter, the descendant of an old Montgomery family, had been with Weil since it was a partnership. He too habitually sported a dour expression but did occasionally manage an angelic smile. Gunter's desk adjoined that of Washburn, who not only ran the books but performed the crucial functions of transferring funds and securing collateral for Weil's borrowings, while Gunter kept track of the bottom lines of the various operations. Usually mild and soft spoken, Gunter rarely gave vent to his temper. But when an issue was at stake, he could be fairly vehement, even with Adolph. This happened once when Al Grayson fretted that he'd been losing money all season. Gunter, after the books were closed, was dispatched to Dallas to run a profit and loss statement. To everyone's surprise, not the least Grayson's, the audit disclosed that Dallas had actually done very well for itself. When Adolph heard this, he concluded that Gunter must have made a mistake and sent him back to Dallas a second and third time. Again and again Gunter came up with the same results. When Adolph wanted to have him check the Dallas books yet a fourth time, Gunter finally had enough. "Now Adolph," he said in a tone that brooked no contradiction, "I don't want to hear any more about this or I'll resign. The figures are correct and to go back to Dallas would be another wild goose chase." Adolph was so stunned by Gunter's outburst that he surrendered without another word. Needless to say, Al Grayson was immensely relieved that he'd been running in the money all along.

11

The Long and Short
of Hanover Square

THAT COTTON'S WESTWARD CHANGE of venue had its impact on futures trading is to be expected. Traditionally, the exchanges in New Orleans and New York had written futures in terms of Eastern Belt fiber, whose staple generally ran an inch or shorter. As futures trading rallied after the price-support hiatus of the 1950s and early 1960s, the standard of the surviving New York Cotton Exchange became 1⅟16-style cotton, and that's what's been trading ever since.

Charles Storrow had set up the Weil's first New York operation under Isidor, initially for the purpose of sales to the mills in the Northeast and those in Canada, names that by now are recalled only by nostalgia freaks flipping through old magazines in grandmother's attic: Oneida Knit, Utica Knitting, Dwight, Drummerville, and many more. Edwin Shields, adept at hedging, became the New York office's first in-house manager. He stayed on as floor trader when, after World War I, Al Grayson briefly held forth in Gotham, and after him came Shap Dowdell. Then, as now, the cotton pit was a scene of organized confusion, comprehensible only to its initiates, and even they sometimes made mistakes. In the pandemonium of shouts and pantomime of gestures, Dowdell once got stuck with a substantial trade because he'd been absent-mindedly scratching his nose, the cliché kind of no-no that greenhorns at auction markets are warned about half in jest. But it wasn't the scratching, to put it politely, that did him in: it was the preparatory movement of his hand toward his face: palm in, this motion signals "I am buying" (while palm out, hand waving at bidders, means "I'm selling").

Shap Dowdell (left) and his erst-while assistant and successor, Bob Murray (above) were New York managers in the 1930s and 1940s, and both served as presidents of the New York Cotton Exchange. Dowdell was the grandson of the founder of the Shapard Banking Co. in Opelika, later the Bank of Opelika and now the Bank of East Alabama.

Dowdell was an unpretentious man, forever a country boy at heart, even if he did live the life of a Wall Street commuter (to Pelham Manor) when commuting was still pleasant. He always wore sober business suits: dressing up was not his style. When Rodolfo Kronauer, then the Weils' Milan agent, dropped in on his periodic visits to the States, the New York office staff always marveled at the contrast: Rodolfo in his long-fitted overcoat with Persian lamb collar looking like an opera impresario, and Shap Dowdell, in his drab three-piece, like a bank clerk from the boonies. Once, when the Kronauers, who were friendly with Gatti Cassaza of the Metropolitan, asked Mr. and Mrs. Dowdell to join them in the manager's box, Shap had to admit that he hadn't seen his white tie and tails since they were married.

Dowdell's erstwhile assistant and successor, Bob Murray, a red-faced Irishman, was a hard drinker and staunch Catholic, one of the few papists in the Weils' predominantly Protestant retinue. At lunch on Fridays, Murray would always order ham. He insisted that blessing the dish turned it into salmon. Murray held the fort during most of Adolph's and Leonel's reign. After World War II, Carl Baquie replaced him, but was soon diverted to other enterprises: first, sales to China, and later the establishment of Cia. Algodones Extranjeros in Nicaragua. As Baquie became increasingly involved in Central America, his assistant, James D. "Pick" Butler, took over in New York in the early 1950s.

Almost predictably, considering Pick's place in the continuum of cotton, he was Memphis-bred, just as his father, Chauncey Butler, who had served as the first president of the American Cotton Shippers Association in 1924, hailed from New Orleans. Chauncey Butler, like the Weils, had been a cotton merchant, if on a smaller scale: he was the American partner of the old Liverpool firm of Mellor & Fenton. Pick, born in Memphis in 1912, graduated from the University of the South and spent the first part of his career in his home town, working for McFadden. He was a highly experienced cotton man by the time he joined Weil in New York after World War II service as a navy officer. But for his telltale Delta accent, you'd never know that he wasn't a New Yorker. Tall and loosely elegant, debonair even when there's plenty to worry about, he typifies the old Wall Street establishment whose members fight for cabs on lower Broadway in the afternoon rush hour, then frequently end up as strap-hangers on the East Side IRT as they flee to the presumed safety of the Silk Stocking District. This is indeed where Pick makes his home in a large, cozily old-fashioned apartment with his Austrian-born wife, Liesl.

Pick is vice-president of the New York Cotton Exchange, a not inconsiderable honor as well as more than occasional headache: in any organization that governs the flow of real money, policy is far more important than pomp and ceremony. Weil executives have traditionally been involved in cotton-exchange matters, and fre- quently in key positions. Shap Dowdell, in fact, was the first man elected to the presidency of the New York Cotton Exchange (1932–34) who didn't own his own firm. Bob Murray also gained the presidency (1940–43) as an employee, and Carl Baquie served on the board of directors. Nor was the Weil crew's participation limited to New York. Al Grayson served as president of the Dallas Cotton Exchange in 1930, and later A. M. Crawford, Sr., (1949–50) and Thomas C. Adams (1975–76) headed the Memphis Cotton Exchange.

No less important to Weil in New York than the managers—and sometimes perhaps more important, as when Bob Murray treated

Mildred Schwab in the New York office in 1973.

himself to "blessed ham" at Delmonico's—was Mildred Schwab, who had started as a twenty-one-year-old secretary in Shap Dowdell's time, and kept the office running and the accounts straight until a year before her death of cancer in 1977. She would willingly have worked right up to her last day had that been possible. As she wrote wistfully to Bucks from her sickbed, "A few days ago I had to go to my bank...which made me think I could soon return to Wall Street, but I had to stop for a long nap and I don't think my bed would be welcome in the office." She added, "I do hope to be able to return though in the not too distant future. It would surprise the doctor who has suggested to me...that I make my will, etc. while my mind was still clear!" Alas, her exclamation mark was a futile protest.

When Mildred had first worked for Weil, Isidor advised her to pay close attention to the letters she transcribed. This, he said, was the best way to learn what made the business tick. One day, he told her, she "would be able to buy and sell cotton like a man." She might indeed have been given that opportunity had she herself felt confident enough. But she had grown up in a time when much of the world was still closed to women. A. M. Crawford, in New York to expedite the delivery of some contract cotton, was so impressed with Mildred that he was about to arrange her transfer to Montgomery. Shap Dowdell, intent on keeping her, argued Crawford out of that. But, as she remembered, neither man asked how she felt about it: "All I could have told them was that my father would have had a dim view of anyone taking his daughter to live in a strange town. He would have equated it with sin."*

As it was, Mildred's responsibilities soon extended far beyond office routines; she became, in effect, the Weils' New York agent for their personal affairs. Isidor, an inveterate smoker of Cuban cigars, sent her on shopping expeditions to tobacconists all over the city: he was constantly trying to find the cheapest way to buy them, and engaged in computations of postage versus tax plus mark-up with the same intensity he applied to setting limits. He repeatedly wrote letters charging Mildred with making sure that Shap always turned out the office lights at night; like Emil, Isidor always fretted about bills being too high. Indeed, such penny-wise frugality seems to be a Weil family trait. Bucks, who wouldn't think of flying in the back of an airplane, drives a car that's well beyond its prime and compulsively turns off lights in empty rooms. Bobby, between lavish parties, lunches at hamburger joints that give you wax paper instead of plates. Adolph used to spend as much time selecting a five-cent fish hook as he would on a real estate investment. A telephone call he made from the New York office on one of his frequent visits left the staff agog—and made them respect him all the more, for here, evidently, was a man who knew he was important but didn't think that spending money foolishly was the way to prove it. In the middle of dictation, he picked up the phone and asked the switchboard operator to get him the men's department at Saks Fifth Avenue. When the call came through, he said, "This is Adolph Weil from Montgomery, Alabama"—as if everyone would promptly recognize him by that introduction—"I'm in New York right now and we're staying at the St. Regis and I happened to be walking down Fifth Avenue this morning when your store was closed, and I saw in the window that you're having a sale on some ties. There was one with a stripe on it sitting in

---

*From a letter of recollections Mrs. Schwab wrote to Bucks Weil in September 1976.

the back in the window and it was marked down to a dollar ninety-five. Do you still have that tie out in the window? You do? Wonderful. Please have it wrapped up and sent over to me at the St. Regis. Now, make sure that it's the one that's reduced. That's the one I want."

Many of Adolph's visits to New York before World War II were stopovers on his annual summer trips to Europe with his family, and it was Mrs. Schwab's duty to arrange all bookings. During the war, and in the last months before Hitler sealed off the Continent, she was Isidor's emissary to receive and look after distant relatives and other refugees from Germany, friends, and friends of friends, for whom he had provided immigration affidavits and whom he supported until they found work. In those days it was almost impossible to get private bedrooms on trains, and Adolph, on his New York journeys, had to travel in a lower or an upper. It was up to Mrs. Schwab to play detective and find out all she could about his prospective partner on the Southern Railway: Adolph wouldn't share berths with just anyone.

In 1951, when Weil Brothers–New York was still in the old Cotton Exchange Building at 60 Beaver Street, Mildred Schwab hired a part-time assistant—a young lady by the name of Mimi (born Miriam) Randolph, who, it turned out, was a closet actress. Mimi's father, who had moved to New York from Montreal, was a cantor and occasionally sang opera, and Mimi had fallen in love with the stage early in life. For years, after leaving the Weil office when it closed in the afternoon, she caught the IRT to Times Square, gulped a snack, and rushed to the theater to change for whatever part she was playing at the time. For some reason she was self-conscious about it and never told anyone at Weil, and since there were no weekday matinees in those days, she never had to ask for time off. Summer stock was no problem either: that's not a busy time in cotton.

In 1967, when the Exchange perked up and basis operations once again came into its own, Weil was short on floor staff and Mimi was asked to clerk at the Exchange, i.e. to serve as phone intermediary between the office and the floor trader. As it happened, she was the first woman ever to be admitted to the Cotton Exchange floor. "I was told in no uncertain terms," she says, "that I had to wear a smock. I suppose that was so I wouldn't be distracting." There were other complications as well: she had to "run almost a mile" to the ladies'

New York Times photograph (below) recorded the day in February 1967 when Mimi Randolph, of Weil's New York Office, was the first woman ever to be admitted to the floor of the New York Cotton Exchange, then still at 60 Beaver Street. It was the story that went with this picture that made the Weils aware of Mimi's other career, until then carefully hidden from her fellow staffers: she was a Broadway actress. Top right is how she appeared with Buster Keaton in 1961 in "Once Upon A Mattress." Above she is Golda in "Fiddler On The Roof," a perennial role she was offered as a result of the *New York Times* story.

room, since there were no facilities for the gentler sex at the Exchange. This proved interesting enough for the *New York Times* to dispatch a reporter and photographer, and the next day Mimi's picture was in the paper, along with a feature story, and that's how the Weils found out about Mimi's moonlighting behind the footlights.

Something else happened, too. Mimi's agent, delighted by the publicity and using it to full advantage, called her that same day and said, "You've got *Fiddler on the Roof*." Her first reaction, now that she had such an exciting and responsible job, was "I can't do that," for it involved going on the road. In any event, she thought she'd be playing Yenta, the matchmaker in the show. "You're crazy," her agent said. "This is for Golda," and Mimi couldn't turn that down, of course, "especially when he told me what the money was going to be."

From then on, Mimi took off years at a time for Broadway, off-Broadway, tours, and TV, but always came back to Weil between parts. She liked the work, enjoyed the people, and besides, it must have been fun to be an in-house celebrity. One day, Manuel Held, in charge of the Montgomery clerical staff, called her with glee to tell that the local dinner theater, reviving *Fiddler*, had put up an old poster for atmosphere: "Starring Jan Pierce. Also starring Mimi Randolph." Whenever she went near Weil territory on tour, flowers were waiting for her in the dressing room.

Adolph, on a visit to his daughter's family, the Pat Uhlmanns, in Kansas City shortly before his death, called Mimi, then playing there with Pierce, to come to a party at the Muehlebach Hotel. They hadn't seen each other in several years, and at first the seventy-nine-year-old Adolph didn't recognize her. She'd had her hair dyed red in the interval for *Redhead* and kept it that way. "When I arrived, I was the first one there," she recalls, "and when he ordered drinks for us, I noticed how he subtly tried to keep the door open because he was entertaining a lady in his room." Afraid of being swamped by offers to play one Jewish mother after another, and not wanting to be typed, she later accepted roles only in other genres: in *Funny Girl* and *A Majority of One*, Beatrice in *As You Like It*, Hippolyta in *Midsummer Night's Dream*, and Lady Macbeth.

Mimi is less busy in the theater now, and since Mildred fell ill has been working for Weil full time. The two women were close friends despite the disparity in ages. Above all, they shared a great interest in music. It ran in both their families: Mildred was a cousin of William

Schumann, then director of Juilliard (and now with Lincoln Center). Aware of this closeness, the Weils charged her with looking after Mildred Schwab during her fatal illness. Mimi was instructed to fulfill all of Mildred's wishes. "Keep checking if she wants anything," Bucks repeatedly reminded her. "Don't ask any questions. Just get it and charge it to our account."

At the World Trade Center, where the Cotton Exchange moved from the building on Beaver Street that it had previously sold, the cotton pit shares an immense hall with the New York Commodity Exchange, the Coffee & Sugar Exchange, and the New York Mercantile Exchange; everything is traded here from silver dollars to soybeans, and the resulting din resembles that of an ice hockey arena when the home team scores. Even so, the volume of futures traded here does not match those at the Chicago Board of Trade and the Chicago Mercantile, which together handle about three-fourths of all commodity contracts. Cotton, which unlike most other major commodities is traded only in New York, is small potatoes compared to grain and pork bellies. On an average day, only about 4,500 cotton contracts, each for a hundred bales, change hands.

The New York Cotton Exchange had opened its doors in 1870, when Isidor and Emil were still peddling dry goods in Huntsville, Alabama. It then occupied the street floor of a narrow four-story building at 142 Pearl Street. B. C. Baker Son & Co., a cotton merchant, rented the floor above it, and two other cotton houses were in a building next door: Carter & Hawley and L. Hirschhorn & Co.—all names that have become famous in other endeavors since. The house on the other side was occupied by wine merchants, Edward Hart & Co., who evidently were bigger than any of the cotton people because they had the whole building to themselves. But 142 Pearl was only temporary. By 1872, the Exchange had moved into a stately building on Hanover Square, subsequently known as India House, and three years later it moved into a yet more opulent structure, also on Hanover Square at William and Beaver Streets, whose imposing entrance was recessed into a rounded corner with a broad flight of stone stairs leading up to it. That's where Edwin Shields did the first futures trading on behalf of Weil around the turn of the century. In Shap Dowdell's time, in 1923, the New York Cotton

Exchange finally erected its own quarters at 60 Beaver, near Hanover Square, and many cotton houses leased space in the building, including Weil. Since the building's sale (it's now a condominium) and the Exchange's subsequent move to the World Trade Center, Weil Brothers first went to 82 Wall and later to the ornate Trinity Building, one of two side-by-side twins with sculpted lobby ceilings, ormolu fretwork, until recently hand-operated elevators, and bland, dim hallways on their office floors. As usual, the Weil quarters are scant and simple: two rooms with but a minimum of furniture.

Over the years, as might be expected, sales of actual cotton by the New York office have decreased dramatically. With most American mills having gone south and the remaining Canadian mills buying largely through Memphis, Weil's biggest customers now are Johnson

The New York Cotton Exchange had its beginnings in 1870 on the ground floor of 142 Pearl Street in lower Manhattan (left). Note the other shingles whose proprietors have also since outgrown their modest quarters: next door, "Carter Hawly," today's Carter Hawley Hale Stores, Inc., and L. Hirshhorn & Company, spelled two ways, with and without the c, by the artist who evidently wanted to make sure that he got at least one of them right. The picture below shows the sumptuous trading floor, sketched by Chester B. Price, when the Exchange erected its own quarters at 60 Beaver Street in 1923.—*Courtesy New York Cotton Exchange*

& Johnson, which buys short-stapled drugstore cotton, and Kendall Mills, whose specialty is the cotton that's stuffed into the necks of pharmaceutical and vitamin bottles to absorb moisture.

Butler, as the New York office is known, also handles sales to some foreign countries, like Chile, as well as to a number of nations with government economies, such as Yugoslavia and Romania, which send purchasing agents to New York. These usually do their whole year's buying all at once.

Thus, in the past decade, New York's primary activity has been to handle futures for the Weil organizations. As a sideline, Weil Brothers and Butler, as the New York office is known, also acts as a cotton futures brokerage for a small number of outside customers, whose transactions are kept in accounts that are totally separate from the house business. That's necessary not only for bookkeeping purposes—all that goes on the Weil books are the commissions earned through these external transactions—but also to keep the firm inviolate from unrelated adventures, and in that sense to follow the regulations laid down by the Commodities Futures Trading Commission (CFTC), whose function it is to ascertain that everything happens on the up and up.

Until 1936, the commodities exchanges operated virtually without controls. At that time, after a cotton-market scandal that we'll deal with shortly, Congress established the Commodities Exchange Administration (CEA), an agency ruled in theory by the secretaries of agriculture and commerce and the attorney general. In practice, however, it was run by the Department of Agriculture. This eventually precipitated pangs of jealousy on the part of the Small Business Administration, which wanted a piece of the action, and this in turn flustered the all-powerful House Agricultural Committee. In the subsequent interdepartment hassle so typical of bureaucracies, an untypical solution was found. Congressman Robert Pogue, an old Texas hand, succeeded in pushing through the present CFTC, which is completely independent of any government department. Since then (1974), the governing of the exchanges has been a bit saner, at least in the view of people who should know about such things; the only conundrum is, as ever with politically appointed boards, that some of the commissioners are not exactly experts in the field.

But, expert or not, they'd be hard put to solve the major problem: the relationship, partly symbiotic and partly adversary, between the

Edgar Degas. *Cotton Office in New Orleans*, 1873 (Musée des Beaux Arts de Pau).

people actually involved with commodities and those who merely speculate in them. On the Cotton Exchange, the speculative interest averages about 45 percent, with the weight sometimes on the long and sometimes on the short, but in either case essential to maintain liquidity. Yet speculators can create considerable mischief. At the least harmful level, a speculator with access to the exchange floor may try to make a quick profit by "running ahead on orders." When such a speculator spots a floor trader for a merchant or a farmers' cooperative who is trying to fill a big order—one so big that it can't be bought in all at once—he will bid a couple of points ahead of the professional trader, thus running up the price; then, while the professional trader is still trying to fill his order, the speculator will sell the cotton he has just bought. In short, he creates a position that's not based on fundamentals and then tries to skim off the top before it's too late. On a more serious level, some speculators try to profit by taking big positions, often with disastrous results.

True enough, basis operators also sometimes get carried away by the lure of easy profits, as Tom Adams did in 1977, which proves that even the best of them can go off half cocked. Even old A. M. Crawford, who was as astute as they come with futures, once fell into such a trap. It's a story worth retelling, for it illustrates that markets have the habit of acting contrarywise. One Friday afternoon in 1951, after the Exchange closed, he called Allie in Fresno and told him, "I think the market is going up the limit. See if you can go out and buy some fixed cotton at today's close." This was against Weil policy, of course, since this cotton wouldn't be hedged. But if Crawford proved right and the market did rise the two-cents daily limit, the firm stood to gain ten dollars a bale. Crawford's target was 50,000 bales—a cool half million dollars.

Tells Allie: "I called Helmut Kruse in Arizona. I called my New Mexico man. I called everybody I knew. I told them to buy, and no limit. Just go ahead and buy everything you find. That was on a Friday. On Saturday we were going down to Los Angeles for the weekend, and again I called everybody. By that time we had seventy-seven bales. Get moving, I told them. Down in Los Angeles on Sunday we went to a football game, and then we went out and partied pretty good.

"The market in California opens up at seven-thirty in the morning with the difference in time between the East Coast, and I didn't wake up until about an hour later. Right away, still in bed, I called this futures house over in the Biltmore Hotel and asked them to give me December cotton. On Friday it had closed at something like forty-three and a half cents [per pound] and from what my father had said, I thought it was going to open up at forty-five and a half. But this guy said it was forty-one and a half, which was the limit down. I said, 'No, no, that can't be right.' He said, 'Yes it is. That son of a bitch is down the limit.' And I said, 'What in hell happened?' and he said, 'I don't know. Word was that it was going up the limit.'

"Now I was really scared. I didn't know how much cotton had been bought after I left: maybe the whole fifty thousand bales. Can you imagine? Half a million dollars in the hole! I got Helmut Kruse on the phone. I was sure he had at least ten thousand. But he said, 'Hell, I didn't buy anything. I couldn't get anybody to sell,' and I said, 'Bless your sweet heart.' Then I called the others. Same story. And I knew just what had happened. My father had fallen for a tip, sharp as he was, and everybody else had gotten that same tip and that's why nobody would sell cotton. So we were lucky. We only had that first seventy-seven bales."

Rumors like that make the rounds all the time. The story might be that Mainland China is going to buy 200,000 bales at a fixed price that evening, or that Japan was going to pick up 100,000, or whatever. This means that someone the next day will have to cover those bales with futures, and the market isn't flexible enough to absorb that many orders without taking a jump. Anyway, that's the theory, and usually that's how it works, and if the rumor is correct and you get it soon enough and act on it quickly and decisively, you can laugh all the way to the bank. But, astoundingly enough, the market sometimes turns ornery and does precisely the opposite of what's predictable. And that's what happened here.

Still, there's great psychological pressure to follow tips or even to obey one's own educated reasoning, and this often makes it difficult for basis operators to stick to policy, even at Weil Brothers. Bucks, who, despite his generally happy nature, is basically a pessimist and therefore fairly unflappable, has the best answer to the inside-know-how dilemma. When Weil executives argue convincingly for taking a position, Bucks calmly tells them, "Just this once you may be right. But look. Here we have a big organization, dozens and dozens of people on the payroll, paying rent all over. If we wanted to be speculators, we wouldn't need any of that. All we'd need is a telephone." Which was exactly what Adolph used to say when faced with such temptations. This firmness has saved Weil more than once; in the firm's 100 years there have been several drastic breaks that ruined less cautious merchants.

When cotton broke the daily limit of two cents two days in a row on March 11 and 12, 1935, it was a disaster of unprecedented proportions. Nowadays, four cents a pound doesn't seem all that much (with cotton climbing toward a dollar at the time of this writing), but then the price was just a little more than ten cents, and a four-cent drop meant nearly 40 percent—as if the Dow, in just two days, would plunge to 600 from 1,000. As it happened, this break came shortly after Cotton Ed Smith had given a speech before the Exchange extolling the purchase of cotton futures. Convinced that he'd been right and that someone done him wrong, he demanded a Congressional investigation. This cry was echoed with equal fervor by Bankhead and Thomas. The resultant hearings lasted weeks on end and produced a two-volume record, each volume nearly one inch thick. But the only conclusion anyone could reach was that mysterious market forces had been at work; perhaps, as some jesters suggested, the market had been overbought after Cotton Ed's speech. In any case, the cotton break contributed mightily to the formation of the Commodities Exchange Administration the following year.

But it isn't always just natural forces that put the market in a tantrum, and the CEA, in all its wisdom, was unable to foresee cotton's next tailspin. In October 1946, with the market at a twenty-seven-year high, Tom Jordan, a New Orleans speculator, bought thousands of futures through a dozen different houses, a stratagem designed to mask his activities. Eventually the market peaked, as it always does, and started giving ground. Jordan, overextended, couldn't put up margin and was sold out, practically all at once, along with a number of other smaller operators who had also bet long. In this avalanche of offers, each lower than the previous, no buyers could be found. By the time the slaughter was over, the price of cotton had plunged fifty dollars a bale, the daily limit of two cents a pound for five days in a row. At the end of the third day, the Exchanges (New Orleans was still operating then) halted trading. The hope was that

Britain would step into the gap, much as one country's central bank often does to prop up another nation's currency during panic selling. But the Liverpool Cotton Exchange, once the world's most important, had been closed early in World War II as the United Kingdom began buying its cotton in bulk through a government agency. The Exchange had remained closed under the Labour Government that took over after the war, and in this moment of crisis the Labour-dominated House of Commons rejected a hurried motion to save the world's cotton markets by allowing British spinners to engage in free buying. All W. R. Brownell, then president of the dormant Liverpool Exchange, could do was to dispatch telegrams expressing "fraternal sympathy" to his American opposite numbers. Weil and other big basis operators were not greatly hurt, except that the "Jordan Break," as it came to be called, made it temporarily difficult for anyone in the cotton business to obtain credit. In fact, along with Anderson Clayton and a few other major houses, Weil Brothers did its best to help soften the blow by purposely going long into the declining market. Luckily, the market soon recovered. By the end of that season, the paper losses Weil had taken on the way down were compensated for as prices once again were on the rise.

Since 1971, Weil's floor trading has been largely in the hands of Jack Rutkay, who is not a Weil employee but an independent floor broker. Rutkay, a spunky septuagenarian, alternately brash and sentimental, is the kind of character Damon Runyon liked to put in his stories. As anyone can tell who's heard him talk, Jack was born in Brooklyn. In 1926, when he was seventeen, he started as a runner for Clayton, and in the evenings, to make more money, worked in that company's shipping department; New York was then still a delivery point for cotton. Jack began clerking on the floor of the New York Cotton Exchange a few years later, and, after World War II, was made a partner in the firm of Anderson, Clayton & Fleming, the New York clearing firm for Anderson Clayton & Co. Jack was lucky in that Clayton also dealt in other commodities. During the years cotton futures were in limbo, he kept busy trading sugar.

Then, in 1971, while he still worked for that gigantic enterprise, Pick Butler, short of floor talent—there weren't many cotton traders left after the hiatus—asked Jack if he also could handle the Weil account along with his regular tasks. Clayton most generously had no objections. In fact, Jack was told by its chairman that he "couldn't work for better bosses." Perhaps, by then, Clayton's management had already decided to get out of the cotton business, which they did in 1973. Since then, Rutkay has handled most Weil transactions. Interestingly enough, long before Jack knew he'd ever work for Weil, he'd met young Bucks on the floor of the Exchange when Bucks was putting in his apprentice stint learning the ins and outs of the futures business. It was largely Jack who taught him the differences between Garside's theories and the day-to-day routines of the Exchange.

The superficial mechanics are simple enough. Butler, in his office, gets an order to buy or sell so-and-so many contracts in a certain month. The order may come from Montgomery or Memphis or from one of the outside clients. He records the order even as he telephones on the direct line to John McAlick, the Weil clerk on the floor of the Exchange. The clerk hurriedly scribbles the order and slaps it into the hands of a runner, who chases over to Rutkay, one of about fifty men "in the ring" around the "cotton pit." This is a slight depression in the floor which has no other purpose than to prevent bunching of the traders. When they stand around in a circle like this, even if occasionally two or three feet deep, there is enough separation to see their gestures and tell their voices apart. As soon as an order, or part of an order, is executed, Rutkay jots it on the slip, hands it to the runner, and the runner rushes back to the clerk, who calls Butler. Butler, in turn, confirms the execution of the order to its originator. The whole process, beginning to end, often takes less than a minute, and it is almost routine for Butler to keep both lines open until the deal is completed, even when the order comes from overseas.

When Rutkay has a market order, he'll pay the offered price if he feels it's fair. If the offered price is too high, he will bid up, a point at a time, until the offer comes down to meet his bid. Everything is done "open outcry," which means that no private trading takes place. Every bid and offer is announced and the traders develop the skill to hear them and tell one from the other. In a volatile market, this is sometimes difficult, and it can happen that a buyer pays above the offer or a seller sells below the bid. All bids and offers are called in points. When Rutkay calls "fifty for ten March," it signifies that he wants ten March contracts at fifty points above the current cent price; for example, if the price for March has been 60 plus cents, it means that he's willing to pay 60.50 cents. If the only offer is at fifty-two (60.52 cents) and he has a market order, he may yell "take it at fifty-

In the hectic last minutes before the bell that stops the day's trading (below), Jack Rutkay, Weil's floor trader, gesticulates wildly to bid on cotton futures (left). After the market's close, as other traders resolve differences (in background, bottom right), he takes time out to pose for portrait in front of the cotton pit with Pick Butler, manager of Weil's New York office.—*Author's photographs*

two" and frantically wave toward himself. That consummates the trade and the exchange reporter assigned to the pit immediately flashes the details by means of finger signals to the rostrum. The trade is instantly recorded on an electronic board, which also shows the highs and lows of the day and the prices of the last three transactions. Simultaneously, the quotations go out on the ticker.

But there's more to it than that. Floor traders, even when they are not buying or selling at the moment, carefully watch other traders so they may notice patterns in their trading. Everybody knows, of course, who all the others are and whom they represent, and it can make a great deal of difference to them whether a merchant is buying heavily or some speculator is going out on a limb. Off the floor, this intelligence work continues. All the traders lie like hell to each other, scattering wrong information; the skill comes in deducing the correct information from the spurious plants.

Hectic as life is around Rutkay's cotton pit, it seems an infinitesimal arena when you consider that cotton, despite its partial replacement by synthetics, remains one of the world's major commodities. Ever since the demise of the New Orleans Cotton Exchange, New York was the only place where cotton futures were traded for many

years. This held true until 1981 when the New Orleans Commodity Exchange introduced a new cotton contract. Meanwhile, the Cotton Board of Trade has also submitted a cotton contract to the CFTC, which eventually turned it down.

12

The Viles of Opeleeka

ALTHOUGH WEIL HAS BEEN KNOWN primarily as a domestic cotton house, it already engaged in export when Isidor and Emil still operated out of Opelika. There is some indication that the first foreign sales might have been to Japan via agents in New Orleans, Charleston, and Savannah. Quite early, too, some cotton must also have been shipped to Europe: by 1899 Isidor had established a sufficiently close relationship with Federico "Fritz" Kronauer, a broker in Milan, to be entrusted with the care and training of Kronauer's seventeen-year-old son, Rodolfo—the firm's first foreign squidge. It was a relationship, as so many others in the close-knit cotton world, that soon burst through the boundaries of business and became a personal alliance, a faithful friendship between clans. To-day, four generations later, assorted Weils and Kronauers still visit each other at least once a year. Rodolfo's witty wife, Piera, who came to Montgomery with her husband in 1923, has been credited with the saucy pronouncement (saucy because she spoke exquisite English), "Here I came to see the famous Viles of Opeleeka, and meet the Weals of Opelika. Veal, vile, weal, wile, it's all vile to me." To this day, thanks to Piera and the idiosyncratic phonetics of the English language, the Weils are known in northern Italian cotton circles as the Viles of Opeleeka, which is how untutored Europeans would pronounce these names.

Precisely when and how the Kronauers and Weils first got together is impossible to pinpoint. Like Isidor, Federico started his business in 1878. A native of Winterthur, the center of Switzerland's textile

The Kronauers have been the Weil's agents in Italy and close family friends for three generations. Brothers Carlo, shown at left with his wife Maria, and Rodolfo, above with his wife Piera, represented the firm in Adolph's and Leonel's time. Today, Carlo's son, Federico "Chicco" Kronauer, right, runs the Milan company.

manufacture, he had come to Italy three years earlier to hire out his expertise to the spinnery Cotonificio Cantoni, which, like many Italian mills, was of Swiss ownership. The first Kronauer, Friedrich, who later changed his name to Federico but was called "Fritz" throughout his life, soon realized that he would make out better on his own. To start with, he launched a small factory near Venice for the making of gauze. When this enterprise proved less than successful, he opened a cotton sales agency in Milan.

In 1880, when Fritz was twenty-nine, he married the Barcelona-born daughter of Temistocle Solera, a gentleman of many parts and endowed with a fine Italian hand. Solera, an Italian patriot and all-around politician, had been jailed by the Austrians who then ruled

northern Italy. He escaped to Spain, where he found a royal welcome in Queen Isabella II's bed. Dispossessed and deported when this dalliance was discovered, he next managed to be named chief of the gendarmerie of Sicily and later contracted to organize the awakening of Egypt's new constabulary. In between, he composed a little music, devised a sideshow act that had chickens dancing to his flute (glowing coals hidden under the metal floor of the cage provided the incentive), and found time to write several librettos for Verdi operas, including *Nabucco*. All these diverse talents, plus Fritz Kronauer's staunch German-Swiss heritage, came together in his and Amalia Solera's seven children, among them Rodolfo (1882–1966) and Carlo (1894–1960) Kronauer, who operated the cotton agency in Adolph's and Leonel's time.

Yet more adventurous Italian blood leavened the next generation when Carlo Kronauer married Maria Forlanini, the daughter of Henrico Forlanini, inventor of the autogyro, the helicopter's antecedent, after whom Milan's older airport, in suburban Linate, was named. The eldest son of this union, Federico Rodolfo (Chicco), born in 1922, is the current Kronauer, and, in turn, a close friend of his Weil contemporaries, Bucks and Bobby.

The friendship between the two cotton clans was nurtured on the Weils' between-seasons trips to Europe, and on Kronauer visits to the States. Chicco Kronauer, after half-starving for six years in Italy during World War II and the economic chaos that ensued, lived it up in Memphis and Montgomery when he came over to learn the cotton business in 1947. Awed by America, which was then still never-never land, he borrowed $3,000 from the Weils to buy a loaded Studebaker Commander (it was given to him in $1,000 bills). Most recently, Chicco's daughter Marzia, an art student, lived with Bobby's family while touring the United States, and Carlo Mor, the son of Chicco's sister, Federica Antonia, completed his training in the Weil organization.

That the exigencies of business will not rend the bonds between the Kronauers and Weils has been demonstrated time and again in recent years. Ever since Isidor's and, later, Adolph's times, Italy has been one of Europe's major textile producers. Its imports of United States cotton rose as high as 800,000 bales a year in the mid-twenties and rarely dropped below 600,000. France imported still more, exceeding one million bales in 1926. The Netherlands and Belgium also were substantial users. But the real champion cotton consumers were Britain and Germany, whose annual imports, except during the Depression and the war years, ranged around 1.5 million bales each and sometimes approached 3 million, Kronauer alone could not tap these markets, and shortly after World War I, Weil sent its own expeditionary force abroad in the person of Shap Dowdell. Adolph's objective was to sell (hopefully) about 50,000 bales in each of the big textile countries. Shap was to establish his first beachhead at Liverpool, an ambitious undertaking since that port was the Gibraltar of the cotton world, a veritable maze of entrenched interests whose complex fraternal rituals were as effective as machine guns in making mincemeat of the cheekiest intruder.

Liverpool had been Britain's cotton port since the 1790s, when the almost simultaneous invention of the spinning mule, power loom, and cotton gin catapulted cotton to the throne of textile fibers. Not only was Liverpool the harbor of choice for the island's sailing-ship commerce with the American Colonies, but the soft, damp climate of its region ideally suited the physical process of spinning. Just as Yorkshire had been the hub of Britain's wool manufacture, so adjoining Lancashire now spawned hundreds of mills for spinning cotton yarns, fine and coarse, and nearly as many weaving mills to make those yarns into cloth, functions that were originally performed under separate auspices and only later combined under one roof. The powerful Liverpool Cotton Association dated back to 1842, a cabal of merchants, brokers, and shippers, whose collective wealth challenges the imagination. In its own way, Liverpool epitomized the British Empire. Its rules and quality standards governed international cotton dealings. Its merchants were bankers as well, and invested their fortunes in colonization: the profits derived from American cotton were assiduously plowed back into cotton-growing enterprises in Africa and India.

Between the exchanges of Liverpool and Manchester, the city (thirty-eight miles inland) closest to the cotton mills of Lancashire, more than double the number of futures contracts were traded than on all the American exchanges combined. Like the Empire (and unlike mill-hand Manchester), Liverpool was ruled by gentlemen in tall hats, butterfly collars, frock coats, and cravats with stick pins, an attire that only slowly gave way to immaculately tailored business suits and bowler hats. If a young man dared to don sport flannels, the commissioners of the Liverpool Exchange would usher him aside from view. Every morning before the market opened, the bellboys (runners) were mustered like soldiers to have their uniforms, hats, buttons, and shoes checked for cleanliness and gleam. Everybody spoke the King's (as opposed to the Beatles') English. As a saying had it, the Liverpool *gentleman* called a spade a spade, while the Manchester *man* referred to it as a bloody shovel.

Into this sun-never-sets setting trooped Shap Dowdell, of New York, Montgomery and Memphis. He rented a small office in the Orleans House, an overflow building of the Liverpool Exchange, filled it with Weil-style rickety furniture, and bravely hung out a Weil Brothers Agency shingle. As manager, he installed F. S. Porter, formerly chief salesman of D.F. Pennefather & Co., a venerable Liverpool firm. Porter, in turn, hired a young man by the name of George H. Way, who had gained considerable experience in handling American and Indian cottons on consignment since his return from the World War I trenches. The agency had a twofold function. One was to sell forward cotton; the other, to procure commissions for trading futures on the New York Cotton Exchange. To accomplish the latter, Shap arrived at an arrangement with Hornby Hemelryk & Co., then Europe's largest futures firm, for a substantial portion of its New York contracts. Just how Shap went about this is a mystery. All we know is that it involved some kind of reciprocal accommodation with a Hornby Hemelryk trader, a Greek of enormous proportions with jewel-encrusted fingers and gold teeth, whose name was Gussi Galati. There's no doubt that Isidor, who visited in 1923, and A. M. Crawford and Al Grayson, who dropped in a few years later, must have found the workings of this branch of considerable puzzlement.

The other, more important function—to sell large quantities of spot and forward cotton procured by Weil in the United States—was not so easily achieved. As stated before, the goal was 50,000 bales a year, but the hope was really for 100,000. Anderson Clayton had done it. So why not Weil? In an exhaustive memoir, penned for Leonel in 1976 by the then eighty-five-year-old George H. Way, he summarized the problem in his meticulous, if somewhat shaky, script:

> What you could not see or measure situated away back in Montgomery was the big number of Importing Agencies [his

capitals] in Liverpool some of them already large in volume. With up to around 50 such Importing Shippers' Agents, it is obvious that as far as American Cottons were concerned, 50,000 bales per Agency would total around 2½ million bales. Added to this C.I.F. type business came many 1000s of bales of consignment cottons. Between them, the number of Shippers' Agents and Agencies, and the availability of consignment cottons in quantity made an extremely competitive C.I.F. Market; and, in turn, qualified a Shipper's ability to reach 50,000 bales annually. Such as Anderson Clayton did it (and much more) quite easily. They got right behind consignment cottons for example....[Also] *Price* would decide whether you reached that figure, or not. Again, cheapness of a Shipper's *Forward* offering basis could enable him to exceed the 50,000 bales. Some shippers would offer "seller's call" for up to 6 or 9 months ahead. This suited certain Spinners who in turn could trade ahead with their Yarns, Weaves and Finished Goods.

The problem encountered by the Liverpool agency was twofold: one, that Adolph and Leonel were unwilling to compromise price on forward transactions, and the other, that they would not deal in consignment cottons, i.e., to act as intermediary in spot cottons of largely foreign growths. At that point, Weil was interested only in U.S. cotton—remember, these were the 1920s, long before New Deal legislation all but priced American fiber out of the international market. Given this approach, there was no way for Weil to become the biggest boy on the British block, but there was enough volume available to sustain a profitable business. On one single, evidently memorable day, Way placed 12,000 bales with The Manchester Raw Cotton Co. and had no sooner phoned Liverpool to get the cable off to Montgomery when Bushby Son & Beazly ordered 15,000. In addition, there were numerous smaller bids. Such triumphant days were rare, of course; in part because Memphis, whose cotton was in most demand, found it too expensive to conform to the Liverpool practice of demanding complete lots of "Actuals" for classing, not just representative portions of lots. As for Dallas cotton, which was perfectly acceptable on the Continent, it did not, for the most part, meet the Lancashire mills' requirement of "Liverpool Good Strong Character," one of the standards that justified the claim "None Finer" for British finished goods.

The procedures of doing business in Liverpool presented complexities unheard of on our side of the Atlantic. George H. Way wrote:

The market *did* have a strict etiquette in those days, and it was fatal to ignore it. For example the Market and Association comprised certain well-defined compartments such as Shippers (Inward) Merchants, Mills' Brokers and Futures Brokers. The strict code was, Shippers or their Agents could only sell through, and deal with, a Mill Broker. If a Shipper or his Agent broke the chain, and even offered, to go more direct such as to a Mill Broker or a Mill itself, that Shipper or Agent was blackballed by the Merchant fraternity. Similar treatment awaited a Merchant who tried to by-pass a Mill's Broker. The Brokers would no longer look at his Cottons for all other Mills. With this in mind such as ourselves working the market we had to keep well away from the Broker's premises.

Then from the Associations' point of view, at that time Mills could not be Members; and CIF Agents found great difficulty in becoming Members. The Association classified everybody and marked out what they could or could not do. Hence, Full Members (*Local* Merchants and Brokers); Restricted Members (A Local Concern with no facility to Trade in the Ring); and Associate Members (categories of non-local etc. etc.) with a different Set of Brokerage Fees attached, compared to "Member-with-Member" Trading.

Again with the foregoing in mind we had to watch our step. WB [Weil Brothers] were not Members (Galati *was*, and duly Registered); Mr P [Porter] nor I were Members at that time, so we had no access to the Cotton Exchange Floor. When we were instructed to Fix 'On Call' cotton sales we had to stand at the Entrance and request the Commissionaire to call out from the "Ring" the Buyer's Ring Trader to whom we then gave the "calling" instructions. All this meant unavoidable delay; and, in a falling Market could mean an expensive fixing. We soon realized we had to get this angle of the business straightened out; and the cheapest way eventually was for Mr P to become a Member and me in my turn to become a Member. But neither of us could take this step *with WB's name up*, and where both of us were nominated as employees.

The association with the glinting Mr. Galati eventually disintegrated, as it was bound to, when he tried to finagle Weil into paying a higher commission than had been originally agreed. But to everyone's pleasant surprise, the futures business did not collapse as a result of his departure: not only Hornby Hemelryk but even most of Gussi's Greek friends stuck with the Weil Agency. At this point, to enable Porter and later Way to become members of the Liverpool Cotton Association, the branch lowered its Stars and Stripes and raised the Union Jack. The Weil Brothers Agency ceased to exist only to be resurrected the same day as F.S. Porter Cotton Agents, with offices in the Cotton Exchange Building itself. This tactic was essential. Weil had to be represented on the floor of the Exchange, especially between 2:45 P.M. and 4:00 P.M., or else much futures business would be missed. Again George H. Way:

> With New York coming in at our 3 P.M. (GMT) the Ring Traders required to have their New York contact at their elbow...to open or close a straddle between Liverpool and New York. Obviously the Ring Trader couldn't afford to leave the Ring searching for someone to take his urgent instruction. With this in mind, New York Futures Agents...tended to hover at Ringside to catch the eye of any would-be straddle operator. There were quite a few such....If we were not as prominently available as these others we would not secure "New Business," and would be blamed for not being on hand to liquidate "Old Business."...Speed of action is vital...both getting in and getting out. Between 3 P.M. and 4 PM., New York Futures prices of their active months were quoted alongside our Liverpool American Futures Board for the Ring Traders to evaluate the various straddles. The prices came through every 3 minutes...from the New York Floor by a direct cable link. In addition to that 3 minutes price service, individual prices of any month traded within any 3 minute period were also quoted. The Rate of Exchange was also chalked up. It was our job to keep momentary Straddle figurings for the active months aided by certain 'tables' we carried about with us. When the Ring Trader sprinted out of the Ring, tempted by what appeared a profitable two Market Difference, he would dash to his chosen New York agent....

Porter's retirement not long thereafter left Way in charge of operations and the name of the firm was changed appropriately to George H. Way & Co. Among the functions that fell to him was the periodic hosting of Weil emissaries. He took A.M. Crawford, Sr., shopping in Manchester to find an overcoat of Crawford tartan, sponsored a stuttered speech by Al Grayson before the Liverpool Cotton Association during the latter's term as president of the Dallas Cotton Exchange ("which was," wrote Way, "of great help in furthering the sales of Texas cottons"), and accompanied Adolph on assorted troubleshooting trips to France and Belgium. Way's friendly ways were not forgotten on this side of the Atlantic. When the Luftwaffe launched its Blitz on British cities, Grayson cabled Way to send his two children immediately to the safety of Dallas; in the excitement, Al had completely forgotten that those kids must have grown up since his Liverpool visits nearly two decades earlier. Way's boy, in fact, was serving in His Majesty's forces by that time. Still the generosity was appreciated and so was Leonel's shortly after World War II when the latter insisted on taking Way to a store in Paris to replace his ragged wartime wardrobe.

By then Liverpool was no longer the Liverpool of yore. The Liverpool Cotton Exchange had existed in name only since the British government's Raw Cotton Commission (RCC) began procuring imports at the start of Hitler's war. All that effectively remained was its arbitration and appeals board; even the Labour government realized that the RCC couldn't do its own arbitrating. The commission carried on for several years at the exclusion of private traders, and even when such trading resumed, the government did not sanction the reopening of the exchange. During this period, Weil used Porter's office to sell to the RCC, and at the same time set up George Way to offer cotton in the name of W. J. Reckling, then the firm's pseudonymous Houston operation.

Thus matters stood until 1954, when the Attlee government fell and Winston Churchill was brought back as prime minister—the Empire's last postmortem gasp. Churchill set about denationalizing industries that the Socialist government had nationalized. This gave Liverpool another, albeit short-lived, lease on life. The rebirth was celebrated with great fanfare, for much as Britain had sacrificed in the Attlee years, it hadn't lost its knack for ceremony. The reopening of the Liverpool Exchange in 1954 was attended by 1,500 high-powered visitors from all over the world, who were introduced by a lion-voiced toastmaster, dressed in striped trousers and a bemedaled cutaway of regal red, as they strode down the elaborate marble stairway of the Exchange building to meet the local dignitaries in the receiving line.

"This isn't bad for a couple of country boys," Bobby Weil remarked to Chuck Hohenberg after their names had been announced. "Don't you think we ought to go up and do it again?"

Pomp aside, it was old-home week. Prominent in the receiving line was the Exchange's president, Kentish Barnes, who had been an old business associate of Pick Butler's family. The banquet that night, on the eve before trading commenced, opened with a toast to the Queen. There followed a five-course dinner, so meticulously arranged that all tables were served at exactly the same time, and with each course came a separate wine. Toast followed toast, by Chuck Hohenberg for the American Cotton Shippers Association, by the vice-president of Peru for his country's cotton association, by representatives of every organization in the business everywhere. Sir Selwyn Lloyd, later to be named foreign secretary, delivered the keynote address. He was a spellbinding orator who disdained the use of notes. His subject, appropriately, was the resurgence of free enterprise, and in pursuing the theme he managed to twit the attending cotton nabobs of Egypt in such a subtle way that his remarks amused even them—a major rhetorical accomplishment, for their situation under Nasser was highly precarious; not long afterward they had to flee Cairo and set up shop as exiles in Geneva, whose cotton community they now dominate.

The opening of the floor was no less festive. Chairs had been set up all around the trading ring and in the balconies above. Traders, as in bygone days, wore formal morning dress. Shortly before noon, Kentish Barnes and another trader, in their gray top hats, cutaways, and ascots, faced each other in the ring. At high noon the bell rang and the two men began to trade. As they traded, light applause rose to a roar, and soon the British reserve gave way as everyone rose to his feet clapping and shouting. Other traders then entered the ring, and in the tumult it was hardly noticed that some of them, having been out of practice for fifteen years, were rusty on their hand signals.

With the liberation of the cotton trade, the problem arose how Weil Brothers would do business. Lancashire did most of its purchasing through buying brokers, with each in control of several mill accounts, and not infrequently there were tie-ups between the brokers and the selling agents. Liverpool's inherent caste system also presented difficulties. Men like Porter belonged to certain clubs, to which former clerks like George Way were not admitted. The latter had indicated even before the Liverpool reopening that he wanted to retire. His assistant, Gabriel Coury, a World War I Victoria Cross winner and proud participant in the coronation parade of Queen Elizabeth II, also did not want to continue. One of Bobby's missions on this particular Liverpool trip, therefore, was to scout for a replacement. In that, he was none too successful. Liverpool's agents—actually merchants—had little money left in 1954 to set up any kind of merchandising operation. Weil would have to invest capital in England, which it was not prepared to do. Ergo, a rich firm must be found.

The prime candidate in this respect was Reynolds & Gibson, which got its start running the Civil War blockade. One of the partners, Leslie Orme, a Mayfair Britisher, already had made overtures to Weil; his son Michael had trained in the Memphis office. But Bobby was turned off almost the minute he arrived at the Reynolds & Gibson offices. After Sir John Reynolds offered a limp hand and invited Bobby to come in, "Sir Jack" glanced over at George Way, who naturally accompanied Bobby everywhere in Liverpool, and said, "Mr. Way, Mr. Weil will be through in about an hour. Please wait here." Devoid of an old-school tie, Way evidently was not welcome in the inner sanctum. The ensuing conversation convinced Bobby that his first impression had been correct. "They had power, money, and prestige," he says, "but as far as doing business, I was reminded of Al Grayson's saying, 'Fat dogs don't hunt'."

Nor did a visit to Kleinwort's, the eminent London merchant bankers, yield the hoped-for results. Bobby went to Kleinwort's almost as an afterthought. From Liverpool he had gone to Denmark, Sweden and Finland before meeting his wife, Virginia, in Paris for yet more Continental rounds. Later, in Zurich, he remembered having stayed at the Dolder Grand with the Alvin Weils. The hotel's bar had seemed as steeped in intrigue as any Hitchcock movie. One of Alvin's acquaintances had explained some of the deals in progress at other tables: wool being shipped from Argentina to Rotterdam, then forwarded to the United States and sold there at a much lower price in dollars than would have to be paid FOB at Argentinian ports. It was

This is only part of the festive crowd of 1,500 cotton people from all over the world who attended the reopening of the Liverpool Cotton Exchange in 1954. Sir Selwyn Lloyd (he is the younger of the two gentlemen in front of the letter C above), was keynote speaker at the banquet. The next day, futures trading resumed with great formality (left) which soon turned into jubilant pandemonium. Note time on clock in background: Liverpool coordinated its trading hours with those of the New York Cotton Exchange.

all a paper-money game, using commodities as vehicles to switch out of soft currencies at black market rates. As sophisticated a firm as Weil was, such manipulations, a European specialty, were beyond its ken, even though cotton might have lent itself as readily to fleece as wool. Later, when Bobby and Virginia returned to London en route home, Leslie Orme came by for one more talk on behalf of Reynolds & Gibson. Introduced to Virginia, he expressed his surprise that Bobby had not brought his stunning wife to the Liverpool opening. Apparently he was not quite convinced that a cotton man like Bobby deserved such an elegant mate; when Bobby was paged to answer a phone call, Orme played it out of Noel Coward: gloves in his hands, his hands folded on top of his cane, leaning forward so that his chin rested on the back of his hands, he raised his eyebrows and in all seriousness asked Virginia, "*Are* you Mrs. Weil?"

Reynolds & Gibson being out of the picture, Bobby hoped that Kleinwort might fill two of Weil's needs—that for a Liverpool agency and for insurance. The Bowring firm at Lloyd's of London, Bobby was to learn, did not write the two kinds of coverage that Weil most sorely needed—war risk onshore and credit—and Bobby thought that Kleinwort might oblige. This bank, dating back to voyages of Sir Francis Drake, had built its fortune on West Indian cocoa and sugar. It now wanted to open a cotton department and was willing to hire a man to act as Weil's Liverpool connection. This, however, was not enough for Bobby, who wanted exclusive representation, at least so far as American cottons were concerned. And Kleinwort's didn't write credit insurance and war risk onshore either.

But the inability to come to terms did not hamper cordial relations between the bankers and the cotton firm, despite the fact that Bobby committed an unforgivable breach of etiquette, at least by old British standards, in arriving late for the appointment. He had scheduled his Kleinwort visit for the last day of his stay in London, and Virginia pressed him to first accompany her to Partridge's to inspect an antique sideboard before she bought it. Upon leaving Partridge's, he had trouble finding a taxi to take him to the bank. When he finally did arrive for the meeting, he was greeted by Sir Cyril Kleinwort, the chairman, who then phoned the Bank of England to request a thirty-minute postponement of a session of its board of governors, of which he was a member. "Whenever I look at that sideboard," says Bobby, "I think of how Virginia must have been the only woman ever to hold up a meeting of the Bank of England."*

Weil did not establish a new Liverpool connection until two years after the reopening of the Liverpool Exchange. It was a last-ditch stand; by then, the British market for American cotton was sliding inexorably downhill. The Liverpool Cotton Exchange, briefly revived, had closed again, this time for lack of business. The mills of Lancashire were dying in droves, dragged under by antiquated machinery, the high cost of union labor, and the United Kingdom's "redundancy" program, which eliminated spindles by decree as British textiles were replaced by Oriental imports. Such mills as struggled on purchased the cheapest growths they could find: high-quality medium staple from Russia and Turkey and slightly shorter staple from Brazil. Besides these, only assorted "exotics"—from Egypt, Peru, Syria, and Pakistan—were in demand to any degree. Their import was dominated by a handful of international merchant companies that traded in all manner of commodities and were able to hedge their transactions by playing the currencies—firms like Cassir, Bunge & Co., Bunzl & Biach, Louis Dreyfus, Duncan Fox & Co., Forbes Cabell & Co., Ralli Bros. Ltd., and Volkart.

Russian cotton and Turkish cotton were particularly competitive with Memphis cotton in quality, and in some years Bunzl & Biach, formerly of Vienna, practically swamped the UK market. The only way Weil could hope to survive in this maelstrom was to merchandise foreign growths together with its Memphis cotton. George Way, persuaded not to yield his post despite advancing age, wrote long memos to that effect, to which Adolph sternly replied: "Mr. Way! We don't have time to read long letters. Whatever you have to say, say it in *one* page." By then, Central American cottons had become part of Weil's stock in trade but the advent of Algodonera Weil was not enough. Weil had to get together with one of the importers of exotic growths on some kind of commission-sharing basis.

---

*Bobby's assessment of a woman's place in the British scheme of things turned out to be fairly on the mark. In September 1978, back in England to attend the annual meeting and dinner of the Liverpool Cotton Association, the wives of the cotton men were not invited to attend the dinner—and this in a country whose monarch as well as prime minister, Margaret Thatcher, were women. So, for that matter, was the mayor of Liverpool.

This Adolph arranged on a trip in 1956, establishing a channel with Cassir & Co. for Algodonera Weil and with Deltapine Ltd. for Weil Brothers. Deltapine seemed better situated, since it owned a group of Lancashire mills in addition to the aforementioned seed business in the United States, while Albert Cassir, originally from Egypt, was primarily interested in the import of Turkish cotton, being able to obtain it through an ingenious barter arrangement that permitted him to fill orders very cheaply. But Cassir eventually ended up with both accounts when, on a trip in 1959, Bobby was informed by Deltapine that it would no longer carry representations, and that the relationship was to be severed immediately.* It was at this point that Bobby also handed the agency for domestic cottons to Cassir. However, this connection proved tenuous as well. It became increasingly apparent that Cassir was interested in the Weil relationship more for prestige than for profit; the firm was geared to merchandising its own cottons, not to the sale of someone else's. The Weil business then went to Meredith-Jones, and later to Eccles & Stern, whom Weil would have preferred in the first place had Eccles & Stern not had other American clients.

Eccles & Stern, or, more specifically, its associated firm, M. & B. Stern Ltd., now transacts what little business there is left to be done in Britain. Already in 1958, imports from the United States had been down to 210,000 bales. By 1980, Britain's worldwide cotton imports were hardly more than that, and the use of American cottons had dwindled to very much less than 50,000. However, the Liverpool Cotton Association not only still exists but remains the world's most prestigious. It continues as the central point of reference for the international cotton trade, and more contracts are subject to Liverpool rules and arbitration than any other.

Britain was the only European country where Weil ever operated—however briefly—under its own name. In Germany and Belgium it had always sold through exclusive agents. The first representative in

---

*Meeting Bobby in London a few days later, Steven Bowkett, the head of Deltapine's cotton department in Liverpool, expressed his wish to come to work for Weil. There was no opening at that time and Bowkett subsequently became the general agent in Europe for Calcot, the California cotton producers cooperative.

Weil's business in the United Kingdom is in the hands of David M. (left) and Philip J.M. Stern, of M.&B. Stern Ltd., of London, Manchester, and Liverpool.

Bremen, Germany's Liverpool, was George Hartmann, a superb cotton man who easily marketed between 50,000 and 100,000 bales a year. But this volume lasted only a few seasons. Once Hitler came to power, Adolph and Leonel refused to do any more business with Germany. Had it not been for a letter from George Hartmann to Isidor in the early 1930s, Weil might not have severed the connection so abruptly—after all, crackpots come and go—but the Hartmann letter brought home to the Weils that Hitlerism was more than an aberration: it was a state of mind one had to reckon with. Hartmann had known Isidor since before World War I, and the two Germans (for Isidor was a German after all) had become quite attached to one another. Hartmann lived in England then, and in fact sold some cotton there for Weil. During World War I, although a naturalized Briton, he was apparently badly treated in his adopted country, a victim of the same mentality that makes people change the names of streets and even cities in wartime. As a result, Hartmann, once a citizen of the world, became a nationalist German. He left the Britain he now hated and returned to Germany, which was fine with the Weils who wanted a good man in Bremen. Then, about 1934, he wrote Isidor the kind of soul-searching *Weltschmertz* letter that Germans used to specialize in. He wanted Isidor to understand why he was for Hitler: Germany deserved its place in the sun once more. Of course, Hartmann wrote, he was entirely opposed to Hitler's policy regarding Jews, "but. . . ." And that was the end of the relationship. There is, however, a sad footnote to this story. Several years later, just before World War II, Hartmann again wrote to Isidor, carefully mailing the letter from Switzerland, where he was visiting his daughter. He confessed that he'd been all wrong about Hitler, and he could see nothing ahead but destruction. No further correspondence was exchanged.

For about a decade, starting in 1949, Weil tried to reestablish itself in the post–World War II German market through a new Bremen agent, Theodor Riepling, who seemed devoid of nostalgia, however suppressed, for the Third Reich. Indeed, a rather close relationship developed, and Riepling sent his sons to the United States to train with Weil. Gentleman though that Riepling was, and perhaps because of that, he was extremely conservative and careful as only meticulous Germans can be. Consequently he never pushed for volume, and German business remained minimal. The association finally dissolved, and sales to Germany did not pick up until Weil established an affiliate corporation in Europe some time later.

Weil's man in Belgium, Willem "Willie" Brementhal, of Brementhal Frères Cie., was an entirely different sort from either Hartmann or Riepling. Unlike Hartmann, he couldn't have cared less about politics, and, unlike Riepling, his aim was to maximize sales, for he was concerned only with the good things in life and the wherewithal necessary to acquire them. As if to advertise his preoccupation, an especially hand-woven rug, replicating a dollar bill, adorned the hallway of his home. His corpulence, all of one solid piece, evidenced his gourmandise. The gleam behind his rimless spectacles testified to his shrewdness in business and his appreciation of après-business. Whenever he saw an attractive woman, he'd nudge Adolph and say, "Ah, voilà, dot iss streect meedling strong staple." But thanks to Willie's equally sharp eye for cotton, the mill people held him in great esteem and trusted his advice. He rarely handled less than 20 percent of the approximately 250,000 bales of U.S. cotton that Belgium imported annually in the 1950s, thus making Weil the biggest single shipper to that country by

Willie Brementhal was the largest seller of American cotton in Belgium for
many years.

far, and himself one of the wealthiest of agents. At his 1 percent commission, a season's sales of, say, 50,000 bales at $125 a bale—and the price was often higher than that—earned him about $62,500, equivalent in Belgian purchasing power at that time to almost one quarter of a million dollars today.

If Willie had one drawback, it was that his wife—formerly the mistress of his brother Louis—rather nonplussed the highly respectable gentry that controlled Belgium's old-line mills. She was the kind of stagey blond whose every sentence was a sexual allusion. The Weils were occasionally taken aback too, as when she once slipped off her panties at a dinner party and draped them over Bucks' head. The lady's story had an unhappy ending: Willie was too bright a man to remain interested for long in so blatant an organism, and he soon drifted on to other liaisons.

For the Weils, the Belgian business was as trying as it was amazing, since the Belgians tended to make a social event out of every transaction. They would prolong trading for days, knowing all the while what the price was going to be, but enjoying convivial dinners accompanied by immense quantities of champagne (which they called Belgian soda water) along the route to agreement. Adolph was always appalled at the cost of such entertaining. On his first business trip to Europe in 1949, Bobby took Alvin Weil, Willie Brementhal, and a mill owner, Tony Herbert, and everybody's wives to dinner at the Belgian seaside resort, LeZoute. That meal for eight cost $200, an astronomical sum in those days, and Adolph would refer to the tab for many years to come. The Belgians had no such scruples when it came to expenses, and moreover paid the visiting Weils the ultimate European compliment of not merely entertaining them in restaurants but inviting them to their homes. On one such occasion, at the weekend villa of Gustav Willems, of the Cotonnière de Flandres, Bobby and Virginia were guests at an intimate family lunch that lasted three hours, after which Bobby was expected to trade with Willems over yet another bottle of Belgian soda water. Bobby had enough French for light conversation, but with all the bubbly on his brain, did not trust himself when it came to business and tried to make Willems converse in English. Willems, big and pouchy, a comfortable man, pretended to listen to whatever Bobby had to say, and would only belch loudly and repeat again and again, "*Parce que vous êtes le fils de vôtre père...*", offering to Bobby, only "because he was Adolph's son," the generous price of 300 on December for 1,000 bales of Matamoros Middling Inch when Bobby knew that 310 was what he should get.

On his next trip to Belgium in 1954, Bobby showed Willems a sample of Weil's highest-grade Nicaraguan cotton, called CAMN. This was in June and Willems asked Bobby when this crop came on the market. Bobby told him that it would first be available in December and probably could be shipped through February or March. "Ah," said Willems, "it is beautiful cotton. What will you offer me 1,000 bales for?" At that time it was Algodonera Weil's unalterable policy never to sell Latin American cotton until after it had been harvested because there were too many risks, political and otherwise. Consequently, Bobby had to tell Willems that he could not quote a price for the new crop but would offer the cotton in November or December. At this, Willems stood up at his desk, opened his palms wide beside his big stomach, and said dramatically, "First you show me a beautiful virgin, and then you tell me I cannot have her."

While Weil worked with agents in most European countries, the firm took an entirely different tack in France. Here, in 1933, Weil Bros. went into silent partnership with one of Le Havre's oldest and most respected cotton houses, which had found itself sorely squeezed by the Depression and needed an infusion of capital to survive.

That company was Maison Du Pasquier, whose antecedents in the textile business dated back to 1751 when its founding fathers were engaged in the making of dyed cloth. In the cotton world, while no roads lead to Rome, many start in Switzerland. Like Federico Kronauer, the original cotton du Pasquier also was a Swiss. This gentleman, Claude du Pasquier (1717–1783), built his factory in Neuchâtel, in the Jura, and soon established branches in France and Austria. His descendants were yet more enterprising. In order to obtain cotton for their factories more expeditiously, they opened buying offices in the ports of Havre and Rouen. By 1815, the du Pasquiers had gone into shipping as well, operating sailing vessels that brought cotton from New Orleans, Mobile, Savannah, and

Charleston. Merchandising was the next logical step, selling fiber to the mills that were mushrooming around Rouen and Lille in northwestern France, and around Thann, Münster and Mulhouse in Alsace and the Vosges. The fact that one of the prolific du Pasquiers had meanwhile established a bank in New York, Du Pasquier Lenthilon & Cie., helped considerably in these transactions.

The first purchases from Weil Bros. were made in the 1909–10 season, one merchant buying from another, as is often done. Not until after World War I, however, did the two family firms begin to develop a closer relationship. At that time, two of the du Pasquiers, Hermann and his son Pierre, were sent to the United States by the French government to buy as much cotton as they could lay their hands on in order to speed the recovery of the French textile industry. Adolph, through Shap Dowdell, managed to secure a large percentage of the French orders, a most welcome source of revenues since Weil's overhead had increased greatly with the firm's postwar expansion. From then on, as had happened with the Kronauers, the Weils and du Pasquiers became personal as well as business friends.

The idea to pull Weil into a partnership with the French firm was Robert du Pasquier's, later chairman of the board of Maison Du Pasquier S.A. when that partnership was transformed into a corporation after World War II. In 1933, Robert, a native of Le Havre, was twenty-seven years old. He had studied economics at the Sorbonne and apprenticed for one year in a private bank in Geneva before squidging for Albrecht, Müller, Pearse & Co. in Bremen, Germany. He reasoned quite rightly that, apart from supplying the money needed to prop up Du Pasquier, the partnership would enhance the prospects of both parties. For the French firm, it would ensure a substantial flow of cotton, while eliminating the need for shopping around, at least among American sources. For Weil, in turn, it would provide direct entry into what was then the Continent's second largest market—France—and a no less effective pipeline to Du Pasquier's customers in the other countries. Only two American cotton houses maintained selling agencies in Le Havre: George H. McFadden and Anderson Clayton. Between them, they preempted the largest share of the market. Weil–Du Pasquier should be able to pick up a substantial portion of that business.

Robert du Pasquier, Weil's former partner in France, descended from an old cotton family. One of his ancestors is reportedly among the men in the famous Degas oil of a New Orleans cotton merchant's office—his only painting purchased by a museum during his lifetime—which is reproduced at the end of this chapter.

Robert du Pasquier set off on the long journey, by train and ship, to Montgomery, where he broached his proposal to Leonel. The very next day he had the 600,000 francs (then $150,000) he required, and Weil had a solid base in France. Specifically, this meant that the firm was no longer merely one supplier among several on an outside agent's roster. Henceforth, when Du Pasquier sold American cotton, it would be first and foremost Weil Bros. cotton. Before long, Weil also was one of the top American merchants in France.

At the end of World War II, just as it had after World War I, the prominence of Maison Du Pasquier stood Weil in good stead. Once again, in late 1945, the French government recruited its cotton-industry ambassador from that old house, and Robert was sent to America "to consolidate and clarify the trade in staple fibers with American suppliers." As may be expected, Weil was among the first American merchants to be authorized to ship directly to French mills.

Conditions were hectic, to say the least. A veritable barricade of government reglations, some dating back to the Vichy days, made the resumption of normal commerce almost impossible. The French mills, many of them severely damaged in air raids and the seesaw battles of the Vosges and Alsace, couldn't go back into even partial operation unless they received raw cotton. But to buy cotton, they needed dollars (the franc was worthless outside of France), and the French government cast an evil eye on anyone in possession of dollars; at the very least, dollar holders had to pay a 35 percent tax to "legitimize" their foreign lucre. Moreover, they faced the chance of going to jail if they couldn't explain where the money came from. The adventures of a mysterious M. Silberstein exemplified the tribulations of those troubled times.

Silberstein, a German refugee and naturalized French citizen, was the lucky owner of a suitcase stuffed with greenbacks of uncertain origin. He wanted to convert said greenbacks into finished cotton goods. The spinner he approached, a Du Pasquier client, was delighted at the prospect of an order, but for the aforementioned reasons there was nothing he could do. Robert du Pasquier then devised the following stratagem. Silberstein was to send his attractive daughter to Brussels with the suitcase, instructing her to mail the money to a New York bank. Meanwhile, Robert finagled passage to

America for M. Silberstein. No sooner had the latter rushed from the pier to his New York hotel than he frantically began dialing every Silberstein in the phone book: he needed a "relative," preferably with the same last name, willing to front the ownership of the funds and place an order for goods with a French mill. Anywhere else, such a search would probably have proved fruitless, but in New York, it yielded almost immediate results. Carefully tutored, the long-lost American "cousin" next approached the French economic attaché, who was happy to help out. A cotton import license was granted almost on the spot, whereupon the funds were transferred to Weil Bros. and Weil Bros. in turn delivered the required cotton through Du Pasquier to the Alsatian cotton mill. A few weeks later, M. Silberstein, once again back in France, took possession of the merchandise. Business, even if not back to normal, was at least amenable to improvisation.

The Weils were no more aware of the shenanigans behind this transaction than was the French government. If they had been, they'd have refused to sell the cotton. It wouldn't have been the first time, nor the last, that the firm turned its back on profits based on less than perfectly clean deals. From Isidor's time on, and right down to the present, the merest suspicion (often unfounded) that one of their contacts, whether he be supplier, customer, or agent, wasn't completely on the up and up ruled out any further relationship. That Weil became a major force in international cotton trading despite this straight-laced attitude is all the more surprising, since, outside the United States, such moralistic precepts are considered not merely unrealistic but utterly naive. There can be little doubt that the firm sometimes benefited from practices it would not have condoned had it been apprised of the details. After all, Weil dealt with and was represented by businessmen nurtured in Old World traditions: until the late 1950s, the firm's activities abroad were largely in the hands of foreign nationals.

Personal loyalty, freely offered, was an important aspect of Weil's relationships with its intermediaries abroad. In 1952, for instance, Bobby was hurriedly dispatched to France when Robert du Pasquier, after weeks of daily complaints about quality claims, announced abruptly that he was going to quit. The claims that bothered du Pasquier were easy enough to settle, if not always in the best interests of Weil: here Bobby learned once and for all that whoever had to represent the good will of a firm was ill equipped to stand up to even the most outrageous claims—an important bit of knowledge he would put to good use many years later in dealing with the Chinese People's Republic. But even as the claims were being settled, it was plainly apparent that du Pasquier's depression was not due to these disputes. He finally admitted that he was extremely worried; now that Russia had exploded its atomic bomb, he feared that Europe would be invaded soon, and that this would be the end of his family. Bobby assured him that if anything were to happen, du Pasquier would always have a place with Weil Brothers in America. Adolph was taken aback that Bobby could make such an offer without first consulting him, but then quickly agreed it was the right thing to do. Robert du Pasquier, much relieved, stayed on, and business in France, then Weil's most important foreign market, soon returned to normal.

From almost the beginning of the firm, Weil executives had traveled overseas periodically to consolidate relationships with agents, firm up contacts with customers, and occasionally to take a direct hand in major transactions. But only two staffers had been assigned to Europe for any length of time. The first was Shap Dowdell, who spent a year in Liverpool after World War I. The other was William J. Reckling, later manager of the Houston office, who had been sent to Le Havre when Weil invested in Maison Du Pasquier. Bill Reckling was an unusually able man, not only with cotton but with languages. Although his English was endowed with a distinct Savannah lilt, he managed to speak French almost like a native within a few months of his arrival.

While working with Du Pasquier on selling the mills of Alsace-Lorraine, Reckling was often involved in arbitrages between the Le Havre and Liverpool futures markets, then still going strong, and the New York Cotton Exchange. But an apprenticeship is all it was. He was eventually brought back to help Texas do business with foreign markets. There, first under Al Grayson in Dallas, and later managing the Houston office, he became close friends with Harmon Whittington of Anderson Clayton, and when Clayton's Paris manager retired, Reckling was offered the opportunity to succeed him in a position that involved not only cotton but also other commodities. Reckling was unable to resist this opportunity. He'd always wanted to work in Europe anyway. And thus Weil lost one of its best men ever— and also one of the most principled. As a close friend of the du Pasquiers, he could easily have taken the account with him to Clayton, which would have been a feather in his cap since Maison Du Pasquier undoubtedly was the best agency in France. But he never attempted to do so, and that's a rarity in any business.

Yet, as good as Reckling was, he probably could not have accomplished as much for Weil as the man finally chosen to manage the firm's affairs in Europe. Just as Richard Nixon realized that a foreigner with Harvard experience would do better dealing with foreign politicians than a Harvard man with foreign experience, so the Weils eventually picked a naturalized American as their secretary of state. To this day, Peter Frank, head of Unicosa, makes fun of the fact that he was hired largely because he could speak five languages: even European hotel clerks usually manage at least three. But much as Frank might take the mastery of foreign languages for granted, Adolph Weil did not, and for a good reason. He knew that, other things being equal, such linguistic flexibility (Frank speaks even Schwyzerdütsch without an accent), and the cultural adaptability it implied, were essential to real success abroad. As for the intricacies of cotton merchandising, including the fine art of classing, any intelligent man could be trained in the required skills.

It's not surprising that Peter Frank appealed greatly to the Weils. He was a German Jew of good family, well educated, steeped in literature, art, and music; he was Jewish by proud principle only, and otherwise totally assimilated. Indeed, his Germanic pedantries and somewhat ironic sense of humor must have reminded Adolph and Leonel of their father's similar proclivities. Yet Frank was almost as American as European. As a young man, he had worked for publishers in New York City, but more important, he had, before being commissioned in the field, served as an enlisted man in the Eighty-second Airborne. No experience other than being a GI in a gung-ho division could so effectively imbue a non-Southerner with an understanding of Southern ways, for such outfits drew heavily on Dixie. And understanding Southerners was essential for anyone who would bridge the cotton worlds of America and Europe.

Peter Frank was born in Nuremberg in 1923. His father, a prominent lawyer, was more astute than most German Jews. Or perhaps less optimistic. He sent Peter to school in England in 1936 when it was still relatively easy to get out of Nazi Germany. By 1941, Peter was working as a proofreader and writing occasional book reviews for *Horizon*, the magazine edited by poet Stephen Spender and critic Cyril Connolly, which at the time was the showcase for

Peter Frank (right), then a lieutenant in the One-hundred-first Airborne, aided in the capture in May 1945 near Berchtesgaden, Germany, of war criminal Julius Streicher, publisher of the notorious anti semitic porno-propaganda newspaper, *Der Stürmer*. The Nazi fugitive, who grew a beard in an effort to escape detection, is being questioned here by Lieutenant Colonel Paul Danahy, G-2 of the One-hundred-first. Streicher was later convicted at Nuremberg and hanged.—*U.S. Army Signal Corps Photo*

young George Orwell and C. D. Lewis. At that point, Peter's literary career was interrupted when his maternal uncle in New York, Emil Schwarzhaupt, vice-president of Schenley Distilleries (I.W. Harper bourbon), sent him an affidavit and passage money to the States. There, Peter joined his parents and brother Claude, the concert pianist, who had escaped the holocaust via France, Spain, and Brazil. Still plagued by literary ambitions, Peter first obtained a job with the advertising agency that handled the I. W. Harper account, and then went to work for the trade publication *Printer's Ink*.

His draft board sent him greetings in January 1943, whereupon he was assigned to the Army Intelligence School at Camp Richie, Maryland, and from there went back to England, first as a prisoner-of-war interrogator with the Fourth Infantry Division and later, after volunteering for parachute training, with the Eighty-second Airborne. And that's how Peter Frank, in a roundabout way, jumped from a Dakota over the Netherlands and landed in the cotton business.

It so happened that in November 1944, after the Eighty-second was dropped near Arnhem, Peter, then a master sergeant, was second in command of a night reconnaissance patrol that stumbled into a German strong point and took more than thirty prisoners without firing a shot—all by virtue of the fact that Peter spoke native German: in the dark, the Krauts couldn't see that Peter's men wore American uniforms. A stint at Bastogne (where he translated "nuts" for the Germans), a chest covered with fruit salad, and a field commission followed, as did an article about the patrol in *Life*. Among the people who saw the story was Walter Wolf, the owner and president of SAPT (Société Anonyme Produits Textiles), another old family friend, to whom Peter's father, by then a life insurance salesman in New York City, had just sold a hefty policy. Wolf told the elder Frank that he wanted the young man to come to work for him when he got out of the army. Since Wolf was considerably more generous about salaries than *Printer's Ink*, Peter joined SAPT, first in New York, then at the company's headquarters in Zurich, and finally as SAPT's representative in Brussels.

SAPT's business was, and is, cotton waste—the cotton that's swept up from sample room and spinnery floors, the vast quantity of leftover fiber (as much as 10 to 15 percent of raw weight) combed and carded out in spinning. There is a big market for this waste, which is made into furniture stuffing, sterilized into medical cotton, mixed with wood pulp in the making of rag paper, and sometimes respun into inferior yarns. But the waste business is less a matter of cotton expertise than of astute trading: buying low and selling high, tapping new sources and finding new customers. Still, cotton-waste merchants operate in the same arena as regular cotton merchants, and the same agent often represents both. Such also was the case in Belgium, where Brementhal handled SAPT as well as Weil. Willy himself devoted most of his time to the bigger Weil account. He had another man in his office to take care of the waste business, and when this man died in 1953, it was arranged between SAPT and Brementhal to share Peter Frank's services as their waste specialist, working both the Belgian and Netherlands markets.

It was during his tenure of this post that Peter was introduced to Adolph on one of the latter's European trips. Almost the first thing Adolph asked Peter when Willy introduced them was what languages he spoke (English, German, Italian, French and Dutch). There the matter rested until Peter's 1956 Christmas visit to his mother in New York. When he arrived at her West End Avenue apartment, he found a message from Pick Butler to call him at the office: the Weils wanted Peter to come down to Montgomery as soon as possible to discuss a position as the firm's general representative in Europe. The terms were agreed on in short order, and a few weeks later Peter found himself at Murdoch's in Memphis, the only Weil staffer ever to be trained as a squidge while already an executive.

To establish its own man in Europe had become increasingly important to the firm. Before World War II, Adolph and Leonel used to rotate their summer selling trips, and the cycle was revived after the war when Leonel went to Europe in 1948, Bobby in 1949, and Bucks in 1950. Within a few years, however, with business in Central America growing and the international market patterns beginning to change, the scope and tempo of Weil's activities precluded the absence of Bucks or Bobby for eight to ten weeks every year. What's more, by the mid-1950s, as the government initiated programs to work off its cotton surpluses, export was picking up so fast that Bobby and Bucks had to devote a disproportionate amount of time to supervising the foreign merchandising activities. A full-time executive in Europe could do the year round what the Weils had crammed into short summers, and work more effectively with agents at the same time.

Peter's first assignment was to establish a Weil Selling Agency, headquartered in Brussels, that would coordinate all of the firm's marketing on the Continent. Europe's mills then still used between two and three million bales a year of U.S. cotton. Since by then most agents, including Kronauer in Milan, represented not only Weil but other American merchants as well, a centralized effort such as Peter's would be of great help in increasing Weil's share of the volume.

This is indeed what happened, except that by the late 1960s most of the Continent's textile mills, like Britain's before them, were moribund, and the consumption of U.S. fiber had dropped to less than one million bales a year. Of Europe's total annual cotton use of approximately 4.5 million bales, all the rest were imported from other countries, primarily Russia, and in the long staples, from Egypt, Peru, and the Sudan. The great post–World War II surge of American cotton exports to the Continent was finished.

13

Shanghai Checks

By a quirk of historical circumstance, Weil's single biggest foreign customer during Europe's cotton boom wasn't any of the Continental textile countries. It was China, one of the world's three largest cotton producers itself. What occasioned the 300,000-bale honeymoon was that this vast country, then only recently liberated from the Japanese, was so disorganized under Chiang Kai-shek that her own cotton could not be transported to the mills of Shanghai.

Carl Baquie was then manager of Weil–New York, a lean man of medium height, sinuous and athletic, a recent Coast Guard two-striper who had skippered LSTs in New Guinea and in the first wave that landed in the Philippines, as Douglas MacArthur had so dramatically promised. A sailor at heart, Baquie had the contradictory makeup of the rough-and-tough mariners of fiction: often brusque and short tempered, a no-nonsense man's man, but gentle with his friends. A New Orleans Frenchman, he was born in 1907, the third generation of his family in the cotton business at this old cotton port. When Carl was a boy, Memphis and Delta cotton still floated down the Mississippi on barges, to be sold from tables in New Orleans factors' offices. The New Orleans Cotton Exchange stood at the corner of Carondelet and Gravier Streets, and all the cotton business took place within a radius of about four blocks from that location. Carl took a stab at college, then went to work for Sylvan Newberger & Son, the son being Kirby Newberger, eventually one of

Carl's very best friends. The man who hired Carl was the Nathan Rosenfield who later worked for Weil. Nathan was then head classer at Newberger's. Before Carl pulled his first sample, Nathan lectured him about the sample room porters, the Negroes (New Orleans people didn't say "Nigger") whose function it was to unwrap and reroll the samples and to keep track of them. "Don't you go out," Nathan said, peering sternly in Carl's eyes. "Don't you go out and make trouble for those Negroes. We need them, but we don't need you."

After two years, as customary, Carl was sent out into the country to buy a few bales here and there from farmers, ginners and country cotton merchants, small middlemen most of whom also ran general stores so they'd have something to carry them through bad crops. The second time Carl went out, he bought one hundred bales from a "very proper gentleman," a deacon in the church, altogether as respectable as they come. Afterwards, sitting around with a few of the older, more experienced cotton buyers, he was asked how he had bought the cotton. Carl replied that he had purchased it on warehouse weights, i.e., on the weights that the merchant's warehouse had put on the receipts. The older men shook their heads in mock disbelief, had a good laugh, and told Carl he still had a lot to learn. Sure enough, when the cotton reached New Orleans, it was short by about twenty pounds a bale. Says Carl, who is now retired at Sewall's Point on Florida's east coast and given to months-long voyages on his forty-two footer with this wife, Virginia, a Red Cross girl he'd met in Australia during the war, "You get no medals for that kind of buying. But that's the way to get the hang of this business." Highly principled himself, he hasn't been altogether trustful of most people since.

Much to Carl's regret, Newberger soon went on the rocks, and Carl, then twenty-one years old, took a job as classer with H. R. Gould & Co., which, like all other New Orleans cotton houses, has since gone out of business. This job lasted until 1932 when Carl quit and found himself out on the street along with countless other men at that time. But he had good connections. Kirby Newberger introduced him to Alvin Weil, and Alvin spoke to A. M. Crawford, Sr., up in Memphis. John Wagner gave Carl a classing test, which he passed even though he had just sprained the joint on his right index finger, and he spent the next year working for Weil at this inland port. But being a saltwater man at heart, the Mississippi River struck him as a dull puddle. He disliked living so far from the sea and said so. Now something happened that sheds an interesting light on Crawford. Remember, he was considered a hard man. Yet he sympathzied enough with Carl actually to create a job for him: he established the young man in New Orleans as forwarder of the cotton Memphis handled. To begin with, there were only two local mills, Lane and Maginnis (both since out of business) that did any buying of consequence. But as the Depression abated and war clouds darkened Europe's skies, the export business picked up, and soon Carl had two people working for him, an assistant, George Brown, fresh from the Memphis office, and a New Orleans maiden lady, Evelyn Burt, who had previously worked for another forwarder. Handling export cotton was right up Carl's alley. With his lifelong interest in ships, he had absorbed the intricate details involved in transporting ocean freight: the interplay of insurance rates and nationalities of ships, the vicissitudes of schedules, the pros and cons of mixed cargos; in short, how to figure out the least costly, most efficient way to get one's goods to where they were supposed to go and get them there on time. This, combined with his knowledge of cotton, would prove to be invaluable in Carl Baquie's future and to Weil's expertise not only as an exporter of American fiber but as a merchant of foreign growths.

Carl's first experiences in export while still with Newberger had their humorous aspects. The Russians were big buyers then, and, as with Leonel and Greengrass in Corpus Christi, they manifested their ignorance also in New Orleans. Quite naturally, the Russian buyers were nervous; if they made mistakes they wouldn't just be fired but quite possibly be fired on. They wouldn't take cotton on samples but insisted that the samples were cut from the bales in their presence. So the bales, one by one, would be brought before the Russian who sat behind a desk, glowering, and the American sampler would cut into the bale and the Russian would pull the sample. Every once in a while, he would reject a bale. The rejected bale was then removed, taken around the back, and eventually brought in again, turned around so that the earlier hole wouldn't show. That time, or the time after, or the next day (with the hole now sewed up), the Russian would be sure to buy the bale. Lest an unfamiliar reader conclude this was unethical, let him be informed that this was fair and square: the cotton hadn't been doctored or switched, and if the Russian buyers had really known what they were doing they either wouldn't have rejected such samples the first time around or, conversely, would have continued to reject them every time they were presented: either the cotton was good or it wasn't; it certainly didn't change in the process of being moved around. It should be pointed out in this connection that presenting rejected bales a second, or even third time, to the same buyer is not unknown in domestic business either. Buyers, especially young ones still trying to show how important they are, sometimes tend to be quite unreasonable at the first go-round, rejecting nearly everything they look at. Out of one hundred bales, such a buyer might take forty and turn down the rest. Those sixty would then be married with the next set of samples shown to him the next day, and the buyer, having demonstrated his perspicacity and now an equal among equals, would accept them for shipment without question.

The New Orleans forwarding office was closed as exports petered out after the Nazi armies overwhelmed France and the Low Countries. Five years later, as soon as Carl Baquie had swapped his uniform for civvies, he was assigned to the New York office, whose Bob Murray was about to depart for Bunge & Born, the once Belgian, now Argentinian cotton giant. Carl's window, on the fourteenth floor of the Cotton Exchange Building, overlooked the East River, and many were the times when, with great longing, he watched ships coming in and puzzled why it took their captains so long to maneuver them to dockside; he'd done better than that, even under fire. But this period didn't last long. In June 1946, Adolph and Leonel proposed that he go to Shanghai, the capital of China's textile industry, to sell its mills which were now ravenous for cotton. It was expected that Carl would be absent for some time, and Bucks was dispatched to replace him temporarily as manager of the New York office.

Japan's defeat had not brought peace to China. The Russians, who had occupied Manchuria in their last-minute war on Nippon, refused to leave the newly taken territory, and in the meantime provided tacit, and occasionally also overt, support to Mao Tse-tung and his Communist minions. On the other side of the fence, the United States backed Chiang Kai-shek's Kuomintang. Trying to forestall a full-scale civil war, the new U.S. ambassador, Patrick J. Hurley, with the help of George C. Marshall, had arranged meetings between Chiang and Mao, but to no avail. Fighting continued between the two factions and steadily grew in intensity. Shanghai, although the front lines were still hundreds of miles away, teetered on the edge of wholesale starvation. There was no transportation system to bring food from the interior to this port city of some seven million, nor even any infrastructure that could try to tackle this problem. Masses of people, many of them homeless, jammed the streets; at night they sheltered in the doorways of the splendid commercial buildings that stood as monuments to the era of Western extraterritoriality, which had ended in fact, if not yet in law, with the Japanese occupation. In this seething sea of misery flourished islands of untold wealth. The lordship of Nippon had by no means diminished the fortunes of the truly rich Chinese. Nor had the Japanese interfered to any great degree with the lives of European nationals whose countries were not at war with Japan. These neutrals included numerous exiled Russians, Tsarists, and other refugees from the Communist regime, who not only survived but sometimes even prospered under Japanese rule.

As usual under such anarchic circumstances, the infusions of U.S. aid benefited mostly those who needed help the least. The "China Lobby" effectively filtered all criticism of Chiang's administration. Warnings of the inevitable consequences went unheeded even when they came from such respected statesmen as Joseph E. Davies, the former ambassador to Russia and then chief of Truman's War Relief Control Board, and Clarence E. Gauss, the former ambassador to Chungking, whom the Chinese had graced with the sobriquet, "the honest Buddha."

In the Shanghai area, textiles were the one industry that could provide any significant employment. All the mills were intact. The terror bombings of 1937, concentrated on the downtown area, had not touched them, and they had been operative, under Japanese auspices, throughout the war. Interestingly enough, unlike the mills in Japan proper, they had not been stripped of their machinery to make room for war production. Yet, while cotton was in fairly good supply in the Chinese hinterland, there was no way to bring it to the city. The only course to get the Shanghai spinneries back into spinning was to import massive quantities of cotton by ship from abroad. Clayton had been the first to supply the sorely needed fiber. Even before the subdued Japanese warlords trooped aboard the U.S.S. *Missouri* in their stovepipe hats to sign the surrender, Anderson Clayton, astute as always, had consigned boatloads of cotton for Shanghai to arrive the minute the shooting was over. Its man on the scene was a Swiss national who had lived in Shanghai before the war. Rumor had it that he was paid a dollar for each bale he sold, plus all expenses. In one year, he was reputed to have made close to one million dollars in commissions, tax free, considerably more than the combined salaries of that company's top executives.

When Carl arrived at long last in Shanghai, he put up at the Cathay Hotel, along with all the other visiting Westerners.* Getting to Shanghai, while hardly cheap, had not been a major investment. Staying there was. Restaurants frequented by the rich locals and expense-account Americans billed on the basis of signed chits that were delivered to the Cathay and charged to the guests' accounts. Carl's palatial room looked out on the Wangpoo River, the Yangtze tributary that sloshes past the city. The river was nearly obscured by junks tied abreast, freeboard against freeboard, an undulating slum. Carl had seen dead GIs and Marines stacked like cordwood on Pacific beaches. Now he had to watch "dead wagons" cruising the streets, picking up hunger-shriveled corpses. At the half-empty Cathay, at the Long Bar of the Shanghai Club, in the mills' offices, and at the banks, life masqueraded as normal—normal, that is, by Shanghai standards, a mix of the Oriental and continental European, cynical and devious.

Only a trickle of Americans had so far reached postwar Shanghai. Being one of them opened many doors for Carl. Even so, to have operated blindly in Shanghai's chaos would have been impossible. But Carl had not come unprepared. He carried introductions from Ambassador Gauss (later a director of the Export-Import Bank) and, while still in New York, he had arranged contacts with two long-established Shanghai merchant firms, S. E. Levy & Co. and Arnhold Trading Co. A Wall Streeter by the name of Buchan, the Levy partner in New York and associated with White, Weld, had arranged entree to his Shanghai principals: Rudy Koppelman and Nat Concoff, stateless Russians who had lived in Shanghai since the Bolshevik Revolution. The fact that they were Jewish had made no difference to the Japanese, to whom the Nazis were merely allies of convenience;

---

*The old Cathay is now the Peace Hotel.

there was no ideological link. Thus Rudy and Nat survived the Holocaust at safe distance, and while not getting richer seemed to have had a fairly amusing time. Rudy's mistress was a statuesque English showgirl type who had first come to Shanghai before the war as the wife of an influential Chinese. When war broke out, her husband clapped his hands to finish that union, and left with their children for Chungking to join the Generalissimo's entourage. The young lady then moved in with a Chinese puppet radio broadcaster, resisting Rudy's invitations to join him instead, until the radio man decided to commit suicide when it became obvious that the Yanks were about to move in on Shanghai and would no doubt arrange for his prompt departure by way of a war criminal's noose. That's when the lady finally succumbed to Rudy's more enduring charms. Not that those charms were eternal. When Rudy showed up broke in Montgomery a few years later to borrow some money from Adolph, the lady had long since departed. Adolph did help him out; like Isidor he was tightfisted only in business. Rudy then disappeared from the Weil scene, never to be heard from again.

Much as Carl Baquie was eager to get away from Shanghai's there-shall-be-no-night existence—his wife, back home, was awaiting their first child—he spent some time investigating the possibility of opening an agency there for sales to Chinese mills. But he soon gave up the idea as it became increasingly apparent that the Generalissimo's China dangled by a precarious string. Almost every Western businessman Carl met advised him against making any permanent commitment. There was no doubt that Mao would eventually take over; the only question was when. All things considered, the course was to sell as much cotton as possible and get out while the gettin' was good.

The selling was easy enough. The problem was getting paid. Almost immediately, Carl placed 17,500 bales, a whole shipload, with one of the largest Shanghai mill groups. That lot at $200 a bale was worth 3.5 million dollars, but Weil didn't see the money until many months later.

The contract, intermediated by Rudy and Nat, called for payment three days before arrival of the vessel. When the mill did not pay as agreed, Weil faced a difficult choice, one that cost everyone involved many a night's sleep. With the agreement violated, Weil could refuse

Shanghai was ruled by Chiang Kai-shek (see poster on Nan-king Road below) when Weil sent Carl Baquie to China in 1946. That teeming port, the West's outpost on the mainland until the Japanese occupation, still looked like a metropolis, with boulevards like the Bund (left) reminiscent of European capitals, but it was moribund. Teetering on the brink of disaster—and soon plunging into it—Chiang's China lacked the infrastructure to feed Shanghai's millions, much less transport cotton from the interior to the city's many mills. Within a few weeks, Carl sold some 300,000 bales, a veritable record, eventually to be unloaded along Shanghai's waterfront (top left) and cleared at the Customs Building (right). Carl even managed to make sure that Weil was paid in full for every single bale.—*All photos except Baquie portrait by United Press International*

to deliver and instruct the ship's master to change course and steam for Europe; there would be no problem selling cotton on that continent, but the additional freight charges would end all prospects of profit and perhaps even result in a loss. Or Weil could take the chance of putting the cotton ashore in a Shanghai "godown," as warehouses are called in the Chinese Orient, and hope for eventual payment. This alternative was potentially more profitable but entailed a twofold risk: one, that the mill might never pay; and two, that the cotton could be destroyed in an act of war, not an impossibility under the circumstances. If the latter were to happen, Weil would not be covered by insurance, since cargoes destined for war zones are covered only so long as they are aboard ship. In either eventuality, Weil would lose not merely the freight charges, but the cotton as well.

After long and tense considerations, Adolph and Leonel finally decided to deliver the cotton. The U.S. Government had guaranteed, if somewhat ambiguously, to compensate exporters for possible losses suffered in dealing with the Chinese, and the Weils figured they might as well trust Uncle Sam. This almost turned out to be a 3.5-million-dollar mistake.

Meanwhile, Carl Baquie, much as he had been amused by Rudy's and Nat's company, no longer had much faith in the Levy partners' judgment, and he increasingly relied on Arnhold Trading Co., whose Shanghai manager, a Briton by the name of William Russell, was of less adventurous bent. This was a wise move. Russell's input proved invariably correct. When he said that with certain mills Weil could count on being paid at shipside, that's what happened. And when he wasn't absolutely certain that a mill was good for payment, then no deal was struck. Of the 350,000 bales Baquie would sell to Shanghai's spinners before the Communists took over in 1949, only those first 17,500 bales were ever in jeopardy.

Carl Baquie, guided by Willy Russell, initiated most of the connections himself. His greatest coup was to get a share of the business of the Wing On mill group, China's second largest textile complex. The Kwoks, who once owned these mills along with a number of other enterprises (including Shanghai's one big department store), had until then dealt only with Anderson Clayton. Baquie's courtship of David Kwok, a tall, dour Chinese who, like all the other members of his family, spoke superb English, took considerable patience. Time after time, Baquie met with Kwok, who kept on telling him what a great company Anderson Clayton was. All this time Baquie never mentioned business. Finally, one day, having invited Carl to lunch, Kwok asked him, "Don't you wish to sell us any cotton?" As Carl recalls, "It took a lot of willpower to refrain from showing too much enthusiasm. That just wasn't done."

Carl contracted so much cotton for forward delivery that, at times, Weil could not supply all that was required. In those cases, always with Adolph's and Leonel's consent, Carl would buy cotton "guaranteed through" from competitors, among them Cook & Co., Allenberg, Goedecke (the same who shares Greengrass' fame for inventing blending), and Grunow, Hogg & Co. Of all these, only Allenberg is today still in the cotton business. In order to effect his sales most profitably, Carl applied all the shipping knowledge he had garnered in New Orleans. He foresaw and carefully avoided the dangers of chartering, which puts the charterer at risk of heavy demurrage penalties for delays in loading and unloading. Instead, he booked on "liner" terms where the freight rate was fixed, regardless of the difficulties that might be encountered at the ports. This was a major consideration in Chinese waters, and particularly so when tramp steamers were used, since they were not always totally dependable. Moreover, Carl made it a point to book full cargoes; that way he had complete control over the ship.

His performance in Shanghai was a veritable tour de force. He flew back to the States just four months later, leaving local Shanghai arrangements in the care of Arnhold's Willy Russell. He himself attended to the shipping contracts out of New York. The remaining challenge was to collect the 3.5 million dollars owing on his first sale.

Luckily, however, Carl Baquie had always been an extremely careful operator. When he had obtained the order, Red Reed, then vice-president in charge of the National City Bank branch in Shanghai, had advised him that it would be a good idea to get the contract countersigned and sealed by the Chinese government's Central Bank. Baquie complied. Suppressing his natural impatience, he waited for more than three hours until one of Chiang's bureaucrats finally found the time to impress the "chop"—the official Chinese seal—upon the contract.

The seal proved of little use in Washington, however. Nor did letters from National City and Chase do much good. Finally, in his meanderings through the corridors of governmental power, Baquie encountered a department head in the State Department, Thayer White, who, unlike his superiors, took the trouble to look at the Shanghai contract. "When he'd read through it," recalls Baquie, "he asked if the seal was that of the Central Bank. I told him it was, and he said in that case he would see to it that we received our money, plus interest of six percent."*

Unwittingly, Carl's persistence in obtaining the seal had saved the day for Weil, for it so happened that the "Aid to China" program embodied a provision that any contract between U.S. and Chinese nationals, which had the official approval of a Chinese government agency, was to be guaranteed by the Chinese government. The State Department now got behind the claim, and the firm was paid.

Some final notes to close the Shanghai chapter:

Most of Carl's cotton contacts managed to flee the city before and after the Communists marched in. Willy Russell established himself in Hong Kong, which soon produced more textiles for export to Western nations than Shanghai ever had, and, conversely, imported more cotton, including considerable quantities from Weil. Along the way, Willy became Arnhold's chairman and acquired a beautiful Russian wife. His trading activities were by no means restricted to cotton. When Carl Baquie visited him in 1967, Willy had just sold one million dollars worth of Swiss watches to the People's Republic of China.

Oriental wonders never cease: David Kwok. after escaping Shanghai and moving to Hong Kong, decided to return and manage the family's mills for the Communists. This, he was convinced, would be the only way that the family might ever get their properties back if and when the Communists were ousted.

---

*Carl Baquie, in relating these events, wanted to be sure the following comment found its way into print: "After the payment matter was settled, I had my brother, then executive vice-president of Brown Foreman Distilleries, send Thayer White a case of 'personalized' Old Forester at Christmas—heck, I would have sent him a Cadillac in gratitude. Anyway, shortly afterward, Thayer sent back the gift. He said that as a government employee he could not accept it. There weren't many like him around."

As for Occidental accidents: Rudy Koppelman, of S. E. Levy, also got out by the skin of his teeth—as a Russian, he could well have ended up in more trouble with Mao than with Tojo. In New York City, some time before he went to Montgomery to hit Adolph for the loan, his taxi cab was struck by a stray bullet in a shootout between gangsters near Times Square. The bullet nicked his knickers and their contents.

In Japan, unlike in China, Weil Brothers was to establish a permanent base, the Weil Selling Agency in Osaka, which was originally headed by Russell Eaton. More recently, it has been under the direction of Masahide Yoshida, with Rujuhei Nishi as office manager, Ahira Hanada as salesman, and Mrs. Katsuko Abe as secretary. The Weil Selling Agency is not a subsidiary of Weil Brothers, but a separate legal entity, which acts as an agent for Weil.

Japan, with imports of some three million bales a year, is one of the five major textile producers in today's Orient, along with the PRC, Korea, Hong Kong and Taiwan. This is in large measure due to the efforts of General Douglas MacArthur, who pursued the revitalization of Nippon with the same vigor he had applied to defeating the country. The Japanese textile industry had all but been destroyed in World War II. Mills that had survived the bombings had been stripped and their equipment scrapped for use in ordnance. Under MacArthur's military government, the wrecked Japanese spinneries were rebuilt and refurbished with the world's finest, most modern machinery almost overnight.

MacArthur also broke up Japan's great cartels, among them Mitsui and Mitsubishi, whose efficiencies had so enhanced that country's military potential. Both, Mitsui and Mitsubishi, were involved in cotton, as in just about everything else, but in this particular arena, Mitsubishi was the more important. One of its separate segments, a cotton merchant establishment, seemed at the time the most promising candidate to represent Weil in Japan. The use of a merchant, rather than an agent, was necessary since under Japanese law the country's mills were not permitted to buy cotton from other than Japanese merchants.

The arrangement with Mitsubishi worked very well until the occupation ended in 1951. Then Mitsubishi and the other cartels promptly put themselves back together again, and it became increasingly difficult for Weil to sell cotton to the mills of the other combines through a Mitsubishi splinter. In 1954, Adolph decided to sever the Mitsubishi connection and to retain the services of Russell Eaton, a former Weil staffer, who had been the prime mover in the resurrection of the Japanese textile industry under MacArthur's reign.

Russell Eaton, a slightly chubby gentleman of happy disposition, had begun his career with Weil in Memphis, and later managed a textile mill owned by William M. Vermilye, a vice-president of the National City Bank (1937–1944), whose daughter, Neni, he eventually married. Still later, he entered the U.S. Foreign Service and served a tour in Greece, with particular responsibilities in the textile area—additional experience that made him a prominent member of the postwar military government.

To ask Eaton back aboard proved to be a most fortuitous choice. As the great benefactor of Japan's mills, their owners regarded him almost as a demigod. As soon as he became Weil's agent in Osaka, most of them insisted that their Japanese suppliers buy their cotton from Weil.

The success of any enterprise depends in equal measure on luck, perception, timing, and hard work. This magic combination also fell into place here. As Russell Eaton rejoined Weil, the firm was just hitting full stride on a new and unprecedented venture: the merchandising of cotton grown in other countries, specifically, at that time, those of Central America. Under Eaton's auspices, the Weil Selling Agency became the big mover of these growths. By the time other merchants caught on to what was happening, Weil held the advantage that accrues to those who get there fastest with the mostest.

14

Samples from Managua

LIKE SO MANY IMPORTANT ENDEAVORS, Weil's expansion into foreign growths—which would culminate years later in the formations of Algodonera Weil and Unicosa—had a most insignificant beginning. A man with an Hispanic accent came to the New York office one day in 1948 and announced that he had some Nicaraguan cotton to sell. To show that he meant business, he plunked a bag containing samples on Pick Butler's desk.

At the time, Carl Baquie was off on a trip to Akron, Ohio, helping Alvin sell cotton for cordage to Firestone. Pick, then still assistant manager, thought the Nicaraguan's proposition somewhat nebulous. The visitor, Gerardo Salinas, admitted he had no financial backing; still, the samples in his satchel appeared salable. They were FAQ cotton, which means fair average quality without specifying any one particular grade or staple, but, even so, suitable to the requirements of many mills.

Under normal circumstances, Weil would not have taken action on so vague an approach. The risks of doing business in Central America seemed to outweigh any possible gain. For one thing, Central American crops were hardly impressive in volume. Nicaragua then harvested no more than 5,000 bales a season. El Salvador, which grew about 20,000, sold all its cotton through its *Cooperativa* to Britain, which, as you will recall, had begun to purchase its requirements through a government agency. Guatemala and Colombia harvested barely enough most years to keep their own mills going;

303

sometimes there was a little cotton left for export, but usually they had to import it. Costa Rica was a minimal producer. In short, there wasn't a whole lot to be had anywhere in the region. Financing, too, would be a problem. In the United States, banks backed Weil all the way, but south of the border the firm had no standing whatsoever.

Even more important, having missed the boat in Mexico earlier, no one in the Weil organization had any experience in dealing with foreign countries at the rural level. Doing business with foreign mills and merchants was something entirely different: in that stratum, everyone spoke the same language. But not so at the farms and gins, particularly in the "banana republics," which were in many ways less developed than are some of the so-called "underdeveloped" countries of the Third World today. Add the dangers of social unrest: in Central America, coups and revolutions followed each other in perpetuity.

So it is hardly surprising that Pick did not commit himself on the spot. The situation was far too tenuous for that. To begin with, there had to be assurance of delivery in sufficient volume to generate a margin of profit; by the same token, Pick had to find customers willing to take up the Nicaraguan cotton and pay enough for it. Thus, Weil's entry into this new arena was extremely tentative.

After Pick had lined up some mills to buy the Nicaraguan FAQ cotton if it became available, Leonel sent him to Managua to bring back samples that he himself had cut. By then, that year's crop was almost finished and all Pick could obtain through Salinas' somewhat feeble contacts was a couple hundred bales. Considering the time and cost involved, this barely was worthwhile. Pick promptly returned to New York and devoted his attention to more important business.

There the matter would have rested had not another Nicaraguan visitor, Gabriel Horvilleur, poked his head in the door two years later. Unlike Salinas, Horvilleur sported impressive credentials, including a letter of introduction from the Chase. Gabriel Horvilleur, a bespectacled rotund gentleman, was the son of a Frenchman who had come to Nicaragua at the turn of the century with Dreyfus & Cie., to this day one of the world's leading commodity merchant firms. The sophisticated Horvilleur family quickly established itself within the wafer-thin upper crust of Nicaraguan society, founding an alliance with the Palazios, one of several illustrious clans that had immigrated from Italy. Together with the Palazios, several of whom were close to the coterie of General Anastasia "Tacho" Somoza, the Horvilleurs formed Palazio, Horvilleur, & Co., an offspring of which was Industria Nicaragua Agricolas (INA), with Gabriel Horvilleur as the managing partner in charge of cotton activities. If any organization could make sure of delivery of more than token quantities of cotton, it was INA, the largest single factor in Nicaraguan commodities from seed to sale.

The two samples Horvilleur brought with him to New York had been grown in the Granada area of southern Nicaragua where INA had its gins. Horvilleur's cotton, like Salina's, was also FAQ, but he offered it at only thirty cents a pound net weight, which in the 1950–51 season—the one time in all history when the United States found itself so short of cotton that exports were embargoed—made it an exceptional bargain. If Weil could bring foreign growths to market even in small quantities, the firm could only gain. To get things rolling with INA, Carl ordered 300 tons on the basis of the samples, bales unseen, a modest $180,000 transaction. Like the earlier Nicaraguan cotton, it was sold forward.

Now another coincidence came into play. It so happened that at almost the same time Horvilleur visited the New York office, the Continental Gin Co., a maker of gins in Prattville, Alabama, on the outskirts of Montgomery, received an order to build a gin for the Duque-Estradas, a family of Nicaraguan entrepreneurs who had made their money in the hardware business and owned lands in the León area, about fifty miles north of Managua. This perked Adolph's and Leonel's interest considerably. Between Gabriel Horvilleur's INA and Don Estaban Duque-Estrada's gin operation, Weil had the chance to cover much of the cotton-growing acreage in Nicaragua's fertile strip along the Pacific. Adolph arranged a meeting between Carl Baquie and Carlos Duque-Estrada, one of Don Esteban's sons who had been sent on the mission to Continental Gin. Shortly thereafter, Baquie flew to Nicaragua to make arrangements with both organizations.

On January 1, 1951, still sleepy from New Year's Eve, Pick Butler joined him to buy and take up the cotton, which already had been contracted by the thousands of bales to Japanese mills through Russell Eaton and to European mills through the Kronauers of Milan, Du Pasquier in France and Brementhal in Belgium. There had been no shortage of takers. With the American cotton embargo and Europe's economies racing along in high gear, spinners were in a panic, and the price of fiber rose with every passing day as they all tried to outbid each other.

Despite the temptation of higher bids, INA certainly wouldn't lay down (as the cotton term goes) on its commitments: United States currency was a most precious commodity. As for distinguished, utterly honest Don Estaban, Carl had no doubt that he would deliver to the letter of the contract. And Nicaraguan weather was nearly predictable as California's: there would be no problem with the crop.

But trouble erupted, quite literally, within two weeks of Pick Butler's arrival, during which time one of his checks was filched, promptly cashed, and cleared before he was even aware of the theft. He was on his way to León when the black cone of Cerro Negro, which had been dormant for decades, suddenly started spewing untold tons of volcanic ash over the cotton fields of the very farmers who had contracted with Duque-Estrada. Cerro Negro kept spitting for two weeks, permeating the fiber with its cinders. The cotton, heavy with grit, was rushed to Don Esteban's new Continental gin, in which he had invested all his cash, counting on a huge return. But now the brand new gin was ruined the first season. The volcanic particles chewed up the blades in the suction pipe, and friction heat from the laboring machinery did further damage. The fans of the blowers overheated and often didn't even last out a whole day; there was no way to keep enough spares on hand, and makeshift repairs, welding together the fractured parts, only worsened the situation. Still, the moribund gin labored along, sounding like Dante's inferno. Outside, meanwhile, the ginned-out volcanic ash piled up higher than the building.

The dirty cotton made it shipside at last and eventually reached the mills as promised, even if not in prime condition. Some months after the dusty shipments had been delivered to the spinners, Carl heard comments from Japan and Europe that there was a lot of "sand" in the bales that caused them to lose weight. But with the market price for cotton considerably higher by the time those bales arrived than what the spinners had to pay for them, complaints were minimal and there were no claims.

Far more serious was the fact that most of Duque-Estrada's farmers who possessed undamaged cotton, as well as some of those with gritty fiber, refused to deliver their crops at the contracted prices. To be sure, Nicaragua was primitive; chickens cackled and hogs snuffled all over the streets of León, its second largest city, entering houses as they pleased and even attending services at the fine old church. But there were radios and of course the eternal jungle telegraph, and it didn't take the Nicaraguan growers long to find out that the world was paying premium rates for cotton. Naturally they demanded more money, and could not care less if the gringos they were dealing with lost out in the process.

However, the loser in this instance was Don Esteban, a fine gentleman but hardly a walking business encyclopedia. Gabriel Horvilleur at INA had anticipated that some of the farmers might lay down, and he had gone long to protect himself against that eventuality. This Don Esteban had not done, and thus he left himself wide open. Being of the old school, he made sure that Carl and Pick got their cotton as per contract, regardless of what it would cost him in the end, which turned out to be $130,000, not a great sum by U.S. business standards but a fortune in Nicaragua. This was the amount due Weil, for that's what was needed to cover the cotton sold to Weil but not delivered by Duque Estrada. Don Esteban told Carl that if he were forced to the wall on the issue, he'd have to go bankrupt. But if Carl gave him time to work it out, he would make up those losses. Carl, no less a gentleman, and with the backing of Adolph and Leonel, agreed to put his faith in the old man on the line, and within two seasons Weil got back every single cent. Henceforth, Weil worked with Duque Estrada on joint account, an arrangement that lasted until a year after the old gentleman's death in 1956. Then Weil pulled out: Don Esteban's sons weren't quite of the same caliber.

A letter written by Pick on February 14, 1951, to Carl Baquie, who had returned to New York, evidences the frustrations of this first year in Central America. "In view of the high prices," he reported, "there is probably more jealousy, hostility, snooping, lying, etc. here than ever before.... I'll give you a brief summary of my activities.... On arrival I went to Manticas' (the gin manager's) office. He was ready to offer about 200 but wanted me to class before buying. I told him I

would look at a few samples and give him an idea what to expect but
he was afraid the owner (the farmer) might think he and I were
gypping him and if the price was higher later would refuse to deliver. I
told him they had the protection of the U.S. arbitration and he said
he himself still had every confidence in my class but the farmers... were suspicious of everyone. Anyway he asked me to return at 5
and he offered the cotton which turned out to be a defaulter's and I
turned it down. He agreed with me and claimed he was not aware of
this. I had found out that this farmer was a defaulter from Carlos. I
thought he (the gin manager) was going to stab me in the back when I
turned down that business...."

Prices kept rising and the laydowns continued into yet another
season. To expedite delivery of orders by now contracted to Europe
and Japan, Carl finally resorted to letting farmers set their own class.
Inevitably, they graded their cotton higher than it actually was. But
the way Carl figured it, any cotton was better than no cotton at this
point, and he knew that the fiber, even if not of high quality, couldn't
be below a certain grade. The farmers lugged their sacks of samples
into the gin office, where under normal conditions they'd be opened
and classed by the buyer. The first few times Carl did go through the
sacks and said in his kitchen Spanish, "It's not Strict Middling but
we'll take it." After a while, this didn't seem worth the bother. He
simply kicked the sacks as they were placed before him and grunted
"Strict Middling," hoping to conclude the deal before the farmer
changed his mind and walked out. When the samples reached
Montgomery, Adolph was understandably upset, and he instructed
Carl to force the Nicaraguan farmers to deliver correctly. "But all
these guys in León are packing guns," Carl said, whereupon Adolph
replied, "Oh don't worry about that. They only carry them to protect
themselves from wild animals." Said Carl, "I'll be sure to tell them
that."

Folkloric as Nicaragua may have appeared in the de la Varre–type
travelogues of that era, such was not the case. General Somoza's since
much maligned regime was the first that had brought a semblance of
order to the country since the U.S. Marines had moved out in 1925
and left hapless Nicaragua to its own devices. León was still
pockmarked from bullets fired a century earlier when filibuster
William Walker, the adventurer from Nashville, Tennessee, briefly

gained control of the country and made his headquarters in this city. When Carl and Pick first went to Nicaragua, the Pan-American Highway had not yet been built. Traveling between Managua and León, or between Managua and Granada, they had the choice between taking their chances in a flimsy biplane of ancient vintage, piloted by a former carnival barnstormer from the States; or riding aboard a *gasolino*, a railroad "hand cart" powered with a carbon-clogged internal combustion engine that thundered fitfully along the single track. The *gasolinos* always carried armed guards to protect the travelers from bandits; when a real train came along, which didn't happen all that often, everybody dismounted and lifted the cart off the rails.

Shipping the purchased cotton to port also presented problems. Somoza, by his own decree, was the only Nicaraguan permitted to export cattle. Moreover, he preempted all freight trains whenever he had cattle to ship to Corinto, the country's only rail-served port. All other goods had to wait until the general's cattle were safely aboard ship. Those were the official orders. Thus, if you had cotton or coffee to ship, you had to make your own unofficial arrangements. Gabriel Horvilleur knew all about that: he knew a dispatcher who could be bought for about $100 per car.

Carl, a man of principle, had reservations about such dealings; despite Shanghai he remained the proverbial American innocent abroad (which is intended as a compliment, not as an insult). "Gabriel," he said, "suppose I come to you and say I've got a limit from the firm of thirty cents to pay for cotton, but we can buy it for twenty-eight cents, so why don't we buy it at twenty-eight, invoice the firm thirty, and you and I each take five dollars a bale. What would you say?" Gabriel answered, "I'd say you'd be a crook." Well, Carl wanted to know, isn't it equally crooked to bribe the dispatcher? Said Gabriel, "You gringos just don't understand. With you, the government decides what's crooked. Here it's different. That fellow is a poor man, he doesn't make much money. He is entitled to a little handout."

When in Rome do as the Romans do, Uncle Sam notwithstanding; or, put another way, if you want to catch foreign fish, cut their kind of bait. So Carl cut the bait, Horvilleur went fishing, and the cotton moved to port.

That first season, Carl and Pick picked up from Duque-Estrada and INA what they had bought by prior arrangement with Weil. Next, Weil engaged in a joint venture that involved all three parties. This turned out to be unsatisfactory since Duque-Estrada received a larger share of profits than his deliveries warranted. Finally, Weil formed separate joint ventures with Duque-Estrada and INA, and that worked out fine.

Weil initially handled its Central American business through a Delaware-chartered "Western Hemisphere Corporation," an entity for which the Congress had provided certain tax advantages as part of the Good Neighbor Policy. This corporation, Cia. Algodones Extranjeros, Ltda., was eventually superseded by a Panamanian corporation, Algodonera Weil, S.A., and most recently by Weil Hermanos.

Bucks first became familiar with the Latin American operation in the early days of Algodones Extranjeros when he was assigned to the New York office to sub for Carl while the latter went off on vacation. Bucks accompanied Carl to Nicaragua and El Salvador many times in the ensuing years. On one trip, he recalls, he and Carl traveled all the way by jeep from Managua to León to visit the elder Duque-Estrada. Then they jeeped on to Corinto. Their return trip to Managua, a matter of less than eighty miles, took eight hours by train. On that visit too, they went to Granada where the father of Gabriel Horvilleur had his home, and saw Gabriel building cotton-seed warehouses by digging cubic holes twenty feet in each dimension in the limestone, a device to avoid the spread of fires that Gabriel had learned from cotton people in Brazil. Bucks was particularly impressed by INA operations at Chinendega whose manager Señor Montealagre displayed great ingenuity in adapting imported U.S. machinery to severe local conditions. Bucks' forays in Latin America were not without humorous aspects. Once, as he landed in Managua, his plane was met at the airport by the Guardia Naçional complete with band. Carl quipped that he hadn't realized how important Weil was to Nicaragua. What he and Bucks didn't know was that Tachito Somoza, son of Nicaraguan dictator Tacho Somoza, also was aboard.

On another occasion, which did not lend itself to jest, Bucks had stopped off in Guatemala en route to Nicaragua when the Managua office called, advising him to delay his trip since someone had just tried to assassinate Tacho Somoza and that the situation was pre-carious, to say the least. Bucks proceeded anyway, roadblocks between the airport and Managua notwithstanding, and after going through a control where some passengers were rudely searched, arrived in the city just in time to bid farewell to Henk Dewit of the Dutch mill Van Heek & Zonen, Weil's best customer for Nicaraguan cotton. The Dutchman had experienced the Nazi occupation of the Netherlands and couldn't wait to get out of Nicaragua. This did not deter him from his interest in the local cotton. At the earliest opportunity he flew to Panama to negotiate a purchase with Carl, who by that time had an office there.

Carl had operated Extralgo, as Algodones Extranjeros often was referred to, from the fourteenth floor of the old Cotton Exchange Building in New York. As the exigencies of business dictated, he made periodic trips to Nicaragua, as did Pick Butler out of New York, and Alex Carothers, Otis Odom, and Pick Dozier out of Montgom-ery. But communications were poor and commuting laborious. To ease at least the latter, Adolph and Leonel had decided initially to move Carl and his Central American operation to Houston, at which point Pick took over the New York office. But at about that time, attorneys advised Weil that because of location as well as tax laws a Panamanian corporation would be more suited to the firm's purposes than the somewhat ambiguous Western Hemisphere setup, which in any case could be abridged at any moment with the stroke of a government pen.

Panama had long been a tax haven for mailbox companies, a Liechtenstein with palm trees. But Adolph and Leonel wanted none of that. If Weil were to engage in such an extraterritorial enterprise, then, by gosh, it would be a Panamanian company in deed and not just legal lingo. So Carl Baquie moved to Panama City with Virginia and their little girl Lynn (now a U.S. Army nurse), and he staffed up the new headquarters with a contingent that included Thomas J. Carney as office manager, the same position Tom had held in New York. Bucks accompanied Carl to Panama to set up the office and to lease homes for the staff. To assist Carney with the shipping and invoicing, Lee Yarwood, who had trained under Crawford in Memphis and worked with Baquie in Houston, was sent down in

1954. But Yarwood, then thirty-four years old, was tied to Front Street and didn't take to the lifestyle of the Latin countries. Homesick, he was reassigned in 1957, and is now Tom Adams' office manager.

As his own assistant, Carl imported Fritz Ficke, the son of an innkeeper in Blumenthal, Germany, who had apprenticed as a young man with S. Bulley & Son in nearby Bremen, the German cotton port. Fritz had been lucky to get a job when that Liverpool firm reopened its German branch after Versailles: as the Weimar Republic's infamous inflation beat Werner von Braun to the ionosphere, Fritz was paid five dollars a week in U.S. currency, enough to fill several wheelbarrows with billions of marks. Even so he had enough dimes and quarters left to save for his passage to America: "To amount to anything in the cotton business," he says, "you had to spend some time in the U.S." It took Fritz several years to get the fare together and he arrived in Dallas just in time for the stock market crash of 1929. After having a number of cotton jobs collapse under him, he finally found a more solid position in El Paso with R.T. Hoover & Co., handling its export end. Martin Cotton Co. in Phoenix was next on his itinerary, and when World War II broke out he joined Anderson Clayton, which had just opened a branch there to deal in Arizona's premium-priced Pima cotton, an American-Egyptian hybrid of extremely long staple and fine fiber that was in great demand for military parachutes, now that ratcatcher shirts had temporarily gone out of style. Fritz joined Weil in 1949, when Leonel lured him to Montgomery to take charge of the export department, which processed all foreign sales, whether from Memphis, Houston, Fresno, or New York.

From Nicaragua, Carl Baquie rapidly expanded into the other Central American countries, at the same time handling some of Weil's Mexican buying, mostly from gins near Matamoros, in the state of Tamaulipas, which previously had been part of Nathan Rosenfield's territory. First on the list was Guatemala, where the United Fruit Company had begun to release land from its huge holdings to allow the cultivation of cotton. This process was speeded up when Jacobo Arbenz-Guzmán ousted his predecessor, Juan José Arévalo, in 1951. Arbenz, by expropriating Guatemala's large estates, and most specifically those of United Fruit, turned the country into a substantial cotton producer almost overnight. Apart from the drastic expropriation measures, Arbenz's strong-man regime did little to interfere with free enterprise; whether this was because of inefficiency or because of an understanding that the now-Communist country needed capitalist dollars to survive is impossible to say. His agents butchered (literally) a fair number of people they didn't like, but otherwise life went on pretty much as before. The cotton growers, most of them members of old, established families, were almost uniformly reliable, and Carl's man on the spot, Manuel Ortiz, had no problem with deliveries despite all the political turmoil.

Ironically, trouble did not strike until Colonel Carlos Castillo Armas, with covert U.S. backing, toppled Arbenz in the spring of 1954—only to be assassinated himself three years later. At the time of the Castillo Armas coup, Carl was still headquartered in Houston and spending a rare evening at home. He'd been on the road about 240 of the previous 365 days, and he figured it was time to take a breather. With Fritz Ficke en route to Gautemala City to help with the shipping of 3,000 recently purchased bales to Holland, he didn't even think about Guatemala. What he did not know was that Guatemala City's main street, Sixth Avenue, had that morning resumed its traditional role as a shooting gallery, and that Fritz's Pan Am had been turned back from the city's airport without being allowed to land. When Carl turned on the TV to watch the news, he nearly had a heart attack: The S.S. *Springfjord*, a British vessel, had just been bombed and sunk at San Jose, Guatemala's cotton port. "My God!" he yelled, "We've got cotton on that ship!"

Carl was not worried about the cotton already aboard; those bales were covered by insurance. But he knew that in San Jose, a lighter port, the loading process was lengthy and laborious. With the harbor too shallow for vessels of deep draft, cargoes had to be transferred from the docks on lighters, small bargelike craft. Thus there was a good chance that some of the bales were still ashore and hence not covered by war-risk insurance. If, as the newcaster said, the docks had been bombed as well, Weil's loss could be considerable—as much, perhaps, as a quarter million dollars.

Quite naturally, Carl remembered the raids of World War II, and such were the visions the report conjured up in his mind. What actually happened was that the anti-Arbenz pilot of a light plane had dropped a hand grenade on the S. S. *Springfjord*. By a million-to-one fluke, the grenade fell into the funnel and exploded deep inside the ship, setting it afire. It sank without loss of life, but the 1,500 bales aboard went into the briny. As for the other 1,500 bales still ashore, they were unharmed.

Carl's third venture, El Salvador, turned out to be the most successful. That country's last strong man of note, Maximilliano Hernandez, had been overthrown in 1944. Since then, coups had become a national pastime. This, however, didn't faze the Cooperativa Algodonera Salvadorena, which, along with almost everything else, was run by members of the country's fifty or so most prominent families. All Carl had to do was wean the Cooperativa from selling their fiber to Britain's Raw Cotton Commission, and this he accomplished with great dispatch. During one of his first talks with the Cooperativa's manager, who claimed he'd learned English from comic books, the door suddenly swung open and the windows started to rattle and pretty soon Carl's chair started to dance. The manager, a stocky little fellow, kept right on talking, explaining how things were done in Salvador. Finally, Carl could contain himself no longer. "Look," he said, "it's been years since I've had a drink. If this is an earthquake, we'd better get out of here." The Salvadorean nonchalantly waved him off. "Don't pay any attention," he said. "We have those all the time." The first time Bucks visited San Salvador, there was yet another quake which he found somewhat alarming but didn't seem to bother anyone else. On that occasion, he was hosted by Garcia Parieto, then chairman of the Cooperativa and a big cotton and coffee grower. Visiting him at his office finca in the mountains, Bucks found him an utterly charming man, tranquil among the vicissitudes of Latin American life.

As sanguine about tremblors as about coups, the Cooperativa was the most efficient of Central America's cotton operations. It controlled acreages in each of Salvador's three fertile valleys, maintained its own fleet of some twenty crop-dusters, kept its gins in top-notch condition with a fine staff of expert mechanics, and always had its warehouses in perfect order. Its head classer at the organization's offices in San Salvador, the capital, was an elderly New Englander who had once worked for one of the great American mills. As this complex enterprise grew ever more finely tuned under its capable manager and Carl's ministrations, Salvador cotton soon earned the reputation as being the best-classed, best-handled, best-produced cotton in that part of the world, and demanded a premium over other Central American growths.

Within a relatively short time, Algodonera Weil handled the bulk of Salvador's cotton, sometimes as many as 100,000 bales a season. Indeed, for a number of years, Weil was the only merchant that bought Salvador cotton for export, and almost the entire offtake went to Japan under Russell Eaton's auspices. With his eminent position in Osaka, Eaton not only stimulated a lively interest in this Central American growth, but was also able to furnish Carl Baquie with advance information regarding the buying intentions of the Japanese merchants who did the importing—as pointed out earlier, Nippon's mills never bought directly. Carl's value to both sides was that he could put the business together and was in the best position (as opposed to Russell Eaton as the selling agent) to negotiate claims. The latter function was far more important than it sounds: Claims, if successful, reduce the cost of purchases and thus are of significant value to any importer. That the Japanese merchants maintained fully operative claim departments separate from their buying departments illustrates how seriously they took this aspect of the business. Nonetheless, it was a joy to deal with the Japanese, for they were impeccably honest. They would trade hard, they would claim without mercy, they would fight for every advantage, but like samurai with swords and daggers, they would always abide by the rules. Without fail, their word was their bond.

It was this Japanese integrity that enabled Carl Baquie to pull off one of the most remarkable feats of his career. At that time, around 1960, Mitsubishi was still Weil's largest customer in the Osaka market. The chief of the buying department was Z. Okamoto, the successor of a Mr. Minami, who had run Mitsubishi's cotton business when that branch of the cartel still acted as agent for Weil. Okamoto, sensing that prospects were bullish, decided to buy a large quantity of Salvador cotton. Eaton so informed Carl Baquie, and Carl, as was his routine, began to feel out the Cooperativa. But the price the

Cooperativa gave was unrealistic. Still, Carl had the hunch that if they were presented with a bid for a sufficiently large quantity, Salvador would be willing to sacrifice price for volume. Meanwhile, Okamoto gave Eaton a bid for 40,000 bales, good for the standard forty-eight hours Carl required to receive a reply from the Salvadorans.

Okamoto's bid was cheap, way below the Cooperativa's ideas. Recognizing this, Carl decided to put only the most minimal margin in the price to Mitsubishi and to make money out of the deal by increasing the quantity to 50,000 bales, taking 10,000 of them on his own position. In other words, he was going to use the volume buying of Mitsubishi as a vehicle to buy cotton for Algodonera Weil at a cheap price.

This was a most promising maneuver, since the margin of profit in transactions with the Japanese was extremely small as a rule, the business being practically back-to-back, i.e., purchase and sale were put together with the Cooperativa guaranteeing both quality and weights. But on those extra 10,000 bales, Carl would have leverage. So he deducted ten points (fifty cents per bale) from the Mitsubishi price and put in his bid.

The next day, at midnight, the phone rang at Bobby's house in Montgomery with a call from Osaka. Middle-of-the-night calls from the Orient are now routine, but in those days they were reserved for special occasions such as this: it was Russell Eaton with the bad news that Okamoto had had second thoughts and decided to withdraw the bid.

Bobby knew that there was no point in trying to cancel Carl's bid in Salvador. If the Cooperativa knew that Weil was anxious to get out of the deal, they'd be sure to accept the bid within the forty-eight hours it was good, and Weil would find itself 50,000 bales long of Salvador cotton—an overwhelming prospect. There was only one thing to do—and it was hardly the best PR vis-à-vis a major client—and this was to insist that Okamoto stick with his bid. Bobby told Russell Eaton to call Okamoto on the other phone to inform him that Weil had taken the bid on good faith and that Mitsubishi now had to live up to its obligation. Bobby nervously hung on the open line while Eaton talked with Okamoto. But, lo and behold, there was no problem. Of course, Okamoto said, the bid would be good if a

On the other side of the Pacific, Russell Eaton, formerly a member of General MacArthur's reconstruction team in postwar Japan, sold Carl Baquie's Latin American cotton to Nippons' cartel merchants. The Baquie-Eaton pass, from El Salvador to Osaka, scored season after season, drubbing all competitors. It was one of Weil's most successful plays ever.

commitment had already been made against it, and he would wait for a reply within the specified time.

The next day, Carl's bid was accepted by the Cooperativa, and Mitsubishi took its 40,000 bales as agreed. Okamoto's integrity was rewarded. He did very well on his position, as did Carl, who made more money on the 10,000 bales than he would normally have profited on 50,000.

Only once in all the glory years of Salvador cotton did Carl Baquie strike out. This happened in 1958. That season looked just great in the beginning, but then, quite suddenly, nobody wanted cotton. Carl had purchased 5,000 Salvador bales in February, and he still had them sitting around in June. Carl finally let those bales go at a twenty-dollar loss, the first and only time in his life that he'd had to take such a licking, and he moped about it for weeks. Adolph set him straight. "In our kind of business," he said, "these things happen. Forget it. If you get bogged down feeling guilty, you'll never make another nickel."

It was a bad year all over. Europe wasn't interested in cotton either. Bucks went over to Milan that summer, hoping to sell Nicaraguan growth to some of Kronauer's customers. Bucks remembers calling on one Italian mill, where Chicco tried to place several hundred bales. But the spinner only wanted 100, and said he didn't even need that much. So Chicco and the mill man played this hand game they have in Italy, with the rock blunting the scissors, the scissors cutting the paper, and the paper wrapping the rock. Chicco Kronauer lost the game, and he and Bucks sold the hundred bales, taking a substantial loss the way the glutted market had been dropping. Bucks was no luckier with Mexican cotton that summer. In Bremen he could have sold 300 bales if Montgomery had allowed him to cut his price by ten points, and in Belgium he had to sacrifice a really big sale—15,000 bales—which would have been phenomenal considering the circumstances. But, remembers Bucks, Nathan Rosenfield was adamant about setting his own prices and Adolph backed him and there was nothing Bucks could do although he was on the scene and could see what was happening. Much to his dismay, Esteve then copped the sale. Still, the season's beginning had been fine and Algodonera Weil scraped by with a small profit even in that miserable year.

As Central American growers increased their cotton acreage, Weil easily handled 200,000 to 250,000 bales a season. From 1951 to 1964, Nicaragua's harvest alone grew more than twelvefold from 47,000 bales to 565,000. Guatemala's increase was yet more dramatic: from 11,000 bales that first year to 40,000 when the *Springfjord* was sunk, to 312,000 in 1964. Weil consistently marketed at least 10 percent of the crops of these countries; that plus the hefty Salvador volume made the firm the leading merchant in the region for a number of years, as well as the most reliable and secure, for it was Carl's steadfast policy never to sell any cotton until the crop was actually being harvested.

His business with the other Central American countries was minimal. One year, shortly after he'd moved to Panama, Carl bought that country's entire cotton crop—five or six poorly packed bales. It was the only time Panama had ever raised cotton; there were no gins, and not a large enough farm population to support a crop. Colombia, with its own mills, didn't produce enough for consistent export until the late 1950s; only in recent years has its growth become significant to any degree. Costa Rica was an on-and-off proposition, and its volume too small to warrant the financial and physical risks entailed.

In Panama, President José Antonio Ramón, elected in 1952, had been shot while watching a horse race the year after Weil opened its Central American office. In November 1958, on the fifty-third anniversary of Panama's independence, the campaign to push out Americans began in earnest when mobs invaded the Canal Zone to protest the U.S. presence. In the ensuing years, riots became ever more frequent and violent. Carl's daughter, Lynn, attended Balboa High School in the Zone; to get to her classes she had to ride a school bus through the turbulent city twice a day, a situation that was hardly conducive to Carl's peace of mind. Nor was Balboa High School a safe haven. Leftist teachers constantly egged on the native students until riots flared also in school. By 1963, the situation had become untenable. When the anti-American incidents progressed from tearing down the Stars and Stripes to physical assault, including the murder of U.S. servicemen, Bobby Weil, Sr., greatly concerned, rushed to Washington to call on the State Department's Central American desk so that he might get a clear a idea of what was going on. To his surprise, he was advised to call the Chase, which, it seems, was kept better informed than the government, largely thanks to Luis Gomez, an Englishman who was in charge of the bank's operation in that region.

Carl Baquie, of course, knew Gomez quite well, not only from business but from encounters at social gatherings of the U.S. community. In any event, Carl needed no urging to get out. There wasn't even a good business reason to stay. At the beginning, Panama had been a convenient location. Mexico had reverted to Rosenfield's Houston office, since it was almost hopeless to fly there from Panama, but there were ample plane connections to all Central American capitals, and it was possible to travel on annual visas rather than wait around for weeks for temporary permits, as Carl and Pick had been forced to when they still operated out of New York. But, by 1964, the necessary facilities to conduct international business were to be found in a number of other extraterritorial locations. Carl opted for Nassau; it had been Adolph's policy all along to let his executives, and particularly Carl, make their homes wherever they wanted within the territories assigned to them.

But by the time Carl had moved himself, his family, and his staff to the Bahamas, the bloom was off the bougainvillea. Russell Eaton's

Anti-American riots in Panama prompted Weil to close its office there, and in 1963 Carl Baquie moved his headquarters to the Bahamas.—*United Press International*

death from heart disease in 1963 had been hastened by the pressure and frustrations he lived under, for the Japanese were increasingly bypassing Weil and purchasing their cotton directly from the Cooperativa. Weil still sold them Salvador fiber, but the volume was drastically diminished and grew ever smaller. At the same time, other merchant houses, prompted by Weil's Central American tour de force, also had become interested in the area and sent their emissaries. For once, Clayton surprisingly fell on its face, but eventually just about everybody else came in to carve out a slice of the pie— Cook, Hohenberg, Starke Taylor, Bunge, Ralli, Schwabach, Perutz & Co., Esteve, and Cotton Import-Export. Indeed, with the big increase in cotton acreage, there was sufficient volume to make Central American business worth pursuing. But, for the moment at least, the urgency was gone for Weil, and so was the excitement intrinsic to pioneering. The Nassau office was soon closed, and Carl Baquie retired to Florida and tranquil sailing.

Today, Weil Hermanos, its buying expanded to South America, is in the hands of Jack Wilson, who runs the business out of Montgomery and spends his spare time handcrafting elaborate doll houses with the same meticulous patience and skill he applies to his cotton operations. Among other attributes, Jack Wilson bears the distinction of being Weil's only senior executive who speaks Spanish well enough to

converse with Latins without taking too much of a chance of misunderstanding them or being misunderstood. Yet, Jack's background is strictly Memphis, as anyone can attest who had ever heard him speak his native tongue. Born there in 1924, he first squidged for John Wagner, later for Joe McAteer, and finally for Bird Bridgeforth, in what was probably the longest cotton apprenticeship on record: it lasted nearly ten years as a result of World War II and the Korean Conflict, in both of which Jack served as a pilot, first training bombardiers and later flying paratrooper transports. At long last, in 1952, he was made a country buyer, and A. M. Crawford was quick to let him know that he still had a lot to learn. On his first trip, Jack had found a "real cheap lot of cotton" and proudly returned to Memphis to show off the samples. "Well, son," old Crawford said, "even a blind hog will stumble across an acorn onced in a while."

Nor did Crawford let young Wilson ever take his ease. Jack recalls: "Working out of the Memphis office, when my territory was dead, I'd come in and maybe sit around in the dugout reading a newspaper. I would hear Mr. Crawford coming down the hall and feel his eyes on me. About ten minutes later the switchboard would call and tell me Mr. Crawford wanted to see me. I'd walk in and he'd have his atlas out and he'd say, 'Son, I want you to run down to Shreveport, Louisiana, and talk to Raymond Little. He said he had some cotton down there to look at.' I'd get in the car and head down there and there wouldn't be anything there and I'd call Crawford and he'd say, 'Well, run over to Pine Bluff and talk to Bob Cherry and see what's going on over there.' I'd drive all the way over to Pine Bluff, Arkansas, and the first thing you know I'd been gone about two weeks and put about 5,000 miles on the car not doing anything. I was convinced he did it just because he didn't want me sittin' around doin' nothin', and I'm still convinced of it."

Jack Wilson's first executive experience, and indeed title, had come to him when he was still a squidge. Shortly after World War II and fresh out of his Air Corps uniform, he'd been sent down to New Orleans, to Carl Baquie's former shipping office, where George Brown now sat trying to keep up with the sudden burgeoning of exports to European mills. To accommodate the vast quantity of fiber going through the port, Weil had spun off a little storage outfit, The Delta Warehouse Co., of which Jack Wilson suddenly found himself "general manager." After a few phone calls to Memphis, he thought he might have it figured how a warehouse was run. Most important, there had to be a signed receipt for every bale that came in. With 3,000 bales or even more arriving every day, this was obviously impossible. So Jack had the brilliant idea of having a rubber stamp made up with his signature on it, and he fairly machine-gunned through his paperwork.

But Jack hadn't reckoned with Uncle Sam. Delta, being a bonded warehouse, was occasionally inspected, and when the government men saw Jack's labor-saving device, they accused him of violating all sorts of regulations. Jack thought he was about to land in federal prison. This was his first experience with government bureaucracy; as boss of an international company, he would have many more.

From country buying, he graduated into the Memphis shipping department, and in 1954 was assigned to Brownsville, Texas, to take charge of buying Mexican cotton for the Houston office, where Nathan Rosenfield had just regained control of that territory from Carl Baquie, who gave up the franchise happily enough. W. J. Reckling had been the first of the Weil contingent to explore the possibilities south of the border. This was back in the 1930s after Reckling, having been on loan from Weil to Maison Du Pasquier in France, was assigned to Grayson in Dallas and subsequently opened a separate Houston office. But after Reckling's resignation to return to France with Anderson Clayton, Mexico was given low priority. Rosenfield had more fertile fields to plow and, in any event, had little understanding for dealing with Latins. Meanwhile, ubiquitous Anderson Clayton had preempted much of the Mexican crops after World War II, and Esteve, Cook and Hohenberg also had carved out substantial niches for themselves. Thus, Weil ended up johnny-come-lately and missed most of the postwar Mexican bonanza.

Carl Baquie had tried his best to help Weil catch up with the other merchants when he briefly took charge of the Mexican operation in the summer of 1952. In Sonora, where he was joined by Bobby Weil, the firm formed a joint account with Faustino Felix, later to become the governor of Sonora, who was then head of the Union de Cajeme, and thus able to get the farmers to go along. For Bobby, accustomed when he traveled to the comforts of Continental hotels, this was no pleasure trip. The airport at Ciudad Obregon, the capital of West

Mexico's cotton region, was a gravel strip, on which Mexican pilots landed DC3s as if they counted on the planes to fly themselves. Cows strolled on a makeshift runway that, not inappropriately, ended at a cemetery. On checking into his motel, Bobby found that a contingent of fat frogs had moved into the room before him. "If I were you," the manager said, "I'd leave the frogs alone. They eat the insects." Bobby's diet consisted of grilled cheese sandwiches and Coca-Cola; anything else was likely to give gringos the green-apple two-step.

In the sample room of the Obregon "office"—a flat-topped hut— Bobby and Garland Roberts, from the Fresno office, would class cotton, stripped to the waist and wet with sweat. Carl and Bobby went to call on a Señor Ruiz, who owned a very elaborate gin at Huatabampo. Ruiz controlled the water supply in the area, so the farmers had to sell to him, at his low prices, or do without. Adolph's emissaries tried to make an arrangement with Ruiz to buy all his cotton, and he was as cutthroat with them as with his farmers. Walking through the warehouse upon leaving his office, Carl and Bobby passed a tomcat singlemindedly straddling a female. "See that?" Carl said. "The one on top is Ruiz."

Trying to buy cotton at Los Mochis, Bobby Weil and Guillermo Ibarra, the man appointed to run the Obregon operation, were caught in a gunfight. As they pulled onto a highway near the El Fuerte River, two men dressed in white ran toward the car, pistols blazing. One jumped in the back seat. Bobby thought he was done for, but after an excited conversation in machinegun Spanish between Ibarra and the intruder, he was informed that the two armed men were police officers chasing a big truck that had just sped by. The Weil automobile was commandeered to chase the fleeing vehicle, with Ibarra driving and Bobby instructed to hug the floor as they passed the truck en route to the next police barricade, where this adventure finally ended.

That same summer, in East Mexico, Carl Baquie established a relationship with Tamaulipeca, a Matamoros company that operated six gins in the State of Tamaulipas, one of Mexico's most productive cotton territories. Tamaulipeca never had the money to buy enough cotton to keep its gins busy, so a deal was made under which Weil would do the purchasing. For Carl, those few weeks proved to be a miserable experience. He suffered from an undiagnosed illness that often left him prostrate, he could not stand the heat, he felt oppressed by the poverty on the other side of the Rio Grande, and, at the same time, he was driven to distraction by the way the Mexicans did business—and, of course, he could not afford to show his anger. With no way of running the Matamoros operation out of Panama, he was only too glad to turn this responsibility over to Jack Wilson.

But Jack, the easygoing sort, a patient, careful man, had a great time. As a country buyer out of Memphis, he had picked up perhaps 10,000 bales a season, mostly in tiny lots from small farmers. But in Tamaulipeca, where fewer than a dozen gins controlled that region's annual output of around 500,000 bales, the smallest lots to be found were about 500 bales, and it was not unusual to buy as many as 5,000 bales in one single afternoon. Jack gloried in being in a position to take up so much cotton. But for the fact that Mexican cotton sold far below the price-supported U.S. cotton, the operation was off to a good start. By the following summer, the Brownsville office had been made permanent, and suboffices had been established in Matamoros, in Torreon in the interior south of El Paso, and in Ciudad Obregon, Sonora.

In a normal year, the Matamoros operation alone handled as many as 30,000 bales, the large volume being mandatory to compensate for an extremely small profit margin. Getting all that cotton in was far from easy. The season lasted only from June to mid-September; by July, the gins were operating at peak capacity. Days were long and arduous. Jack would often start at seven in the morning and not get to bed until two o'clock that night. "At that time," he recalls, "there were three ways to buy cotton in Matamoros. You could make a contract with a big farmer or ginner, which were mostly cooperatives of a sort. Let's say you'd buy ten thousand bales from them and they'd deliver it sometime during the season. They had a classer who always pushed the cotton [classing it at a higher quality than it actually was]. You had to develop a real knack for that game. It would get to the point where you'd scream and holler and storm out and come back later. If I'd let it get to me, I guess I would have gone crazy because every bale of cotton you took up had to be fought over.

"Then they had what they called a *subasta*, which is auction in English. They'd call you on the phone, call all the buyers, and say they're going to display some samples at a certain time and want you to make an offer in a sealed envelope. There might be sixty bundles of cotton, with fifty samples to a bundle, laid on a table, and all the buyers crowded around. You really weren't doing much classing. What you were doing was putting a value on the cotton that might give you a little profit.

"The third way was equally chancy: you'd buy the cotton in the seed as it's picked off the farm and delivered to the gin. This they called *hueso*. In Central America it's called *rama*. That way you bought the seed and the trash and the cotton all at one time, and you'd hope that the percentage of lint was very high because that's the most valuable part."

As in the Opelika days and later in Ben Barnes' time in Savannah, Weil once again went into the ginning business as a sideline, but this time the venture proved less successful. To begin with, Jack Wilson bought a gin at Rio Bravo, about twenty miles south of the Texas border by road. The gin fulfilled its intended purpose, which was to provide access to additional cotton, but the extra fiber thus obtained did not compensate for resulting headaches, for no one at Weil knew anything about ginning. Another gin, this one at Torreon, came to Weil by default. The firm had financed a ginner, and when he could not pay back the advance, Weil took possession of the collateral. Both gins were sold within a few seasons. The one at Rio Bravo was turned over at a modest profit, but the other had to be disposed of for its parts and the land on which it stood; between the two operations, it was a washout. The joint venture with Tamaulipeca also eventually collapsed as a result of having sold more forward cotton than was ginned, forcing Weil to go into the open market to make up the deficit.

With Carl Baquie in Panama, and Jack Wilson ensconced in Brownsville, Bobby took on Obregon in addition to his other duties. This was pretty good business for a while until Faustino Felix opened up a couple of new gins at Caborca to the north. That crop froze in 1956, after which Faustino Felix, who had lost $135,000 in the Caborca debacle, gave up on cotton and turned increasingly to politics. Weil broke up the joint account in 1957, but still maintains an Obregon office under Humberto Castillo, who reports to Jack Wilson.

Jack supervised the East Mexican buying out of Brownsville until 1966, when that office closed and he was reassigned to Houston where he later replaced Tom Adams as Nathan Rosenfield's assistant manager. Rosenfield died shortly afterward, which left Jack in charge during the last year of the Houston branch's existence. He then went to Montgomery to handle all of Latin America.

Since that time, the volume of the operation has never been less than 100,000 bales a year, and in good years has gone as high as 250,000. The flow depends to a great degree on the political situation. At this writing, for instance, El Salvador, caught in the throes of an agrarian reform program unsatisfactory to both right and left, is out of the picture. Here, in any case, the purchasing had been sporadic in recent years, depending on whether Weil felt that the cotton could be marketed at a profit to merchants other than the Japanese cartel buyers, who dealt directly with the Cooperativa.

Nicaragua, where most recently Ramon Sevilla has been in charge of the Weil office, used to contribute around 50,000 bales. Here, too, the volume has been minimal of late. To begin with, INA canceled its contract with Weil and went instead with Balfour, Guthrie & Co. At that time, in 1967, Adolph and Bucks visited the Manticas, another important Nicaraguan cotton clan. The Weils hoped to make an arrangement with them similar to the one with INA. But because the Manticas worked closely with Volkart, the most Adolph and Bucks could accomplish was to have Weil treated as just another customer. Exclusivity was out of the question. The fact that many of the gins, like INA's and the Manticas', had special arrangements with specific merchants made marketing more difficult as it became necessary to employ buyers to buy from growers, instead of having the gins in charge of exclusive purchasing. More recently, terrorism has been on the increase in Nicaragua, making it impractical to engage in heavy buying. Not that the cotton would not be available, but Weil prefers not to take chances on war risks that cannot be covered by insurance.

Guatemala, under Karl Fangmeier, has generally been good for about 50,000 bales. The volume never goes much above that since Weil does not like to advance money to growers, which is the usual practice in that country. By and large, Fangmeier sticks to the firm's longtime suppliers who can be handled without advances or for whom financing can be arranged directly with banks. Fangmeier, who was born in Bremen in 1941 and apprenticed there with H. O. Schubeler, a German cotton firm, first went to Nicaragua in 1964 for Esteve and was transferred to Guatemala five years later. Weil recruited him in 1974 through Jo Haack, then the firm's Nicaragua representative.

Colombia has been a comer of late. Jack Wilson first went there on Carl Baquie's behalf in about 1960 to make sure that an order of about eight or ten thousand bales was properly shipped. Wilson has been interested in Colombia ever since, and no wonder. He found that taking up cotton here was, at least for him, like going on vacation.

In a Guatemalan sample room, cotton for sale to the Far East is inspected by (left to right) David Hardoon, Carlos Solares, Akira Hanada, and Karl Fangmeier, manager of the Guatemala operation. Carlos Solares is one of Fangmeier's staff of five. Hardoon and Hanada came from Osaka to help select specific qualities.

While waiting for a ship to pick up his cargo, he was quartered for two weeks at a fine hotel in Cartagena, that country's Caribbean cotton port and also one of its favorite tourist destinations. Jack went swimming in the mornings, then ambled to the docks around noon to see if anyone had filched some of his bales. "On the docks down there," he explains, "your cotton was just sitting out in stacks, and if somebody needed some to fill a shipment, they just went and got it. If you waited until the port authorities found your cotton, you'd never get it out. My competitors would take it from my stacks and I would get it out of theirs. This was standard procedure." That reshuffling might take an hour, and then Jack would head back to the swimming pool. In the late afternoon, he'd have another look at the stacks, and by then it was time for cocktails. Tom Adams, on similar Colombian missions, wasn't quite that lucky. Once bandits held up the hotel where he stayed; the other time, in February 1966, there was an earthquake.

Weil's annual Colombia volume, now about 10,000 bales, has been as high as 20,000, thanks to the exuberant wheeling and dealing of Roberto Herrera V. (the V. stands for his mother's maiden name, a common Latin American practice). In his mid-fifties and resembling nothing so much as a happy Mephistopheles, Herrera is what the Germans call a *Lebemann*, a fellow who really knows how to live. This requires a certain amount of money, and Herrera knows how to make it. In the late 1950s, when Colombia first started exporting cotton in earnest, at the rate of about 10,000 bales a year, he was in the rice business, the son of a prominent family whose commercial interests encompassed the Colombian spectrum. He joined forces with Weil some three years later, when he began trading cotton not only on his own account but also Weil's. This arrangement lasted until the mid-1970s. Since then, Herrera has bought exclusively for Weil. Unlike buyers in other Latin American countries, Herrera has the advantage of being able to handle a variety of grades and staples, something to fit almost every market—medium staple from the Caribbean region, long staple from the Orinoco Plateau, and superior grades from the Cauca Valley, whose climate is like Hawaii's and allows the year-round harvesting of cotton.

After Colombia, Weil next tried to establish itself in Brazil. This turned out to be a disappointing episode. The Brazilian government put an embargo on cotton just as the firm started to make a little money after spending three years trying to break into that market. With the embargo suddenly in effect, it took so long for Weil to clear the bales on hand that the carrying charges had eaten up most of the profit by the time the cotton could be shipped. But recently there have been some indications that Brazil might open up again. If so, Jack is ready. Meanwhile, Weil also has started to buy in Paraguay as well as Argentina and is flirting with expanding into Bolivia.

In Mexico, the firm now obtains between 25,000 and 50,000 bales a season. After several frustrating years, during which the Japanese trading companies set up local operations, most of them quit the scene, including Nissho-Iwai and Marubeni. They found that direct buying was a lot more trouble than going through merchants—and just as costly. So Jack Wilson, one of the safest, most steadfast operators in the business, hopes for an increased share of market.

Jack's right-hand man at Weil Hermanos is Wallace L. "Wally" Darneille, a Houston native and sometime cowboy on his family's ranch in Arkansas, who joined the company in 1974, the year after his graduation from Dartmouth. Wally had attended school in Spain for one semester and spent his summers in Honduras as a volunteer in the *Amigos de las Americas* program. He speaks almost perfect Spanish, and after a stint handling special statistical projects for Bobby Weil Sr. and attending Murdoch's, he was immediately assigned to the Latin American operations.

Jack Wilson and Wally Darneille market some of the Weil Hermanos cotton in Latin America, primarily in Mexico and Venezuela, but most of it is shipped to the Orient through the Weil Selling Agency in Japan, and to Europe through Peter Frank's Unicosa in Switzerland. There, Peter's second in command is no stranger to Central American growths. He is German-born Joachim "Jo" Haack, who had gone through his basic training in international cotton dealings as Clayton's man in Nigeria, joined Weil in Nicaragua in 1967, and stuck it out there for nine years, gunplay and tremblors notwithstanding. Jo even refused to leave—as did his family—when Managua was wrecked by the big earthquake of December 23, 1972, and Karl Fangmeier flew in by hired plane from Guatemala City intending to pull the Haacks out of this typhus trap.

Ever struggling to cope with political
upheavals, Jack Wilson, Weil vice-president, and his assistant, Wally
Darneille, manage the firm's Latin
American operations.

The Christmas earthquake of 1972 wrecked much of Managua, and typhus threatened in its wake. Even so, Jo Haack and his family refused to leave when Karl Fangmeier flew in from Nicaragua in a hired plane to pull them out.—*United Press International*

Jo Haack had come to Weil in the most critical period in the history of the firm. Not critical in terms of financial survival—the early 1950s, with their artificial cotton prices, had been the toughest years in that respect. But critical in terms of organizational viability: the structure Adolph and Leonel had so carefully constructed was threatening to fall apart.

Carl Baquie retired in 1965. Tom Carney, his assistant, left for Balfour, Guthrie about a year later. Then, in 1967, A. M. Crawford, Sr., retired and Nathan Rosenfield died. James L. "Jimmy" Loeb, the nephew of Adolph and Leonel, found himself dissatisfied with not playing a more dominant role in the organization and went into business for himself. He resigned in 1969 to form his own cotton merchant firm, Loeb & Company, Inc., also in Montgomery. But even before this split occurred, Weil already was thin in executive backup, particularly in the field of foreign growths. In this hiatus, Adolph, although nearly eighty years old, traveled with Bucks to Central America in November 1967 to reorganize the staff and hire Jo Haack. It was to be Adolph's last journey.

In late December, shortly after his return from Nicaragua, he was unable to rise from his bed one morning. He knew instinctively that this was the end. To his houseman and chauffeur, Arthur James, who had been with him since 1946, he issued careful instructions on how to take care of his wife's grave, aware that hard-pressed Bobby and Bucks would not have much time to attend to this themselves. Adolph was taken to St. Margaret's Hospital, where he died a week later, on January 4, 1968.

His had been an illustrious career: board chairman of Weil Brothers–Cotton, Inc., since its incorporation in 1950, member of the New York Cotton Exchange, past president of the Atlantic Cotton Association, past vice-president of the American Cotton Shippers Association, chairman of the Birmingham branch of the Federal Reserve Bank of Atlanta, trustee of the National Jewish Hospital in Denver, member of the National Board of Christians and Jews, cofounder and director of the Southern Research Institute, and officer of and adviser to a great number of civic organizations. As has been said of him, he always kept his foot on the accelerator, while his brother's was poised cautiously and wisely over the brake.

15

Cavalcade II

THAT ADOLPH KEPT DRIVING hard almost until his dying day, and was indeed still productive in his late seventies, is not cited here only as a matter of record, or for its anecdotal value, or even as an insight into his character. All this is true enough, but there's far more to it than that, namely that Adolph's lifelong involvement provided the Weils, as a family and as a business enterprise, with a continuity rare in our time.

This continuity, a veritable blending of the generations, goes back to Isidor, who went to the office every day for at least an hour or two until he was nearly ninety. The last time he came was on March 28, 1946, and he died two days later. Now it's Leonel who shows up every morning, except Thursdays when he looks after his farm. He remains an active member of the Board of Directors of Weil Bros.–Cotton, Inc., and of the family holding company, Weil Enterprises, and it is to him that Bucks and Bobby often turn for advice. The fact that the old gentleman takes his time speaking up has nothing to do with his age. It has always been Leonel's specialty to sit and listen. Once in a while he nods, and everybody knows that when he asks, "Do you all really want to do that?" it's time to start thinking extra-hard. Thus, as the older Weils have always participated in the present, the younger Weils are ever guided by the past.

Not a week goes by without Bucks and Bobby, Sr., quoting their elders. Isidor's: "Never shoot craps with bales of cotton"; "If it's not worth hedging, it isn't worth buying"; "There's nothing more unsure than a dead sure thing"; and Adolph's "If it's a good thing, you've got enough, and if it's a bad thing, you've got too much"; "Nobody hands you anything on a silver platter. You've got to take a chance"; "Let's ask ourselves, what have we got to lose and what have we got to gain?"; and "All that twitters doesn't twatter," which was his inevitable reaction to anything that looked too good to be true.

Nor are their lessons forgotten. One of the last times Isidor came to the office, the government had just announced its first closed-bid auction sale of accumulated loan cotton that was stored in warehouses all over the cotton belts. He'd recently had a stroke, and his lips refused to move as quickly as his brain, especially when he was excited. Old Mr. I. pointed his shaking finger at Adolph and Leonel. "Lookahere, you buy!" he finally got out. "Lookahere, you buy all the banks will let you buy. This is the biggest opportunity I've ever seen. Lookahere, you buy!" As it turned out, Adolph and Leonel didn't buy nearly as much as Isidor would have wanted them to, and afterward regretted that they hadn't.

Some years later, when the government staged another of its periodic sales during a scarcity of low-grade cottons, Bucks noticed that Clayton and Cannon Mills had gone in heavily for the low grades on the first bidding. With a short crop in prospect, it looked to him as if there might be a squeeze, and he proposed that Weil also ought to buy some. Adolph studied the government catalog and Bucks' supply projections. Then he looked around the room. A company meeting was going on at the time, and all the officers and managers were present. "How much would you buy?" Adolph asked A. M. Crawford, Sr. Crawford said, "Oh, I might buy five thousand bales." Next, Adolph turned to Rosenfield: "How about you, Nathan?" Rosenfield replied that he didn't want any. Most others felt pretty much the same way. Bobby, more adventurous but nonetheless basically of con-servative bent, suggested that Weil bid just enough to cover the firm's current short position of low grades, something like 25,000 bales. When Bucks' turn came, he proposed bidding for twice as much as Bobby had suggested, his rationale being that Weil would probably end up with only about half the cotton it bid for. Adolph clearly was disgusted. He frowned, shook his head in disbelief, and said, "You are all a bunch of pikers."

On his instructions, bids were placed for more than 200,000 bales. Adolph then went off fishing somewhere in Michigan, and Bucks left for a vacation on Cape Cod. Both phoned Bobby in Montgomery every day to find out if he'd heard yet how the bidding had turned out. "One day," tells Bucks, "I called Bobby and he was very excited. He had been notified that our bids had been taken up for close to a hundred and fifty thousand bales. That's a lot of cotton, and we were long on almost all of it. 'Does Dad know?' I asked him. 'Yes,' Bobby answered, 'and you know what Dad said? Dad said, "Now we're in business!"'"

It was scary for a while. Nobody wanted the cotton. What if the new crop was heavy with low grades, and the old cotton still not sold? This would have meant a disastrous loss.

But the new crop also was short in low grades, and all of a sudden apprehension turned to triumph. The scarcity Bucks had spotted now materialized with a vengeance and Weil was well supplied. "We made

"Lookahere," said Isidor, making his point with a characteristic gesture at a family gathering in 1938, as Leonel (left) and Adolph's Rossie permitted themselves to smile indulgently.

Isidor Weil (left), as he appeared in his eighties, elegantly taking his ease in Atlantic City. At right, Ma Eda celebrating her ninetieth birthday in 1949. In their last years, they lived in the fourth-floor corner suite of the Exchange Hotel at Montgomery and Commerce Streets (top right). Long the city's leading hostelry, it was reopened in 1906, replacing its smaller predecessor (above), from whose columned balcony, on February 16, 1861, Jefferson Davis, president-elect of the Confederacy, addressed Montgomery's citizens on the eve of his inauguration.— *1887 hotel scene from Algernon Blair Collection, courtesy of Elizabeth Blair Pannell; hotel photo, Montgomery Advertiser/Alabama Journal*

a potful out of that purchase," Bucks recalls, "and it gave us momentum. We kept on buying lower grades and next lower grades, and when the season was over we had moved about a million bales. Up until that time, it was the biggest year we'd ever had."

The influence of the older generation has not only been that of mentors. Fathers and sons, uncles and nephews, protectors and adversaries, pleasant companions and sometimes disagreeable partners—their relationships were all of these.

When Bobby, fresh out of the army after World War II, negotiated for a job with the family firm, he had to "trade" with Uncle Leonel, just as Adolph and Leonel had to have it out with Emil, not Isidor. Bobby wasn't at all convinced he wanted to go into the cotton business. He had a number of other offers, all at higher salaries than Leonel was willing to pay. Their trading lasted for several weeks and Leonel finally offered $150 a month. Bobby reminded him that he'd graduated from Harvard Business School. "Look," he said, "you pay your secretary more than that." Leonel's response was irrefutable: "Can you take dictation?" and Bobby threw up his hands.

Still without a job, he visited Isidor a few days later, and his grandfather asked him why he hadn't seen him around the office. When Bobby told him, Isidor said, "Lookahere, I'll make it up to you. What do you think I worked for all these years if not to hand the business down to you?"

Isidor and Eda, who was to survive her husband by eight years, had lived since the early 1920s in a suite at the once elegant but now steadily deteriorating Exchange Hotel, on the corner of Commerce and Montgomery, across from the First National Bank. In his last years, Isidor was nearly blind. His detached retina had been operated on in middle life, but he now suffered from cataracts, and the techniques to remove these had not yet been perfected. Forced to give up reading his beloved classics, business remained his only interest. His speech was impaired, too, and he was not strong enough to walk the stairs at the office, where an elevator had to be installed for him.

But for Isidor, by then, it was business for business' sake, not for the money. He had lost all interest in possessions. Eda, slightly confused, often thought they were poor. When a doctor told her that, to save her own eyes, she'd have to put drops in twice a day for the rest of her life, there was a big scene: she insisted she could not afford the treatment. On one occasion, she gave a handout fountain pen with advertising on its shaft as a graduation present. Another time, it was a book with pages missing. When the recipient suggested taking it back to the store for an exchange, Eda said this couldn't be done; they'd given her a discount on the book because it was damaged. "Ma Eda," as everyone in the family called her, had been a strong-willed woman, albeit with a fine sense of humor, who ruled at home with the same determination that Isidor applied to business. She never hesitated to speak her mind, and Isidor always yielded. Nor did she hesitate to oppose him in public. Once, at the Temple Beth Or, the congregation was split over the issue whether only the family of the deceased should rise when the prayer for the dead was offered. This had been the temple's tradition, and Isidor, the congregation's president for many years, favored continuation of the custom. Eda, no less prominent as president of Montgomery's Council of Jewish Women, disagreed. She felt that death was a loss to all, making them equal mourners—a minor matter of protocol perhaps, but the arguments were heated on both sides, as frequently they are on such formalities. Needless to say, Isidor eventually gave in, and Eda's side won.

Her grit did not desert her in old age. Although she constantly fretted about her loneliness after Isidor's death, she insisted on remaining independent and refused to move in with her daughter. Not until nearly the end did she even give in to the family's demands to take on a female companion. The old lady, headstrong as ever, died in the hotel in 1954, at the age of ninety-three.

All three of Isidor's and Eda's children lived in Montgomery and were as much part of the firm as of the family, inseparable concepts in the Weils' lexicon. There were, of course, Adolph and Leonel, who ran the show. Their sister, Helen, Isidor's youngest child and daughter, was married to Lucien Loeb, a childhood friend, who had become a Weil partner four years after their wedding, and largely handled the company's finances and all-important banking relationships with the Guarantee Trust Co. (later Morgan Guaranty Trust), National City Bank (later Citicorp), Bankers Trust, and Chase National (later Chase Manhattan).

Lucien, born in 1888, was the scion of a family that had been intertwined with the Weils since the previous generation and would so continue into the next, much as the Hills and Carters of the Tidewater plantations in Virginia kept mating with each other. Indeed, the Loebs and Weils, along with the Greils (related by marriage to both the Loebs and Weils), and the Winters (related to the Loebs) constituted the gentry of Montgomery's Jewish community. Lucien's maternal grandfather, Henry Weil—of a different Weil family, although he also hailed from the Palatinate—had arrived in Montgomery in the 1840s. Along with the Lehman brothers, Henry, Emanuel and Mayer, the erstwhile peddlers and cotton factors who made it big on Wall Street after the Civil War, Henry Weil had been one of the founders of Kahl Montgomery, the Reform Jewish congregation, in 1852. On the paternal side, Lucien was the descendant of a family from Reichshofen, Alsace, that had dispatched three boys and two girls to Montgomery circa 1870. One of Lucien's uncles, Michel, a hardware wholesaler, had married Lena Weil, Isidor's sister. The other Montgomery uncle, Ben, was in the tobacco business with his cousin and brother-in-law, Leon, as Loeb & Loeb. Lucien's father, Jacques, had gone into advancing and retailing with the other brother-in-law, Isaac Winter. This enterprise eventually evolved into a wholesale house, the Winter-Loeb Grocery Co., which was soon joined by Victor Loeb, a Reichshofen cousin and prospective father of Virginia Loeb, acclaimed as the most beautiful girl in Montgomery, who would in turn become a Weil via Adolph's son, Bobby. As for the Greil connection: Lucien's sister, Cecile, was married to Gaston J. Greil; and Lawrence Weil, the two-*n* Hermann's eldest son, won the hand of Juliette Greil. As a parochial Montgomery pun has it: if you aren't a Weil or a Greil, you are a shlemiel. Stephen Birmingham could have written *Our Crowd* as easily in Alabama.

Leonel also married a Birmingham girl, Cecile Rich. But Adolph, like Isidor before him, chose to go far afield to fetch his bride. In fact, he went considerably farther than Cincinnati. Rossie (Rosina) Schoenhof was her name, and she lived in Boston. Gently rounded, dreamy, and endowed with mischievous brown eyes, altogether as delicious as a bonbon in her 1910 finery, she swept him off his feet. If

Adolph needed an excuse to go courting in Massachusetts, it was tailor-made: there was plenty of business to discuss with Charles Storrow, who sold the New England mills. As circumstance would have it, Rossie's father, Carl Schoenhof, the son of a rabbi and teacher, was a native of Oppenheim, a small town in the Palatinate less than thirty-five miles from Otterstadt, the cradle of the Weils. There is some indication that Schoenhof had heard of the Otterstadt Weils; old Abraham, the *Amerikafreund*, must have had quite a reputation. But the two families did not know each other. In any event, this geographic coincidence, still a subject of wonderment among the Weils, must have delighted Adolph and Rossie as they, like all lovers, greedily searched for things in common and found kismet.

To gain Carl Schoenhof's consent to their marriage could not have been easy. Not only would his daughter move far away, to a dusty hick town in the Deep South, but in his eyes, the Weils must have seemed crassly commercial. After emigrating to the United States, Carl had joined a maternal-line relative, Samson Raphael Urbino, an abolitionist, in a Boston bookshop that specialized in foreign-language works and served as the rendezvous of the literary lions of the late 1800s. Longfellow, Emerson, and Thoreau, all published by nearby Houghton Mifflin, used to hang around pontificating when the writer's cramp hit them, and Carl took pride in corresponding regularly with Dickens. Carl's older brother, Jacob Schoenhof (1839–1903) had been a noted free-trade economist and author, and had served as an adviser to Thomas F. Bayard, President Cleveland's secretary of state. In Schoenhof's family, everybody spoke at least one or two foreign languages, attended concerts more religiously than Friday night services, and was expected to master a musical instrument. Carl's was the flute; Rossie was a pianist. But even if by Carl's elitist standards (that's what we'd call them today) the Weils might have appeared somewhat pedestrian, the separation from his twenty-one-year-old daughter bothered him far more. To a relative, he wrote, "It will be a good match, not only financially, but also because the fiance and his family are very respectable. I would be satisfied with her choice, if only her future residence would not be so far from ours. It takes 32 hours to get there.... However, what can be done? The children love each other...."

This bewitching portrait of Rossie must have been made about the time Adolph courted her in Boston.

Carl Schoenhof never got the chance to ride the Southern to Montgomery. He died four days before the wedding, in May 1911, at age sixty-eight. Adolph and Rossie took a house at 906 South Perry, down the street from Isidor's, and Carl's widow, Minnie, seventeen years younger than her husband, moved right in with the bridal couple, a built-in grandmother, who by all accounts was unusually sweet and kind. Her grandchildren would call her "Minnie-Ma" (as opposed to Eda, who, when safely out of hearing, was known as "Maxi-Ma"). Much to the family's subsequent merriment, Adolph and Rossie's first child, Carol, was born nine months to the day after their wedding. Bobby, the last of their four children, arrived seven years later, in 1919.

To have these kids to care for must have been a blessing to Minnie-Ma. Here she was, a Northern lady of artistic interests, as sheltered in her own way as a Southern belle, suddenly transplanted into the heartland of Dixie; for the anti-Yankee citizenry of this one-time capital of the Confederacy, then a town of about 45,000, the War Between the States was not yesteryear but yesterday. Minnie had no friends, no outside interests; there were no writers, painters and musicans to mingle with at decorous teas. As has been said somewhat unkindly, in the Montgomery of those days you were thought an art lover if you kept a painted turtle.

Unlike her mother, Rossie loved giving parties. She and Adolph had guests several times a week. Their fêtes, for which Adolph insisted on supervising the cooking, often included luminaries like Jack Dempsey, a friend of Louis Whitfield, Jr., one of Adolph's buddies. Admiral Richard E. Byrd was among the visitors; his wife, Marie, had grown up with Rossie and they were very close.

Even before Adolph wrested full partnership for himself and Leonel from Uncle Emil, he had moved his family to a new house at 1308 South Perry, then still at the city limits and with the sidewalk in front half completed. The rambling two-story Georgian mansion was designed by Frank Lockwood, a prominent local architect in his day. It cost $28,000 to build, a rather respectable sum in 1917. * Even so,

---

*The house number was later changed to 1540, a familiar sight for several years to latter-day downtown commuters, for the mansion was partly destroyed by fire in the mid-1970s and left to stand as a ruin for several years.

Adolph had to cut a few corners, such as settling for brick facades. However, the home was exquisitely finished and furnished with fine antiques, and that's where Adolph and Rossie would spend the rest of their lives, and where their children would be born and the grandchildren come to visit on Sundays.

Those who knew Rossie remember her as somewhat fey, which is not an adjective they'd use, but what their memories of her add up to. To her grandchildren, who called her "Grandear" (for Grandmother Dear), she was a sweet, patient, forgiving little lady, as Minnie-Ma had been to hers, but with the added dimension of conspiratorial youthful levity. Deep inside her, there seemed to reside a happy child. Inclined to chubbiness and afraid to be caught munching, she hid candy in her hatbands, under the mattress, and behind boxes in closets. Every time Adolph peeked in the back of a drawer, he found a cache of good things to eat. She was an eternal innocent, that much is certain, a gentle, pliant counterfoil to her intense and temperamental husband. In her efforts to be with it, she called homosexuals "odds" because she couldn't remember the expression "queers." At parties, she broke up over risque jokes only to ask afterward in private what those stories were about.

But this doesn't mean she was naive. In fact, she was probably quite brilliant: she accommodated herself expertly to what was expected of upper-crust Southern ladies of that time, and if she ever felt a longing for the heady intellectual atmosphere of Boston, she never let on. She read voraciously and spent many hours listening to music, but discussed such matters with only a select few, such as her son-in-law, Pat Uhlmann, Helen Jane's husband. She taught the governesses how to handle the children, her servants how to set the table and how to clean: she was one of the last of a generation still able to make demands of their staffs without being either overbearing or apologetic. As if to prove her accomplished domesticity, she sewed her daughters' dresses, all gingham, challis and dotted Swiss, adorning them with pains-taking embroidery and smocking; the girls didn't wear shop-bought silk until they were well into their teens. She insisted on ironing her personals, which Adolph disapproved of because she nearly always burned herself. One time—probably the last time he caught her at it—he had a servant bring the ironing board into the dining room and smashed the plank to smithereens before he settled down to eat his salad.

Unlike his father, Adolph was the undisputed boss also at home. What made this palatable, if not always pleasant, was that he assumed his leadership in all matters as a droit de seigneur. There was none of the bluster in him, born of uncertainty, that stigmatizes mini-Napoleons. His explosions, while momentarily intimidating, left no lasting rancor; everyone understood that he'd merely been caught up in his visions of perfection, that he would soon calm down again and make up for his intransigence with innumerable kindnesses that he freely, if sometimes brusquely, dispensed. It's interesting to note that

Rossie and her first-born daughter, Carol, who would later marry Myron J. Rothschild.

this characteristic made him a less effective manager than even-tempered Leonel, who never raised his voice. Weil staffers forgot Adolph's outbursts the minute he walked out the door, but one disappointed look from Leonel was long remembered.

At home, Rossie's bridge game in particular drove Adolph to distraction. Totally in character, he played by the book, methodical and calculating in his strategies, while she bid on intuition: if she held several face cards, she automatically called a two. Surprisingly, and much to her husband's frustration, this often worked as well as his studied game. In their daily life, she handled him by indirection, never arguing, usually agreeing, and then simply doing what she wanted to do anyway, a trick that Bucks was to learn from her; thus Bucks, unlike Bobby who talked back, mostly had his way.

Inevitably, as in all marriages, there were frictions, but Adolph and Rossie were exceptionally close. She had infinite faith in his judgment, so much so that even their attorney was surprised. Once, as they were getting on in years, Adolph had new wills drawn, and Rossie went to the lawyer's office to sign hers. She didn't give it so much as a glance before she picked up the pen. "Don't you want to read it first?" the attorney asked her. She countered with the question, "Did my husband read it?" and when the lawyer answered in the affirmative, she set the pen to paper without another word.

How dependent they were on each other did not become fully apparent until Rossie died of heart failure in 1965. She passed away at home and did not suffer long. According to Arthur James, Adolph's chauffeur and all-around man Friday, much as John Carver had been to Isidor in the context of the office, Rossie smiled like a girl to the last and "looked like she was twenty when she must have been sixty." What makes Arthur James' recollection so poignant is not that he thought she looked like a young girl but that he presumed her to be sixty. Actually, Rossie was seventy-five when she died.

After she had been taken away, Adolph, who had rarely gone to temple except on high holidays, made her room into a shrine. He placed a prayer book on the pillow of her deathbed, brought fresh flowers every day, and kept the door closed to others. Only his granddaughter Rosalind, Bobby's younger girl, ever ventured into the sunny, silent room, so delicately feminine with its pastels and creams and frilly French decor that it seemed the small, pink lady would come bustling in at any moment. Rosalind used to sit there on Sundays, dreaming her girlhood dreams, while the rest of the family visited downstairs. In the first year after Rossie's death, Adolph only left his house to go to the office or the cemetery, and he shunned most parties even after that, in the short time he himself had left to live. His grandchildren were his main interest, and remained so even after he decided to handle personally the Central American operation after Carl Baquie's departure.

When the grandchildren were still small, they had called him the "Candy Man." Later he was Pop-Pop. Spending the night at his house, then joining him for an early breakfast, was one of the kids' great thrills. That and when he took them fishing. Except on those outdoor expeditions, when they were permitted slacks, the girls always had to wear proper dresses and stockings in his presence. But these Victorian strictures bothered them not at all. They felt Pop-Pop understood them. No one else ever asked them to sing the trashy tunes they'd picked up from the radio and TV, and then listened with evident enjoyment. With Grandear gone, he was the favorite of all their relatives, of which there were battalions, and his disapproval counted far more than lectures from their parents.

"What are you doing, going to Dartmouth on a blind date before your exams?" he wrote to Rosalind when she studied biology at Wheaton. "You know you are riding for a fall! [He was very fond of exclamation marks.] You should work before you play!" Laurie Jean, Bucks' eldest, remembers that Pop-Pop warned her parents about a young fellow she was dating. "I don't like the look in his eyes," he said. "I've seen it before on others. I don't trust him." Needless to say, Laurie was upset when her parents told her about this conversation; she thought Pop-Pop presumptuous, and kept seeing the boy anyhow. "I should have trusted his judgment," she says now. "Pop-Pop was absolutely correct. It wasn't his style to say something nasty just for the sake of saying it, like so many people do. He wasn't interested in taking other people apart. But he took himself seriously enough, and he took us seriously enough, to always come right out and say what he thought. He was being far more perceptive than my folks were at that time." One of the suitors of Helen Jane's daughter, Patricia, also bit the dust. The boy had failed to stand up when Pop-Pop entered the room. The old man administered a truly Adolphian chewing out on the spot, informing him that only gentlemen were welcome in his house. After that, the fellow didn't have a chance.

Adolph's and Rossie's ménage had been dominated by females: Rossie, Minnie-Ma, a protective Mammy who had been born a slave, a mademoiselle, a cook, a couple of servant girls, plus two little daughters, Carol and Helen Jane—a heavy load of the gentle' sex for boys like Bucks and Bobby. It was perhaps precisely for this reason that Adolph, as the only adult male, so profoundly influenced his sons. He was their idol for all his skills and macho pursuits, the angler who caught more fish than anyone else on the lake, the unfailing bull's-eye hunter. In the tradition of old, he was the wellspring of rod and reward. That his punishments were far harsher than modern pedagogues would approve did not diminish his sons' love but only enhanced their respect. Once, when Bucks rode his tricycle over the Mammy's corn-encrusted toes and she screamed in agony, Adolph not only gave him a sound thrashing, but held the little boy's head under water (his bath had just been drawn) until he could hardly breathe. Overkill? Perhaps. "But," says Bucks, "I never ran over anyone's feet again." Carol and Helen Jane escaped such indignities. The separate but equal doctrine still pertained in all aspects of Southern life.

When Bucks was about five, he was sent to Miss Gussie Woodruff's classes. From there he went on to Barnes, another old Montgomery private school. Adolph next dispatched him to Culver Military Academy, which he had selected over Exeter, Andover, Lake Forest and Lawrenceville after a long inspection trip: Culver's discipline appealed to him. Along the way, Bucks, born Adolph, Jr., picked up the nickname that was to stick with him for life. It was bestowed by a camp counselor in Wisconsin. Bucks graduated from Culver at sixteen and was admitted to Dartmouth, one of the youngest in his class.

One college summer, cozy at the Dartmouth Club, he clerked for Shap Dowdell at the New York office. That's when he learned the rudiments of futures trading from Jack Rutkay, then still with Anderson Clayton. Another summer, he helped around the Montgomery office. On alternate vacations, as he had done most of his life, he traveled abroad. Like Isidor and Emil before them, Adolph and Leonel took turns visiting their European representatives, and their families came along. By the time Bucks went to college, he spoke fair French, albeit with a drawl that made Parisians think he was a Basque. But more important, these trips had spawned his avocation: the appreciation and collection of fine art. Unlike most youngsters dragged around museums by their mothers, Bucks got to like it, and by his late teens had developed into something of a connoisseur. That's why he didn't major in art at Dartmouth; he read enough books in that field on his own. He majored in English, tried to improve his French, and took his B.A. in 1935.

Next on his agenda came Harvard Law School, which turned out to be less of a success. He flunked criminal law in his first year and had to repeat it. Likewise, agency in his second. He played bridge more often than he attended classes, and finally graduated with one single A. He clearly had little interest in becoming an attorney. Not that this mattered. Adolph had only sent him to law school anyway because he'd been afraid that the cotton business could not survive the New Deal. But Weil was still there, and Bucks went to work as a squidge. Nonetheless, his legal training was to pay off within a few weeks.

From his taxation course, Bucks remembered that the heavy "excess profits tax" originally had been instituted as an enforcement device to keep businesses honest when they declared their capitalization. The capital value of a firm had long been subject to a nominal levy, the so-called "capital stock tax," and many companies had underestimated their worth so as to cut this liability to a minimum. Only recently, as the government tried to derive additional revenues from surging war production, had the excess profits tax become a patriotically acceptable device to procure revenue.

What was involved in this instance was a company in Mobile, Alabama, that Weil had organized, together with Hohenberg Bros. and Manget Bros., with very little capital. This company served strictly as a convenient conduit. The three merchants had agreed to put all the cotton they exported from Mobile through that warehouse. Bucks reasoned quite correctly that if this warehouse company declared a high capital value for capital stock purposes, which it had every right to do, it would not be subject to sky-high rates of the excess profits levy. He so informed Vasser Gunter, the firm's longtime controller, who was so trusted by the Weils that the company books had not been audited by an outsider for years. Vasser at first couldn't believe what Bucks told him: he was unable to conceive of anyone being clumsy enough to devise such foolish legislation. Uncle Leonel couldn't either—but then these men were in the cotton business, not in government. They did, however, ask a Selma attorney, who also represented Hohenberg and Manget, to check into the matter. Sure enough, Bucks turned out to be right, which saved the three companies a small fortune. Hohenberg and Manget never expressed their appreciation tangibly, but Weil did and Bucks could well use the bonus. His salary as a squidge was less than fifteen dollars a week.

Money became yet more important to him when, at the end of 1939, he was transferred to Dallas to get some experience under Grayson. At the start of the season, he had to trade for his pay like everyone else in the business. And, as previously explained, he had to do his trading with Uncle Leonel, not with his father. Recalls Bucks: "He tested me with a lot of questions, and I thought they required very involved answers when they were really very simple. One that I remember he asked me was what I would do as far as foreign exchange was concerned if I sold cotton to England at six pence per pound on six months delivery. I don't know how I messed up, but the answer obviously is that you sell sterling for delivery six months from now so that when you get paid in sterling you can convert it immediately into dollars without taking an exchange risk. I guess that pence business threw me off, and I never thought of converting it into U.S. cents per pound. But that's typical of Uncle Lee. He always reduces a problem to simplicity before he does anything, and he wanted to teach me not to get involved with red herrings either."

In Texas, Bucks went down to Corpus Christi with Charles Greengrass, learning about the shipping of export cotton, how to move it from compress to steamer, knowledge that soon would be useless for some years. Bucks had no sooner returned to Dallas from the port than the Germans invaded France. Trust Al Grayson. Only the Sage of St. Paul could have provided comic relief at this depressing moment. Bill Reckling, Weil's former ambassador to France, sitting across their partners desks from Grayson, shook his head sadly and said, "I suppose all my friends from Le Havre are now fighting; that is with the exception of Chardines." Pierre Chardines was a tough French cotton merchant with a lot of brass. "What's the matter with Chardines?" Grayson asked. Reckling explained that Pierre had been badly shot up in World War I and had lost most of his liver. "Hell," Grayson stuttered, straight-faced as always. "Th..Th ... That don't ma..ma..matter. He still has a lot of g ... g ... gall."

Bucks remained in Dallas for a year, working with George Hedick, who later left for Reinhart, and with Manuel Held, now in Montgomery. The Dallas office handled 75,000 to 100,000 bales a year, about one fifth of the Weil volume at that time, and less than half of Memphis', where most of Weil's apprentices were trained. When Bucks was transferred there for his third and last year as a squidge, the office was full of college kids, former football players at Southwestern, of which Alvin was a busy booster. For Bucks, in many ways, it was like going back to school, between his rooming-house adventures with Tom Adams, playing practical jokes on John Wagner, and taking assorted girls to the roof-garden nightclub of the Peabody for big-band dancing. The fact that on his twenty-fifth birthday, on February 8, 1940, Adolph presented him with his first car, a maroon four-door Buick, proved of considerable advantage in all departments.

The then customary "Greetings" soon put an end to this idyll, and Bucks went off to Camp Lee (later Fort Lee), Virginia, while Robert Mangum, proud behind the steering wheel, delivered Bucks' car to Montgomery for the duration. Eventually Bucks found himself in OCS at Carlisle Barracks, Pennsylvania, whence the fortunes of war brought him to the New York Port of Embarkation as a medical supply officer to help expedite the shipment to the ETO of ready-to-assemble field hospitals. Not until after the last shot had been fired did he arrive in Paris, duded up in brand-new combat boots, which caused no end of mirth among his fellow company-grade officers who were all dressed for night patrols on the Champs Elysées. But Bucks' sojourn to the war zone was of short duration, and he was soon transferred back stateside. Here the comedy of dress errors came to a no-win climax. His old buddies at the New York Port of Embarkation

Lieutenant Bucks Weil in his dress
uniform before he went overseas.

had rigged up a "Welcome Home Bucks" banner, and in the reception
committee was First Lieutenant Bobby Weil, fresh out of Command
and General Staff School and briskly attired in an Eisenhower jacket,
the uniform item that until recently had distinguished ETO veterans.
Bucks, on the other hand, had shed his combat boots; he was dressed
in regulation dress greens and stood there neglected, while all the
Gray ladies fussed over Bobby, their supposed hero returned from
overseas.

That Bucks would return to the cotton business was a foregone
conclusion. As his first assignment as a full-fledged staffer, he was sent
to the New York office to fill in for Carl Baquie while the latter spent
the summer of 1946 in Shanghai, laying the groundwork for selling
the Chinese mills. Bucks still had a lot to learn, and he learned it the
hard way. For a considerable period he left Montgomery, Texas, and
Memphis dangling without hedges, not because he was attempting to
speculate, but because he believed that the long transactions of one
office washed out the shorts of another. In theory, this was true
enough, but the Weil offices were, in effect, running separate
businesses, with the respective managers participating in their offices'
profits. To protect them, Bucks should have arranged ex-pit hedges, a

practice recognized by the Exchange for such in-house transactions. Another time, he nearly fell for a con game when an unknown caller told him on the phone that he could arrange a sale of 400,000 bales to a certain war-torn country; he would acquaint Bucks with the details at a hush-hush meeting in a room at the Hampshire House on Central Park South. All excited, Bucks immediately called Adolph— 400,000 bales was then nearly one year's volume for the firm. Adolph straightened him out in a hurry: the very fact that this mysterious deal involved such a monumental quantity marked it as a ruse, possibly for some sexual entrapment. Sadder but wiser, Bucks never went to the secret rendezvous.

Bucks' preoccupation with the still largely mysterious world of large-scale cotton merchandising almost cost him his bride-to-be. At that time Weil was doing considerable business with Daniel F. Rice & Co., a firm of grain merchants and grain futures traders, some of whose customers also were in cotton. The head of Daniel F. Rice in New York was Ralph Kaufman. When Bucks called on him, he spotted the picture of a lovely young lady on the desk. She turned out to be Kaufman's daughter, Jean. Bucks subsequently met her and asked her for a date. It so happened that the second time he took her out to dinner there had been a tremendous crash in the cotton futures market. Rumors were flying that some houses were in trouble, and all through Bucks' and Jean's tête-à-tête in the Maisonette Room of the St. Regis, Bucks kept imagining all kinds of terrible things he might have done on that fateful trading day. In short, he was a fretful bore, and Jean told him later that she'd decided never to see him again. This contretemps passed quickly, however. Jean soon found out that Bucks could smile after all, and they were married the following February.

It wasn't long before the vivacious young bride, once a talented art major at the since defunct National Park College in Maryland, found herself a busy cotton wife. Almost immediately she accompanied Bucks on a tour through the Carolinas, calling on Weil's agents and customers. It is expected in the cotton world that wives help husbands on business trips; for most of them this is an ordeal, unless they manage to become involved with the people they meet, for the business part itself is bound to be a mystery. Jean, like her sister-in-law Virginia, Bobby's wife, responded with enthusiasm. Bucks and Jean

called on Gordon McCabe of J. P. Stevens, and his wife, Lydia; the
E. P. Murrays and the Robert Chapmans of the Enoree mill group;*
the John Hamricks of the Hamrick Mills at Asheville; E. P. "Fleece"
Murray, the agent in Spartanburg; Charles Couch and John La-
bouisse, the firm's representatives in Charlotte; and Andrew "Dutch"
Gullick, who sold Weil cotton in Belmont and Gastonia.

The following year, only three months after their first daughter,
Laurie, was born, Bucks and Jean made a similar tour of Europe,
leaving the baby and its nurse with Jean's parents in Scarsdale for
almost three months. When the Weils' Enschede agent, Herman
Scholten, took them around to the Dutch mills, Jean at first insisted
on staying in the car while the men went inside to discuss business.
An invitation by mill-owner Chris Gelderman soon broke through
her reluctance, however, and after that she participated in all
meetings, as with Henry Vanderhorst, then buyer for the Spinnerij
Roombeck and later a Weil agent, and with Roombeck's owners, the
Menko family, whose mansion, interestingly enough, was subsequently converted into a hotel, called the Memphis—probably the
only hotel with a cotton name in Europe. †

Before Bucks was married, he had been recalled to the main office,
where the joint account records had fallen into total disarray. It was
his assignment to put them back in order. Between endless days of
analyzing all individual entries, Bucks took on tasks that no one else
seemed to have time for. He bought many small lots of cotton, often
only two or three bales, which the shareholders of Callaway Mills in
La Grange had received in settlement when that firm liquidated. On
another occasion, he brought Raleigh Williams of Pepperell back into
the fold; an argument with Adolph over staple had prompted
Williams to withdraw that mill's business from Weil. Most important,
however, was the reorganization of the books, which required not only
an eye for detail but a thorough understanding of every transaction.
When, after many month's work, Bucks finally completed that

*Robert Chapman, initially E. P. Murray's partner, later became the cotton buyer and
an officer of the Chapman family company, Inman Mills.

†The hotel was named for Memphis, Tennessee, which had dispatched aid to
Enschede after World War II.

project, he knew that now, at last, he had become a cotton man. Neither his father nor Uncle Lee were given to praise. When a man failed, they told him so, but when he did right, they took it for granted. Bucks heard only indirectly that Leonel had told his wife Cecile that "Bucks knows more about the cotton business than I thought he did." He still considers this the finest compliment he has ever received.

While Bucks quite naturally slipped into his intended niche, Bobby's role in the family business was by no means certain. Even after he joined the firm and was being groomed as one of the next set of Weil brothers, there were times when he seriously considered quitting and seeking his future elsewhere. As a high school youngster, he had wanted to become a doctor. In college, he flirted with an advertising career. Later, the corporate life beckoned. And throughout it all, he had a suppressed desire to become a writer. A half-finished novel gathers dust in one of his closets.

The fact that Bobby was not so firmly caught in the web of family tradition may have been due to his being the youngest of four children, and the widened scope for individual expression such placement usually entails. Moreover, with an older boy having preceded him, he was not the first on whom the new was tried. Essentially, Bobby's upbringing had followed the same course as Bucks': the household full of loving womenfolk, the stern father (even sterner with Bobby since he was more obstreperous), the intellectual exercises at the dinner table (anagrams and rote memory contests), fishing on Lake Martin. Adolph took great pride that by the time Bobby started the first grade at Miss Gussie Woodruff's he knew the multiplication tables, the capitals of every state, and spoke and read English and French. Bobby skipped second and fourth grades and entered sixth grade at the age of eight, and then moved over to public school, the only one of the Weil children to have done so. Thus, at Bellinger Hill School, Montgomery Junior High and Lanier High, he was thrown in with youngsters several years older than he, and this worked to his disadvantage. In 1934, he would have been in his senior year at Lanier when the public schools were threatened with closure for lack of money, and Bobby was sent to Culver Military Academy where he took an extra year so he would not graduate at the early age of fifteen.

Attending public schools during the Depression made him conscious that the Weils were of a tiny privileged minority. Among the friends he brought home for lunch, one was not used to eating hot food, and another did not know how to handle knife and fork. Several of his friends went barefoot even in winter. Often a dish of watery soup was their main meal.

Adolph was highly sensitive to the poverty of those days. Almost every evening, the doorbell would ring repeatedly as poor people came by to ask for food. One day Adolph, while en route to a compress then on the north side of Montgomery, saw children eating out of garbage cans. According to Georgia Brown, one of the Weils' longtime retainers, he was so upset that he couldn't eat his lunch when he came home. Adolph told Leonel afterward, and Leonel told their sister Helen, Lucien Loeb's wife. The ladies and several of their friends then organized a lunch and food-supplement program at the Lovelace and Billingslee Schools in the poorest sections of the city, and the pupils were instructed to bring in their dilapidated shoes so they could be fixed, and frequently replaced, at the Weils' expense.

To a Spartan like Adolph, self-denial was a virtue; he did not allow Bobby to own a bicycle because his friends had none. Above all else, the poverty that Bobby saw around him convinced him of the need to make money to pay his own way. Once, when his mother joked that she was broke, he took it seriously. Then only about nine years old, he got himself a magazine route for the *Saturday Evening Post, Ladies Home Journal* and *Country Gentleman,* and on Rossie's birthday gave her his savings, a total of two dollars.

If Adolph was tough on his boys, he was equally tough on himself. He was a great believer in training his boys for leadership. He liked to say, "You cannot order others to do things unless you have done them yourself. Others will not follow you unless you do them yourself." But as rigorous as Adolph was in his upbringing of the boys, he was a marvelous companion. Bobby loved to go fishing and on early-morning shoots with his father, who was an enthusiastic outdoorsman and a great sport. In the field they were buddies, and there was a great solidarity between the father and his two sons.

When Bobby was eight, he started going to camp every summer.

Once he nearly died of a streptococcus infection in his knee while his parents were traveling abroad. Thus, when Bobby was thirteen, Rossie and Adolph took all their children to Europe with them, so that if any were to fall ill, they wouldn't be an ocean away. Not having anything better to do with Bobby, they stuck him in a camp, just outside of Geneva, the L'Institut Juillerat. This was a fancy international camp with about thirty boys from a dozen different nations, who wintered at the Le Rosey school near Lausanne. Nearly every boy had a title except for Bobby and two other Americans. One of the campers was the then Crown Prince of Iran, Pahlevi, later to become the Shah. Pahlevi's brother was there too. Bobby, with the help of his counselor, earned acceptance by claiming that he was Franklin Roosevelt's cousin, and that his father owned a plantation called "Alabama" in the southern part of the United States, which he proudly showed them on a map.

Bobby had excelled at Culver Military Academy, but at Dartmouth College, which he entered in 1936, his studies suffered because of his work on *The Daily Dartmouth*. He earned sufficient money in his senior year as advertising manager of this publication to have paid all of his college expenses, but since Adolph footed all the bills, Bobby had $1,500 to invest when he graduated. He wanted to buy about fifty acres on the east side of Montgomery along the Atlanta Highway, near what is now burgeoning Eastdale, but he was dissuaded from that venture by Adolph, who favored the Socratic method of teaching.

ADOLPH: When you buy this land, what are you going to do with it?

BOBBY: Just let it sit there.

ADOLPH: You'll have to pay property taxes.

BOBBY: I didn't know that.

ADOLPH: And you can't collect any interest on your money.

BOBBY: I'll farm it.

ADOLPH: You can't farm it. You're away at school.

BOBBY: I'll get a tenant.

ADOLPH: Who is going to make sure that tenant's doing the right thing?

BOBBY (shrugging): You are.

ADOLPH: No, I'm not either.

Adolph advised Bobby to study stocks and to invest in the stock market instead. There followed high-level discussions between Isidor, Adolph, Leonel, and Lucien, to debate Bobby's choices. In the end, he bought ten shares of seven different stocks which did well but not so well as the $30,000 per acre which the East Montgomery land brings now.

Adolph was an expert when it came to pedagogic stratagems. Bobby was given an allowance at Dartmouth, on the condition that he would file a monthly expense account just as if he were in the business. These expense accounts had another purpose, for Adolph could easily keep track of his son's activities by the way he spent his money. The thought dawned on Bobby as well, who began slowly to conceal some adventures by including an item entitled "GOK." After many months, as this item began to grow in size, Adolph demanded to know what this "GOK" was that Bobby kept spending his money on. Bobby answered, "God Only Knows."

Bobby's sojourn at Dartmouth provided him with something no less important than a liberal arts education, experience as a newspaper executive, a modicum of money for investing, and the know-how of expense accounts. It was here that he solidified friendships that were to last a lifetime. Moreover, all but one of his five roommates in Fayerweather Hall married into the Weil family: R. Hugh "Pat" Uhlmann, who later became Bobby's brother-in-law and perennial vacation companion; Ed Oppenheim, formerly Bobby's detested corporal at Culver, who eventually married the widow of Bobby's cousin, Walter H. "Bunks" Weil, Jr.; Louis Oberdorfer, who subsequently married Leonel's daughter, Elizabeth; Richard L. "Dick" Weil, Bobby's best friend since childhood, whose father, Lawrence Weil, also had been Adolph's closest friend; and Bernei Burgunder, of Baltimore. Bernei was the only exception in one of Bobby's favorite pleasantries of later years. As he put it when another friend, H. F. "Jimmy" Levy married Mary Lynne Weil, "I've lost all my friends; they've become my relatives."*

---

*Pat Uhlmann, of the Kansas City Uhlmanns, who are to grain what the Weils are to cotton, was by then a senior and engaged to Bobby's sister Helen Jane, whom he had met earlier when his sojourn at Dartmouth overlapped with Bucks'. Ed Oppenheim came from Oklahoma City. Louis Oberdorfer, both of whose grandfathers had been Confederate soldiers, hailed from Birmingham, and his parents had known the Weils for many years. Dick Weil (a grandson of the two-*n* Hermann) also was a Culver graduate.

From Dartmouth, Bobby went to Harvard Business School, whose case-study approach proved a powerful tool in sharpening his naturally analytical mind. Toward the end of his first year, in 1941, the school instituted a wartime program that enabled its students to earn their degrees while training for commissions in the Army Quartermaster Corps. With Culver in his background, Bobby had no difficulty qualifying. Meanwhile, a girl he had known since early childhood, Virginia Loeb, daughter of the aforementioned Victor Loeb, was attending college at nearby Wheaton. They became engaged in the summer of 1941 and were married in January 1942.

At Dartmouth, Bobby Weil (right) sat for a formal picture with his buddies (from left) Richard Weil, Louis Oberdorfer, and Edgar R. Oppenheim. Missing are college friends Bernei Burgunder, whom Bobby had only just met when this photo was taken, and Pat Uhlmann, who by that time had already graduated.

Reeling from the shock of Pearl Harbor, Virginia, although already a senior with an exemplary record as an art major, May Queen and Madonna, had decided to sacrifice her college career to be with him. *

On graduation from Harvard that June, Bobby reported to Fort Warren, Wyoming, ready for shipment to the Pacific as one of the replacements for the many Corps casualties on Bataan. But, as it happened, the entire officers class was shipped to interior depots, and the newly hatched second lieutenant proceeded to Philadelphia to fight the war there. Virginia was able to live with him, and during their tour in Philadelphia, Vicki (Virginia Ann), their first child, was born in 1943. Bobby never made it overseas. He was sent to Fort Leavenworth to prepare for the invasion of Japan, and while he was there, the bomb was dropped on Hiroshima.

If Bobby, as a boy, had finished his formal education well ahead of his contemporaries, he now felt an old man, entering business at twenty-six. It was thus with a sense of urgency that, before he returned home, he looked for jobs in New York and Boston, trying to find out what alternatives he might have to joining the family enterprise. But once back in Montgomery, there was no way he could resist his grandfather's entreaty that the only reason for a family business is its continuity. Soon Bobby was aboard.

Having worked some of his youthful summers in the sample room, he was familiar, at least to a degree, with the physical aspects of cotton. As a student, he had often asked his father how money was made in the cotton business. Adolph's cryptic answer was that there were many ways, and he left it at that. Thus the merchant side of the business had remained an enigma to the young man until he came aboard the firm full time. Weil Brothers, Bobby soon found out, wasn't at all like business school, for the cotton world must function without any of the predictable elements inherent in manufacturing, wholesaling, and retailing. Cotton merchants do not budget costs (although there are costs in distribution) the way it is done elsewhere; nor do they mark up on them: commodity prices move in response to

---

*When Virginia was chosen Madonna, she at first declined. Being Jewish, she felt that this honor was inappropriate, and so told the dean, who heard her out, then asked, "But so was Mary, wasn't she?"

supply and demand. The cotton business even involves totally different accounting concepts.

Weil Brothers has always been known for its superb training in cotton fundamentals. When Bobby came to work in early 1946, Bob Collins, as expert and consistent a technician as there was in the firm, headed the sample room, with Arthur Hester as his assistant. Physically, squidging was a menial task that consisted mostly of arranging samples on the tables according to the way they were classed. The secret, however, was in training the eye to see the differences between one class and another, and for the fingers and the eyes to judge the length of staple. Squidges learned largely through the osmosis of experience, but Bobby found that if he trained his mind to analyze precisely what he was doing each time, the learning came more quickly. He discovered, moreover, that this analysis lent itself to the same visual and mental processes that college art courses had taught him.

Summers, when the sample room was not so busy, he apprenticed on clerical jobs, and by the end of his second summer, he had mastered all functions well enough to pinch-hit for vacationers. Eventually, he was assigned a desk in the room shared by Nathan Rosenfield and Helmut Kruse. Rosenfield ran the cotton operation, Kruse was in charge of exports, shipping and stock control, and they were, both intellectually and in the disciplinary sense, among the trade's finest and most demanding teachers. "I want you to follow them around like a puppy dog," Leonel told Bobby. "Watch everything they do until you can do it yourself."

Learning to figure was crucial: outturns upon outturns in the sample room, and the cost-to-land under Rosenfield and Kruse. Export offers were written by Adolph and Leonel with prices for shipside, i.e., landed at the port of shipment. These prices were then translated to the terms of the individual buyer, such as CIF–North Continent and FOB. Each price was figured and checked individually to the nearest five points, an exacting and laborious process and if Bobby was so much as one point off he was instructed to do it all over again without being told how far off he'd been in the first place (today all this is done by computer). Bobby went out to every buying office in Alabama, because the buying was done a little differently, whether one was in Decatur, Huntsville, or Sand Mountain, or in Arab, where Bobby finally bought his first bale. Rosenfield didn't like to buy in Montgomery because of the unfavorable terms and weights given by the local warehouses. Heartened by his Arab purchase, Bobby went out to the Montgomery market anyhow, and came back with his first lot of 150 bales. He was soon deflated. It seems he had classed the cotton next to a red brick wall, whose reflection concealed the presence of light spot. Rosenfield made him feel as if he had broken the firm, although the loss came to only about $250.

From Helmut Kruse, Bobby learned the mechanics of export: use of the Buentings Code, how to send cables, issue shipping instructions, process letters of credit. All exports were then handled in Montgomery. Cables were extracted and conveyed to the appropriate shipping offices first thing every morning. In the afternoons, after the market closed, the shipping offices would call in their offers to Adolph and Leonel, who wrote the cables to be sent to customers.

When Kruse fell ill with his second bout of tuberculosis in 1948, Bobby was assigned to take over his desk, at the same time serving Rosenfield as general assistant. But he was not yet firmly established; nor was he altogether sure of himself. One thing was certain however: he had no desire to remain a mere export manager indefinitely. Then it so happened that, in January 1949, Memphis came through with a second crop of low grades of all different styles and colors. This was an excellent opportunity to learn that aspect of the business, and Bobby was sent to Crawford's domain for six weeks to work with Joe McAteer, the low-grade expert. This trip turned out to be a watershed in Bobby's career. Once when a broker brought cotton to the Memphis sample room and spread it out on the tables for inspection, McAteer asked Bobby what he thought the lot was worth. Impetuously Bobby quoted a price. He could feel himself blushing, afraid he sounded ridiculous. But McAteer turned to the broker, who was trying to dicker. "You heard Bobby," he said. "That's our price." From that moment on, Bobby counted himself a cotton man.

Bobby's sojourn in Memphis also contributed indirectly to his status in the export field. Until that time, when he had written letters to agents, he'd been told in no uncertain terms by Leonel that he could only prepare drafts for the two old partners' approval; after all, Bobby had never met the agents and was not familiar with their problems. But while in Memphis, Bobby met Robert du Pasquier, over from France on a visit. Du Pasquier apparently had a private word with Adolph, for shortly afterwards Bobby received a confidential letter from his dad that he would soon be sent abroad.

In previous years, Adolph and Leonel had taken turns traveling to Europe. They always carried with them a black book, which they used interchangeably. The book, with a page for each mill—its requirements, the idiosyncracies of its buyers, its claim records, etc.—became Bobby's primer prior to embarking on *Nieuw Amsterdam* in April 1949, accompanied by his wife, Virginia, and Alvin and Trudy Weil and their daughter Ann. For Virginia, it was the first of many such journeys; in future years, when Bobby served in effect as the firm's ambassador-at-large, she was nearly always with him, whether in Europe or the Far East. On this occasion, at a time when fastidious Americans still packed soap and toilet paper on journeys to the war-shattered continent, they concentrated on Belgium, France, the Netherlands, Germany and Italy. Robert du Pasquier and Pierre Chardines met them when they docked at Le Havre; they ate their first dinner at the Rouen home of Marcel Fremaux, World War I ace and mill owner. Next in Paris, du Pasquier and his elegant wife, Alix, hosted a big party for more mill people. Then the journey turned hectic. While the Alvin Weils trundled off to Spain, Bobby, with Virginia in tow, visited thirty-five Alsace mills in four and a half days, accompanied by agents Jean Schmidt of Epinal and Daniel Olivier of Mulhouse.

Bobby's visit to eastern France left him with a memory he still treasures nearly half a century later, for it embodies for him the kinship that, he feels, binds Americans and their traditional European allies, despite occasional squabbles. One of the Vosges mills he called on was situated in a narrow valley between two bulging mountains. The mill's owner, a M. Chavannes, told him that in the fall of 1943 he huddled in terror in the basement of his mill for two days, while the Germans on one mountain, and the Americans on the other, bombarded each other with artillery, and shells from both sides often fell into the valley. All he could do was pray, Chavannes said, and he never thanked God so much as when the Americans prevailed. As Bobby and du Pasquier climbed back into their car,

Chavannes, after already having wished them farewell, suddenly ran out the door again, with his fist held high and exclaiming, "Vive l'Amerique! Vive l'Amerique!"

The Frenchman's emotional gesture was on Bobby's mind for days, all the more so since everyone he met was talking about the Marshall Plan. As the father-in-law of Willie Brementhal's associate, Marc Serck, told Bobby on his next stop in Belgium, "I don't think you Americans realize what a great thing you have done. No other country in history has won a war and then given its own substance to rehabilitate other nations, even its own enemies." This hadn't quite occurred to Bobby in those terms, but now that he'd heard a European's perception of the program, he felt ever more closely drawn to Europe.

From Belgium, Weil's primary export market before the war, he proceeded to Bremen, where Alvin rejoined him. The purpose was to interview Theodor Riepling as Weil's potential representative in Germany, whose mills were beginning to revive—thanks to the Marshall Plan. Sufficiently impressed, Bobby made the appointment on behalf of the firm. Virginia, meanwhile, had been in Thionville, France, visiting her first cousin, Raoul Loeb, who had been orphaned in the war when his parents were taken off to Auschwitz. That was the other side of the German coin, which now glittered with renewed promise. Finally, everybody headed for Milan to cover Italy with the Kronauers.

Upon Bobby's return from Europe, his position in the company changed radically. During his absence, Fritz Ficke had been hired as Weil's export manager. Liberated from these routines, Bobby was now able to spend more time with Nathan Rosenfield in cotton operations. Moreover, Adolph and Leonel gave him the chance to handle some of the executive aspects of export, which the two elders had heretofore jealously kept to themselves. Like Bucks, Bobby was on his way, his apprenticeship nearing completion. For the next three years, the two brothers would spend many hours every day sitting with Adolph and Leonel to listen in on their phone conversations. As time went on, they began to take some of these calls, discussing prices with Grayson, Reckling, and Crawford. Afternoons, Bobby would take their export offers and make up the outgoing cables.

Bobby Weil in the mid-1960s when he was president of the American Cotton Shippers Association.—*Leon Loard*

But for Bobby's early reservations about tying his life to the firm, the line of succession at Weil Brothers was predestined by the circumstance of birth. In the lottery of lineage, Adolph's side held all the winning cards. Although Leonel's union had been blessed with three children, they were all girls—Elizabeth, Margaret Lee, and Mary Lynne—who grew up in the all-pervasive aura of their father's tranquillity. At Leonel's and Cecile's home, there were none of the tensions so manifest in Adolph's household, and while life with Leonel was rarely exhilarating, neither was it subject to the frequent donnybrooks that were inevitable with someone of Adolph's temperament. Often, when Adolph and Rossie were off on trips, their children were sent over to Leonel's large Tudor-style house at Fairview Avenue and Hull Street to share their cousins' sleeping porch. There was nothing they liked better than such visits: it was their second home, and they reveled in its gaiety and informality, its lack of didactic discipline. Of course, a houseful of little girls is less likely to bring out the Hun in a father than a couple of rambunctious boys given to mayhem.

Leonel was too wise and kind a man ever to hurt his daughters by letting on that he might also have wanted a son. Only once did he let it slip, probably quite unconsciously, for it happened in a business conversation. Carl Baquie, early in his career, had made the mistake of buying ⅞ staple, which, on closer inspection, turned out to be only ¹³⁄₁₆—too short to fetch a decent price. After examining the samples, Leonel didn't blow up at Carl, as Adolph would have. All he said was, "My little boy wouldn't have bought that as seven-eighths," and then he corrected himself and added, "if I had a little boy."

Almost equally discouraging, none of Leonel's sons-in-law was interested in cotton. Thus Leonel's line stopped with him. This was probably the major reason why he retired at an exceptionally young age for a cotton man. He was barely sixty when he gave up his partnership in 1951; with a son to push along, he might have stuck around. There was yet another consideration: some years earlier— before antibiotics were developed—Leonel had almost died of septicemia after he scratched himself on a thorn while hunting. Ever since, his wife Cecile had been trying to tell him that there was more to life than business. Now she insisted it was time to quit. He vacated his desk across from Adolph's (who wanted him to keep sitting there anyway), and moved to the room next door, to Isidor's old desk, where he continued as busy as before, taking care of his own investments.

With Leonel's retirement, Bucks and Bobby moved into overall management. They had been partners in the firm all along, and upon Weil Brothers' incorporation in 1950 had become directors and officers, at least in name. Now title became fact as, serving as Adolph's assistants and deputies, they were increasingly involved in top-level decisions. This happened none too soon, for Weil was suddenly caught in a maelstrom of crises. One was financial and the other managerial, and they aggravated each other as such circumstances will.

As may be recalled, Al Grayson, Weil's prime mover in Dallas, died in 1951—the same year Leonel retired. Then, less than a year later, Bill Reckling, Al's counterpart in Houston, left for Anderson Clayton, necessitating the transfer of Nathan Rosenfield from Montgomery to replace him. Also in 1952, Lucien Loeb retired, yet another loss to the firm. Lucien had befriended Adolph in the late 1890s when both were about ten years old. At that time the Weils had

Jack C. DeLoney. *Riverbottom Cotton*, 1975 (Weil Brothers Collection).

still lived in Opelika, but the families were already connected, and the Loebs, like many other Montgomery families, always fled the low country for Opelika during yellow fever epidemics. In Lucien's early life, despite his eventual marriage into the Weil clan, he'd had no interest in becoming involved in cotton. After graduation from Cornell, he had gone with his family's grocery wholesale firm and did not join Weil as a partner until he was thirty-six. Then, however, his business experience and financial acumen had served to fill an important niche as he concerned himself with the company's ever more complex administration and the vital relationships with its banks. These functions now fell largely to Bucks and Bobby.

Meanwhile, soon after Rosenfield's move to Houston, it became apparent that James L. Loeb, Lucien's son, was not thriving there. He was recalled to Montgomery in 1953 to take over the Eastern operation under Bucks' and Bobby's direction. It did not turn out to be a propitious time for a new, relatively inexperienced manager in this arena, which was in dire need of Nathan Rosenfield's honed skills: the 1953–54 season, coming at the height of the CCC doldrums, resulted in such disastrous losses to the Eastern operation that Adolph wanted to discontinue that part of the business and establish a new base for the firm in Memphis or Houston. Only combined pressure of the three young men—Bucks, Bobby, and Jimmy, who also held a partnership—made Adolph yield on both counts, and then only under the condition that there would be no bonuses that year. It became Bobby's unhappy duty to so inform the employees; needless to say, being forced to play the role of hatchet-man did not enhance his popularity.

For Bobby and Bucks, the decision to oppose removal from Montgomery was not an easy one. It was not the first time that such a change had been considered. For years Adolph and Leonel had flirted with relocating in Atlanta and resisted this temptation only because Isidor would have refused to come along. The possibility of transferring headquarters to Memphis or Houston had been broached to Bucks and Bobby as early as 1950 when the Eastern operation was still comfortably in the black. Now, with the East in the red, the arguments against a change of venue were much harder to refute. But the two brothers still had faith in the Eastern business because here the firm faced less interference from direct mill buyers, largely because the cotton was harder to buy. And while they did not discount the advantages of being in a market hub, they could not agree that, given modern communications, physical distance was necessarily detrimental. "Sometimes," says Bobby, "there is a disadvantage in being with all the others. You tend to lose your objective point of view and are much more open to the observation of competitors." On the other hand, with key people running offices in Memphis, Houston, or Dallas, Weil could get the news of what was going on easily enough. What's more, while Montgomery was no longer in the heart of cotton country, it was conveniently near the southern concentration of domestic mills, which still constituted the major part of the firm's business.

Nor could personal reasons be discounted. Bucks and Bobby and their wives loved Montgomery, and found it an ideal city in which to raise their families. They were well known, but could live comfortably just being themselves; they did not relish the social and financial competition so prevalent in larger centers.

At the height of the where-do-we-belong crisis—aggravated by rumors in the trade that Weil was in serious trouble with its internal upheavals and Montgomery losses—Bucks and Bobby happened to be visiting the cemetery. It was April 24, 1954, the anniversary of Isidor's birthday, and they had gone to put some flowers on his grave. The sun was just setting, birds were singing, spring scented the air. Montgomery was at its tranquil best. They stood there, silent for a spell, and then Bucks said to Bobby, "You know, it's even a wonderful place to be dead in."

16

Reconstruction

TODAY, WITH MONTGOMERY still the Weils' home, Bucks and Bobby share the top executive functions of the Weil companies. Following Adolph's death, Bucks became chairman, and Bobby president, of Weil Brothers–Cotton, Inc. Upon the formation in January 1980 of a holding company, Weil Enterprises and Investments, Ltd., Bucks and Bobby assumed the corresponding positions in the new organization while Bobby took over as chairman of the cotton company and Bucks became its president. At the same time, they have been partners in Weil Hermanos (and its predecessor companies) and the Weil Selling Agency, and control the Swiss-based Unicosa.

Problems, both direct and indirect, resulting from the ever-increasing powers of government were to characterize their tenure as the Weil Brothers of their generation. The pervasive federal presence in the cotton business, as in all others, plus a plethora of unprecedented challenges made theirs the most difficult period (so far) in the firm's history. In Isidor's time, free enterprise still reigned unchallenged, and while cotton was no longer king, it remained the characteristic staple of American agriculture. Adolph and Leonel also could still operate freely during much of their careers, restricted by little but their own principles. The big changes did not come until the 1930s when the New Deal legislation, previously discussed, began discouraging American cotton culture and thereby promoted foreign production. All the trends then incipient came to full force in the

1960s and 1970s, making it necessary for Bucks and Bobby to operate in an entirely different context.

But the pressures on them did not only come from without. The management crisis of the early 1950s was but a pale precursor of the professional climacteric that would jolt them in mid-career. Where the earlier rash of retirements, resignations and reassignments had only given rise to rumors that the firm might founder, this time Weil truly was in trouble. Not that, as in the earlier pinch, profits were a problem. In fact, the company was doing exceedingly well financially. But no organization can long survive without a pool of talent being readied for key positions, and Weil lacked such a reserve. Thus, when a sudden rush of deaths and resignations depleted Weil's executive echelons in the late 1960s, the company not only found itself pushed to the wall for lack of upper middle management, but without a lower middle management cadre to insure orderly succession in the future. Bucks and Bobby, in effect, practically had to rebuild the organization from scratch.

The dearth of new blood had its roots in the years of the first management crisis, when, under the bureaucratic banner of the CCC, the cotton business was so poor that Weil Brothers—as all the other firms—did not encourage young men to enter the trade. Even in the early 1960s, when prospects began to brighten, the idea of taking on college students during the summer and then recruiting the most promising among them as potential executive material was anathema to the economy-minded Jimmy Loeb, who rejected such staffing methods as being wasteful.

To recapitulate: after Carl Baquie retired in 1965, Adolph took the Latin American operations under his own wing. In 1967, when Allie Crawford resigned to move back to California, Tom Adams was pulled in from Houston to take over Memphis. That very summer Nathan Rosenfield succumbed to a sudden illness, and Jack Wilson, with no prior experience in Texas cotton, was designated to replace him. Then, only five months later, Adolph passed away and there was no one in line to run the Latin American business.

During the ensuing year, besides running the company and looking after the many personal matters that naturally followed Adolph's death, Bucks tried to fill the Latin American void with an assist from Bobby, and Bobby looked over Jack Wilson's shoulder.

After that strenuous season, the two brothers decided to retrench, both operationally and from the standpoint of making the best use of the executive material remaining to them. The Houston office was combined with the Montgomery office, with George Clay reassigned to Dallas to supervise buying. In closing Houston, Weil made sure that every employee was offered a new post which, if accepted, would result in no loss of income. Manuel Held returned to Montgomery to manage that office. Nell Lawrence, the bookkeeper, went to Memphis, and Jaydee Tobias took charge of the new Texas sample room in Montgomery. At the same time, Jack Wilson, who had done a most creditable job in Texas cotton that year, also was brought to the head office. He would take on the Latin American responsibilities, with which he already had some familiarity from his work in Mexico and periodic missions to Central America.

Meanwhile, the Texas operation was put under the supervision of Jimmy Loeb, who shouldered this function in addition to his duties as manager of the Eastern operation. But the arrangement was short-lived. He had occupied the new post for barely a year when he announced his resignation in January 1969.

A few months later, he launched his own cotton company, also in Montgomery, taking with him five other Weil employees, including Alex Carothers, who had been his right-hand man. Jimmy Loeb's departure—and that of the staffers who went with him—came as a blow. Now the Montgomery office, which was just beginning to digest the Texas operation, could only limp along, and with the executive ranks decimated by the Loeb exodus, no leader was at hand to give it impetus: Bucks and Bobby had their hands full as it was. True, one esteemed cotton expert remained in the Eastern fold. This was Roland A. "Jim" Hester, who had been born in Franklin City, Alabama, when Alabama still made cotton, and had learned the trade in Decatur, then an important inland market. Hester had joined Weil in 1933 after working for the Farm Bureau Cotton Association, and he rose rapidly to head the Montgomery sample room. But by now Hester was in his late sixties, and too old to take on the strenuous responsibility of handling both the Texas and Eastern operations.*

---

*Roland Hester retired in 1978 but still shows up at least once a week to sniff the sample room and visit with old friends.

It was finally decided to offer the position to the aforementioned Bill Wyatt, who had some experience in the shipping offices. When Bill moved to Montgomery, Tommy Pitts, another member of the Dyersburg contingent and former assistant to Ray White, was moved to Greenville to run that show. Frank Bailey, previously stationed in Lubbock to buy for Rosenfield, was brought to Montgomery to direct the Texas buying (which he does to this day), and he took on the sample room as well when Jaydee Tobias left the firm to go into the real estate business in his native Houston. Frank Bailey was then in his early forties. A native of Clarksdale, Mississippi, he had worked as a country buyer in the heart of the Delta and later in Lubbock for a competitor until he joined Weil's Texas operation in 1961. He was as experienced a buyer as they come; indeed, he was soon to be instrumental in the largest single West Texas purchase Weil had made up to that time—28,000 bales, all in one day, from Carlock & Murdough, a Lubbock FOB merchant. But even with men like Bailey and Wyatt on hand, there were not enough mature staffers to fill all the vital slots. The older management team had simply disappeared from the scene.

Bucks and Bobby realized that any rebuilding for the future would have to be rooted in a quest for talented youngsters who could be trained to rise from the ranks. To begin with, however, some experienced men had to be hired from the outside. One of these was Gordon Redmond, a Bailey contemporary, the son of a Briton who had been sent to Dallas to represent a Liverpool firm. Redmond had squidged for Sternberg, Martin & Co., fought as a marine in Korea, then worked for Mitsubishi's merchandising office in Houston until the Japanese firm shut down that operation in 1970—just in time for Redmond's recruitment by Weil. After a year in Montgomery, he was sent to Dallas to replace George Clay, who had resigned to go with Dunavant. Since the closing of Weil's Dallas office in 1975, Redmond has made his headquarters in Lubbock.

There was yet another resignation from a key slot to be coped with. After several years, Bill Wyatt decided that cotton merchandising was not his cup of tea. Thus, when Lowenstein's top buyer, Bob Smith, retired and Wyatt was approached to replace him, he accepted and moved back to Greenville. His parting with Weil was friendly but traumatic nonetheless, for staff rebuilding had not yet advanced to the point where there was anyone in-house able to take on the complex job of running the combined Texas/Eastern operations.

Luckily there appeared a bright and vigorous young man, Marvin Woolen, Jr., who had been trained most thoroughly in all the fundamentals by his father, formerly a vice-president of Anderson Clayton and famous as one of the most astute merchants in the business. One of Marvin's strengths was his knowledge of domestic mills. His weaknesses lay in his limited experiences with Texas cotton and lack of export expertise. But these proved to be no handicap. From the day he stepped into the Montgomery office, he strove to learn every aspect of the operation, and within a short time was making such phenomenal profits that he was personally confronted with the delightful problem of investment management in dealing with his income. His progress was so extraordinary that in only a few years, at the age of thirty-three, he was made a vice-president of the firm.

Still another young man proved invaluable in getting Weil back on even keel during this difficult transition period. He was James McGhee, who actually dated back to Adolph's time, having joined

Gordon Redmond, Weil's manager in Lubbock, is the son of a Briton who represented a Liverpool firm in Dallas.

Weil in 1966. A native of Camp Hill, a little town between Alexander City and Opelika, he had studied accounting at Auburn and then went with Arthur Anderson & Co., first in Atlanta and then in Birmingham. But the constant traveling involved was not to his liking and he wanted a more stationary job. What he didn't know when Bobby interviewed him was that he'd be journeying even farther afield—to nearly every country where Weil has outposts—if not as frequently.

Jim McGhee sent his resume to Weil at just the right moment. After Vasser Gunter's retirement, G. T. Hill had acted as Weil's auditor, assisted by Al Wilson. When Hill died in 1965, he left a major void, for in the cotton business it's not enough to be an expert accountant; one must have the innate capacity to pick up on the vagaries of the trade. McGhee, then only thirty years old, had such a mind. Jack Wilson, who is rather competent himself when it comes to books, was soon to say that he had never yet met anyone who could look at another man's ledgers and tell you so quickly about things going on in your business that you didn't know yourself. In Jack Wilson's first year in Montgomery, Jim McGhee deduced, simply from examining the figures, that someone was stealing cotton sacks in Nicaragua. The following year, Jim noticed some discrepancies in another Central American operation, which, upon further investigation, revealed the most serious defalcation the firm had encountered in its entire history. As defalcations are often very hard to prove, the bonding company resisted the resulting claim, and it was only Jim's ingenious research, brought to bear on the first day of the trial, which persuaded the bonding company to promptly settle the case.

Today, Jim McGhee holds the titles of vice-president and treasurer, as well as assistant secretary, of the Weil companies. He manages all finances, deals with banks and lawyers, and is general administrative officer. Moreover, he is a highly valued confidante not only of Bucks and Bobby but also of the other executives, and especially the younger men in the firm.

But importing men of an experience level such as McGhee's in the financial field, and of Woolen's and Redmond's in cotton, was not enough to provide backup for the future. To recruit and train promising novices was equally important—yet this was not as simple as it once had been. In the old days, job seekers had been consigned to the sample room for three years to learn the basics, while being paid a nominal wage. More recently, however, beginners were no longer content to be apprentices and demanded more than marginal salaries right from the start, although their contribution wasn't really worth it. Especially enlisting college graduates at scales comparative to those that had been paid to Bucks and Bobby, Tom Adams and Jack Wilson, was impossible. Evidently, the three-year apprenticeship routine had become financially prohibitive. The game now was to seek the best available talent, provide concentrated schooling, and push the newcomers into developmental management positions as rapidly as possible. For this intensive training, recruits were sent to the Murdoch Cotton Classing School in Memphis, which taught the art of classing in four months.

The first and most successful example of bringing young talent aboard in the new way was the hiring of Stuart Frazer, the young man and spinner of tall tales who was later to be chased to the top of his car by a New Mexico ginner's dog and then thought by the ginner to be a foreign cotton buyer.

Organizations like Weil have no personnel department. Applicants are interviewed by Bucks and Bobby, a crossfire interrogation that makes many lose their cool. But not Stu Frazer. That he happened to be a friend of Richard Kohn, who is the son of close friends of the Weils, made his interview no less challenging. His answers to questions were so acute that several times during the session Bucks and Bobby smiled surreptitiously at each other like cats that had cornered a fat mouse. Bucks, who is known to blurt out abrupt but very thoughtful questions, came up with one that would have caught anyone by surprise. Just after Stu had worked out a calculation dealing with cotton costs, Bucks asked him if he'd ever smoked marijuana. With a puzzled look but not lacking in composure, Stu turned to him and said, "Yessir." Now it was Bucks' turn to be taken aback; he had not expected such a candid reply. Stuart added that he hadn't liked the weed, but this didn't matter nearly as much to Bucks and Bobby as the quick answer. Ironically, had Stuart enjoyed pot he couldn't have found a more opportune job, for he was soon assigned as an understudy to Jack Wilson for Latin America, maryjane's

Montgomery's select mob includes Marvin
Woolen (above), vice-president in charge of
Eastern and Texas operations, shown here on
one of his frequent visits to the commodities
teletype; Frank W. Bailey (left), once a country buyer, who handles the Texas business;
Jim McGhee (top center), vice-president and
treasurer, who runs the ever-important money
and tax end; Ethel Farley (top right), the
corporate secretary; Mark O'Connor (center
right), manager of the Export Department;
and Stuart Frazer (bottom right), Woolen's
assistant for Eastern operations, who, like everybody else in the office, chalks the latest
futures quotations on the hallway blackboard
every time he passes the ticker.—*Author's
photographs*

Taking a sunshine break on the levee behind Weil's Memphis office, Clark Burnett sits on cobblestones that long ago were covered with cotton bales, next to the heavy moorage rings on which the Mississippi steamers used to tie up.—*Historic photograph courtesy of John W. Hammett from collection of Wallace R. McKay; Burnett picture by author*

birthplace and perpetual nursery. With his inquisitive mind, extraordinary intelligence, sharp sense of humor, and Jack Wilson's supervision, Stuart Frazer probably learned the business more quickly than anyone else ever had at Weil Brothers. After a relatively short period as Wilson's assistant, he was made manager of the Eastern operation under Marvin Woolen. His successor as trainee was Wally Darneille, Wilson's current alter ego, who had been a classmate of Bobby's son at Dartmouth.

Warren Donaldson, now Gordon Redmond's assistant, came up a similar route. The son of an army pilot, he was born in St. Joseph, Missouri, majored in political science at the University of Missouri, served in the army in Vietnam, and came to Weil through an employment agency after his discharge. As Oklahoma buyer, with an annual takeup of about 50,000 bales, he is in charge of a suboffice at Altus, whose only other staff member is a cotton farmer's wife, Mrs. Nancy Jarnagin—she always has up-to-date information on how the crops are coming. As elsewhere in the Texas territory, Donaldson does

Warren Donaldson handles Oklahoma cotton out of the Lubbock, Texas, office.

all his buying on government class, and the samples are later reclassed in Montgomery for sale by the Texas Department.

Another of the latter-day recruits was Clark Burnett, until recently in the Far East, of whom more shortly. Three young men are currently in understudy jobs: Austin Wade and Mike Keesee in Montgomery, and Hardy Butler, a nephew of Pick Butler, in Memphis.

Being prepared, meanwhile, to serve as the next set of Weil "brothers" are cousins—Bucks' son, Adolph "Andy" Weil III, and Bobby's son, Robert S. Weil II, who is known around the office as "Bobby Two" to distinguish him from his dad, now called Bobby, Sr., by everybody in the shop.

While Weil's dramatis personae inevitably change from act to act, the firm's traditional management style remains the same. This style calls for a finely tuned balance of executive independence on the one hand, and close coordination of all operations on the other. Managers have autonomy to act within the prescribed frameworks of house rules and the limits on prices set by Bucks and Bobby, but they must consult whenever possible and without fail report their actions promptly.

That such reporting is vital came home to Bobby, Sr., early in his career, when he still worked under Nathan Rosenfield. Callaway Mills, of La Grange, Georgia, then had ten mills operating under three divisions. All had their own cotton buyers, who did their purchasing independently of each other, although they were often interested in the same qualities. In one season of the early 1950s, which saw discounts in the market, Weil and other shippers sometimes bought cotton from one domestic mill and sold it to another, as mills with heavy inventories sought to rid themselves of surpluses. At that time, Bobby learned that Callaway's MMC division was looking for Middling $^{15}/_{16}$, while the group's HDV division had Middling $^{15}/_{16}$ for sale. Negotiating alternately with the two mill buyers, he then discovered that he could turn the cotton from HDV to MMC and make a profit of about twenty-five points, which in those days wasn't bad for draying cotton a few miles from one mill to another. Nathan found out what Bobby was about to do and stopped him dead in his tracks. "You're going to make a monkey out of Callaway," he said, "and that'll cost you a hell of a lot more in the long run than a quick twenty-five point profit on five hundred bales."

This taught Bobby an important lesson but not all of it. He told Nathan that he saw his point but that maybe he had better tell Gene Parker, the MMC buyer, that he could get his cotton easily next door in an in-house transaction. This, Bobby figured, would be a real favor to the Callaway people. But again Nathan scolded the young man. "What do want to do?" he exploded. "Tell a lady her slip is showing? You've got to learn that sometimes it's better not to open your mouth."

Bobby resolved then and there that Weil would never be caught with its slip showing. The same day Peter Frank buys Unicosa cotton, Tom Adams in Memphis knows about it, and when Tom is trading, Marvin Woolen and Jack Wilson are sure to know the terms under consideration.

This is not to say that Weil managers must agree on everything they do either privately or in public. They don't even have to be in accord on matters of policy. When Bobby was president of the American Cotton Shippers Association in 1963–64, the recommendation was made at the ACSA convention that the government record the micronaire of each bale on the green cards. Nathan Rosenfield, then manager of the Houston office and president of the Texas Cotton Association, strongly opposed this proposition. Jimmy Loeb, the manager of the Eastern office, was for it, and a hot debate between two Weil executives developed on the convention floor, with motions and cross-motions coming up so fast that the parliamentarian had to be consulted. Finally, it was Allie Crawford, then Weil's Fresno manager, who rose to suggest that the problem might best be resolved at a meeting of the directors of Weil Brothers–Cotton, Inc. How this issue was eventually decided is not important here. What matters is that Weil Brothers did not demand that its managers speak for the firm. Nor does it now—a unique working condition in the cotton trade.

At the 1980 ACSA convention, a similar disagreement between Weil executives was to be aired and this time at the highest level. Bobby, Sr., had made a recommendation that all spot markets should quote all qualities with reference to the New York futures market. At this suggestion, Starke Taylor, Jr., a good friend of the Weils who was sitting with them, rose to object and went on to say that, in a committee meeting the day before, Bucks had expressed the exact opposite view, and why didn't the Weils get their stories together? Smiles passed between Bucks and Bobby as Starke talked, and then Bobby rose in rebuttal. "It's a fact, we do disagree quite often after all," he said, and paused to let the laughter die before delivering his punchline: "You know, if we didn't disagree, there would be no need for one of us."

17

Grand Tour

WHEN BOBBY'S SON, BOBBY WEIL II, went on his export indoctrination trip to Europe in the spring of 1980, he was gone for only four weeks. His father, making the same grand tour of agents and mills in 1949, had been on the road for ten weeks, not counting the lengthy steamship crossings. Bobby, Sr., had spent more than two weeks in Belgium alone, which was then a hub of busy spinners. When Bobby II showed up thirty-one years later, one of that country's last major mills, Van Hoegarden Boonen, had only recently taken receivership.

Statistics kept by F. S. Vandriessche & Co. over the years declaim the Flemish dirge in disheartening detail. The Vandriessches were, and are, cotton controllers—intermediaries between shippers and buyers. Commissioned by the bale, and representing the shipper-seller, they weigh, sample and class newly arrived cotton at the port of destination. Their evaluation constitutes evidence in arbitration courts when, as happens fairly frequently, the quantity and/or quality of a shipment is challenged by a buyer.

Sometimes the shipper is at fault. He may have misjudged the buyer's needs or classed the cotton carelessly or, occasionally, a sharpie might dispatch short bales, hoping that they would gain weight through moisture absorption in transit. Conversely, buyers may make mistakes in weighing and classing, and some have been known to falsify their weights.

But while in domestic transactions buyers may reject a shipment and demand replacement by cotton as contracted, this is unworkable when the bales in question have traveled halfway around the world. The international buyer is required to take up the cotton, but may then file a claim for compensation if the stock isn't all it was supposed to be. Such claims come to only a few points per pound, but with thousands of bales that can mean a lot of money. Hence, the great firms of cotton controllers have been as prominent in the cotton world as the big merchants and mills: E. T. Robertson & Son, originally of Boston and later in Liverpool, Shanghai and Hong Kong; General Superintendence, of Geneva, which handles most of the Weil business in the Far East; and F. L. Vandriessche, in Belgium and France.

The original Vandriessche, whose first name was Florent, had represented Weil Bros. along with numerous other American and

Checking cotton shipments at the ports of arrival is the function of several highly specialized worldwide firms of "cotton controllers" whose judgment is vital in establishing the precise quality, and therefore possible variations in price from contract specifications. The photographer of the picture at left, which was probably taken in the 1930s, posed cotton controllers and pier porters in the sheds of the Southern States Line at Rotterdam, once one of the world's leading cotton ports.

foreign firms, including such diverse enterprises as Anderson Clayton of Memphis and Bunzl & Biach of Vienna, since he had first gone into business at the port of Ghent shortly after World War I.* As so many companies dealing with cotton, it was a family enterprise. When Florent died in 1962 at the age of seventy-one, his sons, Leon and Jean, and his nephew Romain, took over. Their records show that in the late 1970s, already before the difficulties of Van Hoegarden Boonen, Belgian cotton consumption stood well below 100,000 bales a year, about one fifth of what it had been during the peak years of the 1950s. Even at the depth of the Great Depression, in the 1933–34 season, American cotton exports to Belgium had totaled nearly 110,000 bales. In all these years, Weil had been one of the three top-volume U.S. merchants, and in the 1950s, thanks to Willy Bre-menthal, had consistently occupied the number-one spot.† Today, Belgium's few surviving spinneries buy most of their cotton from Turkey and Russia. Some long-staple San Joaquin Valley cotton from California is still imported, but the Strict Middling 1⅟₁₆ from Memphis, which used to be the rule, now is a rare exception.

Bobby II remained but one day in Ghent, largely a matter of auld lang syne. Then he moved on to Holland. His sojourn there was equally brief. The great Dutch mills of Gebroeders (brothers, wouldn't you know) Van Heek, Van Heek Scholco, and Roombeek had long since turned turtle. The Netherlands, which at one time imported nearly 400,000 bales a year, now buys only 80,000. Only one large textile organization, Spinnerij Nederland B.V., which is half-owned and largely subsidized by the Dutch government, still imports cotton from the United States.**

---

*The Vandriessche operation was soon expanded to Antwerp, Le Havre and Dunkirk. Its headquarters have remained in Ghent, although the cotton for Belgium now flows mostly through Antwerp.

†The two other big shippers were Anderson Clayton and the American Cotton Cooperative Association. Some years, Hohenberg Bros. and R. L. Dixon also showed up in the top trio.

**Spinnerij Nederland is the result of a merger of the Bamshoeve, Ten Cate, Van Heek, Tubantia, and Twenthe mills, all giants in their day and once substantial Weil customers. As this is written, three smaller Dutch spinneries, Puyenbroek, Zwaluwe, and Rositta, also still buy a little U.S. cotton.

The French situation was hardly more inspiring. The suave boulevardier Robert du Pasquier, Weil's one-time partner at Le Havre, had been out of the cotton business for the past twelve years and kept himself busy in other, more profitable arenas of international trade as a consultant. Back in the late 1940s, Bucks and Bobby, Sr., accompanied by Maison Du Pasquier subagents Jean Schmidt of Epinal and Daniel Olivier of Mulhouse, had called on more than thirty spinners in that region. By 1980, many of these mills in Alsace and the Vosges were closed. In Lille, hub of the textile territories of the Artois and Picardy in northwestern France, the former sample rooms of the venerable Société Polycoton–France were stacked ceiling-high with boxes containing cashmere sweaters. The current generation of Polycoton's Devilder family, Patrick and Francis, whose predecessors had been lifelong Weil agents as well as merchants on their own, were trying to establish themselves in a new line of endeavor—as sales representatives for Pringle of Scotland. France's cotton imports from the United States had rarely been less than half a million bales even in the Depression years. In the 1950s, they ranged as high as 700,000 bales. Now, although France remains one of Europe's largest cotton users at close to one million bales a year, America's share of this market was down to about 100,000 bales—too insignificant a volume for any single American merchant firm to sustain full-time representation.

Needless to say, Bobby II lingered longer in Milan than in most other cities, spending pleasant hours with the Kronauers, Weil's oldest contact on the Continent. But friendship is one thing and business another, and the latter wasn't what it used to be here either. Overall, the Italian textile industry's cotton consumption still held close to one million bales, making it one of Europe's three major users of natural fiber, along with Germany and France. Germany's mills had managed to prosper partly because of their large affluent market, which demanded nothing but the best and could afford to pay for it. At the same time, the underlying cause of this astounding affluence—the rebuilding from scratch of the German industrial apparatus after World War II—had made the spinneries overwhelmingly efficient. Like Japan's, Germany's mills were brand-new and equipped with the most up-to-date machinery, effectively reducing labor costs. Italy's mills, on the other hand, had the advantages of relatively low wages as well as cheap hydroelectric power, thanks to the industry's location in the foothills of the Alps, near the glacial runoff lakes of Como, Maggiore, and Garda. It also helped that the major Italian spinneries, such as Legler and the Gruppo Tessile NK of Niggeler and Küpfer are owned and managed by the ever-efficient Swiss, who are as adept at "rationalization" as the Germans.

But here, as elsewhere, the use of American cottons was on the decline. Traditionally, the Italian mills purchased their Memphis-quality cotton from the States, their short cheap cotton from India, and their long staple from Egypt. In recent years, however, several countries around the Mediterranean have been growing cotton in increasing quantities and of various grades, and are supplying their fiber at prices with which American cotton cannot compete. Today, only about one third of the Kronauer agency's annual volume of 180,000 to 200,000 bales comes from the Weil companies, and while Chicco might be able to sell more Memphis than, say, Turkish cotton if he chopped off a couple of cents a pound, he can't because price-slashing is against Weil policy. This stubborn stance doesn't always delight Chicco, but he is one of those exceptional Italians (albeit equipped with a Swiss passport) who manage to transact business *serenamente*. No matter what happens, Chicco always keeps his cool.

Not that this has ever been easy anywhere in the world of cotton. Some years ago, after a dinner for the Baquies, hosted by Adolph and attended by several of his managers, Carl's wife noticed that most of the men reached into their pockets for Gelusil. "You know," she remarked, "I don't think my husband's in the right business." This little joke brought down the house with rueful laughter. If anything, the situation in Italy, as elsewhere in Europe by the late 1970s, was even less conducive to tranquility. Chicco was doing very well indeed, but he was now one of only six cotton agents left in Milan, a market center that until fairly recently had supported several dozen.

For one thing, Europe's textile industry was not the giant of yore. Not only had its markets shrunk with the independence of the former colonies—Belgium, for instance, had lost its Congo; Holland, its Indonesia; and Britain, everything. But, as pointed out before, textile manufacture comes on strongly at relatively early stages of industrial development, and the bulk of production had shifted to such awakening areas as Taiwan, Hong Kong, Korea, Thailand, and

Indonesia. For another, the increasing use of synthetics, as in the United States, was preempting cotton's dominant role in fabrics.

As for American cottons, they occupied an ever smaller place within this diminishing market. In 1949–50, foreign production had totaled about fourteen million bales. By 1964, it had risen to thirty-six million bales. In 1978, it nudged fifty million bales, as cotton culture inevitably gravitated to countries with cheap agricultural labor, most of which, as it happens, enjoy precisely the climate that's favorable to growing the fiber. To be sure, the United States remains one of the biggest cotton producers, with a crop of about ten to fifteen million bales, depending on the season. China and Russia are in about the same league, but with one important difference. China imports. Russia exports. India comes next with about six million bales. Then there are Turkey, Egypt, Brazil and Pakistan, with two to three million bales each, followed by Greece, Syria and Spain, with about 700,000. Of these, Russia, Turkey, India, Greece, and Syria are heavy exporters. Russia alone ships three to four million bales a year to other countries, mostly to Europe, but also to Japan, where it is now the number-two cotton supplier next to the United States. As for long staple, California's San Joaquin Valley cotton has to compete against the premium exotics from Egypt, Peru, Israel and the Sudan.

In short, the American export surge after World War II had been of predictably limited duration—predictably, that is, if anyone had really thought about it, and it's doubtful that even Adolph and Leonel did: life in the cotton business is far too hectic to allow for such academic projections. The Weils' venture into Central America was not so much prompted by an appreciation of the coming importance of foreign growths than it was by the need to obtain export cotton at lower prices than parity decreed. That it was a fortuitous move not only for the moment but in the long run—by introducing the firm into the new field of extraterritorial buying—was not of consideration at the moment. True enough, the federal government tried to stimulate the export of American cotton. In the beginning, during the Truman Administration, it was done indirectly through Secretary of State George C. Marshall's Economic Cooperation Administration (ECA), a giveaway plan designed to build up Europe economically so it wouldn't fall prey to Communism. As part (a tiny part) of its program, the ECA financed cotton sales through allocations to the various countries, whose governments, in turn, would allocate sums to various mills. The United Kingdom had its Raw Cotton Commission, France had her GIRC, Germany her JEIA. Italy, Holland, Belgium—they all had similar agencies.

The way this was handled was that the Department of Agriculture would make an announcement to the trade that there would be an allocation of so many millions of dollars for so many bales of cotton to be shipped to Germany, France, Italy, or whatever. Contracting always began no less than seven days after the announcement. As usual when Uncle Sam gets mixed up in financing, there was a multitude of strings attached, some of which made little sense. In 1949, for instance, there was a tremendous crop of low grades and only a small domestic demand. As a result, the ECA specified that exactly 17½ percent of any 100,000-bale allocation had to be in the low grades, whether or not any of the mills in the countries subject to this largess were interested in that kind of cotton. Still, there's no question that these allocations did help to restore the textile economies of Europe and, by the same token, put money in the pockets of American growers and shippers. When, after the Korean Conflict, U.S. surplus cotton bulged the warehouses again, PL-480 took the place of the ECA. In effect, PL-480 subsidized exports by making up the negative difference between the high support price of U.S. cotton and the lower price foreign mills were willing to pay. The red tape attached to such transactions was awesome. Each sale had to be registered with the Department of Agriculture, which determined whether the price charged was excessive. Once that hurdle was surmounted, random sample bales had to be submitted at the time of shipment. Agriculture Department classers then decided whether the cotton lived up to its contractual promise. If they felt that the cotton was too expensive, it automatically went into arbitration: the foreign buyer may have been perfectly happy with the cotton, but he had no say about it. Not surprisingly, this procedure undermined confidence in American shippers: if their own government said that the buyers had a claim coming, then something must be wrong indeed.

When Peter Frank first came aboard in 1957 to sell Weil cotton in Europe, the negative influences had not yet made themselves felt to any significant degree. American export sales were moving at a fair clip, even if somewhat handicapped by the clumsy ECA procedures. In any event, Weil, thanks to having pioneered the Central American territory, had plenty of foreign growths to take up the slack. At that time, Europe still absorbed about 200,000 Weil bales a year, a substantial portion of the firm's business at that time, and Britain was the only country that so far showed a definite decline in cotton imports. Its mills had been the first to succumb to the import from lower-wage countries of finished cotton goods and the domestic production of cheap synthetics. Before long, artificial fiber manufacturers like Courtaulds and International Chemical Industries (ICI) were dominating the U.K.'s textile output, partly through mergers that achieved vertical integration.

But so far this was the only dark cloud on the horizon. Still, in what turned out to be a very astute move, Weil in early 1958 set up a Swiss corporation, Unicosa, whose charter provided not only for the sale but the purchasing of cotton. Like Algodonera Weil in Panama, Algodonera Naçional in Mexico, and Weil Selling Agency Inc. (a Delaware corporation), Unicosa was established as an entirely separate entity.

For its first year, Unicosa lay dormant, and Peter still occupied himself exclusively with handling Weil Selling Agency business out of Brussels. Then slowly, a few bales at a time, he began exercising Unicosa's franchise. Just as the Weils had been cautious when they first went into Central America, they now felt it was the better part of valor to get their feet wet in the Mediterranean one toe at a time. They were not at all convinced that buying cottons in Asia Minor and the Middle East was up their alley, and while Peter might be a natural linguist, Turkish and Arabic surely were Greek even to him. His first transactions, therefore, were more in the nature of intermediation: he would purchase from merchants for resale to mills, a matter of outguessing the market.

Peter's office was on the third floor of the private home he'd rented in Brussels. There was no need for a staff. He did most of his business on trips or by telephone and telex through agents like Kronauer in Italy, H. Vonderhorst in Holland, and Werner Müller (since succeeded by his son, Peter) in Switzerland. Adolph still visited occa-

Crossing on the great liners that used to sail the Atlantic was an annual routine for the Weils as they took turns every summer calling on European agents and mill customers. Bobby Weil, with his wife Virginia (center, above), took his indoctrination trip in 1949 aboard the *Nieuw Amsterdam*, accompanied by Alvin and Trudy Weil. In 1950, Bucks and Jean followed on the *Queen Mary* (below left). Adolph and Rossie (below right) also opted for the art-deco splendors of the *Queen Mary* in 1963. It was their last transatlantic journey.

sionally. Although already in his seventies, he'd bound up the three flights to Peter's informal little *agence* two or three steps at a time without running out of breath. Ramrod-straight, he'd then boom out his greetings. It amused Peter no end that Adolph would often spend hours editing telexes—cutting and abbreviating—to prove to Peter how much money could be saved, although the amounts were insignificant since telexes are very cheap within Europe. Except in Brussels, where Adolph stayed at the Plaza (whose manager was a close friend of Willy Brementhal), he always booked into the very best hotels, like Geneva's Le Richemond and the George V in Paris, but once refused to order fresh strawberries at one of Brussel's more (if not most) expensive restaurants because he felt that fifty Belgian francs, then exactly one dollar, was too much to spend on dessert.

Bobby had been to Europe in 1954 at the time of the reopening of the Liverpool Cotton Exchange, then went again in 1959, this time not only taking Virginia but their older daughter, Vicki, with him. Needless to say, the sixteen-year-old girl was welcomed by the Kronauers and du Pasquiers as if she were a member of the family. Bobby's next stop, complete with feminine entourage, was Copenhagen, where he experienced one of the more delicate moments of his career. It happened that Weil's agent in Denmark, Mr. Jurgensen, of L. Paulsen, was a racehorse fancier. And so was Weil's new agent in Sweden, Knut Brannstrom. The Royal Derby, with horses from all over Scandinavia, was being run just at the time of the Weils' visit and naturally Bobby had to go, flanked by Brannstrom's wife and Mr. Jurgensen. The latter's horse was the favorite, but Brannstrom's nosed him out. Trying to remain friendly with both agents, Bobby was faced with three totally unacceptable choices of behavior. He could root for either horse or none. Luckily, the close finish made it possible for him to cheer indiscriminately.

His next trip, in 1963, was a journey in futility. This time, daughter Rosalind was old enough to come along also, and the three ladies joined Bobby after he had visited some of the tougher markets. But by now they all turned out to be tough. In May of that year, Bobby had been elected president of the American Cotton Shippers Association and, as behooved his office, he addressed assemblies of its sister associations in Le Havre, Liverpool, Bremen, and Milan. His speeches were well enough received, but already by 1963 only a trickle of American cotton was finding its way to European markets, and as a representative of American cotton, Bobby was sadly out of date. He didn't sell a single bale.

In the 1960s and 1970s, as the Weil Selling Agency's European business in U.S. and Central American cottons contracted, Peter's Unicosa function came into its own. Today he spends more than two-thirds of his time on Unicosa transactions, buying and selling around 100,000 foreign bales a year. Unlike in the States, his transactions usually can't be hedged, since the prices of the cottons Peter handles only rarely move in concert with the New York futures. What's more, they couldn't be delivered on New York contracts.* Thus, basis operation is usually impossible, and Unicosa's profitability depends largely on market judgment.

For the most part, Peter anticipates demand, knowing that there are certain mills that will need certain kinds of cotton. He then buys this cotton if he can obtain it at what he feels is a favorable price relationship. In order to avoid storage, he purchases for forward delivery on dates that will coincide with the probable consummation of his sale. But although he tries to move what he has bought promptly, there is usually a considerable interval. Thus, he essentially operates from a long or short position. The only way he can reduce the risks inherent in such exposure is by balancing different transac-

---

*As explained in Chapter 6, today's New York futures are based on Strict Low Middling 1¹⁄₁₆ which is by no means the single most prevalent type of all the world's cottons. Of foreign growths, only those of Central America maintain a relatively consistent price relationship to comparable U.S. crops. There have been periodic conferences, most recently promulgated by the United Nations Conference on Trade and Development (UNCTAD), to establish a world cotton futures market that would deal also in other major types. The apparently insurmountable problem with this proposition is that while day-to-day futures trading is done on paper, there comes a time when contracts mature and then the actual cotton must be deliverable. Evidently, it's not practical to ship, say, Turkish cotton to the United States to deliver on contract. For that matter, it isn't even legal. That normally it doesn't come to delivery isn't the point: for a futures market to exist, delivery must be possible. There is no question that international futures trading, if it can be arranged, would be helpful in smoothing out price fluctuations. Moreover, so far as Weil and other international merchants are concerned, it would enable them to go the more conservative route of basis operation.

tions against each other, in hopes that a good sale here will compensate for a bad purchase there. Peter sets his own prices, but needs Montgomery's approval on the extent of his positions. When Bucks and Bobby think that prices will go up, they encourage him to take greater open-market risks. At other times, they instruct him to lie low.

Peter buys mostly Russian, Turkish, and Israeli cotton. His Russian and Turkish cotton is obtained through other merchants. Elsewhere, he buys directly. Israel has been his greatest triumph. Unicosa handles about one third of that country's exports, or about 50,000 bales a year. Israel currently produces around 300,000 bales, of which half are consumed internally. But plans are being implemented to desalinate water from the Dead Sea for increased irrigation of the Negev Desert, which would greatly enhance the export potential.

Although cotton was already being grown in the Negev back in Biblical times, modern Israel's cotton culture is of relatively recent origin. Sam Hamburg, a prominent California grower, had taken note of the similarity of soil and weather conditions in the Negev and his own San Joaquin Valley before it was irrigated. He brought the SJV seed—itself of Egyptian ancestry—to Israel, taught the Israelis how to irrigate, and how to grow cotton under irrigated conditions. Initially, after producing enough to keep their own domestic mills supplied, the Israelis made their selling arrangements through two firms. Eccles & Stern of Liverpool received the exclusive rights to the U.K. market. Bunge was handed a virtual monopoly for the rest of the world. *

This worked for a while. Then, about 1970, the kibbutzniks, who operate communes within a capitalist framework, became uneasy. As a result of the decline of the British market for natural fiber, they found themselves almost completely dependent on Bunge and wanted other merchants in the picture. So as not to lose its franchise, Bunge at that time approached Weil to see if it wanted to participate in the Israeli business. Bobby, Sr., went to Paris to meet with Nick Thompson, who was then the head of Bunge's cotton operations. It

---

*Small amounts were also sold from time to time through Allcott, an Israeli firm, which had previously represented Weil Brothers in the sale of cotton to Israel.

soon became clear that Bunge was willing to let go only of those markets that didn't amount to a hill of beans. Nor was a scheme of joint marketing acceptable to Bobby, since Weil wouldn't take positions as large as Bunge's and was not about to enter into any lopsided arrangement as a junior partner.

Meanwhile, on a trip to Athens, Bobby had met Zvi Neumark, chairman of the Israeli Cotton Marketing Board, the national cooperative. Eventually another get-together was arranged in New York, at which Bobby defined the Weil position: the firm, through Unicosa, would be happy to handle Neumark's cotton, but since it was directly competitive with California cotton, in which Weil had a substantial investment, it would do so only if Neumark could offer the assurance of a continuing commitment. Bobby had no intention of blazing a trail for Israeli cotton only to be left out in the cold. Neumark took the matter up with his board and Weil was in.

Since then, as Israel's premier outlet for cotton, Unicosa has handled as many as 32,000 bales at one crack, more than even Bunge had ever touched in a single transaction. Now the Negev growths go to practically every country Peter covers through his Weil Selling Agency agents—Germany, France, Switzerland, Spain, Portugal, Belgium, and the Netherlands.

The Israelis, as everybody at Weil was soon to find out, were absolutely delightful to deal with. To be sure, they were hard traders, but at the same time eminently fair, personally cordial and informal, and they never lacked a sense of humor. Zvi Neumark, it turned out, was the elder of an extremely religious kibbutz. Peter Frank's two other contacts, Dov Becher and Ely Englender, of the Israeli Marketing Board, were less traditional. Ely, originally from France, also lived on a kibbutz, but his beliefs tended toward the agnostic. Dov, a German refugee and one of the world's foremost cotton-growing technologists, had first lived in a kibbutz, but now maintained his own home; his wife, a Dutch Jewess, had survived World War II by hiding in a friend's house.

When Bobby and Virginia visited in 1978, the three cotton Israelis gave them a warm welcome. It was on this particular occasion that the 32,000-bale purchase (7,000 tons) was being negotiated between Bobby and Peter on one side and Zvi and Ely on the other, with Virginia in the grandstand. When, after long and tough trading, Peter saw that it was impossible to improve on the price, he wiggled to get the advantage of later shipments and a better selection of qualities. The Israelis yielded inch by inch. Finally, Zvi extended his hand to Bobby to clinch the deal but Bobby still had reservations and wanted to talk in private with Peter before sealing the transaction. Zvi looked at him with a disarming smile and said, "You asked me for a loaf of bread, and I gave you a loaf of bread. Then you asked me for raisins on it, and I gave you raisins on it. Then you tell me you want sugarcoating on it and I give you sugarcoating. Now you wonder whether you want a loaf of bread!" The comment sent Virginia into gales of laughter, thereby saving the impasse. Bobby and Peter quickly saw Zvi's point, and thus the transaction was concluded. When the Weils left Israel, everybody kissed Virginia goodbye, which was to be more or less expected, but as a final touch, Zvi also kissed her husband. Wisecracks Bobby: "That must have been a very good price we paid Zvi. I haven't been kissed by a supplier or customer before or since."

Zvi has since visited the Weils in Montgomery and so have Dov and Miriam Becher. Such friendships spring up quite naturally in the cotton world. On the same trip, for instance, while Bobby and his wife were in Liverpool, where David and Philip Stern, of Eccles & Stern, entertained them, Virginia established a close bond with Philip's mother, Lavendar, who now visits her in Montgomery every spring. The Barcelona agent, Hector Khalo, and his wife also have become friends, as have the Peter Müllers in Switzerland. The Kronauers, of course, occupy a special place in the affections of the Weils, and Zia Piera, in turn, treats the successive Montgomery generations as she would her own. "Ah, Virginietta," she once told Bobby's wife as they looked from one of Rome's hills upon St. Peter's blazing in the sunset. "You must take what you have in your eyes now and put it in the back of your head, and someday when you are unhappy or something is very wrong, you must take this out from the back of your head and put it back in your eyes."

Unicosa is now headquartered in Zug, Switzerland, about twenty minutes by train from downtown Zurich. By 1976 it had become apparent that it was awkward to operate a Swiss company out of

Belgium, and Peter Frank looked around for a new home. Geneva would have appeared the obvious choice. That's where Egypt's cotton capitalists had settled after Gamal Abdel Nasser ousted King Farouk in 1952. But the Canton of Geneva would issue residence permits for Peter and his staff only against guarantees of exorbitant taxes. Zug, a commercial center and growing hub of holding companies, was less exacting, and Peter quickly obtained the two residence permits required—for Jo Haack and himself—out of the fifty-eight issued by the Canton of Zug in 1978. Peter liked Zug's location better anyway. It was closer to his Swiss and German customers, and also to St. Anton, on the Tirol side of Austria's Arlberg, where he and his wife, Liesl, the daughter of the late owner of St. Anton's famous Hotel Alte Post, own a vacation apartment for ski weekends.

Aside from the fact that Peter generally cannot hedge his transactions, Unicosa's business carries another built-in risk, one that's common to all international dealings—exposure to currency fluctuations. With but a few exceptions (Russia, for instance, insists on payment in German marks and French francs), cotton is billed worldwide in terms of U.S. cents per pound. Contracts thus are fixed to the dollar value as it stands at the moment of the commitment. If, in the case of a forward sale, the dollar has dropped, say, three percent by the time the cotton is brought in, the merchant has lost that three percent (other factors being equal). Of course, the currencies can be hedged, but this adds to the cost.* There are also other contingencies. To pay for foreign cotton, Weil must have the appropriate foreign currency available in the country of origin. When the Mexican peso was devalued some years ago, Weil happened to be one of the few lucky firms with minimal peso deposits. Humerto Castillo, the manager at San Luis, Sonora, and Nicolas Garcia, in Torreón, along with their seven Algodonera Naçional staffers, had just been paid, as had their office rents, and no major purchases were anticipated at the moment. But other companies with sizable peso deposits lost thousands of dollars overnight. In April 1978, the rumor spread through banking circles that the Guatemalan quetzal would be

---

*Weil has recently minimized its exchange risks by nearly always transacting its purchases and sales in dollars. Unicosa sometimes still buys Russian cotton in French francs, but here again this is immediately converted into a dollar transaction.

Now with Unicosa in Zug, Switzerland, Joachim "Jo" Haack is the last man Adolph recruited. Then in Nicaragua, Haack had previously worked for Anderson Clayton in Africa.

floated at the end of the month. If this actually happened, a drastic devaluation was likely. The news caught Weil just as the firm had forwarded $250,000 to its Guatemala agent through the Chase Manhattan. Bucks got right on the phone, hoping to stop the transfer. In this instance he succeeded: the payment in quetzals had not yet been made.

Other exposures may not be quite so dramatic, but they can hurt nonetheless. The overhead of foreign offices must be paid in local currencies—Osaka's in yen, Unicosa's in Swiss francs. If, as has happened on several occasions in the 1970s, the value of the dollar should decline as much as 20 or 30 percent in the span of a few weeks, the cost of maintaining the foreign operations goes up proportionately. Similarly, steamship companies in recent years have added currency surcharges to their freight rates to safeguard themselves against fluctuations. These surcharges are billed in hard currencies: the German mark, Swiss franc, and the Japanese yen.

There's of course the temptation to offset such cost increases by

At Austria's most famous ski hotel, the Alte Post in St. Anton on the Arlberg, Peter Frank (right) and his wife, Liesl, both enthusiastic and expert downhillers, party with Karl Schranz, Olympic medalist, in the early 1960s. Liesl, like Schranz, is a native of St. Anton; her family has owned the Alte Post for generations.

taking bigger positions in hopes of great profitability. This is nonsense so far as the Weils are concerned. "Simply because something costs more," says Bucks, "is no reason to gamble. That's like saying I'll fly first class to Las Vegas, but I'll make up for the extra fare by betting hundred-dollar chips instead of fifties. We just don't operate that way. So long as our foreign operations remain profitable despite all the extra costs and contingencies, we'll continue them. If we can't, we'll get out."

That Weil never will be as big an international operator as the big foreign cotton firms is a foregone conclusion. To begin with, these are often able to do business more cheaply because they are not subject to taxation in their countries if they maintain extraterritorial bases. By the same token, American firms are constrained by law from engaging in practices like kickbacks and bribes that are taken for granted in other countries. But even if Uncle Sam weren't so inclined to cut off his nose to spite his face, the Weils would never approve of such shenanigans on the part of their representatives. When it comes to choosing between principle and profit, it is principle that always wins.

Peter Frank occasionally finds this unyielding attitude a little frustrating. It's not that he wants to wheel and deal in the Continental fashion. What tends to bother him is that the Weils expect their customers and suppliers to be as principled as they are themselves. Once a client has treated them shabbily, they will no longer do business with him—an attitude that eliminates numerous prospects. But the Weils know that the future doesn't hinge on doing business the Old World way. As always, their basic thrust is to maintain volume within the United States, and here the fact that the Weils are determined to live up to their commitments has been largely responsible for increasing their share of market.

As will be recalled, Weil established itself in Japan shortly after World War II, first through Mitsubishi, and later by setting up the Weil Selling Agency under Russell Eaton. Already in the days of Mitsubishi, Joe McAteer and Allie Crawford had visited Japan on several occasions, pushing Memphis growths. It was from Nathan Rosenfield, who went in 1954, that the recommendation came for Weil to open its own office.

At that time, Japan was the only Asian country that really counted. Hong Kong was only just emerging, and neither Korea nor Thailand, not Taiwan and even less so the People's Republic, were as yet factors in the cotton trade. Weil did some spasmodic business with Smith Bell, an English company in the Philippines, and eventually shipped a good deal of cotton to India, working with the firm Narandas Rajaram, headed by a Mr. Saraiya, the president of the Indian Chamber of Commerce. But compared to the volume Carl Baquie and Russell Eaton funneled from Latin America to the Japanese mills, all else was more or less marginal.

Adolph went with Rossie on a pleasure trip to the Far East in 1958. But with business always the best part of Adolph's pleasure, this journey marked the beginning of Weil's expansion in the region. He stopped off in Hong Kong to scout for contacts and shortly afterwards Weil acquired two agents in the Crown Colony. One was Lebel, which was owned by Calico Prints of England, and later combined to form Lebel-Hutchinson. Weil's accounts with Lebel were under the names of H. H. Lawler and Gulfcot, pseudonyms used because at this point Weil did not as yet wish to advertise that it was trying to gain a foothold in that market. The other agent was Lawrence Yao.

These arrangements stayed in effect until 1967, when Bobby and Virginia toured the Far East for six weeks to celebrate their twenty-fifth anniversary—a combined pleasure and business trip during which, in his characteristically meticulous manner, Bobby kept detailed records of the time devoted to each. Stopping off in the Philippines, he found out that Smith Bell was one of those diffuse trading firms in the British tradition that maintained numerous departments for various commodities and products. That was all right, but it turned out that the man supposedly in charge of the cotton department had left the company some time ago and that, since then, the department had existed in name only: it was no wonder that there hadn't been any sales. Luckily, through an old army friend, Bobby met Wally Wirth, who had been with Neuss-Hesslein, the big cotton goods distributing company. Although Wirth was not actually a cotton man, he had excellent entree and appeared extremely competent, an impression that was to prove itself out in the coming years when he served as Weil's agent in the Philippines.

Another challenge presented itself in Hong Kong, where Mr. Yao, one of the two agents there, failed to show up at the hotel to meet Bobby and Virginia, thus making it clear that he cared little about the Weil business. The problem of changing over from Yao's Barnett Sales was solved with the help of Brinsley Golding, the prominent Hong Kong controller, who managed to retrieve the Weil types from Yao's firm for consignment to Lebel. The consolidation of all Weil business with Lebel was a significant development, since the quid pro quo of the arrangement was that the firm would be Lebel's exclusive cotton client. Weil's sales in Hong Kong jumped immediately.

It was while negotiating with Lebel that Bobby met David Hardoon—father of the young David Hardoon now working for Weil—who had only recently joined Lebel in Hong Kong after fleeing the People's Republic. The elder Hardoon, of whom more shortly, launched his own Asian Pacific Cotton Ltd. a few years later when

Lebel-Hutchinson, which was a diversified trading company, decided to get out of the cotton business. Asian Pacific has since served as Weil's highly successful Hong Kong agency.

In Taiwan, Bobby firmed up Weil's relationship with the Far East's most successful cotton agent, C. L. Wong, a slender gentleman with a broad face and an even broader infectious smile. Wong is now about fifty years old, although he looks much younger. Back in the early 1960s, long before Bobby's visit, he had worked for the Cheng Yuan Trading Co., whose principal, W. Y. Sun, approached Weil to represent the firm in Taiwan's expanding market. Eventually Sun and Wong had a falling out. Odd as it may seem, Wong, the employee, stayed with Cheng Yuan Trading, while Sun moved out to form a new firm, the W. Y. Sun Company. For several years, Weil did business through both, but then the time came when a choice had to be made. Weil opted for Wong, who had loyally borne the brunt of

David Hardoon, Jr., a journalist turned cotton man, and his wife Chris (right) live in Osaka, his base as Weil's general Far Eastern representative. His father, David Hardoon, Sr. (below), has long been the firm's Hong Kong agent. In Taiwan, supersalesman C.L. Wong sells Weil cottons through his Cheng Yuan Trading Co.; he is shown at left with his wife as they visited Montgomery for the Weil centennial. Knowing the merchandise is vital. In the snapshot, bottom right, Akira Hanada of the Osaka office inspects Nicaraguan crop with Jack Wilson, who is up to his ears in bolls.

the work from the beginning. It was a wise choice. By the time of Bobby's visit, Wong had become so expert in his profession that the mills came to him for certain types of cotton simply because other mills had bought it from him. Thus, Weil's Memphis-Type BORD-A became a Taiwan favorite almost overnight.

Wong doesn't represent Weil exclusively. He also acts as agent for a host of European companies dealing in non-U.S. growths. As a welcome result, Weil has started to merchandise growths it hadn't before because Wong wanted to sell them. Needless to say, a number of merchants that trade in similar cottons have tried to seduce Wong into their fold, but he stayed loyal. In a few short years, he had built Weil into the largest single shipper to Taiwan. With his agency selling about 25 percent of the island's imports, albeit not all for the Weil account, that's far from peanuts.

But Taiwan is merely an island. Beyond it, across the Formosa Strait, looms the Chinese mainland, the most populous country on earth. It is this giant of a nation that may yet become Weil's largest foreign customer. Already the firm's sales here run around 100,000 bales a year.

At first glance, it may appear somewhat surprising that the People's Republic, being one of the world's three leading cotton producers, needs to shop outside its borders. But China traditionally has made most of its clothing from cotton. Even those bulky cold-weather coats are stuffed with cotton waste and pieces of old cotton rags. With its close to one billion population, it would take forty million bales, or about two-thirds of the entire world's annual production, to provide every Chinese with the proverbial one shirt. Not that China has yet tried to make up its thirty-million-bale deficit. The country is not that consumer-oriented. Currently it imports only around two million bales a year. But put into perspective, that's one third of the total U.S. mill consumption. If China continues to follow the course it has taken since Mao's demise, its awakening economy may yet bail out the American cotton business (along with a number of other U.S. industries). That's not to say that China's own cotton production will not increase as a result of farm machinery imports. But this is probably a long ways down the road. So long as ample labor is available, machinery is little used. Even in the United States, cotton had been hand-picked for many years after mechanical pickers were developed by International Harvester.

China has been buying cotton from foreign shippers all along, from firms like Bunge, Ralli, Esteve, Dreyfus, and C. Itoh. Until recent years, however, our Trading with the Enemy Act barred American shippers, along with their foreign subsidiaries, from participating in that business. Nor was it legal to engage in indirect transactions, as for instance selling cotton to Bunge for resale to the People's Republic. All this folderol didn't go by the boards until President Nixon's visit to Peking.

The Chinese, understandably, were still more than a little suspicious of America, and the trade doors opened slowly. For once, Weil was not among the first to cross the threshold. Grower cooperatives, like Calcot, made the first sales after initial contact had been established by the National Cotton Council, which sent a delegation along on one of the early trade missions. In 1973, Bobby, Sr., and Jack Wilson called on the Chinese Embassy in Mexico City, only to be told that considerable documentation was required before an invitation to China could be issued. The Chinese commercial attaché spoke no English, and certainly Bobby spoke no Chinese, and neither spoke Spanish. So they faced each other and spoke with long intervals between sentences, while an interpreter translated the Chinese into Spanish, which Wilson translated into English for Bobby. Then the sequence was reversed. What this Babel finally shook down to was that before any business could be done, Weil would have to transmit a formal letter plus other documentation. This was duly accomplished and there was no reply. Bobby's subsequent visit to the liaison office of the People's Republic in Washington proved similarly unsuccessful.

Meanwhile, Weil did make a sale to Red China, if not under the firm's own name, by participating in a joint account with Bunge in the shipment of 20,000 bales of Strict Middling Inch and Middling Inch of Texas cotton, which Bunge, on its own, was in no position to buy. Christian du Pasquier, Robert's son, at that time working for Bunge, went to Peking to make offers on which the principals of

Bunge and Weil had decided after prolonged conferences and telex consultations. Meanwhile, Piet Janssen, the assistant manager of Bunge-Antwerp, had come to Montgomery. Day after day passed without a word from China. At last, within twenty-four hours of Christian's scheduled departure from Peking, the PRC came through with a bid, and Christian phoned Montgomery where Piet, Bobby and Bucks took his conference call. After some discussion, the bid was accepted, and two of Weil's young men, Austin Wade and Mike Keesee, were immediately detailed to handle every phase of the transaction from the time the cotton was bought to the time it was loaded and invoiced. Unfortunately, all the hard work went for naught. It had been Bunge's feeling, at the time the sale was made, that it should not be hedged by the purchase of futures, and the Weils, against their better judgment, had gone along. Sure enough, the market turned against them, and the laborious transaction yielded no profit.

Finally in 1978, Bill Crissamore, then Weil's staff representative in the Far East, who made his office in Osaka, managed to obtain an invitation from the China National Textile Import and Export Corporation (Chinatex), the government agency that controls all of the country's cotton trade. Crissamore sold them 5,000 bales each of Nicaraguan and Guatemalan growths. It wasn't much, but Weil's foot was in the door.

Then something happened that's not at all rare in international cotton transactions. Weil had contracted to sell Chinatex some Middling 1 1/16 and some Strict Low Middling 1 1/16, and it turned out that the Strict Low Middling was unavailable. After mulling it around a bit, Wilson decided to ship 1,400 bales of lower quality than the contract specified. "We knew we would get a quality claim," Wilson says, "but we didn't think it would be bad, since the cotton wasn't off by all that much and only a small quantity was involved. But they came back with a claim that really shook us."

The Chinese were by no means peremptory about it. They requested that Weil send representatives to have a look at the disputed cotton. This put Weil in something of a quandary. Some months previously, Bobby, Sr., together with Tom Adams and Jack Wilson, had met with the Chinatex people in Memphis. The Chinese delegation, led by Yao Chin-Ching and Sun Dequan, was traveling under the auspices of the U.S. Department of Agriculture to hold a series of conferences with American shippers. "We had a most cordial meeting with them," Bobby recalls. "We were supposed to be with them for half an hour, and the meeting lasted an hour and a half. They are very hard traders, very tough traders. They are putting the screws on you, and all the time they smile. When they trade, it reminds you of a swordsman. You've got to be in there fencing. But their way of doing business is very straight, and once you have a contract with them, they are very good."

But now Weil found itself on the bad side of the firm's own first major contract with a new and important buyer. As previously pointed out, claims are routine in international trading. But the worst thing a merchant can do, if he's interested in selling more cotton, is to settle a claim. The dilemma is this: if the merchant settles to his own advantage, he'll probably lose the customer, and if he settles on the claimant's terms, it costs him more than it should. As one of Weil's principals, Bobby had no intention of getting caught in such a squeeze. He eventually decided to send Jack Wilson, together with Tom Adams' nephew Clark Burnett, who had been reassigned from the Memphis office to succeed Crissamore in Osaka.

Of the new young generation of cotton men, Clark Burnett, born in Tupelo, Mississippi, in 1949, evokes the ambience of his elders, most of whom had been born to the boll. Grandson of a cotton farmer, he'd spent his boyhood summers on the farm, then studied business administration at the University of Mississippi before serving in the navy in Vietnam. He farmed cattle after his discharge, then squidged in Memphis under Rick Wade and Tom Morrow. Before long, he was as peripatetic as the cotton business itself. He was assigned to Fresno as Dewberry's assistant, and subsequently went to New York to work with Pick Butler for nearly a year. The Osaka office was his next stop. Now he is back in Memphis, buying cotton in Mississippi, Louisiana, and Arkansas, selling it to the Japanese outposts in Dallas, and in general running liaison between the home office and the Far East.

But he was still fairly new at the international game when, on their very first day in Peking, he helped Jack Wilson accomplish the

Visiting Peking in January 1979, Jack Wilson, Weil vice-president (center right) and Clark Burnett were among the first Americans to go to Red China after "normalization" of trade relations with the People's Republic. They are shown here with two Chinatex representatives who took them on an outing.

seemingly impossible. Before even getting down to settling the Chinese claim, the two men actually succeeded in selling Chinatex an additional 7,000 tons (some 30,000 bales) of cotton.

Wilson approached this coup in his usual calm manner. Sun had told him about other recent purchases by Chinatex, and how much he'd had to pay. Wilson then phoned Montgomery and suggested that Weil make an offer at more favorable terms. As it happened, the U.S. market was weak that day and Bobby jumped at the chance. A few telexes later—so that the Chinese would have everything on paper and not have to rely on word of mouth—the bid was accepted, Weil covered the sale with futures, and the nine-million-dollar deal was locked up.

There should be no more linguistic problems, like those of the first meeting in Mexico City. Not only do Sun and his associates speak excellent English, but David Hardoon, the young man now in charge of Weil's liaison with Chinatex, speaks Chinese like the Hong Kong native that he is. David Hardoon's Eurasian antecedents go back to China's last dowager empress Tzushih and to Silas Aaron Hardoon, a Mesopotamian Jew, who before World War II owned much of

Shanghai's choicest real estate. One of the many intriguing aspects of David's mission is that his parents are personae non gratae in the People's Republic, but he is most welcome—in part because he represents Weil.

David's grandfather, Silas Aaron Hardoon, had originally gone to China to work for the Sassoons, that legendary Jewish family of Baghdad origin that controlled much of the Asiatic trade, from tea to opium, in the halcyon days of the British Empire. Unlike the Weils, who have kept their heirs across desks from each other, the ancestral David Sassoon (1792–1864) dispersed his offspring, and theirs in turn, from one end of Eurasia to the other, from the Thames to the East China Sea. One of the breed, Sir Philip Sassoon, became King Edward VII's buddy when the latter was still Prince of Wales, a not inconsiderable connection. Another, Siegfried Sassoon, was a sort of dropout: he took to poetry. The rest, though, were soundly commercial, among them David and David Elias Sassoon who established themselves in Bombay and branched out to Hong Kong and Shanghai.

There, Silas Aaron Hardoon rose from the ranks to become manager of the Sassoon Trading Company and married an orphaned French girl who had been adopted by the Empress Tzushih. Having learned all he could from the Sassoons, he set up his own S. A. Hardoon and Co. and adopted eleven children to inherit his wealth. Among them was a boy he named David George, now head of the clan.

David George Hardoon, who later became the Weils' agent in Hong Kong, married into one of Shanghai's immensely wealthy Chinese textile clans, the Yungs. Possibly because the Japanese dropped a bomb on one of the family mills in 1937, the bride's father decided early in the game that Shanghai was not the ideal place to live. He transferred as much of his fortune as he could to Hong Kong as soon as the Japanese surrendered, and there built several mills even as Carl Baquie peddled Weil cotton in Shanghai. (The two gentlemen never met.) When Mao Tse-tung ousted Chiang Kai-shek, David George and his wife, Lilly, luckily were in Hong Kong on a trip, and they haven't been back to mainland China since. As a first venture in their new home town, David George Hardoon fathered the David

Hardoon of this account. Next, he joined a syndicate that tried to corner the Hong Kong gold market. The latter enterprise failed and he was forced to take a job with C. Itoh. Not surprisingly, since David George Hardoon was related to the owners of the Yung mills, C. Itoh put him in the cotton department. After that, it didn't take David George long to recoup. His brother-in-law, who had taken over the family mills in Hong Kong, bought every bale he offered, and David George soon associated himself with Lebel-Hutchinson, where Bobby, Sr, first met him.

Meanwhile, his son David, born in 1949, attended the Universities of Wisconsin and California (Berkeley), studying Slavic languages. In 1972, David stopped short of a Ph.D. and joined a television news service, Visnews of London, a joint venture of Reuters and the BBC. Before he knew it, he found himself back in Southeast Asia, covering the Vietnamese Conflict. David changed his career yet a third time in 1977. He flew from Tokyo to Memphis, attended Murdoch's, and worked for Tom Adams as a squidge. After completing his training there and in Montgomery, he was assigned to Osaka, at the gateway to China.

That Hardoon will make out okay in China is pretty well assured. In April 1979, Bobby, Sr., accompanied by Virginia, had visited Peking to cement Weil's relationship with Chinatex. Clark Burnett and his wife Susan also came along. Throughout their stay, Sun and the top manager of Chinatex, Mao Jin-zhi, insisted on acting as their personal guides, and at one point became terribly upset when they thought Virginia was being mobbed during a promenade on the Chinese Wall; actually she was taking Polaroid pictures and handing out the prints to the curious throng that quickly collected around her. The presence of the two Weil ladies, who were included by the Chinese even in the trading sessions, may well have helped matters along. Sun was especially taken with Virginia; she asked him all about his family, and invited him to send his daughter to the Weils for an American college education. The visit climaxed with a dinner Bobby hosted at the Peking Duck Restaurant ($320 for eight). Here, the inscrutable Mr. Sun, enjoying the duty-free Glen Fiddich that Bobby had brought along, suggested that Weil Brothers establish an office in the trade center for U.S. interests soon to be built in Peking; appropriate space would be arranged. A couple more quaffs of

On their April 1979 trip to the People's Republic, Bobby's wife, Virginia, was mobbed by Chinese who had never seen a Polaroid camera before (right). On another between-negotiations outing on the same journey, host Sun Dequan of Chinatex (below, right) took Clark Burnett and his wife Susan to the recently excavated Ming Tombs between Peking and the Great Wall. It was Clark's second visit to the Chinese mainland in four months.

Fiddich, and Bobby mentioned that Weil intended to change the domicile of Algodonera Weil. "You must domicile it in Peking," Sun joked, "and I will be your manager." They agreed to call this imaginary enterprise "Sun-Weil and Co." and drank another toast to that.

Some months later, when Mao and Sun accompanied David Hardoon on a trip to the United States, they asked him if he could arrange for them to see Virginia. Hardoon took them literally, and the Weil office was busily booking reservations in Williamsburg and Charlottesville when the Chinese explained that they had meant Bobby's wife. Needless to say, they were warmly welcomed in Montgomery the following week.

Since then, Weil has participated in another PRC breakthrough. Peter Frank, in joint account with Eccles & Stern and Weil Hermanos, purchased 13,302 tons (about 60,000 bales) of Peruvian Tanguis cotton in early 1981 through Cotimport, one of the Devilder companies in Lille, and sold it to Chinatex through David Hardoon in Osaka—a thirty-million-dollar transaction. Despite the number and geographic dispersion of the parties involved, the final go-round on pricing took less than twenty-four hours, and the cotton was shipped directly from Peru to China. Luckily, it took only nine days to get there, for the interest meter was ticking at the rate of $10 a minute, or $15,000 a day, and didn't click off until delivery.

Unicosa has been involved repeatedly in joint-account ventures, not only with Eccles & Stern (in this case its Geneva branch, Clement Cohen's Cotunivers), but with several other European merchant houses, like the Devilders' Cotimport and Henry Vonderhorst of the Netherlands. But this was the most complex and voluminous of such transactions. That today's communications made it possible is significant in itself for the future of the cotton business. But the importance of that particular Chinatex sale lay in the fact that Tanguis is a specialty cotton, about 1³⁄₁₆ in length and of extremely high micronaire compared to normal upland styles; it is generally used for knitting yarns, and sometimes blended with California SJV. Prior to this transaction, the PRC had not purchased cotton longer than 1⅛ from the United States or any other country. The new Chinese interest in longer staple—presaging perhaps an unprecedented emphasis on higher-class consumer goods—may well open the door to substantial purchases of Weil's California cottons in the future.

18

Now I Lay Me
Down to Cheat

BEFORE WORLD WAR II, when Bucks first went to work for the family firm, he often heard his father and others of that generation boast that in the cotton business a man's word was his bond. Once a mill had agreed to make a purchase at a certain price, it would live up to its commitment regardless of how much the market might drop by the time of delivery. Even if cotton went down between hand clasp and the actual signing of the contract, no spinner would think of suggesting renegotiation. Conversely, if the market went against the merchant on a forward sale, he would take his licking without flinching and deliver as agreed. But it's been more than four decades since Bucks squidged, and in those years the cotton world's honor code has been severely tested. Adolph would no longer be so proud.

No more than any other arena of human intercourse could the cotton business escape the flaccid morality of modern life. How this ubiquitous pejoration of ethics came about is not the question here; that's for intellectuals to decide between sips of Perrier water. What matters in this account is that in the cotton business the ultimate trial of character occurs when there are tempestuous changes in the market. Such changes have been plentiful of late and the character of many cotton men has been found wanting. In times of rising prices, growers are increasingly tempted to refuse delivery at the agreed on lower quote. In times of falling prices, mills refuse to accept shipments at the agreed higher price. Such transgressions are known in the trade as "laydowns," and it's generally the merchant who gets caught in the middle.

As a modus operandi in human affairs, laydowns are nothing new. Reneging on agreements undoubtedly dates back to when their terms were chiseled in stone. Except that in those days you could pick up the stone and clobber the villain. Obtaining justice with pieces of paper is far more complicated and the cost often comes so high that it's not worthwhile. Legal fees in cotton laydowns can range as high as 60 or 70 percent of recovery. Nor is it always practical to seek compensation. Only once in the entire history of Weil has the firm sued an American farmer. This happened in Arizona, and, surprisingly, the verdict went pro-Weil. Surprisingly, because it's an uneven contest. Such suits must be filed in the federal district court of the farmer's domicile and tried before a local jury. Under those conditions, the international merchant doesn't stand much of a chance, even with all the evidence on his side.

The first major laydowns Weil experienced occurred in Nicaragua when cotton burst through the ceiling during the Korean Conflict. That's when Duque-Estrada nearly went bankrupt. The farmers he'd lined up refused to deliver. A gentleman of the old school, he paid the higher price they asked so he could fulfill his guarantee to Weil. In Mexico, at that time, the government decreed that American merchants must sell a percentage of the Mexican stock to Mexican mills. Weil had never dealt with the Mexican mills and didn't know the good ones from the bad ones. It happened to sell its quota to one of the latter, which then lay down on its one-dollar-per-pound commitment when the market dropped after the Korean flurry. Although only a few hundred bales were involved, Weil decided to sue. It retained the services of Oscar Morineau, one of the deans of the Mexico City law fraternity and associated with Fulbright, Cooker, Freeman, Bates & White of Houston (since joined by Leon Jaworsky of Watergate fame). Despite Morineau's high standing and great talent, nothing ever came of the case since the defaulting mill owner had transferred his assets out of his company and to his family.

In the loan-cotton doldrums of the 1950s and 1960s, laydowns were fairly rare: the incentive for knavery was lacking. Interestingly enough, though, the State of Alabama, whose prisons used to operate cotton mills, tried to lay down on Weil at that time. Adolph, through Lucien, had advised the state's purchasing agent not to buy forward cotton; the price, being at the ceiling, couldn't possibly go higher, and he'd be better off to wait for a downside fluctuation. But the man insisted and signed the top-price purchase contract. Then, when the market dropped as Adolph had said it might, the state buyer wanted to renegotiate. If Weil did not agree to lower its price, he threatened, Alabama would henceforth obtain cotton elsewhere. It goes without saying that Adolph refused to knuckle under to such blackmail, and for the next few years, Weil did indeed lose the Alabama account.

Not until the Arab oil embargo of 1973–74 precipitated the current era of economic uncertainty did laydowns come into their own on a massive scale. Almost instantly, the world's commodity markets went into convulsions as scarcity scares and recession fears alternated like a pendulum gone wild. The first reaction was a general skyrocketing of prices fueled by the rapid deterioration of the U.S. dollar. Of agricultural commodities, cotton was the most seriously affected as adverse weather stunted crops in two major growing areas at the same time: floods hit the Mississippi Delta; drought seared China. In the spring of 1973, cotton sold for about thirty cents a pound. By November, it hit ninety cents. Everybody thought it would go to a dollar. As the season advanced, merchants who had made mill commitments encountered increasing difficulties in taking up contracted cotton from farmers, both at home and abroad. Some farmers demanded renegotiation at higher prices. Others announced that they were summarily abrogating existing agreements, and then sold their already committed cotton to other customers.

Recognizing that defaults on a massive scale could result in the outright bankruptcy of many merchant firms and mills, the American Cotton Shippers Association devised an emergency program that brought together all the disparate groups within the industry—the mills, the cooperatives, and the independent cotton trade—whose members were not normally prone to sit down together. All promptly agreed to participate in a uniform reporting system that would computerize all cotton sold under forward contract.* The resultant catalog listed all such sales, whether by bale or acreage, identifying

---

*A Supreme Court decision of the early 1920s provided authority for this unprecedented measure that otherwise might be construed as a violation of antitrust laws. Three price-fixing suits against the Cotton Shippers Association, two in Alabama and one in Louisiana, were dismissed by the courts.

the buyers and sellers. Nearly 5,000 copies were distributed in the United States and abroad, notifying potential buyers that, if they purchased any of the listed cottons, they were in effect buying something that legally was the property of others. This action alone had a chilling effect on those farmers and buyers who might have been disposed to take advantage of the confusion in the markets. Next, Neal P. Gillen, vice-president and general counsel of the association, identified 500 of the most flagrant cases and aided merchants in retaining the services of lawyers all over the country to file suits. The association won almost every single case. The domestic laydowns were thus largely contained, enabling merchants and co-ops to live up to their contractual obligations. This was indeed a remarkable feat. U. S. exports continued at about thirty-three cents a bale even as cotton was quoted near the magic dollar mark.

More than anything else, this industry-wide campaign exemplified the importance of trade associations in the cotton business, among them the National Cotton Council, which had been organized in 1939 in an effort to stem the increasingly worrisome inroads of synthetics. At that time, Oscar Johnston, a prominent cotton grower and the Council's founder, came to Montgomery to enlist Adolph and Leonel as charter members. This organization, in which the Weils participated heavily until the mid-1960s, went far beyond the customary promotional and lobbying activities of such trade groups. To be sure, the council applied itself to regulatory issues, but it also backed research and technical services that benefited the whole spectrum of the industry, from grower to manufacturer. More specifically, the yet older (1924) American Cotton Shippers Association, as its name suggests, has represented the interests of merchants. Adolph had been a vice-president; and Grayson and A. M. Crawford served as presidents, as have Bucks and Bobby. Many of Weil's senior executives also have held offices in the regional associations. Lucien Loeb, Marvin Woolen, and Stuart Frazer, as well as Adolph and Bucks, have all been presidents of the Atlantic Cotton Association, In the Southern, there was Kenneth Weatherford, currently Tom Adams' assistant manager in Memphis. Al Grayson, Bill Reckling, and Nathan Rosenfield held presidencies in the Southern Cotton Association, and in the Western there were Allie Crawford, Helmut Kruse, and Julian Dewberry.* Without the cooperative effort of these organizations, the laydown crisis of 1973–74 would have had far more destructive consequences.

As it happened, Weil weathered the storm more easily than most merchants. Unlike them, the firm dealt largely with reliable long-time suppliers and was not about to scramble for crops in the helter-skelter market spawned by the laydowns. At Bobby's insistence, it had become a policy never to buy production off a farmer's acres in advance before the yield was known. "That's a crap game," says Bobby. "I wouldn't buy acreage from my brother." Besides avoiding risk, buying "gin-direct" exclusively (i.e. shipping directly from gin to mill) saves warehousing and handling charges. But practically everybody else, from Dunavant to Hohenberg, had been snared into the acreage-buying trap, and these firms were only extricated by Neal Gillen's brilliant strategy.

In fact, Weil Brothers managed to turn potential disaster into profit—a profit that accrued to both seller and buyer. As the market skyrocketed in the 1973–74 season, with laydowns aggravating the cotton shortage, the value of American growths topped that of foreign fibers by a considerable margin. It soon became apparent that some of Weil's customers could profitably sell their contracts for American cottons back to Weil and substitute foreign cottons. When this prospect was discussed with the firm's agents, it was found that a number of mills could make even more money selling back than they could by running their spindles that entire year. At the same time, in buying back the contracts, Weil could achieve substantial basis profits. The way this worked was really fairly simple. As a basis

---

*Terms, except for the Texas Cotton Association where dates are not available, were as follows:

American Cotton Shippers Association: Al Grayson, 1942–43; A. M. Crawford, Sr., 1952–53; Bucks Weil, 1958–59; Bobby Weil, 1963–64. Adolph refused the presidency because of a difference in policy.

Atlantic Cotton Association: Adolph, 1927–28; Lucien Loeb, 1936–37; Bucks, 1957–58; Marvin Woolen, 1977–78; Stuart Frazer, 1980–81. Jimmy Loeb served as president in 1969–70 after he left the Weil organization.

Southern Cotton Association: Kenneth Weatherford, 1978–79.

Western Cotton Association: Helmut Kruse, 1959–60; Allie Crawford, 1963–64; Julian Dewberry, 1969–70.

Million-dollar buy-back check for 5,000 bales Weil had sold forward to Bunge
(Antwerp) in early March 1973. As that year's crop started coming in, the market
exploded. By October, cotton had increased so much in value that it became more
profitable for Bunge, which had been carrying the 5,000 bales in a long position,
to sell them back to Weil rather than market them to a mill. Weil was happy to pay
forty cents a pound, nearly double the price it had originally received, yielding
Bunge an unprecedented per-bale profit. In turn, Weil, having hedged the forward
cotton, had made enough on the covering futures so that the firm showed a profit
even after reacquiring the cotton and selling it to a domestic mill at below-market
price. It was the kind of deal that made everybody happy. Bunge ended up framing
a replica of the check for its Belgian office.

operator, Weil buys futures to cover its forward sales. When the
futures market rises precipitously, as it did that season, Weil can use
its profits in the futures to pay the mills a price that, in turn, allows
them to make money on the sell-back. Meanwhile, Weil has the
bought-back cotton to offer into a rising market that allows an ample
basis profit. The biggest such buy-back Bobby arranged was from
Bunge, which had contracted for a considerable amount of Weil
cotton that year. The Bunge buy-back involved 5,000 bales, a million-
dollar transaction. Proud as Bobby was of this coup, Bunge was even
prouder. A copy of the million-dollar check still adorns the wall of
that firm's Antwerp office.

In Mexico and Central America, however, Weil faced serious
problems. The Mexican government had gone so far as to permit
growers to deliver light-weight bales on outstanding contracts—400
pounds instead of 500. In Nicaragua, a similar stratagem was used by

authorizing the farmers to deliver fewer bales. In Guatemala, one grower tried to organize his fellows to lay down on all their commitments; but fortunately that movement was aborted.

The crisis was overcome to a degree, if not resolved. Most mills, desperate as they were for cotton, agreed to accept the lighter-weight Mexican bales. In Nicaragua, General Somoza intervened at the behest of Armistead Selden, a former congressman from Alabama who had been very active in dealing with the Organization of American States. Selden, accompanied by the head of the different cotton enterprises operating in the republic, flew to Managua, where, joined by Turner Shelton, the U.S. ambassador, they pleaded their case. Somoza then rescinded the authorization for short shipments. Meanwhile in Guatemala, whose cotton culture is dominated by large growers rather than small farmers, it was possible for the merchants to keep track of growers who offered previously committed cotton. Weil, as most other merchants, simply declined to negotiate with them, and the growers, unable to find new markets, eventually delivered on their contracts.

These experiences taught Bucks and Bobby that it could be very dangerous to contract for forward delivery from producers in some areas, and the firm has been far more cautious since. Whenever feasible, forward sales to mills of Central American and Mexican cotton are now hedged with New York futures instead of forward purchases.

But a worse shock was yet to come. As the 1974–75 season got underway, the scarcity hysteria still held sway. But it soon became apparent that cotton would be in ample supply. Not only was there a good crop, but economies dipped almost everywhere, with a consequent lessening of demand for textiles. At first, the cotton market dropped slowly, then it took a nose dive. And now it was the mills' turn to try to squirm out of their commitments—the first time this had ever happened except in isolated instances of threatening bankruptcy.

The largest spinner in Greece, with 2,000 high-priced tons on the Weil books, requested that half the shipment be deferred to the next season. Ralli and Bunge had supposedly agreed to a similar arrangement. Weil refused and the Greek mill honored the contract. But elsewhere—in Thailand, the Philippines, Korea, and Taiwan—one mill after another refused to open credits on the cotton they had contracted.

The first inkling of trouble in the Far East came when Herbert Chang, one of Weil's two agents in Bangkok, notified the firm that a Thai mill, still in the process of construction, had cancelled its order for American machinery and thus would not be able to go forward with its plans: the mill now wanted to cancel the cotton purchase. At this point, the market was down about two cents from where Weil had bought the covering futures. Montgomery cabled that it would be willing to forget the matter if the buyer paid the market difference. Chang's answer was that the mill wanted to see what the market would do before committing itself to such a payment. This response gave Weil cause for concern since it was patently obvious that the more the market dropped, the less likely the mill would be to cough up the difference. Luckily, there was a brief upside fluctuation that soon gave Weil the opportunity to sell out its future hedges without loss, and the mill was notified that the contract had been nullified.

The next word that reached Montgomery was more alarming. K. Cotton & Gauze Company Ltd., one of Thailand's major mills, had refused to open letters of credit on 20,000 bales it had purchased from five American merchant firms, including Weil. Now the fiber really hit the fan. Joining K. Cotton & Gauze in a veritable procession of default were four other mills: Thai Durable Textile Company Ltd. (the country's second largest spinnery complex), Thai Industries Development Company, United Pacific Textile Ltd., and Siam Textile Company Ltd. Between them, the five companies layed down on 65,900 bales, of which 35,400 had been sold by Weil. This was a major blow to Bucks and Bobby—a loss eventually adjudicated by Liverpool arbitration to be in excess of three million dollars.

To check out the situation in Bangkok, Weil first sent Peter Frank, who was then still stationed in Brussels, and later Gordon Redmond, the head of the Lubbock office. But these were merely reconnaissances. No one in the firm's upper echelons had yet met the Thai spinners; the dealings had been left up strictly to the local agents, a routine procedure that had never created special problems elsewhere. Peter Frank and Gordon Redmond were received with customary Oriental politeness but found themselves stonewalled, albeit with smiles. One of the discouraging insights Peter gained on his journey was that Weil could expect little help from agent Herbert Chang. Not only was this gentleman a director of two of the defaulting mills and his assistant the son of one of the mill managers, but Chang's major efforts were directed toward selling synthetic-fiber machinery to the very mills involved in the laydowns. It was obvious that he had no intention of jeopardizing these relationships by taking Weil's side in the confrontation. Indeed, even after the mills had been embargoed by a substantial segment of the international cotton fraternity, Herbert Chang's agency, Thai Textile Engineering, kept selling them other merchants' cotton. The second of Weil's three Bangkok agents, T.S. Young, similarly supported the mills against his erstwhile clients. The one positive aspect of this altogether dismal situation was that Thailand's greatest mill, Thai Blanket Industries Company Ltd., had no intention of abandoning its commitments; nor did a number of smaller mills. Weil has continued to supply these spinners through the only one of the three Bangkok agents who proved completely loyal, David P. T. Yu.

At the time of Peter Frank's trip in October 1974, the situation was not yet defined, however. No one could be absolutely sure which mills would lay down. Peter's observation that the office of one of the potential defaulters reminded him of a "Chinese laundry on the verge of bankruptcy" painted a clearly negative picture but could hardly be construed as evidence of villainy. (As it happened, this mill did default.) Nor did the ⅝-carat diamond stickpin in Herbert Chang's necktie prove anything except that he was good at making money for himself. Peter and Gordon, both, were handicapped by their complete lack of experience with the Thai market and its internal relationships. Nationality alone meant nothing. Most of Thailand's textile people, as elsewhere in the Orient, were Shanghai and Hong Kong Chinese. And while it was true enough that the Japanese-owned mills in Thailand did not default, some of the Chinese did and some didn't. All Peter and Gordon could do is ferret out, largely by hearsay, the financial conditions of the various firms and what cotton they had ordered and from whom.

Meanwhile, the American merchants affected by the Far Eastern laydowns obtained federal authorization to charter the American Cotton Exporters Association (ACEA), an organization specifically exempt from antitrust laws so that its members could cooperate in their efforts to contain the conflagration. ACEA contracted for the services of attorney Victor Friedman, of the New York firm of Fried, Frank, Harris, Shriver & Jacobson, who had previously handled the legal aspects in connection with the grower laydowns in Latin America. European merchants formed a similar alliance, the Association of Cotton Merchants in Europe (ACME).

Friedman and his assistant, Jeffrey Frackman, tackled the problem country by country. Korea was relatively easy, since it relied largely on U.S. cotton imports bought on credit extended by Uncle Sam. With the cooperation of the U.S. government, it was a fairly simple matter to impress on the Korean mills that they would not be considered for credit in the future if they did not honor their contracts. All the Korean spinners eventually came to appreciate the logic of this proposition and complied with the agreements. The situation in Taiwan, whose mills did not depend on U.S. largess, was more precarious. Thanks to C.L. Wong, however, Weil was hardly even inconvenienced. That superb agent had been so consistently careful with his sales that, of all the mills he serviced, only one threatened a laydown. But this problem was solved, too, when Friedman convinced Taiwan's strong central government that the country's reputation would suffer if the laydowns were allowed to spread. It wasn't long before Taiwan's political leaders brought most of the spinners to their senses; the mills that did default were largely bankrupt. Essentially the same approach worked in the Philippines, whose government was also capable of effective leverage. But Thailand, with a weaker government, remained intractable.

In May 1975, during the early stages of the ACEA negotiations, Bobby, Sr., flew to the Orient after first attending a Houston convention of the American Cotton Shippers Association. Jack Frost of Calcot and Sam Reeves of Dunavant joined him in Bangkok, as did Ken Stevens of the U.S. Department of Agriculture. The mission could not have arrived at a less propitious time. The day before Bobby's arrival, President Ford had sent the Marines into Cambodia to liberate the pirated U.S. merchant vessel *Mayaguez*, and Bangkok was in an uproar with anti-American demonstrations. Distraught officials at the U.S. Embassy were of no help; they had more important matters on their mind than the cotton laydown. At this worst possible of all moments, as the crowds outside chanted and jeered and raised a vulture to represent the American eagle, the embassy was in an interregnum; the former ambassador had departed and the new one, Charles Whitehouse, had not yet arrived.

Turning away from this Washingtonian confusion, Bobby went his own way. He first called on Siam Textiles, whose manager, a Mr. Chen, was the father of Billy Chen, who worked for Herbert Chang. Bobby, in his unequivocal manner, made it "very clear that we considered the situation highly unethical," and produced contracts from the previous year when Weil had delivered thirty-three-cent cotton to Siam Textiles as contracted, although by the time of the shipment the market had risen twice as high. Unperturbed by such peculiarly American reasoning, Mr. Chen said that Siam Textile would be willing to open a letter of credit at the current market price. At a subsequent meeting, this position was modified slightly. Chang, as intermediary, assured Bobby that if Weil sold the cotton at the present price, Siam Textile would make up the difference if and when the mill could afford it. With no collateral offered to back up this vague promise, it was of course unacceptable. Visits to other defaulting mills were no more successful. The ultimate rejection came from the Thai Spinners Association which, it was hoped, might be persuaded to put some moral pressures on the mills. Bobby and Victor Friedman were kept waiting for two hours, only to be informed that the association would not meet with them.

Weil and other merchants had in the meanwhile instituted arbitration proceedings in Liverpool, under whose Cotton Association rules the Thai cotton had been contracted. The Thai mills, one after another, refused to respond to Liverpool's invitations to present their side, and the board inevitably ruled in favor of the plaintiffs. On the basis of these Liverpool awards, judgments were obtained first in a British court, and subsequently in Hong Kong, Singapore and Penang, Malaysia, so that cotton bound for the defaulting mills could be seized when ships touched port en route to Bangkok.

The fact that a number of merchants, including Bunge and some Swiss firms, continued supplying the defaulting mills made it all the more difficult to make the sanctions meaningful. It was thus with ironic satisfaction that word later was received that one of the mills had promptly layed down on a violator of the boycott. Such poetic justice, however, did little to help the cause. Nor were the merchants encouraged by the precarious financial state of some of the spinners. Thai Durable, for instance, was deeply in hock to Bangkok Bank Ltd.—an estimated 200 million dollars worth. When Thai Durable subsequently sold off one of its mills, the Bangkok Bank moved quickly to apply the proceeds to this sizable indebtedness. It was a reasonable conclusion that the bank might try to prevent the cotton merchants' claims against its debtors from succeeding. If receivership resulted from a laydown claim, the bank would be forced to share the bankrupt's assets.

Nonetheless, beginning in late 1976, lawsuits were instituted in Thailand against the defaulting mills. In compliance with the country's laws, these were not collective. Each merchant individually sued certain of the mills. Weil took on K. Cotton Gauze, United Pacific, and Thai Durable. To work on the Thai end, Friedman retained Albert Chandler, an American attorney practicing in Bangkok.

Bucks testified in January 1978. The journey, although tiring, turned out to be quite pleasant, a far cry from Bobby's earlier experience. En route, Bucks dropped in on the Osaka office. Next, he went to Hong Kong to meet with C. L. Wong, Weil's highly effective Taiwan agent, and with C. K. Huan, whose Confitex agency sells Weil cotton to the important Japanese-owned mill group TAL. On the way back, Bucks managed to stop once again in Hong Kong to spend a couple of days with George David Hardoon.

Even Bangkok proved hospitable, and the court most courteous. Between lengthy sessions on the witness stand, Bucks visited with the new ambassador, Charles Whitehouse, and an old friend, William Toomey, the commercial attaché, whose daughter Diane had graduated with Bucks' Jan from Wheaton four years earlier. But what his four full days of testimony accomplished, Bucks never knew. He did not hold much hope for recovery, despite assurances from the attorneys that everything was going well.

Not for the first time had he been overly pessimistic. The Thai mills settled in August 1980 for a little more than half of the American shippers' seven million dollars in claims. Evidently his testimony and that of other American merchants had been sufficiently convincing to make the Thai mills doubt that they could win even in a Bangkok court.

John Running/Black Star. *Cotton.*

In a subsequent laydown litigation, however, the Weils did not fare nearly so well. In fact, they lost the case. This discouraging incident concerned a German customer who tried—and succeeded—in nullifying a high-priced purchase during a period of plunging quotations. The German merchant had contracted 2,450 bales of Colombian high-grade Acala for future delivery. While the shipment was pending, prices dropped about fifty dollars a bale. The merchant then cancelled his purchase under Rule 37 of the Bremen Cotton Exchange, which stipulates that the buyer may void a contract if the shipment has not been made by the agreed date. There is no provision under this rule for market adjustments, which are ordinarily taken care of by invoicing back.

In this particular instance, the weather had turned sour and the Colombian crop was sparse. Weil was able to obtain delivery of only about 1,300 bales of the high-grade Acala the firm had contracted for to cover its sale. Those 1,300 bales were shipped well within deadline. Weil promptly notified the German customer that the remainder of the shipment would have to be in the next lower type, and that such would be forwarded at an appropriate discount, This, the merchant categorically refused, although it is the accepted procedure under the various international rules, including Bremen's. Weil then offered Israeli cotton of comparable grade and staple, and the mill turned that down too. While the negotiations were in progress, with the German merchant rejecting each successive substitute, Weil managed to buy back 500 bales of Colombian Acala it had previously sold to another customer, and it also shipped that cotton to Bremen before deadline. In the end, only about 600 bales were thus outstanding, but the Bremen arbitration upheld the buyer in turning down all but the first 1,300 bales.

Despite the disproportionate cost of litigation, Weil has appealed the case. Once again it's a matter of principle. "If the court should uphold the arbitration," says Bobby, "it is in effect legalizing the default. Such a decision is bound to have very serious moral and practical consequences." If nothing else, Weil may well decline to do any further business with Bremen. It wouldn't be the first time.

It appears worthy of note that in the laydown epidemic of the 1970s not a single case of default was reported from Japan, Hong Kong, England, France, Italy, Belgium and Scandinavia. The question arises, how come? Mills in these countries were no less affected. The answer must be conjectural.

Over the generations, the cotton business has been exceptionally honorable, with the trite but true aphorism of a man's word being his bond applying equally to mills and agents, merchants and farmers. In the many decades when the United States was the world's leading exporter of cotton, and Britain and the countries on the Continent the biggest importers, the prevalent Western (but by no means exclusively Anglo-Saxon) morality was heightened by the personal values and social standing of the people who did the trading. Then, when Japan became a major importer, that country's deeply ingrained, staunchly principled ethos was of course operative in its cotton dealings as well, and when Hong Kong first became important, it was governed by strict British tradition, and equally strict Chinese morality.

To be sure, the cotton business even then wasn't all clean. There was cheating on weights and quality, there was chicanery, there were embezzlements. One of the most famous stories—obviously apocryphal because there are so many versions—concerns a bale shipped many years ago to Liverpool. Upon being opened, it was found to contain an anvil; the cotton itself weighed less than 100 pounds. The merchant involved in the transaction, so the tale continues, asked for the tag number of the bale and had the anvil shipped back to the States freight-collect. The farmer was then traced from the tag number and when next he bought sugar from the merchant, he found his old anvil in the keg. One variant of the story, albeit without the poetic-justice denouement, concerns a bale of Indian cotton in which a dead man was discovered when the shipment was opened in the United States. Conversely, yet another gruesome version has an American corpse, similarly wrapped, ending up in India. Nothing exactly like this probably ever happened. But many things like it surely did.

But considering the tens of thousands of transactions taking place in any given year, and the millions of bales sold, transgressions were remarkably rare. As a result, the cotton business operated in an aura of trust without which it could ill function: two parties to a contract could make commitments at a firm price as much as a year or more in advance, and there was never any question that both parties would live up to the letter and spirit of the contract, thus enabling each other to plan future actions within an established framework. While not unique, such systems of business accountability, and hence stability, have been extremely rare in other endeavors. There are few things in this world that can be bought so far ahead, even today, at a set price.

After World War II the cotton business underwent a transformation. Family mills, both in America and Europe, sold out to corporations, and in this consolidation business became less personal. At the same time, a new set of merchants came into the picture. Some emigrated from the Middle East to England. Others, particularly Nasser refugees from Egypt, established themselves in Switzerland. It goes without saying that the majority was scrupulously honest. Nevertheless, they had been trained in a different culture, with different standards. As one of them told the Weils, he would do business with anyone so long as he owed that person money—a puzzling attitude in that it is simultaneously distrustful and undiscriminating.

Then, as cotton consumption moved from Europe and America to the Orient, new markets, such as Taiwan, Korea, the Philippines, and Thailand, sprang up. Many of the mill operators there were cotton Shanghainese who had fled the Chinese revolution. But most were a new breed, and as highly principled as many of them were by training and tradition, they introduced ways of doing business not well understood by those of Western background.

Moreover, when the United States held a price umbrella over the world market in the 1950s and cotton production boomed in "underdeveloped" countries, transactions at the grower level also hinged increasingly on the particular ethics of these regions. Each country had its own way of doing things, whether it was Mexico, Turkey, Nigeria, or Syria; hence, there was soon no predominant culture in the cotton trade, and as trade became internationalized and variegated, so did the standards of doing business.

That about 70 percent of international contracts are still subject to Liverpool arbitration only lends a legal cloak to the proceedings. Under this respectable mantle threatens a situation akin to anarchy— a game whose participants must be as adept at changing rules as at classing cotton.

19

The Root of All Everything

NONE OF THE FOREGOING, from Isidor's first volume purchases to the aborted Thai shipments, would have been possible without extensive, ever-increasing financing. Far from being the root of all evil, money—borrowed money—is the wellspring of Weil's existence.

You don't have to wear Brooks Brothers button-downs to know that cotton is dear. But go from the micro to the macro. Even in the depths of the Depression, the U.S. crop was worth 500 million in 1931 dollars at prices then prevailing. By 1960, the crop's value stood at 2.5 billion dollars. By 1978–79, it had climbed to 4.5 billion. Obviously, Bucks and Bobby can easily afford cotton shirts and wear them as a matter of principle and comfort. But even the combined net worth of the entire cotton trade would be insufficient to finance the turnover of any single season's growth.

That's where the banks come in, and always have. The CCC years were no exception. True, the government financed the farmers' crops, but when a merchant bought cotton from the catalog, he had to rely on his bank lines until it was delivered to and paid for by the ultimate user. Indeed, there is no economic fact of life of which Weil Brothers has been more aware than its dependence on the banks.

Even so, it has been the Weils' long-standing policy never to ask for a "bank line" of open credit. This tradition was handed down from Isidor to Adolph and Leonel, and from them to Bucks and Bobby. As Adolph put it, "Let the banks tell us what they're willing to do, and we will cut the pattern to fit the cloth."

The banking psychology runs strong in the family and so does the sense of responsibility to keep banks strong and safe. Isidor, Leonel and Bucks were all bank directors, and Adolph sat as chairman of the Birmingham District of the Federal Reserve Board. Adolph and Leonel always insisted that the firm would be "out of the banks" between seasons, i.e., that the capital was liquidated and deposits on hand at every institution used. There have been a few exceptions where heavy inventory had to be carried from one crop to the next because new crop prices greatly exceeded the old, but, otherwise, between-crops liquidity has been the rule. Already long before compensating balances became important, Weil Brothers placed these liquid funds on free deposit in a rough ratio to its borrowings during the season.

Inherent in the Weil banking tradition are strict controls on collateral. Adolph would not permit collateral to be withdrawn from a bank and kept in an office safe overnight. He insisted that all collateral, while priced in the most conservative manner, be pledged against loans even in excess of the 90 percent margin requirement. For decades, Weil not only collaterized lines of credit but also free lines. It was the absolute rule that these free lines must not be used except in extreme circumstances, or when collateral was "floating" in the mails or while shipments were out. Moreover, while many cotton firms pledge their sales or collections as collateral, Weil never used its sales, and only in recent years has collaterized its collections, and this only because putting collections through the banks speeds reimbursements.

The firm is equally conservative in its internal finances. Isidor was the first merchant to sell cotton "Cash on Arrival" (to Bremen), the form of reimbursement now standard in Europe. The safety in such a transaction is not sacrificed since the shipper retains a negotiable bill of lading and therefore title to the cotton until payment is received; the cotton is of course insured until payment has been made. And when the trade began to make loans to farmers in Latin America, Weil—as a firm—resisted this trend, although Adolph often financed certain Guatemalan farmers to whom he took a special liking.

Adolph was especially conscious of the value of warehouse receipts. In fact, warehouse receipts were one reason (besides his general pessimism about the cotton business at that time) why he sent Bucks to law school. The firm had lost a court case because some warehouse receipts being held turned out to be nonnegotiable—a hard and expensive way to learn the difference between negotiable and non-negotiable paper. With his pragmatic mind, Adolph figured that his son's three years at Harvard Law would cost far less than the $10,000 Weil lost on those receipts, and would save the firm from similar mistakes in the future.

Weil Brothers today maintains relationships with perhaps a dozen banks. One of its oldest accounts, dating back to 1911, is with Morgan Guaranty Trust, then Guaranty Trust Company, where Bill McGregor, longtime vice-president of the bank, was in charge of the cotton department for many years. Bill McGregor, originally from Hartselle, Alabama, was a dapper man, small but solidly built, and with a bald dome full of banking sense, on which the Weils greatly relied. During his tenure he was possibly Adolph's and Leonel's closest banking friend. When they would ask him how much Guaranty Trust wanted to lend the firm, he would hold his palms out and say, "Take what you like. After your first ten million, take another ten million, and go on from there." A number of assistants came up under Bill, among them Lewis Preston, now board chairman of J. P. Morgan. During his time in the international division, which he also later headed, Lew became a friend and confidante to Bucks and Bobby, who still call him from time to time for his counsel on financial trends. Others who have served in the cotton departments and the international division but have since gone to different positions within the bank are Robert Engel, its executive vice-president and treasurer; John A. Scully, now in London; and Robert Siebel, the dean of New York's cotton bankers, with whom Bucks and Bobby are extremely close.

The Chase Manhattan claims an equally venerable relationship. According to a letter from David Rockefeller, its board chairman, on the occasion of the Weil Centennial, Isidor must have been banking there when he was still in Opelika. "Dear Bucks and Bobby," David Rockefeller wrote, "I don't quite understand how your business got along for 14 years before opening an account with us, but I do hope our 86-year relationship is only the beginning. . . ." David Rockefeller himself had come up through the international division under Charles Cain and Al Schumacher. Many others have followed David's footsteps to earn other high places in that bank, like Bill Ogden, Frank Stankard, James Bergford, and Don Cameron. For many years, the cotton industry's closest "friend at the Chase" was a man who never rose to high title but who undoubtedly had a more detailed technical knowledge of the trade than any other banker. This gentleman, Frank Richards, eventually wrote a book on cotton and its financing, which became a bible in the business.

The Chase has been Weil's bank for Central American operations since the beginning. In the formative years, when Algodonera Weil was starting up in Panama, the Chase's manager there was Luis Gomez—and it was the Chase, by way of Gomez, as will be recalled, that helped Weil get in touch with Carl Baquie during the Panama riots, while the State Department simply shrugged its shoulders. In fact, on that occasion, the officer in charge of the States' Panamanian desk admitted the Chase was far better informed and sent Bobby to the bank.

The firm's personal contact with the top levels of the Chase began long before David Rockefeller's time, when George Champion still ran the bank. Today the link is with Willard Butcher, soon to be the bank's chairman. Not surprisingly, one of the Weils is usually invited to sit at the president's table when the bank holds it annual dinner for customers of the bank's commodity division.

Weil's connection with Bankers Trust may not be on as high a level, but the business and personal relationships with the officers of that bank's commodity division are among the firm's most cordial. For many years, the contact here was Edmund Ebert, who started out as a runner, and brilliantly worked his way up to the rank of executive vice-president. After Ed moved uptown, the Weil account at Bankers Trust was largely in the hands of Roland Charles Beddows, affectionately known to all his customers as "Charlie" until his doctors took him off double martinis because of his tendency to diabetes. Sipping splits, he soon earned himself the nickname "Champagne Charlie."

Beddows was a rough-and-ready, down-to-earth banker, with a rare perception not only of the cotton business in general but of the individual styles of the various firms. In the early fall of 1973, after cotton had risen from forty cents to ninety in barely six months, Bobby went to New York to learn how the banks felt about financing in the upcoming season. Weil has always considered it vital to find out the banks' intentions before the crop started to move, because the firm must make sure that once the sales are on the books and it becomes advisable from a merchandising view to cover them, enough credit is available. This foreknowledge was especially important that high-priced season, since the financial requirements would be more than double if Weil carried the same inventory as in the previous year. However, it was not a case of asking the banks for larger lines. Rather, Bobby was trying to find out at what point Weil would have to curtail its sales and therefore its inventory.

He visited all the institutions, saving Bankers Trust for last. Before he even had a chance to say hello to Beddows, Charlie said, "I know why you're here. With the price of cotton up two-and-a-half times, you can't operate normally unless you have a larger line of credit, and I will tell you before you say anything further that you and Bucks can have all the credit you want, so long as you don't think you're General Motors." Charlies was referring to the fact that all Weil's borrowings at that time were at the prime rate, which then was .5 percent below the "cotton rate" that most of the other merchants were paying. "Charlie," Bobby retorted with a smile, "does General Motors put up warehouse receipts?" Beddows ruefully admitted that General Motors didn't, and Weil continued on the prime. That night, Charlie's assistant, Adrian DeYoung, escorted Bobby and Virginia to the theatre. In the middle of the second act, out of the blue, he turned to Bobby and said, "You know we're going to double your line." Since Charlie's death, Adrian has been in charge of the Weil account. Working with him is Keith Riles, another bright young man out of the same mold.

The fourth bank of long standing is the old National City Bank, now called Citicorp, whose relationship with Weil reaches back at least fifty years. This connection originated with the Importers and Traders National Bank, which was taken over by National City early in the century. In Adolph's and Leonel's time, the Weils' contacts here were William M. Vermilye and Robert Matson, a friend of Shap Dowdell. However, National City was not as oriented to commodities as the other big banks and relationships were far more formal. In fact, George Moore, National City's president in the 1940s, was skeptical of the commodities business altogether. When the cotton market broke sharply in October 1946, all banks were of course concerned about the value of cotton collateral, but most of them realized that there was no real danger if a merchant was hedged or had sales to financially solid mills on his books. National City did not have the same understanding of the business and called Weil Brothers for margin. Instead of remitting the margin, Adolph and Leonel immediately paid up the loan: they had no patience with people who didn't trust them. This was a major setback in the long-standing connection. Even so, Weil Brothers continued as one of National City's few cotton customers, if to a limited degree, as in the 1950s and 1960s the bank was organized along geographical rather than industry lines. In more recent years, however, with James Wallace serving as the Weil contact at Citicorp, matters have improved considerably.

In addition, Weil maintains numerous, less pivotal banking relationships in many other cities, such as with the First National Bank of Chicago and the Bank of America in San Francisco, and with the regional banks that have gained so much prominence in the past two decades. Fred Florence's Republic National Bank of Dallas has played an important role in financing almost every Texas merchant, and Weil's Dallas office was no exception. In Memphis, Weil's lead bank was the National Bank of Commerce, where the firm had a great friend in Claude C. Smith, whose previous affiliation with the Commodity Credit Corporation earned him the nickname C.C.C. Smith. C.C.C. was by far the best-informed banker in the country on the credit-worthiness of U.S. mills. The Union Planters Bank, with whom Weil also has done business over the years, is today its primary Memphis connection; Pick Butler's brother, "Sonny" Butler, was for years its leading cotton banker.

In Montgomery, the Alabama National Bank had been Weil Brothers' bank in the early days when the volume of financing required was still relatively small. But Alabama National has not participated in cotton transactions in more than a decade, and in general, the city's banks do not have the resources for extensive commodity transactions. Nonetheless the firm has maintained close and valued relationships with the First Alabama Bank of Montgomery, on whose board Leonel once served and Bucks now serves, as well as with the Union Bank & Trust Co., whose former chairman, the late John Neill, was a close friend of Bobby.

If anything, Weil's empathy with banks is likely to be enhanced in the future: Bobby's son, Bobby II, apprenticed in management training with Citibank in New York for two years before he returned to Montgomery to start as a rookie in the family shop.

20

Cavalcade III

FAMILY FIRMS ARE FREQUENTLY as mortal as the men who run them. Bobby, Sr., well remembers case studies at the Harvard Business School that pointed up the basic weaknesses of perpetuating hereditary enterprises: the scions have no taste for the trade of their fathers or they lack the ability to pursue them. Often, too, jealousies intervene.

Weil Brothers has been lucky not to face these impediments, at least for its first century. Other cotton firms have not fared so well. The uncertain nature of the business itself had much to do with this. Dozens of fine old names of fifty years ago disappeared simply because of shattering reverses or because other endeavors held out more promising prospects—in oil, real estate, banking, and even poultry. Formerly the world's largest cotton merchant, Anderson Clayton, also originally a partnership, today derives its income largely from food products. Isidor Weil once said that the Bible's "seven fat years and seven lean years" must have been meant specifically for cotton. In the 1950s and 1960s, those seven lean years were stretched, and this is when the business lost some of its best firms, and therefore some of its best people.

All that aside, there is another hurdle that threatens cotton shippers, as it does every other family-owned or closely held entity. This is taxation. Any entrepreneur, be it a rising commodities merchant or a latter-day Henry Ford who plows his profits back into his company, may see his firm accumulate considerable capital

451

during his lifetime, but when he dies his ownership becomes part of his estate and is taxed at its then current value. Since that man's life's savings have been largely retained in business, the only way the estate tax can be paid is from the business: it must be liquidated or the company must buy in the late entrepreneur's share so that his estate can pay his taxes. Either route is detrimental to the enterprise. A liquidated business, by definition, ceases to exist; by extension, it may be merged and similarly disappear. As for buying out the deceased owner, such action more often than not depletes the business of sorely needed operating capital.

Adolph already faced this problem in the early 1960s. He couldn't give his share to his children: the gift tax made this step prohibitive. Nor could he sell out to them, for Bucks and Bobby didn't have that kind of money. What's more, the law of "attribution" would have made a sale of his stock to the company impossibly expensive. Under this legislation, the holdings of all of a principal's close relatives are lumped together with his own, and if the total exceeds 50 percent of equity, the profit from the sale—the money that has been kept working over the years—is taxed as dividends, i.e. at ordinary income tax rates, and not as capital gains. There was only one way to get around this—a signed statement that Adolph agreed never again to participate in the firm's ownership, go into a similar business, or ever work for his old firm. It was the final condition that ruled out taking this course. Working for Weil was Adolph's life.

Consultations with dozens of high-powered lawyers, including Mortimer Caplin, formerly President Kennedy's commissioner of internal revenue, provided no answers. And so the inheritance taxes were paid, which the Weils were luckily able to meet even if it strapped them. If nothing else, Adolph's frustrated quest for a solution testified to the fact that while U.S. tax policy creates problems for family enterprises, it surely provides a fertile field for estate-planning lawyers and accountants. With more than 90 percent (numerically) of U.S. businesses family-owned or privately held, it is astounding that these laws have not been changed but only mildly modified. But it's no wonder that, without such changes being in the offing, the sellout of such businesses continues apace—a boon for the large corporations as the big fish keep eating up the little fish, despite the government's protestations that it favors the minnows.

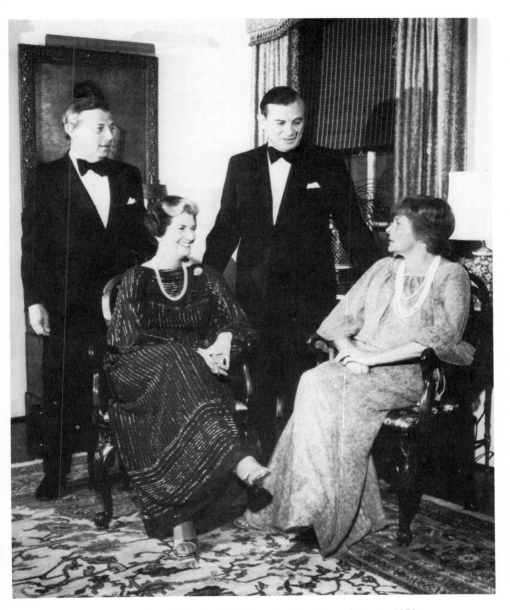

Weil brothers Bobby (left) and Bucks with their wives Virginia and Jean in 1978 when the family firm celebrated its 100th anniversary.—*Montgomery Advertiser/ Alabama Journal*

The problem was not so great between Isidor's generation and Adolph's and Leonel's, when taxation was less punitive. The company was then a partnership and there was plenty of time from 1919, when Adolph and Leonel received their share, to accumulate sufficient capital to keep the growth of the business viable. In turn, Bucks and Bobby were brought in before the incorporation of 1951, and while Adolph's death and the retirement of the other partners surely made serious inroads, the third pair of brothers was successful enough over the years to generate more than had been lost.

Jaydee Tobias, who had come briefly to Montgomery when the Houston office was consolidated, said to Bucks and Bobby shortly before he left to go into real estate, "I have often wondered what would happen to this firm if you two were walking down the street together, as you often do, and the top of a building fell off and killed you both." Bucks and Bobby have since seen dozens of lawyers, but the fact remains that if either one, let alone both, died suddenly in the next few years, there would be no way to avoid grievous tax penalties. Provisions have been made so that there will be enough money to keep operating, but just. After that, it's anybody's guess. Hopefully it will be like old A. M. Crawford said, "Some may come and some may go, but Weil Brothers is like Old Man River. It just keeps rolling along."

Of the two Weil cousins destined to face each other across the firm's venerable partners desks, Bobby II, born in 1951, is five years older than Bud's son, Andy. Along with their fathers and uncles, they serve on the boards of directors of the operating and holding companies. The latter's board, in addition, includes Bobby, Sr.'s, son-in-law (Rosalind's husband) Birmingham attorney Daniel H. Markstein III, and Bucks' daughter, Laurie, who is married to Howard Mandell, of Montgomery. *

---

*Daniel Markstein is a cousin of Julian Adler, the husband of two-*n* Hermann's daughter, Hermione. Daniel and Rosalind have two children, Daniel H. IV, born 1974, and Virginia, born 1976. Bobby's older daughter, Virginia Ann "Vicki," born 1943, is the wife of Thomas L. Langman, of Washington, D.C., a nephew of author Barbara Tuchman. They also have two children, Nicholas W., born 1975, and Andrea, born 1978.

Bucks' older daughter, Laurie, has two children as well: Joshua Francis Mandell, born in 1974, and Charles David Mandell, born in 1977. His younger daughter, Jan, is single and lived for a long time in the Virgin Islands, where she worked with handicapped children.

For the moment, Bobby II and Andy sort of float through the Montgomery office, occupying whatever space happens to be available and doing whatever jobs currently need filling. Bobby II, for instance, subbed for Jim McGhee at the financial end for several weeks when the latter fell ill recently. At the time of this writing, he is in charge of coordinating overseas offers. Meanwhile, Andy, who is still something of a rookie, takes care of details in regard to Pakistani purchases and sales, and is assigned to various management projects, such as statistical comparisons of different markets, which give him an overview of the business. He often parks himself in the conference room, which thus is finally being put to use. This room is about the only place left in the Montgomery office to expand in: everything else is jam-packed full. That the old headquarters at 311 Montgomery Street no longer suffice has long been evident. Architectural studies for a new building were commissioned some time ago and the requisite real estate purchased near the Perry Street exit of the Interstate. But those plans are currently in abeyance, and the former quarters of the Standard Club, however crowded, may yet serve in Bobby II's and Andy's time. Like their fathers, both are tied to Montgomery and have no intention of moving the company elsewhere.

Bobby II was a charter student at the Montgomery Academy, a coeducational day school founded in large part through the efforts of his mother. Then he went to Andover, and from there to Dartmouth to earn a BA with a major in English. For the first two years after his graduation, he worked for the Citibank in New York, an interlude of Manhattan delights before he proceeded to Murdoch's in Memphis and started squidging. To begin with, he was assigned to the Texas Department under Marvin Woolen. One of his early coups, in the fall of 1978, was the sale of 5,000 bales of New Mexico Acala to Bangladesh, which had been buying heavily from Hohenberg. At a profit of about twenty-five dollars a bale, this transaction just about paid for the Weils' 100th-anniversary bash. Since then, Bobby II has wed Winifred Wells, of Albertville, Alabama, a former Atlanta school teacher. In March 1981, Winifred gave birth to a boy, Robert S. Weil III, no doubt to be known someday as "Bobby Three."

Andy came into the firm in 1978 and put in his apprenticeship in Memphis. He, too, had gone to the Montgomery Academy, but Dartmouth held no appeal for him. He wanted to study marine

Cousins Andy (left) and Bobby II are preparing to take over as the Weil Brothers of the next generation.—*Photography by The Robertsons*

biology and opted for the College of Charleston, one of the nation's top schools in that field. Midstream, he changed his mind and switched to business administration with a heavy dose of Spanish. An exceptionally handsome young man and former football player, he has a romantic streak in him: for part of his career, he would like to operate abroad like Carl Baquie and Peter Frank. He has recently been married to Lisa Blach of Birmingham. They had first met as teenagers at the Markstein wedding, but their romance didn't blossom until they encountered each other again several years later.

During Andy's and Bobby's initial training, the criss-cross relationship with their elders continued. Andy reported to Bobby, Sr., and Bobby II to Bucks—an arrangement dating back to the days when Adolph and Leonel reported to Emil rather than Isidor. Then as now it made good sense, since the mutual memories of parenthood and childhood did not influence the business relationships of the respective generations.

Bobby II, who in some ways is intuitive like his grandfather and analytical like his dad, has done a good deal of thinking about the intertwining of family and business. They are, he feels, like yin and yang. The closeness of the family ("I feel like I have a communal father") makes it possible for the Weil business to operate as it does, and the common interest in the business, in turn, draws everyone closer. "What it means, in the end, is this," he says. "When all else fails out there, and you have to come back, it's always there. And I guess it'll be up to Andy and me to keep it in place."

Bibliography

Birmingham, Stephen. *Our Crowd*. New York: Harper & Row, 1967.

Cash, W. J. *The Mind of the South*. New York: Alfred A. Knopf, 1941.

Cohn, David L. *The Life and Times of King Cotton*. New York: Oxford University Press, 1956.

Cox, A. B. *Cotton: Demand, Supply, Merchandising*. Austin: Hemphill's, 1953.

Garside, Alston Hill. *Cotton Goes to Market*. New York: Frederick A. Stokes, 1935.

Morison, Samuel Eliot. *The Oxford History of the American People*. New York: Oxford University Press, 1965.

New York Cotton Exchange 1871–1923. Privately published by the Exchange c. 1923.

U.S. Department of Agriculture Economics Research Service. *Statistics on Cotton and Related Data 1920–73*, and supplements. Washington, D.C.: Government Printing Office, 1974.

Woodman, Harold D. *King Cotton and His Retainers*. Lexington: University of Kentucky Press, 1968.

Appendix A: Weil Staff (1981)

Montgomery, Alabama

Adolph Weil, Jr., chairman, Weil Enterprises/president, Weil Brothers–Cotton

Robert S. Weil, Sr., chairman, Weil Brothers–Cotton/president, Weil Enterprises

Jack L. Wilson, vice-president/manager, Latin American operations

Marvin A. Woolen, Jr., vice-president/manager, Eastern and Texas operations

James E. McGhee, vice-president/treasurer

Ethel H. Farley, corporate secretary

Frank W. Bailey, assistant to Vice-President Woolen

Stuart H. Frazer, III, assistant to Vice-President Woolen

Robert S. Weil, II, assistant to the chairmen

Adolph Weil, III, assistant to Vice-President Woolen

Wallace L. Darneille, assistant to Vice-President Wilson

Michael W. Keesee, assistant to Vice-President McGhee

Mark I. O'Connor, manager, Export Department

Dorothy M. Bailey

Kathryn C. Ballard

Cindy Bennett

Warren Bennington

Sue Bitterman
Christine S. Ennis
Thomas H. Glanzmann
Evelyn M. Hall
Willie James Hawkins
Manuel Held
Joy D. Johnston
Sara N. Lowman
Richard McKenzie
Edward Manora
James B. Mayton
Suzi J. Mills
Janice R. Mulju
David Murrell
Stephen E. Norris

Timothy G. North
Donald A. Odom
James W. Perry
Cleveland Pettway
James A. Poole
Gloria D. Rawlings
Eugenia S. Rittenour
Judith P. Savelis
Elizabeth T. Schaum
Emma A. Stroup
Kenneth W. Talley
Dorothy P. Van Cleef
J. Austin Wade
Vicky R. Williams
R. A. Hester, Jr., retired

Memphis, Tennessee

Thomas C. Adams, Sr., vice president/manager

George T. Wheeler, assistant to Vice-President Adams

Kenneth M. Weatherford, assistant to Vice-President Adams

Mary Frances Adams
Claude Beloch
Margaret A. Bland
Kathy Bradshaw
David Brooks
Peggy Bryan
J. Clark Burnett
Hardy D. Butler
Jack Clark
Joan Dawson
Roger Dawson

James Gaither
Marlin Gitchell
John W. Hammett
John Joiner
Nell Lawrence
Robert Mangum
Thomas G. Morrow
Jeanne Parish
Robert Paxton
Jimmie Russell
James Scruggs

A. T. Shipley
Billie Spickard
Louise Steadman
Richard L. Wade
Esther Williams

Roy E. Williams
Lee S. Yarwood
Thomas R. Moss, retired
F. M. Parker, retired

Lubbock, Texas

Gordon M. Redmond, manager
Warren J. Donaldson

Harry Hetzler
Kate Miller

Fresno, California

Julian R. Dewberry, manager

Barbara K. Dilldine

New York, New York

James D. Butler, manager
Miriam Randolph
John McAlick

Kevin McCarthy
Robert J. Palumbo

Altus, Oklahoma

Nancy Jarnagin

Atlanta, Georgia

Ray G. White, manager

John O. Holt

Attalla, Alabama

O. L. Jackson, manager

Gastonia, North Carolina

Carroll C. Hudson, Jr., manager

Greenville, South Carolinia

Thomas R. Pitts, manager

James D. Klyce

Switzerland

Peter R. Frank, manager
Joachim H. Haack
Eduard Haeller

Margrit Rennggli
Vreni Tanner

Japan

David G. Hardoon, Jr., general Far East representative
Kimitaka Sasaki, manager, Osaka office

Akira Hanada

Katsuko Abe

Colombia

Roberto Herrera V., manager

Luis Fernando Herrera

Guatemala

Karl Fangmeier, manager
Humberto Smith
Alvaro Delgado

Carlos Solares
Rolando Solares
Delmer Davila

Mexico

Humberto Castillo
Nick Garcia
Paco Guerra
Jose Ugalde

Humberto Moreno
Rodrigo Hernandez
Emma Huerta
Miguel Canales

Nicaragua

Ramon Sevilla

Appendix B: Weil Agents (1981)

Australia: Harrisons & Crosfield (Australia) Ltd., Chatswood, N.S.W.

Bangladesh: Jambul International, Ltd. (Mr. Nural Islam Shuja), Dacca.

Britain: M. & B. Stern, Ltd. (Messrs. David and Philip Stern), Liverpool.

Chile: Valdes & Edwards, Santiago.

Greece: George A. Dragotis & Son, Athens.

Hong Kong: Asian Pacific Cotton Limited (Mr. David G. Hardoon, Sr.).

India: Narandas Rajaram & Co., Ltd., Bombay.

Indonesia: P. T. Jaya Guna Engineering Ltd., Jakarta Pusat.

Italy: Federico Kronauer & C.s.a.s., Milan.

Japan: Naudco Company, Ltd. (Mr. R. M. Naudain), Osaka.

Korea: Woo Il Trading Company (Mr. S. C. Kim), Seoul.

Lebanon: Ets. Paget, Beyrouth.

Netherlands: Van Velzen's Produce Company (Mr. M. Groenendijk), Rotterdam.

Philippines: Chem-Cott International, Inc., Quezon City.

Portugal: Francisco da Costa Marques Pinto & Filhos, Lda., Porto.

Singapore: Cotton Distributors, Inc., Far East Branch (Mr. B. Y. Tan).

South Africa: J. L. Clark Cotton Company (Pty.) Ltd., Johannesburg.

Spain: Juan Par y Cia., Barcelona.

Sweden: C. W. Lindeberg, Falkenberg.

Switzerland: Müller & Co. Cotton (Mr. Peter Müller), Uerikon.

Taiwan: Cheng Yuan Trading Company (Mr. C. L. Wong), Taipei.

Thailand: The General Agencies, Inc. (Mr. David Yu), Bangkok.

Gulf Cotton Export Company Agents

France: Cotimport (Messrs. Patrick and Francis Devilder), Lille.

Hong Kong: Confitex International, Ltd. (Messrs. C. Y. King and C. K. Yuan), Kowloon.

Philippines: Textrade Center Enterprises, Inc. (Mrs. R. I. Reyes), Makati, Rizal.

Portugal: Fabricoexport, Guimaraes.

Frescot Company Agents

France: M. Georges Bailleul, Lille.

India: International Cotton Corporation Pvt., Ltd. (Mr. B. P. Thakkar), Bombay.

H.H. Lawler & Company Agents

Japan: Y. Suenaga & Company, Osaka.

Index

Y